TRUSTS, D1322195 *3RARY*

LEWIN ON TRUSTS

Third Supplement
to the Eighteenth Edition

"... a great supplement and lighte to the law"
Sir James Whitelocke, J.K.B., Liber Famelicus

BY

LYNTON TUCKER M.A., B.C.L.
Barrister of Lincoln's Inn

NICHOLAS LE POIDEVIN Q.C., M.A., LL.B.
Bencher of Lincoln's Inn

JAMES BRIGHTWELL M.A., LL.M.
Barrister of Lincoln's Inn

SWEET & MAXWELL   THOMSON REUTERS

Published in 2012 by Sweet & Maxwell, 100 Avenue Road,
London NW3 3PF
part of Thomson Reuters (Professional) UK Limited
(Registered in England & Wales, Company No 1679046.
Registered Office and address for service:
Aldgate House, 33 Aldgate High Street, London EC3N 1DL)
Typeset by YHT, London
Printed in Great Britain by TJ International Ltd, Padstow, Cornwall

For further information on our products and services, visit
www.sweetandmaxwell.co.uk

No natural forests were destroyed to make this product; only farmed
timber was used and re-planted

A CIP catalogue record for this book is available from the British Library
ISBN 978-0-41402-670-4

NOTE TO READERS

This is the second supplement to the text. It takes account of developments to October 26, 2012.

It is intended that after publication of this supplement further updates will be made available online on the editors' website at **www.newsquarechambers. co.uk/lewin**.

CONTENTS

PART ONE

DEFINITION, CLASSIFICATION AND CREATION OF TRUSTS

PART TWO

THE TRUSTEES

PART THREE

THE BENEFICIARIES AND BENEFICIAL INTERESTS

PART FOUR

ADMINISTRATION OF THE TRUST PROPERTY

PART FIVE

BREACH OF TRUST AND REMEDIES

PART SIX

LAWFUL DEPARTURE FROM THE TRUSTS

PART SEVEN

TRUSTS, REGULATION AND CRIME

TABLE OF CASES

TABLE OF STATUTES

References in bold indicate where the text has been reproduced

TABLE OF COURT RULES AND PRACTICE DIRECTIONS

References in bold indicate where the text has been reproduced

TABLE OF STATUTORY INSTRUMENTS

TABLE OF LEGISLATION OF THE COMMONWEALTH AND THE BRITISH ISLANDS

TABLE OF EUROPEAN AND INTERNATIONAL CONVENTIONS, LEGISLATION AND REGULATIONS

CHAPTER 1

DEFINITION AND CLASSIFICATION

1. DEFINITION OF A TRUST

Definitions and descriptions

NOTE 2. Trusts (Guernsey) Law 1989, s.1 HAS BEEN REPLACED BY Trusts **1–01** (Guernsey) Law 2007, s.1 with effect from March 17, 2008.

Sir Arthur Underhill's definition

NOTE 16. DELETE AND REPLACE BY: Underhill and Hayton, *Law of Trusts and* **1–04** *Trustees* (18th edn), § 1.1. The wording of the 18th edition differs slightly from that of the 16th edition, p.3 and earlier editions. For the editors' explanation of the change in the definition, see 18th edition, § 1.2.

Enforceable by beneficiaries

NOTE 21. FOR THE REFERENCES TO Cayman Islands Trust Law, SEE NOW (2011 **1–05** Revision), Pt VIII, Pt VI and s.83(3). FOR THE REFERENCE TO Thomas and Hudson, *The Law of Trusts*, SEE NOW (2nd edn), §§ 42.01 *et seq.*

A proprietary relationship

NOTE 33. FOR THE REFERENCE TO *Snell's Equity*, SEE NOW (32nd edn), § 21– **1–07** 016.

Settlement and will

NOTE 58. AT THE END ADD: Principle applied in *Re AQ Revocable Trust* **1–14** [2010] SC (Bda) 40 Civ [2010] SC (Bda) 40 Civ; (2010–11) 13 I.T.E.L.R. 260 where the statement of the law in this paragraph was approved at [9] and [17].

NOTE 68. FOR THE REFERENCE TO Cayman Islands Trust Law, SEE NOW (2011 Revision), ss.13 and 14. AT THE END ADD: Bermuda: Trusts (Special Provisions) Act 1989, s.2(3) (on which see *Re AQ Revocable Trust*, above, at [17]); British Virgin Islands: Trustee Ordinance 1961, s.86(2); Guernsey: Trusts (Guernsey) Law 2007, s.15.

Trust and contract

Trust or contract debt

1–15 NOTE 72. AT THE END ADD: As to modification of the duty to keep trust property separate from other property, see § 34–34 (Supplement).

2. CLASSIFICATION OF TRUSTS

Bare or simple trusts and special trusts

Powers of trustee for absolute beneficiary

1–25 NOTE 16. ADD: See too *Byrnes v Kendle* [2011] HCA 26; (2011–12) 14 I.T.E.L.R. 299 at [21].

Sub-trusts of absolute trusts and sub-nominees

1–31 NOTE 54. AT THE END ADD: See too *Grey v I.R.C.* [1958] Ch. 690 at 715, CA, where Evershed L.J. spoke of "getting rid of" the intermediate trust. But see *Nelson v Greening & Sykes (Builders) Ltd* [2007] EWCA Civ 1358; (2007–08) 10 I.T.E.L.R. 689, where at [56] and [57] Lawrence Collins L.J. said that the authorities cited to the CA (which included the above statement of Evershed L.J. but not the other authorities cited in this footnote) did not bind the CA to hold that the intermediate trust is determined as a matter of law, though the trustees of the head-trust may decide that as a matter of practicality it is more convenient to deal directly with the beneficiary of the sub-trust.

AT THE END OF THE TEXT ADD: Further, the principle does not prevent the creation of a chain of trusts in cases where the intermediate holder is not a mere repository and has continuing obligations in relation to the property which is the subject matter of the trust of which he is trustee. And so A may hold property in trust for B, and B may hold his equitable interest in the property in trust for C, so that A has obligations in relation to the trust property to B and B has obligations in relation to the equitable interest in the trust property to C.[54a] Nor does the principle apply in a case where A contracts to sell land to B who is acting as nominee for C, and C pays the purchase price to A but B fails to complete the transfer in accordance with the contract between A and B: in such a case A continues to hold the land in trust for B and B holds his interest under the uncompleted contract for C.[54b]

[54a] *Re Lehman Brothers International (Europe)* [2010] EWHC 2914 (Ch); [2010] All E.R. (D) 232 at [226].
[54b] *Nelson v Greening & Sykes (Builders) Ltd*, above, at [58].

CHAPTER 2

PARTIES AND PROPERTY FOR EXPRESS TRUSTS

2. WHO MAY BE A SETTLOR

Minors

NOTE 13. FOR THE REFERENCE TO *Theobald on Wills*, SEE NOW (17th edn), §§ 4– **2–04**
023 to 4–028. FOR THE REFERENCE TO *Williams on Wills*, SEE NOW (9th edn),
Vol.1, Chap.16.

Persons lacking mental capacity

IN THE TEXT TO N.29, AFTER THE WORD "VOID" INSERT: or voidable   **2–09**

NOTE 29. AT THE END ADD: On the question whether a gift, as distinct from a
contract for consideration, made by a person of unsound mind is void or
voidable, a number of modern English cases support the view that the gift is
void, see *Re Beaney* [1978] 1 W.L.R. 700 (but see at 774); *Re Morris* [2000]
All E.R. (D) 598; *Williams v Williams* [2003] EWHC 742 (Ch) 403; [2003] All
E.R. (D) 403 (Feb); *Qutb v Hussain* [2005] EWHC 157 (Ch); [2005] All E.R.
(D) 379 (Apr). But the point was left open in *Sutton v Sutton* [2009] EWHC
2576 (Ch); (2009–10) 12 I.T.E.L.R. 672 at [29]–[51], after a review of the
above English authorities and after reference to *Gibbons v Wright* (1954) 91
C.L.R. 423, Aus. HC (joint tenancy severance deed voidable not void);
Craig v McIntyre [1976] 1 N.S.W.L.R. 729 (voluntary settlement voidable
not void).

NOTE 34. FOR THE REFERENCE TO Heywood and Massey, *Court of Protection* **2–10**
Practice, SEE NOW §§ 20–005A *et seq*. IN THE LAST SENTENCE AMEND THE
OPENING WORDS TO READ: The principal reported cases on the jurisdiction
before Mental Capacity Act 2005 came into force are: AFTER THE PENULTI-
MATE CASE CITED IN THAT SENTENCE INSERT: *G v Official Solicitor* [2006]
EWCA Civ 816; [2007] W.T.L.R. 1201. AT THE END ADD: All these cases
must be read subject to *Re P* [2009] EWHC 163 (Ch); [2010] Ch. 33; *Re M*
[2009] EWHC 2525 (Fam) and *Re D* [2010] EWHC 2159 (Ch); [2010]
W.T.L.R. 1511 concerned with the jurisdiction under Mental Capacity Act
2005. In *Re P* Lewison J. said at [38] that the guidance given in the pre-
Mental Capacity Act 2005 cases can no longer be directly applied to cases
under Mental Capacity Act 2004, while in *Re M* Munby J. went further and
said at [29] that those cases are best consigned to history.

NOTE 35. FOR THE REFERENCE TO Heywood and Massey, *Court of Protection*
Practice, SEE NOW §§ 21–004 *et seq*. IN THE LAST SENTENCE AMEND THE OPENING

WORDS TO READ: The principal reported cases on the jurisdiction before Mental Capacity Act 2005 came into force are: AT THE END ADD: All these cases must be read subject to the cases under the Mental Capacity cited in the previous footnote, all concerned with the jurisdiction under Mental Capacity Act 2005 in relation to statutory wills, but the principles of which are also applicable in relation to settlements.

NOTE 36. ADD: As to the mode of execution of a statutory will, see Mental Capacity Act 2005, s.18(4) and Sch.2, para.3. No specific rules are prescribed about the mode of execution of a settlement, but as to ancillary orders, see Mental Capacity Act 2005, s.18(4) and Sch.2, para.5.

AFTER § 2–10 INSERT THE FOLLOWING NEW PARAGRAPHS:

2–10A What is in the best interests of the person concerned is a different test from the test which applied under the former legislation in relation to statutory wills and which was concerned with what the person concerned might be expected to provide for if he did lack capacity.[37a] What is meant by the best interests of the person concerned is explained in section 4 of the Mental Capacity Act 2005, of which section 4(2), (6) and (7) are most relevant for present purposes. All relevant circumstances must be taken into consideration.[37b] Those circumstances include the past and present wishes and feelings of the person concerned (including in particular any relevant written statement made by him when he had capacity), the beliefs and values that would be likely to influence his decision if he had capacity, and other factors which would he would be likely to consider if he were able to do so.[37c] The wishes of the person concerned carry great weight but are not determinative.[37d] In considering the weight to be attached to the wishes and feelings of the person concerned, regard should be had to the degree of his incapacity, the strength and consistency of his views, the possible impact on him of knowledge that his wishes and feelings are not being given effect to, the extent to which his wishes and feelings are rational, sensible and responsible and, crucially, what can properly be accommodated in an overall assessment of what is in his best interests.[37e] Further, so far as it is practical and appropriate to do so, account must be taken of the views of anyone named by the person concerned, a carer, a donee of a lasting power of attorney and a deputy appointed by the court as to what is in his best interests.[37f] Material which falls outside the specific provisions contained in sections 4(2), (6) and (7) does not fall to be left out of account altogether since it may still form part of the relevant circumstances to be taken into account under the general wording of section 4(2), for instance an oral statement by the person concerned as to his wishes and feelings when he had capacity, and the views of a past carer as to what is in his best interests.[37g] In a case where it is proposed to replace an existing will with one cutting out a particular beneficiary of the

---

[37a] *Re P* [2009] EWHC 163 (Ch); [2010] Ch. 33 at [238]–[239].
[37b] Mental Capacity Act 2005, s.4(2).
[37c] Mental Capacity Act 2005, s.4(6).
[37d] *Re P*, above, at [40] and [44].
[37e] *Re M* [2009] EWHC 2525 (Fam) at [35].
[37f] Mental Capacity Act 2005, s.4(7).
[37g] *Re M*, above at [36].

existing will, regard will be had to the misconduct of that beneficiary in relation to the person concerned.[37h] Though the Court of Protection has no jurisdiction to rule on the validity of an existing will,[37i] it should not refrain, as a matter of principle, from directing the execution of a statutory will where the validity of an earlier will is in dispute. In such a case, the existence and nature of the dispute, and the ability of the Court of Protection to investigate the issues which underlie it, are relevant factors to be taken into account when deciding whether, overall, it is the best interests of the person concerned to order the execution of a statutory will. But it may be in that person's best interests to set to rest concerns about his true testamentary wishes by an order for the execution of a statutory will, rather than to leave his estate to be eroded by the costs of litigation after his death, and his memory to be tainted by the bitterness of a contested probate dispute after his death.[37j]

A statutory settlement may be varied or revoked by order of the Court of **2–10B** Protection if the settlement makes provision for its variation or revocation, or if the court is satisfied that a material fact was not disclosed when the settlement was made, or if there has been a material change of circumstances.[37k]

5. What Property may be Subject to a Trust

General

AT THE END ADD: A share in a company limited by guarantee can be the **2–35** subject of a trust and it makes no difference that the share carries no rights to dividends or distributions or that legal ownership of a share carries is limited to individuals with specified personal qualifications.[90a]

[37h] *Re M*, above, at [44]–[53].
[37i] *Re M*, above at [50]; *Re D*, above, at [15].
[37j] *Re D*, above, at [15]–[20].
[37k] Mental Capacity Act 2005, s.18(4) and Sch.2, para.6.
[90a] *St Vincent de Paul Society (Queensland) v Ozcare Ltd* [2009] QCA 335; (2009–10) 12 I.T.E.L.R. 649. See too *Walbrook Trustees (Jersey) Ltd v Fattal* [2010] EWCA Civ 408; [2011] 1 All E.R. (Comm) 647.

CHAPTER 3

PRINCIPAL METHODS OF CONSTITUTION OF EXPRESS TRUSTS

2. EXPRESS LIFETIME DECLARATIONS OF TRUST

Identification of the property subject to the declaration

3–05 AT THE END OF THE TEXT ADD: It is possible for the court to infer a declaration of trust in circumstances where the directors of a company create a settlement and then treat the company as a corporate trustee carrying on the business formerly carried on by the company for the benefit of a constituted settlement.[23a]

Lifetime declaration, settlor retaining identical assets

3–06 NOTE 24. FOR THE REFERENCE TO Benjamin, *Sale of Goods*, SEE NOW (8th edn), §§ 18–330 to 18–342.

NOTE 27. FOR THE REFERENCE TO Underhill and Hayton, *Law of Trusts and Trustees*, SEE NOW (18th edn), §§ 8.18 to 8.22.

NOTE 28. AT THE END OF THE FIRST SENTENCE ADD: *Re Lehman Brothers International (Europe)* [2010] EWHC 2914 (Ch); [2010] All E.R. (D) 232 at [227]–[234].

NOTE 29. FOR THE REFERENCE TO Hanbury and Martin, *Modern Equity*, SEE NOW (18th edn), §§ 3–022 and 3–023.

NOTE 31. AT THE END OF THE FIRST SENTENCE ADD: (containing an analysis in terms of co-ownership which was treated by Briggs J. in *Re Lehman Brothers International (Europe)* [2010] EWHC 2914 (Ch); [2010] All E.R. (D) 232 at [232] as being the most persuasive analysis of the principle).

AFTER THE TEXT TO N.31 INSERT: In the case of a trust for value the principle in *Hunter v Moss*[31a] may be invoked to create a valid trust of part of a fund of shares to be acquired in the future, so long as the fund to be acquired is sufficiently certain.[31b]

[23a] *Levin v Ikuia* [2010] NZCA 509; [2011] 1 N.Z.L.R. 678 at [10], [43], inferring a declaration of trust by the company over its business, despite the lack of any transfer of the business to the trustees of the express trust. The court considered, at [44], that the business may have been held pursuant to a constructive trust as an adjunct to the express trust, by analogy with the principles discussed at § 3–45.

[31a] [1994] 1 W.L.R. 452, CA.

[31b] *Re Lehman Brothers International (Europe)*, above, at [235]–[248]. On trusts of future property, see § 3–34.

Formal requirements—land

The statute and the defence

NOTE 49. AT THE END ADD: In *Drakeford v Cotton* [2012] EWHC 1414 (Ch); **3–10**
(2012–13) 15 I.T.E.L.R. 144 at [75], the Court referred to this paragraph and
hinted, *obiter*, that it would not have refused to allow the claimant to rely on
s.53(1)(*c*) had that subsection prevented a disposition from taking effect.

Formal requirements—equitable interests

AFTER THE TEXT TO N.77 INSERT: Where A and B hold property on trust for **3–18**
A, A may declare new trusts of the property in favour of A and B or declare
a sub-trust of his subsisting beneficial interest in favour of A and B without
writing as these actions fall outside the statute. If, however, A transferred his
entire beneficial interest for A and B or directed the trustees to hold it for A
and B, then the subsection would be engaged and writing required.[77a]

Formal requirements – personalty

AT THE END OF THE FIRST SENTENCE ADD: and may even be inferred from **3–19**
conduct.[81a]

When section 53 of the Law of Property Act 1925 is excluded

NOTE 88. FOR THE REFERENCE TO Underhill and Hayton, *Law of Trusts and* **3–20**
Trustees, SEE NOW (18th edn), § 12.12.

NOTE 90. AT THE END ADD: *Singh v Anand* [2007] EWHC 3346 (Ch).

NOTE 91. AT THE END ADD: It has been said that some of the older cases on
the Statute of Frauds, such as *Rochefoucauld v Boustead* [1897] 1 Ch. 196,
would now be decided on the principles of common intention constructive
trusts: *Samad v Thompson* [2008] EWHC 2809 (Ch); [2008] All E.R. (D) 165
(Nov) at [128].

3. TRANSFERS TO TRUSTEES

Shares and securities

NOTE 5. Companies Act 2006, s.544 came into force on October 1, 2009: **3–25**
Companies Act 2006 (Commencement No.8, Transitional Provisions and
Savings) Order 2008 (SI 2008/2860). For Companies (Tables A to F) Reg-
ulations 1985, see SI 1985/805, and not SI 1985/1062.

[77a] *Drakeford v Cotton* [2012] EWHC 1414 (Ch); (2012–13) 15 I.T.E.L.R. 144 at [79].
[81a] See *Dhingra v Dhingra* (1999–00) 2 I.T.E.L.R. 262, CA for a discussion of the requirements
for the establishment of a valid trust of personality.

Other things in action

Statutory assignment

3–27   NOTE 10. FOR THE REFERENCE TO *Snell's Equity*, SEE NOW (32nd edn), § 3–007. FOR THE REFERENCE TO *Chitty on Contracts*, SEE NOW (30th edn), Vol.1, § 19–012.

NOTE 11. FOR THE REFERENCE TO *Snell's Equity*, SEE NOW (32nd edn), § 3–007. FOR THE REFERENCE TO *Chitty on Contracts*, SEE NOW (30th edn), Vol.1, § 19–014.

NOTE 12. FOR THE REFERENCE TO *Snell's Equity*, SEE NOW (32nd edn), § 3–006. FOR THE REFERENCE TO *Chitty on Contracts*, SEE NOW (30th edn), Vol.1, § 19–015.

NOTE 13. FOR THE REFERENCE TO *Snell's Equity*, SEE NOW (32nd edn), § 3–008. FOR THE REFERENCE TO *Chitty on Contracts*, SEE NOW (30th edn), Vol.1, §§ 19–016 to 19–018.

NOTE 15. FOR THE REFERENCE TO *Snell's Equity*, SEE NOW (32nd edn), § 3–009. FOR THE REFERENCE TO *Chitty on Contracts*, SEE NOW (30th edn), Vol.1, § 19–011.

Equitable assignment generally

3–28   NOTE 16. FOR THE REFERENCE TO *Snell's Equity*, SEE NOW (32nd edn), § 3–002. FOR THE REFERENCE TO *Chitty on Contracts*, SEE NOW (30th edn), Vol.1, § 19–001.

NOTE 17. FOR THE REFERENCE TO *Chitty on Contracts*, SEE NOW (30th edn), Vol.1, §§ 19–001 and 19–086.

NOTE 18. FOR THE REFERENCE TO *Chitty on Contracts*, SEE NOW (30th edn), Vol.1, § 19–089.

NOTE 19. FOR THE REFERENCE TO *Snell's Equity*, SEE NOW (32nd edn), § 3–002.

Rights incapable of legal transfer

3–33   AFTER THE TEXT TO N.48 ADD: It would seem that the power of a member to make a revocable nomination under a pension scheme is not a debt or other legal chose in action, or an existing equitable interest, capable of assignment.[48a]

Future property

The distinction between contingent interests and expectancies under existing trusts

3–35   IN THE FOURTH SENTENCE DELETE neither A nor B has a contingent interest AND REPLACE BY: neither B nor C has a contingent interest.

[48a]   *Re an Application by the Police Association of South Australia* [2008] SASC 299; (2008–09) 11 I.T.E.L.R. 484 at [66]–[69], approving *Re Danish Bacon Co. Ltd Staff Pension Fund Trusts* [1971] 1 W.L.R. 248.

4. WHEN A TRUST IS FULLY CONSTITUTED ON A TRANSFER TO TRUSTEES

The basic principle—equity will not aid a volunteer

NOTE 74. AT THE END ADD: See too *Antle v R.* [2009] TCC 465; (2009–10) 12   **3–41**
I.T.E.L.R. 314 at [50]–[58] (Canadian settlement of shares failed where the
settlement recited that the shares had been transferred to the trustee but
inadequate steps had been taken to effect a transfer before the date of the
settlement, affirmed on grounds not relating to this point [2010] FCA 280;
(2010–11) 13 I.T.E.L.R. 591).

Nor will a failed transfer be construed as a declaration of trust

AFTER THE THIRD SENTENCE ADD: Where a signed transfer form of shares   **3–42**
without the share certificate was sent to a donee under cover of a letter
stating that the donor held the shares for the donee from the date of the
letter, the letter took effect as declaration of trust since it showed that the
donor intended to make a disposition of the beneficial interest immediately
and not merely intended to make a gift upon registration of the shares in the
name of the donee.[77a]

When equity's aid is not required because the trustee has all he needs

Shares in a company

NOTE 89. AT THE END ADD: *Kaye v Zeital* [2010] EWCA Civ 159; [2010]   **3–45**
W.T.L.R. 913 at [40]. See too *Cheung v Worldcup Investments Inc* [2008]
HKCFA 78; (2008–09) 11 I.T.E.L.R. 449 at [40], *per* Lord Scott of Foscote
N.P.J. (bearer shares).

NOTE 90. AT THE END ADD: The absence of a share certificate will usually
mean that the transfer of shares is not complete. Where the certificate is lost,
the transferee must have done all in his power, *i.e.* to procure the creation of
a duplicate, before a trust in favour of the donee of the shares may arise:
Kaye v Zeital [2010] EWCA Civ 159; [2010] W.T.L.R. 913 at [40]. See too
Curtis v Pulbrook [2011] EWHC 167 (Ch); [2011] 1 B.C.L.C. 638 at [45].

When equity's aid is not needed because the property has vested in the trustee

The rule in Strong v Bird

NOTE 5. FOR THE REFERENCE TO *Snell's Equity*, SEE NOW (32nd edn), § 24–012.   **3–50**

NOTE 22. FOR THE REFERENCE TO Underhill and Hayton, *Law of Trusts and*   **3–51**
Trustees, SEE NOW (18th edn), §§ 9.64 to 9.68.

NOTE 26. FOR THE REFERENCE TO Underhill and Hayton, *Law of Trusts and*
Trustees, SEE NOW (18th edn), § 9.67.

[77a]   *Shah v Shah* [2010] EWCA Civ 1408; [2011] 1 P. & C.R. DG42.

Perfection of gift through promissory or proprietary estoppel

3–56 NOTE 34. FOR THE REFERENCE TO *Snell's Equity*, SEE NOW (32nd edn), Chap.12.

Imposition of constructive trust when it is unconscionable for the gift to be recalled

3–57 AT THE END OF THE TEXT ADD NEW NOTE 44a: The text in this sentence was cited with apparent approval in *Gordon v Hing* [2011] HKCFI 143; [2011] 2 H.K.L.R.D. 506 at [65].

6. TESTAMENTARY AND SECRET TRUSTS

Secret trusts generally

3–77 NOTE 95. FOR THE REFERENCE TO *Snell's Equity*, SEE NOW (32nd edn), § 24–030.

Express or constructive trusts

3–80 NOTE 1. FOR THE REFERENCE TO Thomas and Hudson, *The Law of Trusts*, SEE NOW (2nd edn), § 28.63.

NOTE 4. FOR THE REFERENCE TO Hanbury and Martin, *Modern Equity*, SEE NOW (18th edn), § 5–015.

Acceptance

3–87 NOTE 28. FOR THE REFERENCE TO *Snell's Equity*, SEE NOW (32nd edn), § 24–029.

Death of secondary donee

3–94 NOTE 39. FOR THE REFERENCE TO Underhill and Hayton, *Law of Trusts and Trustees*, SEE NOW (18th edn), § 12.104.

CHAPTER 4

REQUIREMENTS FOR ESSENTIAL VALIDITY OF EXPRESS TRUSTS

1. THE REQUISITE INTENTION TO CREATE A TRUST

Certainty of words

NOTE 8. FOR THE REFERENCE TO *Theobald on Wills*, SEE NOW (17th edn), **4–03** Chaps 15 and 28. FOR THE REFERENCE TO *Williams on Wills*, SEE NOW (9th edn), Vol.1, Chaps 50, 53 and 82.

Inferred or "precatory" trusts

NOTE 13. FOR THE REFERENCE TO *Theobald on Wills*, SEE NOW (17th edn), **4–04** §§ 28–020 to 28–026.

Directions as to maintenance of children

NOTE 18. FOR THE REFERENCE TO *Theobald on Wills*, SEE NOW (17th edn), § 28– **4–05** 027. FOR THE REFERENCE TO *Williams on Wills*, SEE NOW (9th edn), Vol.1, § 82.5.

Conditions construed as trusts

NOTE 43. AT THE END ADD: See *Re Lehman Brothers International (Europe)* **4–09** *(in administration)* [2009] EWHC 3228 (Ch) at [177]–[179] (reversed in part on appeal on other grounds [2010] EWCA Civ 917; [2010] All E.R. (D) 15 (Aug), and a further appeal to the Supreme Court dismissed [2012] UKSC 6; [2012] 3 All E.R. 1) on the distinction between the creation of a charge and the creation of a trust.

NOTE 45. FOR THE REFERENCE TO *Theobald on Wills*, SEE NOW (17th edn), § 29– 002. FOR THE REFERENCE TO *Williams on Wills*, SEE NOW (9th edn), Vol.1, §§ 34.1 and 34.4.

Trusts of the benefit of contracts

No intention to contract as trustee

NOTE 77. AT THE END ADD: *Fluor Australia Pty v Engineering Pty Ltd* [2007] **4–15** VSC 262; (2007–08) 19 V.R. 458.

2. Trusts Held to be Shams

General principle

4–19 Note 86. At the end add: See Conaglen (2008) 68 C.L.J. 176.

Note 86. At the end add: However, this view would not be supported by a recent New Zealand decision, where it was said that sham is part of the common law of fraud, and the question whether a trust is a sham is not resolved by the law of equity: *B v X* [2011] 2 N.Z.L.R. 405, NZ HC.

Note 91. At the end add: a passage approved in *Goldstone v Goldstone* [2011] EWCA Civ 39; [2011] 1 F.L.R. 1926 at [37], [66].

The shamming intent

4–20 Note 94. At the end add: The position in Canada is different. There is no requirement of tortious deceit and it is enough that the parties to a transaction present it as being different from what they know it to be: *Antle v R* [2010] FCA 280; (2010–11) 13 I.T.E.L.R. 591 at [15]–[22].

The trustees or other parties to a declaration

4–22 Note 7. At the end add: It has been said that a common intention is required, but that reckless indifference on the part of the trustee will be taken to amount to the necessary intention: *A v A* [2007] EWHC 99 (Fam); [2007] 2 F.L.R. 467 at [52]. In *Re Reynolds* [2008] NZCA 122; (2007–08) 10 I.T.E.L.R. 1064 at [38], reference was made to recklessness or ignorance on the part of the trustee as being tantamount to intention, but ignorance would not be tantamount to intention unless it involved a wilful shutting of eyes.

The effect of finding a sham

4–23 Note 12. At the end add: That dissent was treated as now representing Australian (as well as English) law in *Byrnes v Kendle* [2011] HCA 26; (2011–12) 14 I.T.E.L.R. 299 at [13]–[18], [60]–[66] and [116], where the statement of the law in this paragraph was approved.

Settlors retaining powers, interests and control

4–25 After the fifth sentence add note 17a: Settlor control may often occur with the view of benefiting the beneficiaries and thus be quite consistent with the existence of an intention on behalf of the settlor that the trust be operative: *Re Reynolds* [2008] NZCA 122; (2007–08) 10 I.T.E.L.R. 1064 at [127].

Note 18. At the end add: *Antle v R* [2009] TCC 465; (2009–10) 12 I.T.E.L.R. 314 at [73]–[74] (agreeing with submissions relying on the statement in the text, affirmed without comment on these submissions [2010] FCA 280; (2010–11) 13 I.T.E.L.R. 591). Evidence of poor administration of a trust is insufficient to establish a sham, although it may show a breach of trust: *Re Reynolds* [2008] NZCA 122; (2007–08) 10 I.T.E.L.R. 1064 at [92], [125].

Further practical considerations in the trust context

Note 25. At the end add: See too *Re Exeter Settlement* [2010] JRC 012. **4–27**

At the end of the text add: An 'alter ego' trust, where a person establishes a trust over the trustee of which he has control, is not, by virtue of this fact, a sham nor does the person with control of the trustee thereby have a beneficial interest in the trust.[26a]

3. Certainty of Objects of the Trust

Certainty of objects

Fixed trusts

Note 32. At the end of the second sentence add: *Pascoe v Boensch* [2008] **4–30** FCAFC 147; (2009) 250 A.L.R. 24 at [22].

Note 33. At the end add: *Public Trustee v Butler* [2012] EWHC 858 (Ch); [2012] W.T.L.R. 1043 ("the deserving materially hardship cases").

Intermediate or hybrid powers

Note 39. For the reference to Underhill and Hayton, *Law of Trusts and* **4–32** *Trustees*, see now (18th edn), §§ 8.86 to 8.88. At the end add: See too the discussion of powers of addition in *Tam Mei Kam v HSBC International Trustee Ltd* [2008] HKCFI 696; (2008–09) 11 I.T.E.L.R 246 at [242]–[249]; affirmed [2010] HKCA 197; [2010] 4 H.K.L.R.D. 69 at [88]–[90]; point not taken on final appeal [2011] HKCFA 34 (but validity of relevant provisions affirmed at [45]).

Conditions

Note 40. For the reference to *Theobald on Wills*, see now (17th edn), **4–33** §§ 29–012 and 29–013. For the reference to *Williams on Wills*, see now (9th edn), Vol.1, § 34.10.

Administrative unworkability

Note 43. At the end add: See too the discussion of administrative **4–34** unworkability in *Tam Mei Kam v HSBC International Trustee Ltd* [2008] HKCFI 696; (2008–09) 11 I.T.E.L.R 246 at [275]–[286]; point not taken on appeal [2010] HKCA 197; [2010] 4 H.K.L.R.D. 69; nor on final appeal [2011] HKCFA 34 (but validity of relevant provisions affirmed at [45]).

Testamentary delegation

Note 44. Delete the wording after the second semi-colon and replace **4–36** by: following *Re Abrahams' Will Trusts* [1969] 1 Ch. 463 at 474–476; applied

[26a] *Public Trustee v Smith* [2008] NSWSC 397; (2007–08) 10 I.T.E.L.R. 1018 at [119]–[120]. See also *Re Reynolds* [2008] NZCA 122; (2007–08) 10 I.T.E.L.R. 1064 at [70]–[72] (alter ego arguments may provide evidence of a sham).

Tam Mei Kam v HSBC International Trustee Ltd [2008] HKCFI 696; (2008–09) 11 I.T.E.L.R 246 at [222]–[241]; affirmed [2010] HKCA 197; [2010] 4 H.K.L.R.D. 69 at [88]–[90]; point not taken on final appeal [2011] HKCFA 34 (but validity of relevant provisions affirmed at [45]).

AT THE END OF THE TEXT ADD: The general rule against testamentary delegation, in the context of fiduciary powers conferred by wills, was a chimera, a shadow cast by the rule of certainty, having no independent existence.[44a] In Australia, however, the general rule against testamentary delegation strikes down powers of appointment, other than general powers of appointment and special powers in favour of a defined class.[44b] Similar considerations may apply in Canada.[44c] But even in Australia there is no objection on the ground of testamentary delegation or uncertainty to a testamentary gift to a pre-existing lifetime discretionary trust, valid in accordance with the rules of certainty applicable to lifetime trusts.[44c] Such a gift has also been upheld in Hong Kong,[44d] and it is thought that in England too there is no objection to such a gift on the ground of testamentary delegation or of uncertainty so long as the trust is adequately identified by the terms of the will.

4. TRUSTS FOR NON-CHARITABLE PURPOSES AND UNINCORPORATED NON-CHARITABLE ASSOCIATIONS

The beneficiary principle

4-38   NOTE 45. AT THE END ADD: *Re Exeter Settlement* [2010] JRC 012, where a settlement with no beneficiaries was rectified to name a charity as a beneficiary (but note that the test for rectification in Jersey differs from that in England); *Equity Trust (Jersey) Ltd v GS* [2010] JRC 013.

NOTE 46. FOR THE REFERENCE TO Picarda, *The Law and Practice relating to Charities*, SEE NOW (4th edn), Pt 1.

Trusts directly or indirectly for the benefit of identifiable persons

4-39   NOTE 54. AT THE END ADD: For a recent example, see *Grender v Dresden* [2009] EWHC 214 (Ch); [2009] W.T.L.R. 379.

[44a]   *Re Beatty*, above, at 1509.
[44b]   *Tatham v Huxtable* (1950) 81 C.L.R. 839, Aus. HC; *Lutheran Church of Australia South Australia District Inc. v Farmers Co-operative Executors & Trustees Ltd* (1970) 121 C.L.R. 628, Aus. HC; *Horan v James* (1982) 2 N.S.W.L.R. 376, NSW CA; *Gregory v Hudson* [1997] NSWSC 140; (1997) 41 N.S.W.L.R. 573; affirmed [1998] NSWSC 582; (1998) 45 N.S.W.L.R. 300, NSW CA. *Tatham v Huxtable*, above, was considered but not followed in *Re Beatty*, above, at 1509.
[44c]   *Re Nicholls* (1987) 34 D.L.R. (4th) 321, Ont. CA (concerned with a general power of appointment) followed *Tatham v Huxtable*, above. And see *Daniels v Daniels Estate* (1992) 85 D.L.R. (4th) 116, Alb CA in which a disposition of residue "unto my executors to distribute as they think fit" was held to create a trust (not a mere power) which failed for certainty of objects (as would also have been the case in England having regard to the principles stated in § 4–35).
[44c]   *Gregory v Hudson*, above.
[44d]   *Tam Mei Kam v HSBC International Trustee Ltd*, above.

Note 56. For the reference to Ford and Lee, *Principles of the Law of Trusts*, see now Vol.1, [5.12710] *et seq.*

Alternative methods

Statutory provision in other jurisdiction

Note 96. For the reference to Cayman Islands Trust Law, see now (2011 **4–48** Revision), Pt VIII. For the reference to British Virgin Islands Trustee Ordinance 1961, see now s.84 (as amended) and s.84A. At the end add: and Guernsey: Trusts (Guernsey) Law 2007, ss.12 and 13.

At the end of the text add: It has also been held in Canada, on the basis of Canadian case law derived from the *Denley* principle, that non-charitable purpose trusts may be created there as long as there is some person with standing to enforce the trust.[96a]

Gifts to non-charitable unincorporated associations

Gift to members subject to the contract between them

Note 5. At the end add: In *Hanchett-Stamford v Att.-Gen.* [2008] EWHC **4–51** 330 (Ch); [2009] Ch. 173 at [29], Lewison J. said that under normal circumstances a gift to an unincorporated association will fall into this second category. In *Re Sam Shui Natives Association* [2009] HKCA 232; [2010] 2 H.K.L.R.D. 649 at [16] this paragraph of the text was approved.

Gifts for purposes satisfying the beneficiary principle

Note 17. At the end add: *Re St Andrew's (Cheam) Lawn Tennis Club Trust* **4–52** [2012] EWHC 1040 (Ch); [2012] 3 All E.R. 746 at [60]–[62].

5. Rectification, Rescission and Cancellation

The functions of the three remedies

Note 21. For the reference to *Snell's Equity*, see now (32nd edn), § 14–007 **4–53** and Chaps 15 and 16. For the reference to Pettit, *Equity and the Law of Trusts*, see now (11th edn), pp.689–710.

Development of rectification and rescission

Note 25. For the reference to *Chitty on Contracts*, see now (30th edn), **4–55** Vol.1, Chaps 5–7. For the reference to Cheshire, Fifoot and Furmston, *Law of Contract*, see now (15th edn), Chaps 8 and 9.

[96a] *Peace Hills Trust Co v Canada Deposit Insurance Corp* [2007] ABQB 364; [2010] W.T.L.R. 83 at [29].

Rectification or rescission on the ground of ignorance or mistake

The nature of the mistake

4-58 DELETE THE SECOND AND THIRD SENTENCES AND NN.31 AND 32 AND REPLACE BY:
In order to invoke this jurisdiction, there must be a mistake on the part of
the donor either as to the legal effect of the disposition or as to an existing
fact which is basic to the transaction.[30a] In addition, in rescission cases, the
mistake must be of sufficient gravity as to render it unconscionable on the
part of the donee to retain the property given to him.[30b] There are two kinds
of mistake which found the jurisdiction. The first is a mistake, which may be
a mistake of law or fact, as to the legal effect of the transaction itself and not
merely as to its consequences or the advantages to be gained from entering
into it.[31] The second is a mistake as to an existing fact which is basic to the
transaction.[31a] Note that the second category of mistake is limited to mistakes of fact,[31b] and so a mistake of law which is basic or fundamental to the
transaction, and which satisfies the gravity requirement, but which is not a
mistake as to legal effect, does not suffice.[31c] For cases within the first
category, the important, and not always clear distinction, is that between
'effects' and 'consequences'.[32] That distinction has been firmly upheld by the
Court of Appeal.[32a]

NOTE 38: AT THE END ADD: See *Ashcroft v Barnsdale* [2010] EWHC 1948
(Ch); [2010] S.T.C. 2544 at [16] where a failure to include a provision in a
deed of variation of a will making a specific gift subject to inheritance tax
was treated as a mistake as to effects rather than consequences in a rectification claim.

AT THE END OF THE TEXT ADD: This was confirmed in terms in *Pitt v Holt*,[40a]
where the Court of Appeal said,[40b] that "the impact of taxation on or as a
result of a particular transaction is a consequence, rather than a part of the
legal effect, of the transaction and is therefore outside the scope of the
factors as to which a mistake on the part of the donor is relevant to the
jurisdiction". Since a mistake as to tax consequences is a mistake of law, it

---

[30a] *Pitt v Holt* [2011] EWCA Civ 197; [2012] Ch. 132 at [210].
[30b] *Pitt v Holt*, above, at [167], [203] and [210], applying *Ogilvie v Littleboy* (1897) 13 T.L.R.
399 at 400, CA (affirmed (1899) 15 T.L.R. 294, HL).
[31] *Gibbon v Mitchell* [1990] 1 W.L.R. 1304 at 1309E. See too *Meadows v Meadows* (1853) 16
Beav. 401; *Stone v Godfrey* (1854) 5 De G.M. & G. 76; *Whiteside v Whiteside* [1950] Ch 65
at 74.
[31a] As in *Lady Hood of Avalon v Mackinnon* [1909] 1 Ch. 476. See too *University of Canterbury
v Att. -Gen.* [1995] 1 N.Z.L.R. 78, NZ HC.
[31b] *Pitt v Holt*, above, at [206].
[31c] The distinction between mistakes of fact and law has been abandoned in common law
money had and received claims seeking relief from mistake (see *Kleinwort Benson Ltd v
Lincoln City Council* [1999] 2 A.C. 349, HL) but survives in England under the equitable
jurisdiction, an aspect of *Pitt v Holt*, above, criticised in *Re S Trust* [2011] JRC 117 at [34]–
[38].
[32] *AMP (UK) Ltd v Barker* [2001] P.L.R. 77 at [70], *per* Lawrence Collins J.: "a formula
designed to ensure that the policy involved in equitable relief is effectuated to keep it within
reasonable bounds and to ensure that it is not used simply when parties are mistaken about
commercial effects of their transactions or have second thoughts about them".
[32a] *Pitt v Holt*, above.
[40a] [2011] EWCA Civ 197; [2011] 3 W.L.R. 19.
[40b] At [209], *per* Lloyd L.J.

will not come within the second category of mistake referred to at the beginning of this paragraph, however basic or fundamental it is to the transaction. It has, nevertheless, been suggested in Jersey that in a case where the settlor overlooks US tax liabilities at rates up to 100 per cent. on US beneficiaries who are to receive distributions from the trust, the mistake is one of legal effect since the practical effect of the tax liabilities is to substitute the US government as beneficiary in place of those chosen by the settlor.[40c] In the Isle of Man[40d] and Jersey,[40e] the distinction between effects and consequences has been discarded in favour of a test whether the mistake was so serious as to render it unjust for the volunteer donee to retain the monies if the payment would not have been made "but for" the mistake, thus allowing a tax mistake to vitiate a transaction.[40f] In *Pitt v Holt* this test has been disavowed, on the basis that the gravity of the mistake is an additional requirement to be satisfied but is not itself sufficient,[40g] and recent decisions made in reliance on it must now be regarded as doubtful in England.[40h] In turn the test in *Pitt v Holt* has been rejected in Jersey and the offshore decisions before *Pitt v Holt* have been followed.[40i]

Indirect effects

AT THE END OF THE TEXT ADD: The Court of Appeal has confirmed that it is **4–59** not possible or desirable to set out hard and fast rules as to when the effect of a mistake is sufficiently serious that the equitable jurisdiction to rescind may be invoked.[42a]

Mistake by trustees as to tax consequences

AT THE END OF TEXT ADD: It is now clear, however, that this jurisdiction may **4–60** be invoked only where the trustees have acted in breach of their fiduciary duties.[46a]

[40c] *Re S Trust* [2011] JRC 117 at [29].
[40d] *Clarkson v Barclays Private Bank (Isle of Man) Ltd* [2007] W.T.L.R 1703, Manx HC at [41]; *Re Betsam Trust* [2009] W.T.L.R. 1489, Manx HC.
[40e] *Re A Trust* [2009] JRC 245; (2009–10) 12 I.T.E.L.R. 866 at [43]; *Re Lochmore Trust* [2010] JRC 068.
[40f] Based upon the decision in *Ogilvie v Littleboy* (1897) 13 T.L.R. 399, CA (affd. (1899) 15 T.L.R. 294, HL), see § 4–64. These courts have proceeded to rescind transactions without considering first whether they are capable of rectification. In *DD v B* [2010] JRC 193 at [16], however, the court considered that if both remedies are available, a remedy which preserves the trust is to be preferred to one which sets aside that which the settlor intended to establish.
[40g] At [207].
[40h] Especially *Ogden v Trustees of the RHS Griffiths 2003 Settlement* [2008] EWHC 118 (Ch); [2009] Ch. 162. In *Pitt v Holt* [2011] EWCA Civ 197; [2012] Ch. 132 at [198] and [206], Lloyd L.J. doubted whether *Ogden* was correctly decided. The Supreme Court has given permission to appeal against the decision of the Court of Appeal in *Pitt v Holt* and so the exposition of its application in this work must be treated as provisional until the Supreme Court has given judgment.
[40i] *Re S Trust* [2011] JRC 117.
[42a] *Pitt v Holt* [2011] EWCA Civ 197; [2012] Ch. 132.
[46a] *Pitt v Holt* [2011] EWCA Civ 197; [2012] Ch. 132. See § 29–238 *et seq.* (Supplement).

Court's discretion to order rectification

4–63 NOTE 60: AT THE END ADD: But see *Ashcroft v Barnsdale* [2010] EWHC 1948 (Ch); [2010] S.T.C. 2544 at [22], where a deed of rectification of a deed of variation of a will did not preclude the remedy of rectification by the court since HMRC considered that the deed of rectification failed to have any effect on the inheritance tax incurred by reason of the deed of variation.

AT THE END OF THE TEXT ADD: The court has a discretion to rectify a trust deed to give effect to the intentions of the parties to the deed and it is not necessary for them to have agreed the precise form of words to be inserted.[60a]

Rescission

4–64 NOTE 61. AT THE END ADD: See, in particular, *Pitt v Holt* [2011] EWCA Civ 197; [2012] Ch. 132, where the cases were subject to a detailed analysis, and the test for rescission reformulated.

AT THE END OF THE TEXT ADD: It has been said that, where a transfer to trustees is made under a mistake, the transfer is voidable and not void and that relief may be refused as a matter of discretion.[73a]

Settlements executed by way of bargain

4–66 NOTE 80. FOR THE REFERENCE TO *Snell's Equity*, SEE NOW (32nd edn), § 16–025.

Rescission on the ground of fraud, duress, mistake, misrepresentation or undue influence

Undue influence

4–68 NOTE 87. FOR THE REFERENCE TO *Snell's Equity*, SEE NOW (32nd edn), §§ 8–008 *et seq.*

Cancellation

4–70 NOTE 96. FOR THE REFERENCE TO *Snell's Equity*, SEE NOW (32nd edn), § 14–007.

[60a] *Stephenson v Stephenson* [2004] EWHC 3473 (Ch); [2009] W.T.L.R. 1467. In *Whalen v Kelsey* [2009] EWHC 905; [2009] W.T.L.R. 1297, an ultimate default clause for a charity was deleted on an application for rectification, when the evidence showed that the settlors' true intention as to the beneficial interests did not require such a clause.

[73a] *Ogden v Trustees of the RHS Griffiths 2003 Settlement* [2008] EWHC 118 (Ch); [2009] Ch. 162 at [34]. Although the decision in *Ogden* is now regarded as doubtful, we consider this statement to be correct.

CHAPTER 5

LEGALITY OF OBJECT OF TRUST

2. TRUSTS AGAINST THE POLICY OF THE LAW

Conditions in restraint of marriage

NOTE 50. AT THE END ADD: In England a provision terminating a bene- **5–13** ficiary's interest in the event of his marriage outside a specified religious faith has been upheld: *Hodgson v Halford* (1879) 11 Ch.D. 959. In the United States, though such a provision may be void, a provision under which a person does not become a beneficiary of the trust at all if he has previously married outside a specified religious faith is valid since it does not seek to restrain that person's future decisions about marriage: *Re Estate of Feinberg* (2009) 235 Ill 2d 256; (2010–11) 13 I.T.E.L.R. 21, Illinois SC.

Name and arms clause

NOTE 61. AT THE END ADD: See too *Howard v Howard-Lawson* [2011] EWHC **5–17** 63 (Ch); [2011] All E.R (D) 172 (Jan).

Trusts created to facilitate an unlawful and fraudulent ulterior purpose

AT THE END OF THE TEXT ADD: For further proposals for reform, see Law **5–30** Commission Consultation Paper No.189 on the Illegality Defence (2009) and Law Commission Report No.320 on the Illegality Defence (2010). By its 2010 Report, the Law Commission proposes to abolish the reliance principle established by *Tinsley v Milligan*[96a] described in §§ 5–31 to 5–33 and to replace it by provisions conferring a statutory discretion on the court. The court is to have a discretion where a trust arrangement is created in order to conceal the beneficiary's interest in the trust property in connection with a criminal purpose, whether or not the criminal purpose has been acted upon, whether it is the beneficiary or the trustee who intends to use the trust arrangement to conceal the real ownership of the trust property and when the trust arrangement is created for other purposes in addition to conceal-ment of the real ownership. The statutory discretion is also to apply where the intention to use the trust arrangement to conceal the beneficial owner-ship for a criminal purpose was formed after the trust was made, but only where the beneficiary has taken steps to ensure that the trust arrangement

---

[96a] [1994] 1 A.C. 340, HL. The application of the reliance principle under the existing law to express trusts is considered in Law Commission Consultation Paper No.189 on the Illeg-ality Defence (2009) at §§ 6.37 to 6.51.

continues in place so that the concealment can be made, and the criminal purpose has been carried out by the beneficiary or by someone else with the beneficiary's consent. In a case where the statutory discretion applies, the court is to declare the intended beneficiary entitled to the equitable interest under the trust but has a discretion, exercisable in exceptional circumstances, to determine that the beneficiary ought not to be entitled to enforce the interest and that the interest should instead vest in the legal owner or, in a case where the settlor and the beneficiary are different people, or if there is another beneficiary, in the legal owner, settlor or another beneficiary.

5–31 NOTE 1. AT THE END ADD: See too *Poojary v Kotecha* [2002] All E.R. (D) 154 (May).

NOTE 2. AT THE END ADD: *Barrett v Barrett* [2008] EWHC 1061 (Ch); [2008] B.P.I.R. 817.

5–32 NOTE 5. AT THE END ADD: The presumption of advancement is prospectively abolished by Equality Act 2010, s.199. See §§ 9–03A and 9–03B (Supplement).

3. PERPETUITIES

The rule against perpetuities

5–35 DELETE THE LAST SENTENCE OF THE TEXT AND N.14 AND REPLACE BY: The Perpetuities and Accumulations Act 2009,[14] which came into force on April 6, 2010,[14a] makes further modifications to the common law rule, principally in relation to most instruments taking effect after the commencement of the 2009 Act, but also in one respect, under section 12 of the 2009 Act, in relation to pre-commencement instruments.[14b] The 2009 Act restricts the operation of the rule against perpetuities[14c] so that it applies only to trusts, powers of appointment and executory bequests.[14d]

AFTER § 5–35 INSERT THE FOLLOWING NEW PARAGRAPHS AND HEADINGS:

The three perpetuity regimes

5–35A Consequently, there are now three perpetuity regimes applicable to trusts:

> (1) *The common law rule regime.* Under this regime the common law rule as modified by section 12 of the 2009 Act has effect.

---

[14]   The 2009 Act implements with modifications proposals made by Law Commission Report No.251 on the Rules against Perpetuities and Excessive Accumulations (1998).

[14a]   Perpetuities and Accumulations Act 2009, s.22; Perpetuities and Accumulations Act 2009 (Commencement) Order 2010 (SI 2010/37).

[14b]   See § 5–36A (Supplement).

[14c]   Perpetuities and Accumulations Act 2009, s.1(1).

[14d]   Perpetuities and Accumulations Act 2009, s.1(2)–(8), and for exceptions see s.2 and s.3. See §§ 5–35D to 5–35H (Supplement). For exceptions, see Perpetuities and Accumulations Act 2009, ss.2 and 3; § 5–92A (Supplement).

(2) *The 1964 Act regime.* Under this regime the common law rule as modified by the 1964 Act and section 12 of the 2009 Act has effect.

(3) *The 2009 Act regime.* Under this regime the common law rule as modified by the 2009 Act (except section 12) has effect.

Which perpetuity regime applies

The common law rule regime applies to following instruments: **5–35B**

(1) the will or codicil of a testator who died before July 16, 1964;[14e]

(2) a lifetime instrument taking effect before July 16, 1964;[14f] and

(3) an instrument made on or after July 16, 1964 in the exercise of a special power of appointment as defined by the 1964 Act[14g] created by an instrument taking effect before July 16, 1964.[14h]

The 1964 Act regime applies to the following instruments, other than an instrument within sub–paragraph (3) above:

(4) the will or codicil made before July 16, 1964 of a testator who dies on or after that date;[14i]

(5) the will or codicil made on or after July 16, 1964 but before April 6, 2010 of a testator dying on, before or after April 6, 2010;[14j]

(6) a lifetime instrument made on or after July 16, 1964 but before April 6, 2010;[14k] and

(7) an instrument made on or after April 6, 2010 in the exercise of a special power of appointment as defined by the 2009 Act[14l] created by an instrument taking effect before April 6, 2010.[14m]

[14e] This is the effect of Perpetuities and Accumulations Act 1964, s.15(5), read with s.15(2); Perpetuities and Accumulations Act 2009, s.15(2)(*a*) and s.20(7).
[14f] This is the effect of Perpetuities and Accumulations Act 1964, s.15(5); Perpetuities and Accumulations Act 2009, s.15(2)(*b*).
[14g] Perpetuities and Accumulations Act 1964, s.7 and s.15(2). See §§ 5–84A and 5–85 (Supplement).
[14h] This is the effect of Perpetuities and Accumulations Act 1964, s.15(5), read with s.15(2); Perpetuities and Accumulations Act 2009, s.15(2)(*a*) and s.20(7).
[14i] Perpetuities and Accumulations Act 1964, s.15(5), read with s.15(2); Perpetuities and Accumulations Act 2009, s.15(2)(*a*) and (*b*) and s.20(7).
[14j] Perpetuities and Accumulations Act 1964, s.15(5), read with s.15(2); Perpetuities and Accumulations Act 2009, s.15(2)(*a*) and s.20(7); Perpetuities and Accumulations Act 1964, s.15(5A)(*a*), inserted by Perpetuities and Accumulations Act 2009, s.16.
[14k] Perpetuities and Accumulations Act 1964, s.15(5); Perpetuities and Accumulations Act 1964, s.15(5A), inserted by Perpetuities and Accumulations Act 2009, s.16; Perpetuities and Accumulations Act 2009, s.15(1) and s.15(2)(*a*).
[14l] Perpetuities and Accumulations Act 2009, s.11 and s.20(2). See §§ 5–84C and 5–85 (Supplement).
[14m] Perpetuities and Accumulations Act 1964, s.15(5) read with s.15(2); Perpetuities and Accumulations Act 1964, s.15(5A)(*b*), inserted by Perpetuities and Accumulations Act 2009, s.16; Perpetuities and Accumulations Act 2009, s.15(1)(*b*), s.15(2) and s.20(7). This differs from the recommendation made by the Law Commission in its Report No.251 on the Rules against Perpetuities and Excessive Accumulations (1998) at 8.23.

The 2009 Act regime applies to the following instruments, other than an instrument within sub-paragraph (3) or (7) above:

> (8) a will or codicil executed on or after April 6, 2010 (but not the will or codicil made before April 6, 2010 of a testator who dies on or after that date);[14n] and

> (9) a lifetime instrument made on or after April 6, 2010.[14o]

If a disposition is made otherwise than by an instrument, the 1964 Act applies, and if provision is made in relation to property otherwise than by an instrument, the 2009 Act applies, as if the disposition or provision had been contained in an instrument taking effect when the disposition or provision was made.[14p]

5–35C The same perpetuity regime does not necessarily apply to all the trusts and powers in the same settlement. For example, if an addition is made by the settlor on or after April 6, 2010 to a settlement made before that date but after July 16, 1964, whether by an instrument of addition, or oral provision directing the added property to be held as an addition to the trust fund, then the 1964 Act regime would apply to the original trust fund and the property representing it, while the 2009 Act regime would apply to the additional trust fund and the property representing it. And if there is a variation on or after April 6, 2010 of a settlement made before July 16, 1964 by agreement between the beneficiaries and the trustees, or by a variation approved under the Variation of Trusts Act 1958,[14q] of the trusts of part of the trust fund, or some but not all of the trusts, the 2009 Act regime will apply to the part of the trust subject to the variation or the trusts so far as varied, while the common law rule regime will continue to apply to the unvaried part of the trusts and the unvaried trusts. But where a variation is effected on or after April 6, 2010 by an exercise of a special power of appointment created before that date, the variation will, contrary to the recommendations of the Law Commission,[14r] be subject to the same regime as that applicable to the instrument creating the power and not to the 2009 Act regime.[14s]

Application of the rule against perpetuities under the 2009 Act

5–35D Section 1(1) of the 2009 Act provides that the rule against perpetuities applies (and applies only) as provided by section 1 of the 2009 Act. So far as

---

[14n] Perpetuities and Accumulations Act 1964, s.15(5A)(a), inserted by Perpetuities and Accumulations Act 2009, s.16; Perpetuities and Accumulations Act 2009, s.15(1), s.15(1)(a), s.15(2)(a) and s.20(7).

[14o] Perpetuities and Accumulations Act 1964, s.15(5A), inserted by Perpetuities and Accumulations Act 2009, s.16; Perpetuities and Accumulations Act 2009, s.15(1) and s.15(2). The different language used in the two provisions does not appear to be of practical significance.

[14p] Perpetuities and Accumulations Act 1964, s.15(6); Perpetuities and Accumulations Act 2009, s.19.

[14q] See § 45–57 (including Supplement).

[14r] Law Commission Report No.251 on the Rules against Perpetuities and Excessive Accumulations (1998) at § 8.23.

[14s] See § 5–35B(3) and (7) (Supplement).

trusts and powers are concerned, and subject to exceptions contained in sections 2 and 3 of the 2009 Act, the rule applies to the following instruments:[14t]

Successive estates or interests

Section 1(2) of the 2009 Act provides: **5–35E**

> "If an instrument limits property in trust so as to create successive estates or interests the rule applies to each of the estates or interests."

For these purposes an estate or interest includes an estate or interest which arises under a right of reverter on the determination of a determinable fee simple, or under a resulting trust on the determination of a determinable interest.[14u]

Estates or interests subject to a condition precedent

Section 1(3) of the 2009 Act provides: **5–35F**

> "If an instrument limits property in trust so as to create an estate or interest which is subject to a condition precedent and which is not one of successive estates or interests, the rule applies to the estate or interest."

This category may include the interests of beneficiaries under a discretionary trust.[14v]

Estates or interests subject to a condition subsequent

Section 1(4) of the 2009 Act provides: **5–35G**

> "If an instrument limits property in trust so as to create an estate or interest which is subject to a condition subsequent, the rule applies to—
>
> (*a*) any right of re-entry exercisable if the condition is broken, or
> (*b*) any equivalent right exercisable in the case of property other than land if the condition is broken."

The remoteness of a condition subsequent does not render the estate or interest void, but rather renders the rights ensuing from a breach of the condition void and thereby frees the estate or interest from the condition. The rights ensuing from a breach of a condition subsequent are, however,

---

[14t] For the purposes of the 2009 Act, an instrument includes an trust or other provision relating to property: see Perpetuities and Accumulations Act 2009, s.19.

[14u] Perpetuities and Accumulations Act 2009, s.1(7). See § 5–84A (Supplement).

[14v] Law Commission Report No.251 on the Rules against Perpetuities and Excessive Accumulations (1998) at § 3.3. If not, the relevant category for such interests is s.1(6) (powers of appointment), see § 5–84C.

subject to wait and see provisions so that they will take effect if exercised during the perpetuity period under the 2009 Act.[14w]

Powers of appointment

5–35H Section 1(6) of the 2009 Act provides:

> "If an instrument creates a power of appointment the rule applies to the power."

Powers of appointment are considered later.[14x]

Traditional perpetuity period

5–36 DELETE THE FIRST SENTENCE OF THE TEXT AND NN.15 AND 16 AND REPLACE BY: Except for dispositions subject to the 1964 Act regime where an alternative period is chosen,[15] and except for dispositions subject to the 2009 Act regime,[15a] the perpetuity period allowed is a life or any number of lives in being at the creation of the trust, plus 21 years, plus any actual periods of gestation.[16]

Alternative periods

5–37 DELETE THE FIRST SENTENCE OF THE TEXT AND N.21 AND REPLACE BY: Where a disposition is subject to the 1964 Act regime and the instrument by which the disposition is made so provides, the perpetuity period, instead of being of any other duration, is of a duration equal to such number of years not exceeding 80 as is specified in that behalf in the instrument.[21]

AFTER § 5–37 INSERT THE FOLLOWING NEW PARAGRAPHS AND HEADINGS:

Section 12 of the 2009 Act—pre-commencement instruments

5–37A Where the common law rule regime applies to an instrument, and where the 1964 Act regime applies and no alternative period has been chosen,[24a] section 12(1) of the 2009 Act confers a power on the trustees, if certain conditions are satisfied, to apply section 12(2) of the 2009 Act so that the trusts of the instrument become subject to a 100-year perpetuity period and to other rules concerning perpetuities (but not accumulations) taking effect under the 2009 Act regime. Section 12 does not apply if the terms of the trust

---

[14w] Perpetuities and Accumulations Act 2009, s.7(3) and (4).
[14x] See §§ 5–84B *et seq.* (Supplement).
[15] See § 5–37.
[15a] See § 5–37A (Supplement).
[16] See *Duke of Norfolk's Case* (1683) 3 Ch. Ca. 1 at 20, 28 and 48.
[21] Perpetuities and Accumulations Act 1964, s.1. The rule applies also to a disposition made otherwise than by an instrument as if contained in an instrument taking effect when the disposition was made: s.15(6), and see § 5–35B (Supplement).
[24a] Perpetuities and Accumulations Act 2009, s.15(2); and see §§ 5–35A and 5–35B (Supplement).

were exhausted before April 6, 2010[24b] or became held on trust for charitable purposes by way of a final disposition of the property.[24c]

Conditions for the exercise of the trustees' power

Three conditions must be satisfied. The first two conditions, contained in **5–37B** section 12(1)(*a*) and (*b*) of the 2009 Act, are as follows:

> "If—
>
> (*a*) an instrument specifies for the purposes of property limited in trust a perpetuity period by reference to the lives of persons in being when the instrument takes effect,
>
> (*b*) the trustees believe that it is difficult or not reasonably practicable for them to ascertain whether the lives have ended and therefore whether the perpetuity period has ended, ..."

The third condition concerns the mode of exercise of the power and is considered in § 5–37C (Supplement). An example of an instrument satisfying the first condition is a trust utilising a royal lives clause.[24d] The wording of the second condition is odd in two related ways. The first oddity is the use of the word "therefore". The end of the lives is most unlikely to be coterminous with the end of the perpetuity period. Normally the perpetuity period will end 21 years after the death of the last surviving measuring life. There may be difficulty in ascertaining whether the lives have ended, but no difficulty in ascertaining whether the perpetuity period has ended. That would be so where it is known that a measuring life, possibly but not certainly the last, has died within the last 21 years. The second oddity is the use of the past tense (twice) in the phrase "whether the lives have ended and therefore whether the perpetuity period has ended". Though this derives from a bill drafted by the Law Commission, the use of the past tense does not accord with the recommendation of the Law Commission. The recommendation was that it would be sufficient for the trustees to believe that it is difficult or impracticable to ascertain the existence or whereabouts of the measuring lives in being so that they could not determine the date at which the perpetuity period would come to an end.[24e] The trustees might have such a belief, for example, in the case of a settlement made in 1927 using a perpetuity period expiring 21 years after the death of the last surviving descendant of Queen Victoria living at the date of the settlement. But on a literal reading the second condition could not be satisfied in the case of such a settlement since at least one of the measuring lives (namely the present Queen) is still living and so the trustees could not believe that there is any difficulty at all in ascertaining whether the lives *have* ended, nor could they

---

[24b] Perpetuities and Accumulations Act 2009, s.15(3)(*a*). April 6, 2010 is the date of commencement, see s.22 and Perpetuities and Accumulations Act 2009 (Commencement) Order 2010 (SI 2010/37).

[24c] Perpetuities and Accumulations Act 2009, s.15(3)(*b*).

[24d] See § 5–42.

[24e] Law Commission Report No.251 on the Rules against Perpetuities and Excessive Accumulations (1998) at §§ 8.19 and 8.20.

believe that there is any difficulty at all in ascertaining whether the perpetuity period *has* ended until 21 years after the death of the present Queen. If
read literally, the second condition is both odd and very restrictive and
arguably it should be given a purposive construction so as to accord with the
Law Commission's recommendation.

Exercise of the power

5–37C If the conditions considered above are satisfied, the trustees may exercise the
power conferred by section 12(1) of the 2009 Act by deed stating that they
believe that it is difficult or not reasonably practicable to ascertain whether
the lives have ended and therefore whether the perpetuity period has ended,
and stating that section 12(2) is to apply to the instrument.[24f] The power
conferred by section 12(1) is conferred on the trustees by virtue of their
office and so is a fiduciary power which must be exercised in the best
interests of the beneficiaries.[24g] It is thought that material factors for the
trustees to take into consideration are the degree of difficulty in ascertaining
whether the lives have ended, the effect of the exercise of the power on
beneficial interests, the effect of the exercise of the power on potential
unborn and unascertained beneficiaries, possible alternative methods of
resolving any uncertainty arising whether through the exercise of other
powers or agreement between the beneficiaries, and the tax position. It is to
be noted that in some circumstances an exercise of the power could have a
dramatic, even perverse, effect on beneficial interests, as where the effect of
the imposition of a 100-year perpetuity period is to eliminate the interests of
beneficiaries who are bound to take under the existing trusts and to vest the
interests of beneficiaries whose interests are bound to fail under the existing
trusts.[24h] It is doubtful whether the power could be properly exercised in
such circumstances.

Which trustees are to exercise the power

5–37D In view of the way section 12(1) of the 2009 Act is worded, it seems that all
trustees must execute the deed even if the terms of the trust authorise the
trustees to act by majority. In view of the wording of the power and the
terms of section 12(2) it seems doubtful whether, in a case where separate
sets of trustees have been appointed for different funds held under different
trusts contained in the same instrument, one set of trustees can exercise the
section 12(1) power as regards the separate trusts.

Effect of exercise of the power

5–37E The exercise of the power in relation to a pre-commencement instrument
causes the instrument to have effect as if it had specified a perpetuity period
of 100 years (and no other period),[24i] and the rule against perpetuities has

---

[24f] Perpetuities and Accumulations Act 2009, s.12(1)(*c*).
[24g] See § 29–19; Parliamentary Explanatory Notes, § 66.
[24h] See supplementary memorandum by Lord Millett filed in HL Appeal Committee Minutes
of Evidence on the Perpetuities and Accumulations Bill dated June 9, 2009.
[24i] Perpetuities and Accumulations Act 2009, s.12(2)(*a*).

effect as if the only perpetuity applicable to the instrument were 100 years.[24j]
Further, the provisions in the 2009 Act concerning the start of the perpetuity
period,[24k] the wait and see rule,[24l] the exclusion of class members to avoid
remoteness,[24m] the saving of expectant interests,[24n] determinable interests[24o]
and powers of appointment[24p] apply to the instrument[24q] in place of the
corresponding provisions in the 1964 Act (if otherwise applicable).[24r]

The perpetuity period under the 2009 Act

Section 5(1) of the 2009 Act provides that: **5–37F**

"The perpetuity period is 125 years (and no other period)."

The perpetuity period applies to an instrument subject to the 2009 Act
regime whether or not the instrument specifies a perpetuity period, and a
specification of a perpetuity period in the instrument is ineffective.[24s]
Although the perpetuity period is fixed there is no reason why a trust should
not contain interests or powers which will vest within a shorter period,
whether or not by reference to lives. For instance, if it is contemplated that
property might be transferred into a trust subject to the 2009 Act regime
from a trust subject to the common law rule regime, a provision for a trust
period ending on the date of expiry of a period of 125 years from and
including the date of the trust instrument, or the date of expiry of a period of
21 years commencing on the death of the last survivor of lives in being at the
date of the creation of the proposed transferor trust, whichever is the earlier,
would ensure that the trust period complied both with the perpetuity period
applicable to the trust subject to the 2009 Act regime and with the common
law perpetuity period applicable[24t] to the property received from the proposed transferor trust.

Start of the perpetuity period

The 125-year perpetuity period starts when the instrument containing the **5–37G**
relevant interest takes effect,[24u] or, if that instrument is made in exercise of a
special power of appointment, when the instrument creating the power takes
effect.[24v] Special rules apply to pension schemes.[24w] A will takes effect on the
death of the testator.[24x] A deed will take effect when it has been signed and

---

[24j] *ibid.*, s.12(2)(*b*).
[24k] *ibid.*, s.6. See § 5–37G (Supplement).
[24l] *ibid.*, s.7. See § 5–38A (Supplement).
[24m] *ibid.*, s.8. See § 5–71A (Supplement).
[24n] *ibid.*, s.9. See § 5–78A (Supplement).
[24o] *ibid.*, s.10. See § 5–84A (Supplement)
[24p] *ibid.*, s.11. See § 5–85A (Supplement).
[24q] *ibid.*, s.12(2)(*c*).
[24r] *ibid.*, s.12(2)(*d*).
[24s] *ibid.*, s.5(2).
[24t] See § 5–90.
[24u] Perpetuities and Accumulations Act 2009, s.6(1). Instrument includes an oral trust or other
       provision relating to property, see s.19.
[24v] *ibid.*, s.6(2).
[24w] See § 5–35B (Supplement).
[24x] Perpetuities and Accumulations Act 2009, s.20(6).

unconditionally delivered by all necessary parties. It is thought that the fact that a deed is revocable by the settlor makes no difference to the time when it takes effect and hence does not suspend the commencement of the perpetuity period.[24y] However, should beneficiaries contract to concur in a variation of beneficial interests if certain conditions become satisfied, for instance if the variation is approved on behalf of other beneficiaries under the Variation of Trusts Act 1958, the relevant instrument will be the instrument effecting the variation and the perpetuity period will start when that instrument is made,[24z] not the earlier time when the contract is made, since the contract by itself does not limit property in trust.

The time to apply the rule

5–38 AT THE END OF THE TEXT ADD: The wait and see rule under section 3(1) of the 1964 Act applies only to dispositions subject to the 1964 Act regime.[29a]

AFTER § 5–38 INSERT THE FOLLOWING NEW PARAGRAPH AND HEADING:

Wait and see under the 2009 Act

5–38A Instruments within the 2009 Act regime are subject to a similar wait and see rule to that which is contained in section 3(1) of the 1964 Act considered above. The corresponding provisions of the 2009 Act are contained in section 7(1) and (2) which provide as follows:

> "(1) Subsection (2) applies if (apart from this section and section 8)[29b] an estate or interest would be void on the ground that it might not become vested until too remote a time.
>
> (2) In such a case—
>
>> (a) until such time (if any) as it becomes established that the vesting must occur (if at all) after the end of the perpetuity period the estate or interest must be treated as if it were not subject to the rule against perpetuities, and
>> (b) if it becomes so established, that does not affect the validity of anything previously done (whether by way of advancement, application of intermediate income or otherwise) in relation to the estate or interest."

Although these provisions are similar to those in the 1964 Act, they apply in a different way in that waiting under the 1964 Act is (if there is no fixed perpetuity period) by reference to a period of statutory lives,[29c] while the waiting under the 2009 Act is by reference to the 125-year perpetuity

---

[24y] Compare § 5–92 as to the start of the perpetuity period under the common law rule.
[24z] See § 45–57 (including Supplement).
[29a] See §§ 5–35A and 5–35B (Supplement).
[29b] See § 5–71A (Supplement) as to Perpetuities and Accumulations Act 2009, s.8.
[29d] See §§ 5–37E and 5–37F (Supplement).

period[29d] applicable under the 2009 Act. The wait and see rule under the 2009 Act is therefore simpler to operate than the wait and see rule under the 1964 Act, though the period of waiting under the 2009 Act may well be substantially longer than under the 1964 Act. The wait and see rules under the 2009 Act concerning conditions subsequent and powers of appointment are considered elsewhere.[29e]

Lives in being for the common law period

No lives expressly chosen

NOTE 37. For the reference to Megarry and Wade, *The Law of Real Prop-* **5–41** *erty*, see now (7th edn), §§ 9–044, 9–045.

Child-bearing age

Under statute

NOTE 63. DELETE AND REPLACE BY: She would be its mother and her husband **5–60** its father under Human Embryology and Fertilisation Act 2008, which is retrospective, see §§ 6–19A to 6–19E (Supplement).

AFTER § 5–61 INSERT THE FOLLOWING NEW PARAGRAPH:

The provisions of section 2 of the 1964 Act considered in §§ 5–59 to 5–60 **5–61A** apply only to dispositions subject to the 1964 Act regime.[64a] There are no provisions corresponding to section 2 of the 1964 Act under the 2009 Act regime since the 125-year perpetuity period under the 2009 Act[64b] is not referable to lives in being.[64c]

Gifts at ages over twenty-one

AT THE END OF THE TEXT ADD: Section 4(1) of the 1964 Act applies only to **5–70** dispositions subject to the 1964 Act regime.[18a] There is no provision corresponding to section 4(1) under the 2009 Act regime since the 125-year perpetuity period under the 2009 Act[18b] is not referable to lives in being.[18c] The omission of any corresponding provision in the 2009 Act means, however, that a gift to a person at an age which he will attain, if at all, after the end of the 125-year perpetuity period will fail and not be saved by reduction to a younger age. This omission will have a significant impact in cases where a gift in favour a person who is born towards the end of the perpetuity period is contingent on attainment of some age such as the age of 25 but the gift fails to provide for vesting of the gift if that person is living and under the age at the end of the perpetuity period.

[29d] See §§ 5–37E and 5–37F (Supplement).
[29e] See §§ 5–35G, 5–86A and 5–89A (Supplement).
[64a] See §§ 5–35A and 5–35B (Supplement).
[64b] See §§ 5–37E and 5–37F (Supplement).
[64c] See Law Commission Report No.251 on the Rules against Perpetuities and Excessive Accumulations (1998) at §§ 8.27 and 8.29.
[18a] See §§ 5–35A and 5–35B (Supplement).
[18b] See §§ 5–37E and 5–37F (Supplement).
[18c] See Law Commission Report No.251 on the Rules against Perpetuities and Excessive Accumulations (1998) at §§ 8.27 and 8.29.

Excluding members to save class gifts

5–71   AT THE END OF THE TEXT ADD: Section 4(3) and (4) of the 1964 Act apply only to dispositions subject to the 1964 Act regime.[20a]

AFTER § 5–38 INSERT THE FOLLOWING NEW PARAGRAPH AND HEADING:

Exclusion of class members to avoid remoteness under the 2009 Act

5–71A   There is no provision corresponding to section 4(3) of the 1964 Act under the 2009 Act regime, since section 4(3) is dependent on the age reduction provisions considered in § 5–70.[20b] Section 8 of the 2009 Act does, however, substantially reproduce the effect of section 4(4) of the 1964 Act. Section 8(1) and (2) provide as follows:

> "(1)   This section applies if—
>
> > (*a*)   it is apparent at the time an instrument takes effect or becomes apparent at a later time that (apart from this section) the inclusion of certain persons as members of a class would cause an estate or interest to be treated as void for remoteness, and
> >
> > (*b*)   those persons are potential members of the class or unborn persons who at birth would become members or potential members of the class.
>
> (2)   From the time it is or becomes so apparent those persons must be treated as excluded from the class unless their exclusion would exhaust the class."

For the purposes of section 8, a person is a member of a class if in that person's case all the conditions identifying a member of the class is satisfied,[20c] and a person is a potential member of a class if in that person's case some only of those conditions are satisfied but there is a possibility that the remainder will in time be satisfied.[20d] Section 8 takes effect subject to the wait and see provisions in section 7 of the 2009 Act and so will become operative only if section 7 fails wholly to save the gift from invalidity. Note that where an age condition must be satisfied, it will be possible to determine at the outset that members of the class born after a certain date cannot take and so cannot be saved by the operation of section 7. For instance, if there is a condition of attainment of the age of 25 years, then no member of the class born more than 100 years after the time when the instrument took effect could take, and there is no reduction in the age so as to allow such persons to take. Where, however, section 7 is capable of operating so as to prevent exclusion from a class under section 8, for example where the contingency is marriage, section 8 does not affect the validity of anything done during the

---

[20a]   See §§ 5–35A and 5–35B (Supplement).
[20b]   See Law Commission Report No.251 on the Rules against Perpetuities and Excessive Accumulations (1998) at §§ 8.27 and 8.29.
[20c]   Perpetuities and Accumulations Act 2009, s.8(4)(*a*).
[20d]   *ibid.*, s.8(4)(*b*).

wait and see period (whether by way of advancement, application of intermediate income or otherwise) in relation to the estate or interest.[20e] In view of the length of the perpetuity period under the 2009 Act, section 8 is unlikely to become of practical significance for many years.

After-born spouses

AT THE END OF THE TEXT ADD: Section 5 of the 1964 Act applies only to **5–72** dispositions subject to the 1964 Act regime.[20f] There is no corresponding provision under the 2009 Act regime since the 125-year perpetuity period under the 2009 Act[20g] is not referable to lives in being.[20h] It is theoretically possible, but improbable, that a person who is living at the commencement of the 125-year perpetuity period under the 2009 Act will leave a spouse living at the end of that period, and the great majority of gifts of the kind at which section 5 of the 1964 Act were directed will in the case of instruments subject to the 2009 Act regime be saved by the wait and see provisions in section 7 of the 2009 Act.

Subsequent trusts

Invalidity by contagion

AT THE END OF THE TEXT ADD: Section 6 of the 1964 Act applies only to **5–78** dispositions subject to the 1964 Act regime.[28a]

AFTER § 5–78 INSERT THE FOLLOWING NEW PARAGRAPH AND HEADING:

Avoiding invalidity by contagion under the 2009 Act

Section 9 of the 2009 Act, however, substantially reproduces the effect of **5–78A** section 6 of the 1964 Act. Section 9 provides as follows:

> "(1) An estate or interest is not void for remoteness by reason only that it is ulterior to and dependent on an estate or interest which is so void.
>
> (2) The vesting of an estate or interest is not prevented from being accelerated on the failure of a prior estate or interest by reason only that the failure arises because of remoteness."

Terminable interests and resulting trusts

FIRST SENTENCE. DELETE THE REFERENCE TO post-June 15, 1964 provisions **5–84** AND REPLACE BY A REFERENCE TO post-July 15, 1964 dispositions.

THIRD SENTENCE. DELETE THE REFERENCE TO a post-June 15, 1964 conveyance AND REPLACE BY A REFERENCE TO a post-July 15, 1964 conveyance.

[20e] *ibid.*, s.8(3).
[20f] See §§ 5–35A and 5–35B (Supplement).
[20g] See §§ 5–37E and 5–37F (Supplement).
[20h] See Law Commission Report No.251 on the Rules against Perpetuities and Excessive Accumulations (1998) at §§ 8.27 and 8.29.
[28a] See §§ 5–35A and 5–35B (Supplement).

AT THE END OF THE TEXT ADD: Section 12 of the 1964 Act applies only to dispositions subject to the 1964 Act regime.[47a]

AFTER § 5–84 INSERT THE FOLLOWING NEW PARAGRAPHS AND HEADINGS:

5–84A   A similar effect to section 12 of the 1964 is produced by section 10 of the 2009 Act, read with section 1(2) and (7),[47b] and section 7(1) and (2),[47c] of the 2009 Act. In view of section 1(2) and (7) of the 2009 Act, an interest which arises under a right of reverter on the determination of a determinable fee simple, or which arises under a resulting trust on the determination of a determinable interest, is subject to the rule against perpetuities, like a gift over in the event of failure of a determinable interest. In view of the wait and see provisions of section 7(1) and (2) of the 2009 Act, such an interest is, however, valid until such time as it becomes established that the determination must occur, if at all, after the end of the perpetuity period. In view of section 10 of the 2009 Act, if it is established that such an interest is void for remoteness, then the determinable fee simple or interest becomes absolute.

Definition of "power of appointment" in the 1964 and 2009 Acts

5–84B   The expression "power of appointment" is defined in the 1964 Act as including any discretionary power to transfer a beneficial interest in property.[47d] In the context of the 1964 Act this definition is mainly of importance for drawing distinctions between the treatment under the 1964 Act of general and special powers of appointment. In the context of the 2009 Act the definition of "power of appointment" is important for drawing similar distinctions under the 2009 Act. But in that context the definition has an additional importance since, under the provisions of section 1 of the 2009 Act, and in particular section 1(6) of the 2009 Act, a power of appointment is the only kind of power to which the rule against perpetuities applies under the 2009 Act.[47e] If a power is not a power of appointment within the meaning of the 2009 Act, the power is not subject to the rule against perpetuities under the 2009 Act regime.

5–84C   The expression "power of appointment" is defined in the 2009 Act as including a discretionary power to create a beneficial interest in property without the provision of valuable consideration and a discretionary power to transfer a beneficial interest in property without the provision of valuable consideration.[47f] It is thought that this definition is wide enough to catch, in addition to conventional powers of appointment, and if exercisable without the provision of valuable consideration, powers of resettlement, powers of nomination, powers of advancement, powers to transfer to other trusts, powers of revocation or variation of interests in property, discretionary powers of application or distribution of property (including income), and discretionary trusts over property (including income) to the extent (if at all)

[47a]   See §§ 5–35A and 5–35B (Supplement).
[47b]   See § 5–35E (Supplement).
[47c]   See § 5–38A (Supplement).
[47d]   Perpetuities and Accumulations Act 1964, s.15(2).
[47e]   See §§ 5–35D to 5–35H (Supplement).
[47f]   Perpetuities and Accumulations Act 2009, s.20(2).

that such trusts do not constitute interests subject to the rule against perpetuities by virtue of section 1(2) or (3) of the 2009 Act. Dispositive powers over trust property exercisable with the provision of valuable consideration, whether or not adequate consideration and whether or not on a commercial basis, are not, however, powers of appointment to which the rule against perpetuities applies under the 2009 Act.

Powers of appointment – general and special powers

NOTE 53. For the reference to Megarry and Wade, *The Law of Real Property*, see now (7th edn), § 9–103.   **5–85**

AT THE END OF THE TEXT ADD: Section 7 of the 1964 Act applies only to dispositions subject to the 1964 Act regime.[53a]

AFTER § 5–85 INSERT THE FOLLOWING NEW PARAGRAPH AND HEADING:

The distinction between general and special powers under the 2009 Act

Section 11 of the 2009 Act contains provisions distinguishing between general and special powers of appointment which are similar to, but more refined than, the provisions in section 7 of the 1964 Act. Section 11(1) and (2) are concerned with powers of appointment exercisable otherwise than by will and provide as follows: **5–85A**

"(1) Subsection (2) applies to a power of appointment exercisable otherwise than by will (whether or not it is also exercisable by will).

(2) For the purposes of the rule against perpetuities the power is a special power unless—

(*a*) the instrument creating it expresses it to be exercisable by one person only, and

(*b*) at all times during its currency when that person is of full age and capacity it could be exercised by that person so as immediately to transfer to that person the whole of the interest governed by the power without the consent of any other person or compliance with any other condition (ignoring a formal condition relating only to the mode of exercise of the power)."

Section 11(3) and (4) are concerned with powers of appointment exercisable by will and provide as follows:

"(3) Subsection (4) applies to a power of appointment exercisable by will (whether or not it is also exercisable otherwise than by will).

(4) For the purposes of the rule against perpetuities the power is a special power unless—

[53a] See §§ 5–35A and 5–35B (Supplement).

> (*a*) the instrument creating it expresses it to be exercisable by one person only, and
>
> (*b*) that person could exercise it to transfer to that person's personal representatives the whole of the estate or interest to which it relates."

Sections 11(2) and (4) are not mutually exclusive since both apply to a power of appointment which is exercisable by will or otherwise. It is possible that a power of appointment might be a special power under one but not both of the sections 11(2) and (4); for example, where a power of appointment is conferred on one person only and is exercisable during his lifetime by deed in favour of himself with the consent of the trustees and is exercisable by will in favour of his personal representatives. In such a case the power of appointment is a special power for the purposes of the rule against perpetuities.[53b]

General powers and appointments under them

5–86 DELETE THE SECOND SENTENCE OF THE TEXT. AFTER THE TEXT TO N.57 ADD: As regards dispositions subject to the 1964 Act regime, section 3(2) of the 1964 Act provides that where, apart from the wait and see provisions of section 3 of the 1964 Act, a disposition consisting of the conferring of a general power of appointment would be void on the ground that the power might not become exercisable until too remote a time, the disposition shall be treated, until such time (if any) as it is established that the power will not be exercised within the perpetuity period, as if it were not subject to the rule against perpetuities. Consequently any exercise of a general power of appointment within the perpetuity period applicable to the disposition under the 1964 Act complies with the rule against perpetuities so far as the time of exercise of the power is concerned.

AFTER § 5–86 INSERT THE FOLLOWING NEW PARAGRAPH AND HEADING:

General powers of appointment under the 2009 Act

5–86A The rule against perpetuities applies to a general power of appointment contained in an instrument subject to the 2009 Act regime under section 1(6) of the 2009 Act. The 125-year perpetuity period starts under section 6(1) of the 2009 Act when the instrument containing the general power takes effect.[58a] Section 7(5) and (6) of the 2009 Act contain a wait and see rule in relation to the time of exercise of a general power of appointment similar to that contained in section 3(2) of the 1964 Act considered in § 5–86. Consequently, any exercise of a general power of appointment within the 125-year perpetuity period complies with the rule against perpetuities so far as the time of exercise is concerned. Trusts created by an exercise of a general power of appointment will be subject to a 125-year perpetuity period

---

[53b] Perpetuities and Accumulations 2009, s.11(5) and (6).
[58a] See § 5–37G (Supplement).

starting when the instrument containing the exercise of the power takes effect, not when the instrument creating the power took effect.[58b] In the case of an instrument taking effect on or after April 6, 2010[58c] under a general power of appointment, within the meaning of the 2009 Act,[58d] created before April 6, 2010, although the validity of the creation of the power and time of exercise of the power will be governed by the perpetuity regime applicable to the disposition creating the power, the trusts contained in the instrument exercising the power will be subject to the 2009 Act regime and so be subject to a 125-year perpetuity period starting when the instrument takes effect.

Appointments under special powers

AT THE END OF THE TEXT ADD: Section 4 of the 1964 Act considered above, **5–89** and section 3(3) of the 1964 Act considered in §§ 5–87 and 5–88, apply only to dispositions subject to the 1964 Act regime.[74a]

AFTER § 5–89 INSERT THE FOLLOWING NEW PARAGRAPH AND HEADING:

Special powers of appointment under the 2009 Act

The 2009 Act regime is concerned solely with special powers of appointment **5–89A** created by a will made on or after April 6, 2010 or by other instrument taking effect on or after that date. The 2009 Act regime is not concerned with any exercise on or after April 6, 2010 of any special powers of appointment created before that date or contained in a will made before that date.[74b] The rule against perpetuities applies to a special power of appointment contained in an instrument subject to the 2009 Act regime under section 1(6) of the 2009 Act. The 125-year perpetuity period starts under section 6(1) of the 2009 Act when the instrument containing the special power takes effect.[74c] Section 7(3) and (4) of the 2009 Act contain a similar wait and see rule in relation to the time of exercise of a special power of appointment to that contained in section 3(3) of the 1964 Act considered in § 5–87. Consequently any exercise of a special power of appointment within the 125-year perpetuity period complies with the rule against perpetuities so far as the time of exercise is concerned. Trusts created by an exercise of a special power of appointments will be subject to a 125-year perpetuity period starting when the instrument creating the power took effect, not when the instrument exercising the power takes effect.[74d]

Advancements

AFTER THE TEXT TO N.75 ADD. A power of advancement (exercisable without **5–90** the provision of valuable consideration) comes within the definition of

---

[58b] Perpetuities and Accumulations 2009, s.6(2) has no application to an instrument made in exercise of a general power of appointment.
[58c] See § 5–35B (Supplement).
[58d] See § 5–85A (Supplement).
[74a] See §§ 5–35A and 5–35B (Supplement).
[74b] See §§ 5–35A and 5–35B (Supplement).
[74c] See § 5–37G (Supplement).
[74d] Perpetuities and Accumulations 2009, s.6(2).

"power of appointment" in section 20(2) of the 2009 Act[75a] and, if vested in trustees, comes within the definition of "special power of appointment" in section 11 the 2009 Act.[75b] Accordingly, if subject to the 2009 Act regime, such powers of advancement will be subject to the same rules as apply to special powers of appointment under the 2009 Act regime.[75c]

DELETE THE THIRD SENTENCE OF THE TEXT AND NN.76 AND 77 AND REPLACE BY: If the new trusts partially contravene the rule, and the remaining trusts cannot reasonably be regarded as beneficial to the advanced beneficiary, the whole advancement will be void,[76] but otherwise the advancement will be valid as to the trusts not rendered void for perpetuity.[77]

Administrative powers and trusts

5–91 AT THE END OF THE TEXT ADD: Section 8 of the 1964 Act applies only to dispositions subject to the common law regime and 1964 Act regime. Conventional administrative powers and trustee charging clauses are not powers of appointment within section 1(6) and 20(2) of the 2009 Act,[78a] nor estates or interests limited in trust within section 1(2) to (4) of the 2009 Act,[78b] and so the rule against perpetuities does not apply to them under the 2009 Act regime.[78c]

Exceptions to the rule against perpetuities

AFTER § 5–92 INSERT THE FOLLOWING NEW PARAGRAPH AND HEADING:

Exceptions under the 2009 Act

5–92A Section 1(2) to (4), (6) and (7) of the 2009 Act set out the estates or interests under trusts, and powers, which are subject to the rule against perpetuities. Section 1(8) provides that section 1 of the 2009 Act takes effect subject to the exceptions made by section 2 and to any exceptions made under section 3. The exceptions in section 2 are of two kinds. First, section 2(2) and (3) contain exceptions about property passing from one charity to another which are similar to the common law exception concerning charities mentioned in § 5–92. Secondly, section 2(4) and (5) contain provisions concerning pension funds and nominations and advancements under them considered in §§ 5–93A and 5–94A. Section 3 of the 2009 Act confers a power, not yet exercised, on the Lord Chancellor to make further exceptions

---

[75a] See § 5–84C (Supplement).
[75b] See § 5–85A (Supplement).
[75c] See § 5–89A (Supplement).
[76] *Re Abrahams' Will Trusts* [1969] 1 Ch. 463; as interpreted in *Re Hastings-Bass* [1975] Ch. 25 at 41, CA; *Pitt v Holt* [2011] EWCA Civ 197; [2012] Ch. 132 at [39]–[45], [57] and [58].
[77] *Re Hastings-Bass*, above; considered in *Pitt v Holt*, above, at [46]–[67]. As to the circumstances in which an exercise of the power of advancement (or other power), though falling within the scope of the power, may be set aside on the ground of breach of duty in failing to take into account relevant consideration or taking into account irrelevant considerations, see §§ 29–238 *et seq.* (Supplement). See further § 32–21 (including Supplement).
[78a] See §§ 5–35H and 5–84C (Supplement).
[78b] See §§ 5–35E to 5–35G (Supplement).
[78c] See § 5–35D (Supplement).

to the rule against perpetuities with the approval of a resolution of each House of Parliament.

Pension funds

AT THE END OF THE TEXT ADD: Section 163 of the Pension Schemes Act 1963 **5–93** was repealed by the Perpetuities and Accumulations Act 2009.[1a] The repeal applies only in relation to instruments made on or after April 6, 2010,[1b] when the 2009 Act came into force,[1c] though not to instruments made on or after that date in exercise of a special power of appointment created before April 6, 2010.[1d] Section 163 will therefore continue to have effect in relation to pre-commencement pension schemes.

AFTER § 5–93 INSERT THE FOLLOWING NEW PARAGRAPH AND HEADING:

Pension funds under the Perpetuities and Accumulations Act 2009

As regards pension schemes subject to the 2009 Act regime, section 2(4) of **5–93A** the 2009 Act provides that the rule against perpetuities does not apply to an interest or right arising under a relevant pension scheme. A relevant pension scheme is an occupational pension scheme, a personal pension scheme or a public service pension scheme.[1e]

AFTER § 5–94 INSERT THE FOLLOWING NEW PARAGRAPH AND HEADING:

Nominations and advancements under the Perpetuities and Accumulations Act 2009

The exception from the rule against perpetuities for pension schemes under **5–94A** section 2(4) of the 2009 Act[6a] does not apply to an interest or right arising under an instrument nominating benefits under the scheme, or an instrument made in the exercise of a power of advancement arising under the scheme.[6b] In relation to such an interest or right, the 125–year perpetuity period under the 2009 Act starts[6c] when the member concerned became a member of the scheme, that member being the member in respect of whose interest in the scheme the instrument is made.[6d] Since a power of nomination or advancement is a special power of appointment within the meaning of the 2009 Act,[6e] these provisions will apply only where the instrument creating the power took effect on or after April 6, 2010.[6f]

[1a]   Perpetuities and Accumulations Act 2009, s.4(3), s.21 and Sch.
[1b]   *ibid.*, s.15(1), s.21, Sch.
[1c]   Perpetuities and Accumulations Act 2009, s.22; Perpetuities and Accumulations Act 2009 (Commencement) Order 2010 (SI 2010/37).
[1d]   Perpetuities and Accumulations Act 2009, s.15(1)(b).
[1e]   *ibid.*, s.15(4) and (5).
[6a]   See § 5–93A (Supplement).
[6b]   Perpetuities and Accumulations Act 2009, s.5. See § 5–37F (Supplement).
[6c]   *ibid.*, s.2(5).
[6d]   *ibid.*, s.6(3) and (4).
[6e]   *ibid.*, s.11 and s.20(2). See §§ 5–84C and 5–85A (Supplement).
[6f]   Perpetuities and Accumulations Act 2009, s.15(1)(*b*), s.21 and Sch. See §§ 5–35A and 5–35B (Supplement).

Rule against inalienability

5–98 AT THE END OF THE TEXT ADD: These rules are not affected by the Perpetuities and Accumulations Act 2009.[26a]

4. ACCUMULATIONS

Statutory restrictions on accumulations

5–100 DELETE THE SECOND TO FIFTH SENTENCES AND REPLACE BY: The statutory restrictions later became contained in sections 164 to 166 of the Law of Property Act and section 13 of the Perpetuities and Accumulations Act 1964. The restrictions are considered in §§ 5–101 to 5–127.

AFTER § 5–100 INSERT THE FOLLOWING NEW PARAGRAPHS AND HEADING:

Repeal of statutory restrictions by the Perpetuities and Accumulations Act 2009

5–100A The statutory restrictions on accumulations under the Law of Property Act 1925 and the Perpetuities and Accumulations Act 1964 were wholly repealed by the Perpetuities and Accumulations Act 2009,[33a] which came into force on April 6, 2010.[33b] The repeal draws no distinction between trusts for, and powers of, accumulation.

Instruments to which the repeal applies

5–100B The repeal of the statutory restrictions by the 2009 Act applies to instruments taking effect on or after April 6, 2010,[33c] with two exceptions. The first exception is that the repeal does not apply to a will[33d] executed before April 6, 2010 of a testator who dies on or after that date.[33e] The second exception[33f] is that the repeal does not apply to an instrument made on or after April 6, 2010 in exercise of a special power of appointment created by an instrument taking effect before that date.[33g] The statutory restrictions continue to apply to pre-commencement instruments and instruments within the two exceptions. It makes no difference that the perpetuity provisions of the 2009 Act apply to a pre-commencement instrument under section 12 of the 2009 Act.[33h] For the purposes of the 2009 Act, a provision made in relation to property otherwise than by instrument, for instance an oral trust, is treated

---

[26a] Perpetuities and Accumulations Act 2009, s.18.
[33a] Perpetuities and Accumulations Act 2009, s.13, s.21 and Sch. The repeal implements with modifications proposals made by Law Commission Report No.251 on the Rules against Perpetuities and Excessive Accumulations (1998).
[33b] Perpetuities and Accumulations Act 2009, s.22; Perpetuities and Accumulations Act 2009 (Commencement) Order 2010 (SI 2010/37).
[33c] Perpetuities and Accumulations Act 2009, s.15(1).
[33d] Includes a codicil, see Perpetuities and Accumulations Act 2009, s.20(7).
[33e] Perpetuities and Accumulations Act 2009, s.15(1)(*a*).
[33f] Made contrary to the recommendations of the Law Commission, see Law Commission Report No.251 on the Rules against Perpetuities and Excessive Accumulations (1998), § 10.16.
[33g] Perpetuities and Accumulations Act 2009, s.15(1)(*b*).
[33h] See §§ 5–37A to 5–37D (Supplement) on Perpetuities and Accumulations Act 2009, s.12.

as taking effect as though contained in an instrument taking effect on the making of the provision.[33i] If it were desired to utilise the repeal of the statutory restrictions in relation to a trust in existence on April 6, 2010, it would be necessary either to have an agreed variation by all the beneficiaries interested in income and being of full age and capacity, or alternatively to have a variation approved by the court under the Variation of Trusts Act 1958.[33j]

Charitable trusts

The 2009 Act contains no replacement statutory restrictions on accumula- **5–100C** tions, save for charitable trusts. Section 14 contains replacement statutory restrictions for an instrument to which the repeal of the previous restrictions applies,[33k] to the extent that it provides for property to be held on trust for charitable purposes,[33l] unless the provision is made by the court or the Charity Commission.[33m] Under the new restrictions, a duty or power to accumulate income normally ceases to have effect at the end of a period of 21 years from the time when the income must or may be accumulated.[33n] However, if the instrument provides for the duty or power to accumulate to cease to have effect on the death of the settlor or of one of the settlors, determined by name or the order of their deaths, that provision will apply in place of the provision for a 21-year period.[33o] If a duty or power to accumulate income ceases to have effect, the income to which the duty or power would have applied must go the person who would have been entitled, or be applied for the purposes for which it would have been applied, if there had been no such duty or power.[33p] Section 14 applies whether the instrument provides for simple or compound accumulation.[33q] There is no requirement for the application of section 14 that the property is held exclusively on charitable trusts. Accordingly, the section will apply while the trust property is held on temporary charitable trusts. But it is not thought that the section would apply merely because trustees have a discretion to apply income for a class of beneficiaries which includes a charity or charitable purpose.

Effect of repeal on non-charitable trusts

In consequence of the repeal, as regards instruments containing non- **5–100D** charitable trusts to which the repeal applies,[33r] income may be directed or authorised to be accumulated for all or any part of the 125-year perpetuity period[33s] under the 2009 Act. It remains necessary to limit accumulation under a settlement to the perpetuity period, since otherwise interests would

---

[33i]   Perpetuities and Accumulations Act 2009, s.19.
[33j]   See § 45–57 (including Supplement).
[33k]   See § 5–100B (Supplement).
[33l]   Perpetuities and Accumulations Act 2009, s.14(1).
[33m]   *ibid.*, s.14(2).
[33n]   *ibid.*, s.14(3) and (4).
[33o]   *ibid.*, s.14(5).
[33p]   *ibid.*, s.14(6).
[33q]   *ibid.*, s.14(7).
[33r]   See § 5–100B (Supplement).
[33s]   Perpetuities and Accumulations Act 2009, s.5. See § 5–37F (Supplement).

fail to vest as required by the 2009 Act. In effect the position is the same as at common law[33t] save that a 125-year perpetuity period applies instead of a period expiring 21 years after the death of a person living at the date of the creation of the settlement.

5–100E   The remainder of this section states the law as it stood before April 6, 2010.

Section 164 of the Law of Property Act 1925

5–101   IN THE FIRST SENTENCE, AFTER 1925, INSERT A NEW NOTE 33a: Repealed as from April 6. 2010 by Perpetuities and Accumulations Act 2009, Sch.1, para.1; see §§ 5–100A *et seq.* (Supplement).

Accumulation during minority

5–102   IN THE FIRST SENTENCE, AFTER 1925, INSERT A NEW NOTE 43a: Repealed as from April 6, 2010 by Perpetuities and Accumulations Act 2009, Sch.1, para.1; see §§ 5–100A *et seq.* (Supplement).

Where section 164 does not apply

Accumulations for portions

5–110   NOTE 70. DELETE THE LAST SENTENCE AND REPLACE BY: That exemption is to be read in accordance with Human Embryology and Fertilisation Act 1990, ss.27–29, and Human Embryology and Fertilisation Act 2008, ss.33 *et seq.*, both of which are retrospective, see §§ 6–15 to 6–19E.

Accumulations to purchase land

5–127   IN THE FIRST SENTENCE AFTER strict rules INSERT A NEW NOTE 24a: See *Re Erskine's Settlement Trusts* [1971] 1 W.L.R. 162, where the direction to accumulate was void but had the effect of excluding Trustee Act 1925, s.31.

NOTE 25. DELETE EXISTING NOTE AND REPLACE BY: Repealed as from April 6, 2010 by Perpetuities and Accumulations Act 2009, Sch.1, para.1; see §§ 5–100A *et seq.* (Supplement).

5. RESTRICTIONS ON ALIENATION AND TRUSTS AGAINST THE POLICY OF INSOLVENCY LAW

The statutory protective trusts

5–151   NOTE 27. AT THE END ADD: and Human Fertilisation and Embryology Act 2008, ss.33 *et seq.*, as to which see §§ 6–19A to 6–19E.

[33t]   See § 5–99.

Attacks by creditors by reason of subsequent events on the ground of public policy or "piercing the veil of the trust" or remedial constructive trust

NOTE 58. ADD: *Re Reynolds* [2008] NZCA 122; (2007–08) 10 I.T.E.L.R. 1064 **5–155** at [66]–[70].

6. TRUSTS THAT PREJUDICE CREDITORS

Section 423 applications

AFTER THE REFERENCE IN THE FIRST SENTENCE TO section 423 of the Insolvency **5–156** Act 1986 INSERT A NEW NOTE 61a: Amended by Civil Partnership Act 2004, s.261(1), Sch.27, para.121.

NOTE 62. DELETE THE SECOND SENTENCE AND REPLACE BY: As to the appropriate county court, see Insolvency Rules 1986, r.6.40A (as substituted by Insolvency (Amendment) Rules 2010 (SI 2010/686), r.2, Sch.1, para.217).

The scope of the section

NOTE 70. ADD: The execution of a declaration of trust over property in **5–157** return for the forbearance to pursue a claim for ancillary relief has recently been held to be a transaction for which valuable consideration was given, such that there was no transaction at an undervalue: *Papanicola v Fagan* [2008] EWHC 313 (Ch); [2009] B.P.I.R. 320. See too *Hill v Haines* [2007] EWCA Civ 1284; [2008] Ch. 412.

AT THE END OF THE TEXT ADD: Where an application is made under this section, trustees should be aware that they will have a right of indemnity in relation to their costs of the application only if they remain neutral.[32a] They should carefully consider whether to make a *Beddoe* application, in order to obtain the directions of the court as to how they should act in response to the section 423 application.[32b]

The settlor's purpose

NOTE 81. AT THE END OF THE FIRST SENTENCE ADD: *Random House UK Ltd v* **5–159** *Allason* [2008] EWHC 2854 (Ch); [2008] All E.R. (D); *Papanicola v Fagan* [2008] EWHC 313 (Ch); [2009] B.P.I.R. 320.

NOTE 83. ADD: The fact that the consequence of a declaration of trust was that the property concerned would be put out of the reach of creditors who later materialised was also not enough where the purpose of the transaction was to protect a matrimonial home against debts and liabilities that might result from the husband's alcoholism and gambling, see *Papanicola v Fagan* [2008] EWHC 313 (Ch); [2009] B.P.I.R. 320.

[32a] See § 21–107.
[32b] See § 21–115.

The order made

5–161 NOTE 90. ADD: *4 Eng Ltd v Harper (No.2)* [2009] EWHC 2633 (Ch); [2010] 1 B.C.L.C. 176.

Time-limits

5–162 NOTE 99. ADD: See too *Random House UK Ltd v Allason* [2008] EWHC 2854 (Ch); [2008] All E.R. (D), at [95], leaving open the question whether a party to litigation became a victim of a transaction whenever it incurred costs which may in due course become the subject of a costs order in its favour, or whether it was when a costs order was actually made.

Sections 339 and 340 of the Insolvency Act 1986

Transactions at an undervalue

5–163 AFTER THE TEXT TO N.1 ADD: The satisfaction of a claim by a spouse or civil partner for ancillary relief, whether by consent or after a contest, constitutes consideration in money or money's worth whose value can be ascertained in order to determine whether a transaction is made at an undervalue.[1a]

NOTE 2. DELETE AND REPLACE BY: Insolvency Act 1986, s.339 (as amended by Civil Partnership Act 2004, s.261(1), Sch.27, para.119) and s.341 (as prospectively amended by Criminal Justice Act 1988, s.170(2), Sch.16).

NOTE 4. AFTER THE SECOND SENTENCE ADD: See too *Papanicola v Fagan* [2008] EWHC 313 (Ch); [2009] B.P.I.R. 320.

AT THE END OF THE TEXT ADD: The court retains a discretion to make no order in respect of a transaction at an undervalue, where the interests of justice so require.[6a]

Preferences

5–164 NOTE 8. DELETE AND REPLACE BY: As defined by Insolvency Act 1986, s.435 (as amended by Civil Partnership Act 2004, s.261(1), Sch.27, para.122, and Companies Act 2006 (Consequential Amendments, Transitional Provisions and Savings) Order 2009 (SI 2009/1941), art.2(1), Sch.1, para.82).

[1a] *Haines v Hill* [2007] EWCA Civ 1284; [2008] Ch 412 at [39].
[6a] *Singla v Brown* [2007] EWHC 405 (Ch); [2008] Ch. 357 at [59], where the court declined to reverse the effect of a notice of severance of a joint tenancy of property which split the beneficial ownership 99 per cent. to 1 per cent. (and which effect was acknowledged by the recipient of the notice), where the parties had failed to appreciate on the acquisition of the property the effect of that beneficial joint tenancy. The decision is significant as it shows that the court can effectively treat a valid declaration of trust as though it had been invalid for the purposes of the Insolvency Act 1986, if satisfied that the parties were mistaken as to its effect.

Other statutory provisions

Inheritance (Provision for Family and Dependants) Act 1975

NOTE 21. ADD: For a case involving the interaction between a claim under **5–167** these provisions and a (potential) claim under Insolvency Act 1986, ss.339 and 423, see *Stow v Stow* [2008] EWHC 495 (Ch); [2008] Ch. 461.

CHAPTER 6

INTERPRETATION OF EXPRESS TRUSTS

1. INTRODUCTION

Scope of chapter

6–01 NOTE 1. FOR THE REFERENCE TO *Theobald on Wills*, SEE NOW (17th edn), Chaps 14 to 28. FOR THE REFERENCE TO *Williams on Wills*, SEE NOW (9th edn), Vol.1, Chaps 49 to 101.

2. EVIDENCE TO INTERPRET SETTLEMENTS

The parol evidence rule

6–03 AT THE END OF THE SECOND SENTENCE OF THE TEXT ADD A NEW NOTE 8a: *Rafferty v Philp* [2011] EWHC 709 (Ch) at [23] (statement in text approved).

NOTE 12. AT THE END ADD: See too *Byrnes v Kendle* [2011] HCA 26; (2011–12) 14 I.T.E.L.R. 299 at [13]–[18], [46]–[66] and [115]–[118].

NOTE 14. AT THE END ADD: *Rafferty v Philp*, above, at [24] (statement in text approved).

NOTE 17. FOR THE REFERENCE TO *Snell's Equity*, SEE NOW (32nd edn), § 16–008.

NOTE 20. ADD: *Chartbrook Ltd v Persimmon Homes Ltd* [2009] UKHL 38; [2009] 1 A.C. 1101.

Evidence of meaning of words

6–07 NOTE 31. FOR THE REFERENCE TO *Theobald on Wills*, SEE NOW (17th edn), § 14–031. FOR THE REFERENCE TO *Williams on Wills*, SEE NOW (9th edn), Vol.1, § 57.18.

Surrounding circumstances

6–08 NOTE 33. ADD: See too *I.R.C. v Botnar* [1999] S.T.C. 711 at 721, 734–738, CA; *Canada Trust Co. v Browne* [2010] ONSC 4118; (2010–11) 13 I.T.E.L.R. 648 at [27]–[30] and [44].

NOTE 36. ADD: See too *Independent Trustee Services Ltd v Knell* [2010] EWHC 650 (Ch); [2010] All E.R. (D) 07 (Apr) at [10].

Ambiguities

Where there is no ambiguity

NOTE 57. FOR THE REFERENCE TO *Snell's Equity*, SEE NOW (32nd edn), § 16– **6–11**
008.

3. INTERPRETATION OF TRUSTS FOR CHILDREN

Construction of gifts to children at common law

NOTE 69. AT THE END ADD: A child is also legitimate at common law if at the **6–14**
time of his birth he is legitimate by the law of the domicile of each of his
parents: *Green v Montagu* [2011] EWHC 1856 (Ch); [2011] W.T.L.R. 1341.

AFTER THE FIRST SENTENCE INSERT: It applies also to the expression "statutory
next of kin",[70a] since by the Administration of Estates Act 1925 the
expression is required[70b] to be construed as a reference to the persons taking
beneficially on an intestacy under that Act and that Act in turn provides[70c]
for those persons to include "children" and "issue".

NOTE 72. FOR THE REFERENCE TO *Theobald on Wills*, SEE NOW (17th edn), § 26–
002 to 26–021. FOR THE REFERENCE TO *Williams on Wills*, SEE NOW (9th edn),
Vol.1, §§ 72.2 to 72.6.

AT THE END OF THE FOURTH SENTENCE, INSERT A NEW NOTE 72a: In the case of a
gift to statutory next of kin, the effect is that the members of the class are
ordinarily identified at the death of the person whose next of kin they are
but in accordance with the law applicable when the trust was created: *Re
Erskine Trust*, above.

Human Fertilisation and Embryology Act 1990

AFTER § 6–19 INSERT THE FOLLOWING NEW PARAGRAPHS AND HEADINGS:

Human Fertilisation and Embryology Act 2008

The Human Fertilisation and Embryology Act 2008, which came into force **6–19A**
on April 6, 2009,[87a] contains new rules concerning parenthood in cases of
assisted fertilisation.[87b] The new rules apply where the assisted fertilisation
(as distinct from the birth) takes place after the commencement of the new
rules in the 2008 Act.[87c] Subject to that, the new rules apply to documents
whenever made[87d] and so have a similar retrospective effect to the rules in

---

[70a] *Re Erskine Trust* [2012] EWHC 732 (Ch); [2012] 3 All E.R. 532.
[70b] Administration of Estates Act 1925, s.50(1).
[70c] *ibid.*, ss.46(1), 47.
[87a] Human Fertilisation and Embryology Act 2008 (Commencement No.1 and Transitional
Provisions) Order 2009 (SI 2009/479).
[87b] Human Fertilisation and Embryology Act 2008, ss.33 *et seq.*
[87c] *ibid.*, s.57(1).
[87d] *ibid.*, s.48(5).

the Human Fertilisation and Embryology Act 1990.[87e] The rules in the 1990 Act continue to apply where the assisted fertilisation (as distinct from the birth) took place before the commencement of the new rules in the 2008 Act.[87f]

Who is the mother under the 2008 Act

6–19B As in the case of the 1990 Act[87g] the woman who carries the child as result of the placing in her of an embryo or sperm and eggs, wherever that takes place, and no other woman, is to be treated as the mother, save to the extent that child is not treated as her child by virtue of adoption.[87h]

Who is the father or other parent under the 2008 Act

6–19C The other parent can be either a man, that is the father, or, in some circumstances, a woman. If the mother is married at the time of the assisted fertilisation, but the fertilisation is not brought about with her husband's sperm, her husband is nonetheless treated as the father wherever the fertilisation takes place, unless it is shown that he did not consent to the assisted fertilisation.[87i] This rule is the same as that applying under the 1990 Act,[87j] and is subject to similar exceptions.[87k] Where this rule does not apply (and a woman is not treated as the other parent under the rules described in § 6–19D (Supplement)), a man whose sperm is not used to bring about the fertilisation is treated as the father if he is alive at the time of the fertilisation, the fertilisation takes place in the course of treatment services provided in the United Kingdom by a licensed person, and he and the mother agree to his being the father in accordance with the agreed fatherhood conditions specified in the 2008 Act.[87l] Where a person is treated as the father under the above rules, no other person is to be treated as the father.[87m]

6–19D We now come to cases where the other parent is a woman. If at the time of the assisted fertilisation, wherever it takes place, the mother is a party to a civil partnership, the other party to the civil partnership is to be treated as a parent of the child unless it is shown that she did not consent to the assisted fertilisation.[87n] Where this rule does not apply (and a man is not treated as the father parent under the rules described in § 6–19C (Supplement)), a woman is treated as the other parent if she is alive at the time of the fertilisation, the fertilisation takes place in the course of treatment services provided in the United Kingdom by a licensed person, and she and the

---

[87e] See § 6–18.
[87f] Human Fertilisation and Embryology Act 2008, s.57(2).
[87g] See § 6–16.
[87h] Human Fertilisation and Embryology Act 2008, s.33.
[87i] Human Fertilisation and Embryology Act 2008, s.35.
[87j] See § 6–17.
[87k] Human Fertilisation and Embryology Act 2008, s.38(2) and (4) The exception in s.38(2) corresponds to the exception in Human Fertilisation and Embryology Act 1990, s.28(5)(*a*) considered in § 6–17, n.84.
[87l] Human Fertilisation and Embryology Act 2008, ss.36 and 37, subject to the exceptions in s.38(2) and (4).
[87m] Human Fertilisation and Embryology Act 2008, s.38(1). See too s.41.
[87n] *ibid.*, s.42, subject to the exceptions in ss.45(2) and (4).

mother agree to her being the other parent in accordance with the agreed female parenthood conditions described in the 2008 Act.[87o] Where a woman is treated as a parent of the child under the above rules, no man is to be treated as the father.[87p] A woman is not to be treated as the other parent merely because of egg donation.[87q]

Effect of provisions

Where a person is treated as the mother, father or a parent of the child **6–19E** under the rules described in §§ 6–19B to 6–19D (Supplement), that person is to be treated in law as the mother, father or parent (as the case may be) for all purposes.[87r] As noted in § 6–19A (Supplement), this applies to any document whenever made, whether before or after the commencement of the 1990 Act or 2008 Act.[87s] In a case where the mother's husband is treated as the father, though the fertilisation was not brought about by the use of his sperm, the effect of his being treated as the father is that the child is legitimate. In a case where the mother's civil partner is treated as the other parent, or where a woman is treated as the other parent under the agreed female parenthood provisions and was the mother's civil partner at any time between the assisted fertilisation and the birth, the child is legitimate.[87t] However, the rules under the 2008 Act do not affect the devolution of any property devolving along with any dignity or title.[87u] There is no provision for exclusion of the rules in the 2008 Act, and on the question whether and how these rules can be excluded or modified by the terms of a trust, similar considerations apply as in the case of the 1990 Act.[87v]

Illegitimate, legitimated and adopted children

We turn now to consider the position of illegitimate, legitimated and **6–19F** adopted children. Different statutes apply to each class of children, the thrust of which is to assimilate the legal position of such children to that of children born in wedlock. As we have said, in general the statutes have no retrospective effect, so that the earlier law continues to apply as it stood when the particular trust was created. It is now necessary, however, to take account of the European Convention for the Protection of Human Rights and Fundamental Freedoms 1950, which forms part of English law.[87w] The European Court of Human Rights has held that the right to respect for private and family life[87x] and the prohibition on various forms of discrimination[87y] preclude disadvantaging children in respect of property rights

---

[87o] *ibid.*, ss.43 and 44, subject to the exceptions in ss.45(2) and (4).
[87p] *ibid.*, s.45(1).
[87q] *ibid.*, s.47.
[87r] *ibid.*, s.48(1).
[87s] *ibid.*, s.48(5).
[87t] *ibid.*, s.48(6).
[87u] *ibid.*, s.48(7).
[87v] See § 6–19.
[87w] Under Human Rights Act 1998.
[87x] Convention, art.8.
[87y] Convention, art.14.

by reason that they are illegitimate, legitimated or adopted.[87z] The constraints imposed by the Convention apply to any "public authority", including a court,[87aa] but not to private individuals, so that settlors remain free to discriminate against children born out of wedlock.[87ab] When construing general expressions, however, it seems that in some cases at least it is possible to adopt a retrospective application of the constraints imposed by the Convention and necessary to do so where that can fairly be done, even though the purely domestic legislation was not retrospective. In England it has been held that an ultimate trust for statutory next of kin should be construed as extending to adopted children even though the settlement had been created before the introduction of any of the legislation assimilating the position of adopted children to natural children.[87ac] The special factors relied on as making it fair so to construe the trust included the special nature of a gift to next of kin, which created only an expectancy and not a proprietary interest; the absence of any evidence that there had been an assignment for value of the expectancy of any of the persons who would have taken in the absence of the adopted children; the fact that those persons were only distant relatives; and the fact that the trust had terminated, so that there would be no continuing difficulty in identifying beneficiaries.[87ad] It may well be that only in rare cases will the human rights legislation require a different result from the other domestic legislation. But it will be necessary to have regard to the possibility and the following sections on illegitimate, legitimated and adopted children should be read with that in mind.

Illegitimate children 1970 to April 3, 1988

6–20 NOTE 89. AT THE END INSERT: and *Upton v National Westminster Bank plc* [2004] EWHC 1962 (Ch); [2004] W.T.L.R. 1339 (held "plainly right" when permission to appeal was refused, [2005] EWCA Civ 1479 at [21]).

Adopted children

1976 to April 3, 1988

6–29 AFTER THE FIRST SENTENCE INSERT: The rules in the Adoption Act 1976 continue to apply in relation to adoptions effected before the Children and Adoption Act 2002 came fully into force on December 30, 2005.[39a] As regards adoptions made on or after that date, the rules in the 1976 Act are replaced by similar but not identical rules contained in the 2002 Act applicable to the same instruments as those to which the 1976 Act applies.[39b] There are thus now two sets of rules under different Acts applicable to the same instruments, depending on the date of the relevant adoption rather than the date of the relevant instrument. References in the text below to the

---

[87z] *Pla v Andorra* [2004] ECHR 69498/01; *Brauer v Germany* [2009] ECHR 3545/04.
[87aa] Human Rights Act 1998, ss.6(1), (3).
[87ab] *Re Erskine Trust* [2012] EWHC 732 (Ch); [2012] 3 All E.R. 532 at [25], [30], [31].
[87ac] *ibid.* For the legislation as to adopted children, see §§ 6–27 *et seq.*
[87ad] *Re Erskine Trust*, above, at [55].
[39a] Adoption and Children Act 2002 (Commencement No.9) Order 2005 (SI 2005/2213).
[39b] Adoption and Children Act 2002, ss.66 *et seq.*

1976 Act include references to the 2002 Act as regards adoptions effected on or after December 30, 2005.

NOTE 40: DELETE AND REPLACE BY: Adoption Act 1976, ss.39(6)(*a*) and 42(1); Adoption and Children Act 2002, ss.67(6)(*a*) and 69(1).

NOTE 42: ADD: Adoption and Children Act 2002, s.73(3).

NOTE 43: ADD: repealed by Trusts of Land and Appointment of Trustees Act 1996, s.25(2) and Sch.4 with savings by s.25(4) for entailed interests created before the commencement of that Act; not expressly covered by Adoption and Children Act 2002.

NOTE 44: ADD: Adoption and Children Act 2002, s.67(6)(*a*), Sch.4, paras.17(1)(*a*) and 18.

NOTE 45: ADD: Adoption and Children Act 2002, s.73(4).

AFTER THE THIRD SENTENCE INSERT: By section 67(2) of the 2002 Act, an adopted person is the legitimate child of the adopter or adopters and if adopted by a couple (or one of a couple under section 51(2) of the 2002 Act) is to be treated as the child of the relationship of the couple in question.

NOTES 46 AND 47: ADD: Adoption and Children Act 2002, s.69(2).

NOTE 48: ADD: Adoption and Children Act 2002, s.69(5).

NOTE 49: ADD: Adoption and Children Act 2002, ss.67(3) and (4) and 69(4).

NOTE 50: ADD: Adoption and Children Act 2002, s.69(4). In *Staffordshire County Council v B* [1998] 1 F.L.R. 261 it was held that Adoption Act 1976, s.42(4) preserved, not only a vested interest in possession of an adopted person but also a reversionary interest of an adopted child expectant upon his natural mother's life interest. Under the different wording of Adoption and Children Act 2002, s.69(2) only a vested interest in possession of an adopted person and an interest of another person expectant upon that vested interest is preserved. An application under Variation of Trusts Act 1958 before an adoption order is made may be a suitable method of avoiding the destruction by the 1976 Act and 2002 Act of contingent interests, and by the 2002 Act of all reversionary interests, see *S v TI* [2006] W.T.L.R. 1461 and § 45–52. The Law Commission has proposed that if immediately before adoption a child has in the estate of his or her deceased parent any contingent interest, other than a contingent interest in remainder, that interest will not be affected by the adoption if made on or after the date of the proposed reform: see Law Commission Report on *Intestacy and Family Provision Claims on Death* (Law Com. No.331, December 14, 2011), paras.4.30 to 4.52 and clause 4 of draft Inheritance and Trustees' Powers Bill in Appendix A to the Report.

NOTE 51: ADD: Adoption and Children Act 2002, s.71.

NOTE 52: ADD: Adoption and Children Act 2002, s.73(2).

NOTE 55: ADD: Adoption and Children Act 2002, s.69(1).

NOTE 56: ADD: Adoption and Children Act 2002, s.67(6)(*a*), Sch.4, paras.17(1)(*a*) and 18.

NOTE 58: ADD: Adoption and Children Act 2002, s.73(2).

NOTE 62: ADD: Adoption and Children Act 2002, s.73(3).

Since April 3, 1988

6–30 AT THE END ADD: Similar considerations apply in relation to the Adoption and Children Act 2002, on which see § 6–29.

5. INTERPRETATION OF EXECUTED TRUSTS

Entailed interests

6–47 NOTE 15. FOR THE REFERENCE TO *Theobald on Wills*, SEE NOW (17th edn), § 28–146.

AFTER § 6–52 ADD THE FOLLOWING NEW SECTION:

7. STATUTORY TRUSTS

Generally

6–53 Where a trust is created by statute, the statute may not create a comprehensive set of rules concerning the rights of the beneficiaries or the duties, rights and powers of the trustees. In such a case it is inappropriate to apply the general rule of interpretation which applies to statutory provisions and non-statutory instruments that if provision is not made for some event, the most usual inference to be drawn is that nothing is to happen.[33] Rather, the general rules of trust law and principles of equity, such as rules concerning self-dealing, the duties of a trustee to account, tracing and pooling of assets, so far as not excluded or modified by statute, are applied by default so as to fill the gap left by the terms of the statute; and where the effect of trust law is to take away private property law rights which would otherwise exist or to confer a power not expressly conferred by the statute concerned, the court will not apply any general presumption that the statute was not intended to take away such rights nor confer such a power.[34]

Application of general statutory provisions concerning trusts

6–54 Similarly, general statutory provisions concerning trusts, such as those contained in the Settled Land Act 1925, Trustee Act 1925, the Variation of Trusts Act 1958 and the Trustee Act 2000 apply to a trust created by statute,[35] so far as not excluded by the terms of the general statutory provisions,[36] or excluded or modified by the terms of the statute creating the trust.

---

[33] *Att.-Gen. of Belize v Belize Telecom Ltd* [2009] UKPC 10; [2009] 1 W.L.R. 1998 at [16]–[17].
[34] *Re Lehman Brothers International (Europe) CRC Credit Fund Ltd v GLG Investments plc* [2010] EWCA Civ 917; [2010] All E.R. (D) 15 (Aug) at [64]–[74].
[35] See *e.g. Hambro v Duke of Marlborough* [1994] Ch. 158 (Settled Land Act 1925, s.64).
[36] See *e.g.* Variation of Trusts Act 1958, s.1(5), on which see § 45–52.

CHAPTER 7

TRUSTS ARISING BY OPERATION OF LAW GENERALLY

1. INTRODUCTION

Distinction between express, resulting and constructive trusts by reference to intention

NOTE 10. AT THE END ADD: The following statement has been judicially **7–02** approved in Australia: "the constructive trust differs in essential respects both from the express and the resulting or implied trust. It differs from the express trust in that it is raised by operation of law without reference to the intentions of the parties concerned and indeed largely contrary to the desires and intentions of the constructive trustee", see Heydon and Leeming, *Jacob's Law of Trusts in Australia* (7th edn), § [1301]; *White City Tennis Club Ltd v John Alexander's Clubs Pty Ltd* [2009] NWSCA 114; (2009–10) 12 I.T.E.L.R. 172 at [65] (reversed on other grounds [2010] HCA 19; (2010–11) 13 I.T.E.L.R. 85).

2. CLASSIFICATION OF RESULTING TRUSTS

The twofold classification of resulting trusts

NOTE 24. FOR THE REFERENCE TO Thomas and Hudson, *The Law of Trusts*, **7–05** SEE NOW (2nd edn), §§ 26.10 and 26.11.

Wide theory of resulting trusts

NOTE 40. AT THE END ADD: The different theories of resulting trust are **7–07** discussed by the New Zealand Court of Appeal in *Re Reynolds: Official Assignee v Wilson* [2007] NZCA 122; (2007–08) 10 I.T.E.L.R. 1064, at [117]–[122], where the view is expressed that there is no resulting trust where a settlor intends a trust to be a sham but the trustee is non-complicit. In such circumstances, the trustee's conscience is bound by the trust instrument, and not by the settlor's subjective intentions: *ibid*, at [118]. As to sham, see §§ 4–19 *et seq.*

3. CLASSIFICATION OF CONSTRUCTIVE TRUSTS AND CONSTRUCTIVE TRUSTEESHIP

Classes of constructive trusts

Subdivision of remedial constructive trusts

7–13 AFTER THE TEXT TO N.59 ADD. These distinctions are particularly important in relation to questions of limitation.[59a]

Fiduciary duty trusts

7–17 AFTER THE TEXT TO N.76 ADD: Where a beneficiary procured an appointment to himself by entering into an agreement with a person whose consent was required for the appointment that the property so acquired would be applied for the benefit of certain grandchildren, a fiduciary obligation was created and the appointee held to be a constructive trustee for the grandchildren.[76a]

NOTE 78. AT THE END ADD: But see now *Sinclair Investments (UK) Ltd v Versailles Trade Finance Ltd* [2010] EWHC 1614 (Ch); [2011] 1 B.C.L.C. 202; affirmed [2011] EWCA Civ 347; [2011] 4 All E.R. 335, discussed at §§ 20–28A to 20–28B (Supplement).

Purely remedial trusts

AFTER § 7–23 INSERT THE FOLLOWING NEW PARAGRAPH AND HEADING:

Move towards recognition of remedial constructive trusts?

7–23A In the recent decision of the House of Lords in *Thorner v Major*,[2a] a claimant was awarded certain land in a claim based on proprietary estoppel, where a deceased farmer had made a series of assurances to him over many years that he would inherit the property. On the facts, the extent of the property was liable to fluctuate during the lifetime of the deceased. In his judgment, Lord Scott of Foscote said that he regarded the claimant's equity as being easier to establish via a remedial constructive trust. He said[2b] that the trust created by the common intention or understanding of the parties regarding the property on the basis of which the claimant had acted to his detriment was a remedial constructive trust. None of the other Law Lords discussed this point or decided the case on this basis. It is at present unclear whether this opens the door for a move towards the recognition of remedial constructive trusts, as suggested by Lord Browne-Wilkinson.[2c] A common intention constructive trust arises at the time of the conduct relied on,[2d] which was not so with the equity awarded to the successful claimant in *Thorner v Major*, where the identity of the property concerned was not

[59a] See §§ 44–47 *et seq.*
[76a] *De Bruyne v De Bruyne* [2010] EWCA Civ 519; [2010] W.T.L.R. 1525. The denial of, or refusal to carry out, the agreement was characterised as unconscionable or inequitable conduct, see at [51].
[2a] [2009] UKHL 18; [2009] 1 W.L.R. 776.
[2b] *ibid*, at [20], relying especially on *Re Basham (Deceased)* [1986] 1 W.L.R. 1498.
[2c] See § 7–23.
[2d] See § 9–66.

capable of precise definition until the death of the representor. Using Lord Scott's formulation, the award would seem to involve the imposition of a trust on the property of a defendant where the claimant has (in the view of the court) been unjustly deprived of that property, thus possibly making it more likely that the higher courts will recognise a purely remedial constructive trust in the foreseeable future.[2e] But for the lower courts, the position would appear to remain that there is no purely remedial constructive trust in English law.[2f] This has, however, not prevented at least one first instance judge from refusing to strike out a claim seeking an award of a remedial constructive trust, on the basis that the authorities, and in particular *Stack v Dowden*,[2g] do not preclude such a trust.[2h]

4. CONSTRUCTIVE TRUSTS IMPOSED ON CERTAIN ACQUISITIONS

Property obtained by fraud or theft

NOTE 6. ADD: See also *Box v Barclays Bank plc* [1998] Lloyd's Rep. Bank. **7–26** 185; *Papamichael v National Westminster Bank plc* [2003] EWHC 164 (Comm); [2003] 1 Lloyd's Rep. 341 at [241]; *Commerzbank Aktiengesellschaft v IMB Morgan plc* [2004] EWHC 2771 (Ch); [2005] 2 All E.R. (Comm) 564 at [36]; *London Allied Holdings Ltd v Lee* [2007] EWHC 2061 (Ch); [2007] All E.R. (D) 153 (Sep) at [275]–[276]; *Bank of Ireland v Pexxnet Ltd* [2010] EWHC 1872 (Comm); [2010] All E.R. (D) 284 (Jul) at [55]–[57].

Rescission and rectification

NOTE 14. ADD: In *Papamichael v National Westminster Bank plc* [2003] **7–27** EWHC 164 (Comm); [2003] 1 Lloyd's Rep. 341, at [241], a contract was described as a "supervening barrier", preventing the imposition of a constructive trust merely because an asset had been obtained by fraud.

NOTE 16. FOR THE REFERENCE TO Thomas and Hudson, *The Law of Trusts*, SEE NOW (2nd edn), § 27.27.

[2e] The question was also discussed, and left open, by Etherton J. in *London Allied Holdings Ltd v Lee* [2007] EWHC 2061 (Ch); [2007] All E.R. (D) 153 (Sep) at [259]–[264].

[2f] *Sinclair Investments (UK) Ltd v Versailles Trade Finance Ltd* [2010] EWHC 1614 (Ch); [2011] 1 B.C.L.C. 202 at [23], Lewison J., saying that such a trust would involve the court taking a proprietary right away from its existing owner; and see the same judge's previous observations in *Ultraframe (UK) Ltd v Fielding* [2005] EWHC 1638 (Ch); [2007] W.T.L.R. 835 at [1546]. The lack of recognition of the remedial constructive trust in English law was also noted by the CA in *Sinclair*, see [2010] EWCA Civ 347; [2011] W.T.L.R. 1043 at [37] and, again, in *Crossco No.4 Unlimited v Jolan Ltd* [2011] EWCA Civ 1619; [2012] 2 All E.R. 754 at [84].

[2g] [2007] UKHL 17; [2007] 2 A.C. 432.

[2h] *Clarke v Meadus* [2010] EWHC 3117 (Ch); [2010] All E.R. (D) 08 (Dec) at [83], Warren J. There was also an arguable claim in proprietary estoppel, and the judge indicated that the claimant still had to surmount the hurdle of showing the availability of the remedy in English law.

Trust arising from pre-existing relationship

7–28 NOTE 20. ADD: This may apply only when the director receives company property, and not where he receives property from a third party in breach of his fiduciary duty to the company: *Sinclair Investments (UK) Ltd v Versailles Trade Finance Ltd* [2010] EWHC 1614 (Ch); [2011] 1 B.C.L.C. 202 at [72]; affirmed [2010] EWCA Civ 347; [2011] 4 All E.R. 335; considered in §§ 20–28A and 20–28B (Supplement).

NOTE 21. ADD: See *Woodroffe v Coleman* [2011] NZHC 1720 at [44]–[47].

Property acquired by unlawful killing

Operation of the constructive trust

7–31 DELETE THE FIRST SENTENCE AND REPLACE WITH: With effect from February 1, 2012,[36a] where a killer is precluded by the forfeiture rule from acquiring an interest in the victim's estate, he is treated for the purpose of ascertaining the devolution of that estate as having died immediately before the victim.[36b] The practical result is that the killer's own children may now inherit despite the killer having forfeited his inheritance and remaining alive. Previously, the victim's will or the intestacy legislation was construed on the basis that the gift of property to the killer was avoided by the constructive trust arising in order to give effect to the forfeiture rule.

DELETE NOTE 41.

Relief from the forfeiture rule

7–33 NOTE 48. AT THE END OF THE FIRST SENTENCE ADD: *Mack v Lockwood* [2009] EWHC 1524 (Ch).

Proprietary estoppel

7–34 NOTE 49. FOR THE REFERENCE TO *Snell's Equity*, SEE NOW (32nd edn), §§ 12–016 *et seq.*

AFTER THE TEXT TO N.50 ADD. More recently, however, Lord Scott of Foscote has expressed the view that proprietary estoppel cannot be relied on to enforce an agreement which is void under section 2 of the 1989 Act for want of writing.[50a]

NOTE 53. AT THE END ADD: See § 7–23A (Supplement) on the comments by Lord Scott of Foscote in *Thorner v Major* [2009] UKHL 18; [2009] 1 W.L.R. 776 on the ability of the court to make an award based on a remedial

---

[36a] Estates of Deceased Persons (Forfeiture Rule and Law of Succession) Act 2011 (Commencement) Order 2011 (SI 2011/2913).

[36b] Estates of Deceased Persons (Forfeiture Rule and Law of Succession) Act 2011. In the case of an intestacy, s.1 inserts a new Administration of Estates Act, s.46A and, in the case of a will, s.2 inserts a new Wills Act 1837, s.33A. The 2011 Act gives effect to the recommendations in Law Com. No.295 (*The Forfeiture Rule and the Law of Succession*).

[50a] *Yeoman's Row Management Ltd v Cobbe* [2008] UKHL 55; [2008] 1 W.L.R. 1752 at [29]. As he points out, there is no exception for estoppel in s.2(5) of the 1989 Act. This supports the view that there is a distinction between proprietary estoppel and the common intention constructive trust, see § 9–81.

constructive trust instead of proprietary estoppel. He did not discuss whether a proprietary estoppel award was itself an institutional or a remedial constructive trust. See too n.50a.

NOTE 55. AT THE BEGINNING ADD: This view would seem to be supported by the approval by Lord Scott of Foscote in *Yeoman's Row Management Ltd v Cobbe* [2008] UKHL 55; [2008] 1 W.L.R. 1752 at [17], in the context of proprietary estoppel, of the statement of Deane J. in *Muschinski v Dodds* (1985) 160 C.L.R. 153, Aus. HC, that a constructive trust remains predominantly remedial. *Cf.* § 7–23.

Unconscionable assertion of title to money payments by agents

NOTE 62. FOR THE REFERENCE TO *Bowstead and Reynolds on Agency*, SEE NOW (19th edn), § 6–41.   **7–36**

AFTER § 7–36 ADD THE FOLLOWING NEW PARAGRAPH AND HEADING

Trust of damages for carer

Following the decision of the House of Lords in *Hunt v Severs*,[67] a personal injury victim holds any damages received in respect of gratuitous services provided by voluntary carers on trust for the carer. This rule, not followed in Australia[68] or New Zealand,[69] means that where the tortfeasor is also the victim's carer, no damages are recoverable (*i.e.* from insurers) in respect of the defendant's care as they would both be payable by the defendant and held on trust for him. The basis of this trust is uncertain, and seems to have been intended largely to bring English law into line with that of Scotland.[70] The trust is an institutional constructive trust which arises in favour of the carer's estate even if the carer dies before the damages in respect of his care have been awarded or assessed.[71] The trust is perhaps best viewed as imposed as a matter of public policy, and not on established principles concerning constructive trusts.[72]   **7–37**

---

[67] [1994] 2 A.C. 350 at 363. See also *H v S* [2002] EWCA Civ 792; [2003] Q.B. 965.
[68] *Grincelis v House* [2000] HCA 42; (2000) 201 C.L.R. 321.
[69] *New Zealand Guardian Trust Company Ltd v Siemonek* [2007] NZCA 494; [2008] 2 N.Z.L.R. 202.
[70] See Administration of Justice Act 1982, s.8 (not applicable in England, see s.77(3)).
[71] *Hughes v Lloyd* [2007] EWHC 3133 (Ch); [2008] W.T.L.R. 473.
[72] *ibid.*, at [29]. See also Underhill and Hayton, *Law of Trusts and Trustees* (18th edn), § 8.259 (suggesting that the victim has the right to change carer despite the imposition of a constructive trust); *McGregor on Damages* (18th edn), § 35–234; Matthews [1994] C.J.Q. 302.

CHAPTER 8

RESULTING AND OTHER TRUSTS ARISING UPON FAILURE OF DISPOSITIONS

2. DISPOSITIONS ON TRUST WHICH FAIL TO EXHAUST THE BENEFICIAL INTEREST

General principle

8–02 NOTE 14. FOR THE REFERENCE TO *Theobald on Wills*, SEE NOW (17th edn), Chap.14.

Examples of application of general principle

Trusts that fail for perpetuity, etc.

8–04 NOTE 21. FOR THE REFERENCE TO *Theobald on Wills*, SEE NOW (17th edn), §§ 22–002 *et seq.*

Surplus assets and surplus income

8–08 NOTE 31. FOR THE REFERENCE TO *Theobald on Wills*, SEE NOW (17th edn), §§ 20–016 to 20–026.

To whom the property results

Resulting trusts affecting residuary gifts in testamentary dispositions

8–14 NOTE 46. IN THE REFERENCE TO *Theobald on Wills* DELETE THE WORDS IN BRACKETS AND REPLACE BY: (not considered in 17th edition: see § 29–032).

Resulting trusts affecting general or specific gifts in testamentary dispositions

8–16 NOTE 50. FOR THE REFERENCE TO *Theobald on Wills*, SEE NOW (17th edn), §§ 22–031 *et seq.*

NOTE 52. IN THE REFERENCE TO *Theobald on Wills* DELETE THE WORDS IN BRACKETS AND REPLACE BY: (not considered in 17th edition: see § 29–032).

Transfer between settlements

8–20 NOTE 68. AT THE END ADD: See §§ 4–59, 29–229 *et seq.* Likewise, where a settlement is rescinded for mistake, see § 4–64.

Circumstances in which a resulting trust does not arise

NOTE 3. FOR THE REFERENCE TO *Theobald on Wills*, SEE NOW (17th edn), §§ 16– **8–30**
003 to 16–005.

Failure of beneficial interest in income—acceleration

Subsequent interest expressed to take effect at time of natural termination of preceding interest

NOTE 16. AT THE END ADD: *Re Sadick* [2009] HKCU 1957; (2009–10) 12 **8–34**
I.T.E.L.R. 679.

Vested but defeasible interests and contingent interests

NOTE 19. FOR THE FIRST REFERENCE TO *Theobald on Wills*, SEE NOW (17th edn), **8–35**
Chap.30. FOR THE SECOND REFERENCE TO *Theobald on Wills*, SEE NOW (17th
edn), §§ 30–008 and 30–009.

Dispositions containing trusts for unborn persons

NOTE 29. FOR THE REFERENCE TO Scott, *The Law of Trusts*, SEE NOW Scott and **8–36**
Ascher, *The Law of Trusts* (5th edn), Vol.11, § 41.1.2.1, n.7.

Effect of acceleration

NOTE 38. AT THE END ADD: *Re Sadick* [2009] HKCU 1957; (2009–10) 12 **8–37**
I.T.E.L.R. 679.

3. *QUISTCLOSE* TRUSTS

Introduction

Testamentary gifts intended to carry beneficial ownership—trust and charge

NOTE 43. FOR THE REFERENCE TO *Theobald on Wills*, SEE NOW (17th edn), § 22– **8–39**
021.

Loans for payment of debts and similar transactions construed as creating trusts

Circumstances in which there is no Quistclose *trust*

AFTER THE THIRD SENTENCE ADD NEW NOTE 66a: It has been held in the Isle of **8–46**
Man that "new money" must be received for the stated purpose in order for
a *Quistclose* trust to arise, and that such a trust cannot arise from the
appropriation of funds already in the hands of the recipient. The reason is
that, unless funds are paid over and accepted for a stated purpose, they
become the recipient's property absolutely (although a trust may later be
expressly declared over them): *Habana Ltd v Kaupthing Singer and Friedlander (Isle of Man) Ltd* (2009–10) 12 I.T.E.L.R. 736, Manx HC at [51]–
[52], [57] (affirmed *sub nom. Du Preez Ltd v Kaupthing Singer and*

Friedlander (Isle of Man) Ltd (2009–10) 12 I.T.E.L.R. 943 at [47], [58]–[59], Manx SGD).

NOTE 67. AT THE END ADD: See too *McManus RE Pty Ltd v Ward* [2009] NSWSC 440; (2008–09) 74 N.S.W.L.R. 662; *Re Lehman Brothers International (Europe)* [2010] EWHC 2914 (Ch); [2010] All E.R. (D) 232 (Nov) at [375]–[379].

Categorisation as a resulting trust

8–49 NOTE 84. AT THE END ADD: For the view that the secondary trust is a constructive trust taking effect whenever it is unconscionable for the recipient to claim a beneficial interest in the property, and regardless of intention, see Smolyansky (2010) 16(7) *Trusts & Trustees* 558. And for a response, see Millett (2011) 17(1) *Trusts & Trustees* 7.

The possibility of a trust rather than a power—when third party has beneficial interest

8–55 NOTE 2. AT THE END ADD: It was held that a purpose trust had arisen in *Cooper v PRG Powerhouse Ltd* [2008] EWHC 498 (Ch); [2008] 2 All E.R. (Comm) 964 at [15]–[24]. Whilst this is plausible on the facts (money had been paid into a company account for the purpose of buying a car for an individual employee), it was assumed that an express purpose trust arises in every instance of a *Quistclose* trust. The same assumption was made in *Kingate Global Fund Ltd v Knightsbridge (USD) Fund Ltd* [2009] CA (Bda) 17 Civ; (2009–10) 12 I.T.E.L.R. 850, citing the decision in *Cooper*. As set out at § 8–47, this is not the correct analysis in the light of the decision in *Twinsectra Ltd v Yardley* [2002] UKHL 12; [2002] 2 A.C. 164.

Payments other than loans for the payment of debts

8–57 NOTE 6. AT THE END ADD: *Cooper v PRG Powerhouse Ltd* [2008] EWHC 498 (Ch); [2008] 2 All E.R. (Comm) 964, where the money was lent to buy a car as part of an employee's severance package.

AFTER THE FIRST SENTENCE OF THE TEXT INSERT: The purpose must be fulfilled by and at the time of the application of the money. The payer, the recipient and the person who benefits from the application of the money for the stated purpose must know whether property has passed.[7a]

NOTE 8. AT THE END ADD: *Kingate Global Fund Ltd v Knightsbridge (USD) Fund Ltd* [2009] CA (Bda) 17 Civ; (2009–10) 12 I.T.E.L.R. 850.

NOTE 9. AT THE END ADD: See *Habana Ltd v Kaupthing Singer and Friedlander (Isle of Man) Ltd* (2009–10) 12 I.T.E.L.R. 736, Manx HC at [57], for the view that the *Kayford* line of authorities should be interpreted as involving the creation of an express trust by a company or individual over its own money, and not the creation of a resulting trust (affirmed *sub nom.*

[7a] *Bieber v Teathers Ltd* [2012] EWHC 190 (Ch); (2011–12) 14 I.T.E.L.R. 814 at [23].

Du Preez Ltd v Kaupthing Singer and Friedlander (Isle of Man) Ltd (2009–10) 12 I.T.E.L.R. 943 at [81], Manx SGD).

AFTER THE FOURTH SENTENCE OF THE TEXT INSERT: It has been said that the effect of the authorities is that a requirement to keep moneys separate is normally an indicator that they are impressed with a trust and the absence of such a requirement, if there are no other indicators, normally negatives it.[10a]

NOTE 14. AT THE END ADD: *McManus RE Pty Ltd v Ward* [2009] NSWSC 440; (2008–09) 74 N.S.W.L.R. 662.

4. SURPLUS ASSETS OF NON-CHARITABLE UNINCORPORATED ASSOCIATIONS AND RELIEF FUNDS

Dormant associations

DELETE THE FINAL SENTENCE OF THE TEXT AND REPLACE BY: It has recently been **8–63** decided that if there is only one surviving member, he is entitled to the assets of the association.[46] Lewison J. held that the members hold the property of the association subject to a species of joint tenancy, but they are contractually precluded from severing that joint tenancy except in accordance with the rules of the association. He said that there was nothing in the earlier authorities[46a] that bound him to the conclusion that where there is one identifiable and living member of an unincorporated association that has ceased to exist, the assets formerly held by or for that association pass to the Crown as *bona vacantia*.[46b]

Relief fund without members

NOTE 67. FOR THE REFERENCE TO Picarda, *The Law and Practice Relating to* **8–73** *Charities*, SEE NOW (4th edn), pp.504–505.

[10a] *R. v Clowes (No.2)* [1994] 2 All E.R. 316 at 325, CA; *Mills v Sportsdirect.com Retail Ltd* [2010] EWHC 1072 (Ch). But see *Re Multi Guarantee Co. Ltd* [1987] B.C.L.C. 257, CA.

[46] *Hanchett-Stamford v Att.-Gen.* [2008] EWHC 330 (Ch); [2008] Ch. 173.

[46a] *Cunnack v Edwards* [1895] 1 Ch. 389; [1896] 2 Ch. 679, CA; *Re Buckinghamshire Constabulary Widows and Orphans Fund Friendly Society (No.2)* [1979] 1 W.L.R. 936. See too *Spiller v Maude* (1864) 13 W.R. 69.

[46b] *Hanchett-Stamford v Att.-Gen.* [2008] EWHC 330 (Ch); [2008] Ch. 173 at [47].

CHAPTER 9

TRUSTS ARISING IN RELATION TO THE ACQUISITION OF PROPERTY

2. RESULTING TRUSTS ON GRATUITOUS LIFETIME TRANSFERS

Presumption of resulting trust and presumption of advancement

9–03 NOTE 6. AT THE END ADD: The rationale for the presumption of advancement was originally said to be the natural consideration of blood and affection: *Grey v Grey* (1677) 2 Sw. 594. Later, the court relied on the presumption that the donor intended to fulfil a "moral legal" obligation to maintain by making the transfer of property: see *Bennet v Bennet* (1879) 10 Ch.D. 474, *per* Jessel M.R. In relation to the problems in ascertaining the nature of the advancement relationship, see Mitchell (ed.), *Constructive and Resulting Trusts*, (Glister), pp.289–314.

AFTER § 9–03 INSERT THE FOLLOWING NEW PARAGRAPHS AND HEADINGS:

Abolition of the presumption of advancement

9–03A When section 199 of the Equality Act 2010 comes into force, the presumption of advancement will be abolished. No date has yet been appointed for the coming into force of this provision. Section 199(1) gives as an example the case where a husband is presumed to be making a gift to his wife if he transfers property to her, or purchases property in her name. It is clear from the terms of the section, however, that the presumption is to be abolished in all circumstances, and not only in relation to property purchased by a man in the name of his wife or fiancée. The abolition of the presumption of advancement, when it comes into operation, will not apply to anything done before that date and will have no effect in relation to any obligation incurred before the commencement of section 199.[6a] In relation to such cases the position will remain as set out in the following sections of this chapter. It is not clear whether the reference to "obligation" includes only legal obligations, or also moral obligations incurred by a husband, parent or

---

[6a] Equality Act 2010, s.199(2). See Glister (2010) 73 M.L.R. 807, questioning the need for this subsection. If the presumption is merely a rule of evidence, there is no reason in principle to limit the repeal to future transfers. Furthermore, it is unclear whether the rule will be amenable to judicial development once it has been repealed, or whether the issue of which 'obligations' may found an advancement relationship will be frozen when section 199 is brought into force.

other person in respect of gifts by whom the presumption of advancement has until now applied.[6b]

Presumption of resulting trust unaffected

The abolition of the presumption of advancement will not affect the **9–03B** application of the presumption of resulting trust. In those circumstances in which the presumption of advancement has hitherto applied, there will now be a presumption of resulting trust. So, where a husband transfers property to his wife it will now be presumed that she is to hold the property on trust for him unless there is evidence that a gift was intended.[6c] In practice, this presumption of resulting trust in the case of husband and wife may well, in many cases, be as weak as the existing presumption of advancement,[6d] with each case in fact usually determined by evidence of the actual intention of the transferor or provider of the purchase moneys.[6e] It should be remembered that the presumption of resulting trust has always been the general rule subject, hitherto, to an exception where the purchaser was under a species of natural obligation to provide for the nominee.[6f]

Significance of the presumption of resulting trust

NOTE 15. AT THE END ADD: The burden of adducing evidence to rebut the **9–05** presumption of resulting trust is an evidential burden. If the donee succeeds in discharging that burden, the claimant will fail unless he can discharge the legal burden of proof by showing an express trust: *Fong v Sun* [2008] HKCFI 385; (2007–08) 10 I.T.E.L.R. 1093 at [26].

Gratuitous dispositions in favour of strangers which raise a presumption of resulting trust

Assurances of land

NOTE 35. FOR THE REFERENCE TO *Snell's Equity*, SEE NOW (32nd edn), § 25– **9–09** 017. DELETE (in contrast to the view expressed in earlier editions) AND REPLACE BY: (in contrast to the view expressed in the 29th and earlier editions).

Transfer of personalty

NOTE 40. FOR THE REFERENCE TO *Snell's Equity*, SEE NOW (32nd edn), § 25– **9–10** 019.

[6b] As to the court's recognition of the validity and effect of moral obligations in the context of the Inheritance (Provision for Family and Dependants) Act 1975, see *Re Goodchild* [1997] 1 W.L.R. 1216 at 1227–1228, CA.

[6c] Explanatory note to the Equality Act 2010 at [633]. See Brightwell (2010) 16(8) *Trusts & Trustees* 627.

[6d] See §§ 9–05, n.18, 9–25.

[6e] See § 9–30.

[6f] *Murless v Franklin* (1818) 1 Sw. 17; *Fong v Sun* [2008] HKCFI 385; (2007–08) 10 I.T.E.L.R. 1093. See § 9–03 (including Supplement).

3. PURCHASE IN THE NAME OF ANOTHER

Generally

9–16 DELETE FINAL SENTENCE AND REPLACE BY: Hitherto, where a purchase has been made in the name of a person who is not in equity a stranger to the real purchaser, such as his wife or child, then a presumption of gift, called the presumption of advancement, has arisen in favour of the nominal purchaser. Where this presumption has applied,[57] the real purchaser has been able to establish a resulting trust in his favour only by evidence of his actual intention rebutting the presumption of advancement. When section 199 of the Equality Act 2010 comes into force, the presumption of advancement will be abolished, except in relation to anything done before, or in relation to any obligation incurred before, that date.[57a] The remainder of this section should be read subject to these remarks.

Presumption of resulting trust

Personalty

9–20 NOTE 69. AT THE END ADD: *Merlo v Duffy* [2009] EWHC 313 Ch; [2009] All E.R. (D) 91 (Feb) at [134].

Presumption of advancement on a purchase by a father in the name of his child

9–22 AT THE END OF THE TEXT ADD: It has recently been suggested that the presumption should not apply where the evidence does not indicate that the parent is under an obligation to provide for the child.[77a]

NOTE 76. AT THE END ADD: This presumption is to be abolished when the Equality Act 2010 comes into force. See § 9–03A (Supplement).

Presumption of advancement in favour of a wife or fiancée

9–25 NOTE 82. AT THE END ADD: This presumption is to be abolished when the Equality Act 2010 comes into force. See § 9–03A (Supplement).

NOTE 87. AT THE END ADD: *Cf. Cheung v Worldcup Investments Inc* [2008] HKCFA 78; (2008–09) 11 I.T.E.L.R. 449 at [7].

Presumption of advancement in other cases

9–26 ADD NEW NOTE 87a: This presumption is to be abolished when the Equality Act 2010 comes into force. See § 9–03A.

---

[57] For the circumstances in which, until now, the presumption of advancement has applied, see §§ 9–22 to 9–33.

[57a] See §§ 9–03A and 9–03B (Supplement).

[77a] *Musson v Bonner* [2010] W.T.L.R. 1369, Ch D at [28], relying on *Pecore v Pecore* [2007] SCC 17; (2006–07) 9 I.T.E.L.R. 873.

Stepchildren and children-in-law

NOTE 98. AT THE END ADD: As to children-in-law, see *Fong v Sun* [2008] **9–29** HKCFI 385; (2007–08) 10 I.T.E.L.R. 1093.

IN THE SECOND SENTENCE DELETE THE FIRST FIVE WORDS AND REPLACE WITH: It **9–30** has until recently been an unresolved question.

NOTE 1. AT THE END OF THE FIRST SENTENCE ADD: *Close Invoice Finance Ltd v Abaowa* [2010] EWHC 1920 (QB); [2010] All E.R. (D) 314 (Jul) at [92]–[96]. AT THE END OF THE SECOND SENTENCE ADD: Equality Act 2010, Explanatory Notes, para.625. AFTER THE FOURTH SENTENCE ADD: In *Musson v Bonner* [2010] W.T.L.R. 1369, Ch D, it was considered at [19] that the presumption of advancement can now apply equally to a mother as it did previously to a father, but held at [28] that the presumption of advancement does not operate in cases where the evidence does not establish that the parent is under an obligation to provide for the child.

Purchase in the name of partner

NOTE 4. AT THE END ADD: Cf. *Cheung v Worldcup Investments Inc* [2008] **9–31** HKCFA 78; (2008–09) 11 I.T.E.L.R. 449 at [9].

Purchase in the name of husband

NOTE 5. AT THE END OF THE FIRST SENTENCE ADD: *Close Invoice Finance Ltd v* **9–32** *Abaowa* [2010] EWHC 1920 (QB); [2010] All E.R. (D) 314 (Jul) at [97]–[98].

Evidence admissible to rebut the presumptions

Subsequent acts and declarations

NOTE 24. AT THE END OF THE SECOND SENTENCE ADD: *Fulton v Gunn* [2008] **9–36** BCSC 1159; (2008) 296 D.L.R. (4th) 1.

Improper purposes

NOTE 29. AT THE END ADD: *Barrett v Barrett* [2008] EWHC 1061 (Ch); [2008] **9–37** B.P.I.R. 817 (purpose to defeat claim of a party's trustee in bankruptcy).

AFTER THE FIRST SENTENCE ADD NEW NOTE 32a: The court should consider of its own motion whether these principles apply, even if they are unpleaded and neither party wishes to rely on them: *Knowlden v Tehrani* [2008] EWHC 54 (Ch); [2008] All E.R. (D) 148 (Jan) at [88].

NOTE 33. AFTER THE SECOND SENTENCE ADD: The Law Commission now proposes the abolition of the reliance principle established by *Tinsley v Milligan* [1994] 1 A.C. 340, HL and its replacement by provisions conferring a statutory discretion on the court. See § 5–30 (Supplement).

NOTE 34. AT THE END ADD: *Anzal v Ellahi*, July 21, 1999, CA, unreported; *Wu Wai Sum v Man Ting Chu* [2010] HKCA 284; [2010] 5 H.K.L.R.D. 125. Likewise, the fact that the purchase moneys have been acquired in a disreputable way or through a prior illegal transaction does not, in itself, prevent the provider of the purchaser moneys from establishing a beneficial interest in the property concerned: *Mortgage Express Ltd v Robson* [2001] EWCA Civ 887; [2001] All E.R. (Comm) 886 at [21]–[22].

NOTE 41. AT THE END ADD: *Q v Q* [2008] EWHC 1874 (Fam); [2009] 1 F.L.R. 935 at [123]–[130].

Provision of purchase money

Provision as purchaser

9–47   AT THE END ADD: Cases where a property is acquired on mortgage are considered in § 9–61 (including Supplement).

4. BENEFICIAL INTERESTS OF TWO OR MORE PERSONS

Introduction

9–48   AFTER THE THIRD SENTENCE ADD NEW NOTE 75a: For an application of these principles to a claim concerning the acquisition of shares, see *Webster v Webster* [2008] EWHC 31 (Ch); [2009] 1 F.L.R. 1240.

Claims to a beneficial interest under the law of trusts

9–50   NOTE 84. AT THE END ADD: *Cf. Kerr v Baranow* [2011] SCC 10; [2011] 1 S.C.R. 269 at [27].

9–51   NOTE 1. AT THE END ADD: It would seem, however, that these principles cannot be used by shareholders to acquire an interest in property owned by a company, for the company is not a party to the common intention: see *Luo Xing Juan v Estate of Hui Shui See* [2008] HKCFA 48; (2008–09) 11 I.T.E.L.R. 218.

NOTE 2. FOR THE REFERENCE TO *Snell's Equity*, SEE NOW (32nd edn), § 12–016 *et seq.*

Express trusts

The general principle

9–53   NOTE 9. FOR THE REFERENCE TO *Snell's Equity*, SEE NOW (32nd edn), Chap.15.

NOTE 10. FOR THE REFERENCE TO *Snell's Equity*, SEE NOW (32nd edn), Chap.16.

NOTE 11. AT THE END OF THE FIRST SENTENCE ADD: *Knowlden v Tehrani* [2008] EWHC 54 (Ch); [2008] All E.R. (D) 148 (Jan) at [71].

AT THE END OF THE FIRST SENTENCE ADD: though there may be room for a claim based on proprietary estoppel relying on events taking place after the declaration.[11a]

[11a]   *Clarke v Meadus* [2010] EWHC 3117 (Ch); [2010] All E.R. (D) 08 (Dec).

Credits for payment of mortgage instalments

NOTE 20. AT THE END ADD: These principles were applied in *Ketteringham v* **9–54**
Hardy [2011] EWHC 162 (Ch); [2011] W.T.L.R. 1367.

NOTE 31. AT THE END ADD: Principles of equitable accounting do still apply,
however, where the co-owner not in occupation has no right to occupy
pursuant to the 1996 Act: *Re Barcham* [2008] EWHC 1505 (Ch); [2009] 1
W.L.R. 1124, see § 37–62 (including Supplement).

Resulting trusts founded on contributions to the purchase money

Circumstances where a resulting trust arises

NOTE 38. AT THE BEGINNING INSERT: *Stack v Dowden* [2007] UKHL 17; [2007] **9–57**
2 A.C. 432; *Jones v Kernott* [2011] UKSC 53; [2011] 3 W.L.R. 1121.

Purchase in joint names—both parties contribute to purchase money

DELETE THE FIRST SENTENCE AND N.44 AND REPLACE BY: The House of Lords **9–58**
considered in *Stack v Dowden*[44] and the Supreme Court considered in *Jones
v Kernott*[44a] the case where a property is acquired by an unmarried couple as
a home and registered in joint names, but where there is no express
declaration of trust.

NOTE 45. DELETE AND REPLACE BY: *Stack v Dowden*, above, at [56], per Lady
Hale, and at [109] *per* Lord Neuberger; Lord Hoffmann agreed with Lady
Hale and Lords Hope and Walker did not expressly address this issue; *Jones
v Kernott*, above, at [15], [51], [60] and [68]. This is consistent with the views
of Lord Upjohn in *Pettitt v Pettitt* [1970] A.C. 777 at 813–814, HL.

NOTE 46. DELETE AND REPLACE BY: *Stack v Dowden*, above, at [56] and [68].

NOTE 47. DELETE THE SECOND SENTENCE AND REPLACE BY: See *Stack v Dowden*,
above, at [58]. AT THE END ADD: For an application of the principles of
common intention constructive trusts to a claim concerning the acquisition
of shares, see *Webster v Webster* [2008] EWHC 31 (Ch); [2009] 1 F.L.R.
1240. Where shareholders purchase property in the name of a company, the
resulting trust analysis is likely to apply: *Rakunas v Scenic Associates Ltd*
[2008] BCSC 444; (2008–09) 11 I.T.E.L.R. 31.

AFTER THE TEXT TO N.47 ADD: In this context a challenge to the presumption
of a beneficial joint tenancy is not to be lightly embarked upon, in part
because the decision to buy a house or flat in which to live together is a
strong indication of an emotional and economic commitment to a joint
enterprise, and in part because of the practical difficulty of taking an

[44] [2007] UKHL 17; [2007] 2 A.C. 432.
[44a] [2011] UKSC 53; [2011] 3 W.L.R. 1121.

account of financial contributions over the potentially lengthy duration of the relationship.[47a]

NOTE 48. DELETE THE FIRST SENTENCE AND REPLACE BY: *Stack v Dowden*, above, at [68] and [69]. AT THE END ADD: By contrast in *Jones v Kernott*, above, the presumption of beneficial joint tenancy applied at the time of purchase but was displaced by subsequent events which had the effect of varying the beneficial shares to a 90%–10% split.

DELETE THE LAST THREE SENTENCES AND REPLACE BY: The presumption of beneficial joint tenancy, rather than presumption of resulting trust by reference to contributions to the purchase price, applies in all cases where a house or flat is bought in joint names for joint occupation by a married or unmarried couple who are both responsible for any mortgage.[50a] But in other contexts, there may still be scope for a presumption of resulting trust. And so where a purchase in the commercial, as opposed to the domestic consumer, context is concerned, the principles in *Stack v Dowden*[50b] and *Jones v Kernott*[50c] do not apply and there is therefore no initial presumption that the beneficial ownership of property follows the legal ownership. Lord Neuberger has said that, "it would not be right to apply the reasoning in *Stack* to ... a case ... where the parties primarily purchased the property as an investment for rental income and capital appreciation, even where their relationship is a familial one".[50d] It has therefore now been established that there remains scope for the application of the resulting trust approach in certain cases, and that it has not been completely emasculated by the common intention principles laid down in *Stack v Dowden* and *Jones v Kernott*.

Quantification where resulting trust analysis applies

9–60   NOTE 61. ADD: *Laskar v Laskar* [2008] EWCA Civ 347; [2008] 1 W.L.R. 2695 at [24].

Mortgage payments

9–61   NOTE 71. AT THE END ADD: It is the incurring of the obligation to make payments to the mortgagee which leads to the analysis that the money borrowed is treated as a contribution to the purchase price. A third party who undertakes to the mortgagor to discharge his borrowing does not acquire an interest under a resulting trust, although he may acquire an interest by virtue of a common intention constructive trust: *Samad v*

[47a]   *Jones v Kernott*, above, at [19]–[22], *per* Lord Walker and Lady Hale. The reasons given explain why the presumption is not to be lightly departed from but not why a presumption of beneficial joint tenancy arises in joint names cases as distinct from single names cases. For the view that the decision could be more easily explained if the presumption in joint name cases were of an equitable tenancy in common in equal shares, see Briggs (2012) 128 L.Q.R. 183.

[50a]   *Jones v Kernott*, above, at [25].
[50b]   Above.
[50c]   Above.
[50d]   *Laskar v Laskar* [2008] EWCA Civ 347; [2008] 1 W.L.R. 2695 at [17]. *Cf. Crossco No.4 Unlimited v Jolan Ltd* [2011] EWCA Civ 1619; [2012] 2 All E.R. 754 at [87].

Thompson [2008] EWHC 2809 (Ch); [2008] All E.R. (D) 165 Nov at [122]; *Close Invoice Finance Ltd v Abaowa* [2010] EWHC 1920 (QB); [2010] All E.R. (D) 314 (Jul) at [100]–[116].

NOTE 72. AT THE END ADD: The view that payments by someone other than a mortgagee should be treated as contributions to the purchase price for the purpose of a purchase money resulting trust was rejected in *Barrett v Barrett* [2008] EWHC 1633 (Ch); [2008] B.P.I.R. 817 at [7], where it was said that no support for it could be derived from the speech of Lord Walker in *Stack v Dowden* [2007] UKHL 17; [2007] 2 A.C. 432. In a case where property is purchased in the name of a person who raises the purchase money by mortgage for which he is liable, save for a deposit which is contributed by another who acquires by way of resulting trust a share in the property corresponding to the proportion which the deposit bears to the purchase money, and the parties contribute to the mortgage instalments and the redemption of the mortgage in amounts which do not correspond to their beneficial shares, principles of equitable accounting (see § 9–54) apply in relation to those contributions: *Close Invoice Finance Ltd v Abaowa*, above, at [118]–[122].

Trusts founded on a common intention

The general principle

NOTE 88. AT THE END ADD: Gardner and Davidson (2007) 123 L.Q.R. 13; **9–66** Etherton (2008) 67 C.L.J. 265; Gardner (2008) 124 L.Q.R. 422; Hopkins (2009) 125 L.Q.R. 310; Gardner and Davidson (2012) 128 L.Q.R. 178; George [2012] C.L.J. 39.

DELETE THE THIRD SENTENCE AND N.89 AND REPLACE BY: The requisite common intention may be shown by virtue of an express agreement between the parties[89] or by inference.[89a] An inferred intention is in the case of each party the intention which was reasonably understood by the other party to be manifested by that party's words and conduct notwithstanding that he did not consciously formulate that intention in his own mind or even acted with some different intention which he did not communicate to the other party.[89b]

---

[89] *Lloyds Bank plc v Rosset* [1991] 1 A.C. 107, HL.

[89a] *Jones v Kernott* [2011] UKSC 53; [2011] 3 W.L.R. 1121 at [31], [51] and [64]. This was the view of the majority, namely Lord Walker and Lady Hale with whom Lord Collins agreed, who sought to resolve apparent ambiguities in *Stack v Dowden* [2007] UKHL 17; [2007] 2 A.C. 432, *e.g.* at [60]. It is noteworthy, however, that in the Court of Appeal, Rimer L.J. had held that the trial judge had identified no evidence justifying this conclusion, "because there was none": [2010] EWCA Civ 578; [2010] 1 W.L.R. 2401 at [83]. The line between a finding of an express agreement and the imputation of one may on occasion be a very fine one.

[89b] *Jones v Kernott*, above, at [51], citing *Gissing v Gissing* [1971] A.C. 886 at 906, HL. For conduct which is relevant to the inference of common intention, see *Stack v Dowden*, above, at [69], quoted in § 9–71.

If the requisite common intention cannot be inferred in this way, the existence of a common intention that beneficial ownership is to be shared, as distinct from the determination of the proportionate shares of the parties, cannot be imputed to the parties on the basis of what the parties would have intended had they addressed the issue of beneficial ownership.[89c]

NOTE 90. AT THE END ADD: Where the common intention is based upon an agreement between the parties, and that agreement follows upon an innocent misrepresentation by one of them, the starting point is to consider what would be the position in equity if an application were made to rescind the agreement upon which the constructive trust was said to be founded. Where rescission would have been refused, it will be an unusual case in which the misrepresentation will be held to have prevented the creation of a common intention constructive trust: *Hameed v Qayyum* [2009] EWCA Civ 352; [2009] 2 F.L.R. 962 at [41].

Common intention from initial discussions

9-67   AT THE END OF THE TEXT ADD: It is, however, necessary that it is possible to discern precisely who the beneficiaries of the trust are intended to be.[97a]

9-68   NOTE 99. AT THE END ADD: But see *Geary v Rankine* [2012] EWCA Civ 555; [2012] 2 F.C.R. 461, where the defendant's excuse was that the claimant's husband might make a claim on the property. This was perfectly rational even if such a claim might not have been given effect.

Common intention inferred from conduct

9-69   NOTE 10. AT THE END ADD: And see *Jones v Kernott* [2011] UKSC 53; [2011] 3 W.L.R. 1121. For a case where a significant financial contribution towards a barn conversion sufficed, see *Aspden v Elvy* [2012] EWHC 1387 (Ch); [2012] 2 F.C.R. 435.

AT THE END OF THE TEXT ADD: ; nor from the fact that the property was used by the parties to run a business together, where it was purchased entirely with money provided by one of them.[14a]

The detriment

9-70   NOTE 16. AT THE END ADD: But there is no requirement that, in a case where the parties have reached an express agreement as to the shares each will hold in the property, the agreement should also prescribe what it is that the claimant has to do: *Parris v Williams* [2008] EWCA Civ 257; [2009] 1 P. & C.R. 169 at [36]–[44].

[89c]   *Jones v Kernott*, above, at [31] and [64]. Lord Walker, Lady Hale and Lord Collins took a broader view of what might be inferred, see at [34] and [65], than did Lord Kerr and Lord Wilson, see at [67], [70]–[77] and [89], who considered that imputation had a significant role, at least as regards the determination of the proportionate shares of the parties. In this context, see *Kerr v Baranow* [2011] SCC 10; [2011] 1 S.C.R. 269 at [26]. See also Gardner and Davidson (2012) 128 L.Q.R. 178.

[97a]   *Tackaberry v Hollis* [2007] EWHC 2633 (Ch); [2008] W.T.L.R. 279.

[14a]   *Geary v Rankine* [2012] EWCA Civ 555; [2012] 2 F.C.R. 461.

NOTE 17. AT THE END ADD: *Thomson v Humphrey* [2009] EWHC 3576 (Ch); [2010] Fam. Law 351 at [95].

Relevant factors where property held in joint names

NOTE 22. AT THE END OF THE FIRST SENTENCE ADD: applied *Jones v Kernott* **9–71** [2011] UKSC 53; [2011] 3 W.L.R. 1121 at [51]. AT THE END ADD: For a case where it was not shown that the beneficial ownership did not follow the legal ownership in such a case, and where there was accordingly a beneficial joint tenancy, see *Edwards v Edwards* [2008] All E.R. (D) 79 (Mar).

Express agreement as to shares

NOTE 26. AT THE END ADD: *Bindra v Chopra* [2009] EWCA Civ 203; (2008– **9–72** 09) 11 I.T.E.L.R. 975.

NOTE 27. AT THE END ADD: In *Samad v Thompson* [2008] EWHC 2809 (Ch); [2008] All E.R. (D) 165 Nov, the claimant was also awarded the entire beneficial interest in the property on the basis of an express agreement. See *Levi v Levi* [2008] 2 P. & C.R. D2 at [56], relying on the text in this paragraph.

AT THE END OF THE TEXT ADD: Evidence of matters postdating the acquisition of the property is unlikely to assist in determining whether there was an express agreement at the outset that each party should have a defined share and should be viewed with caution.[27a]

Quantifying the shares where no express agreement

AT THE END OF THE FOURTH SENTENCE ADD NEW NOTE 29a: *Fowler v Barron* **9–73** [2008] EWCA Civ 377; (2008–09) 11 I.T.E.L.R. 198 at [56].

NOTE 31. AT THE END ADD: For a recent example of the Court determining the shares in which property was held by making inferences from the parties' conduct, see *Gallarotti v Sebastianelli* [2012] EWCA Civ 865; [2012] All E.R. (D) 55 (Jul).

NOTE 37. IN THE FIRST SENTENCE ADD: *Laskar v Laskar* [2008] EWCA Civ 347; [2008] 1 W.L.R. 2695 at [24].

Property in joint names

NOTE 41. AT THE END ADD: *Edwards v Edwards* [2008] All E.R. (D) 79 (Mar). **9–74**

Joint tenancy or tenancy in common

NOTE 46. AT THE END ADD: *HSBC Bank Plc v Dyche* [2009] EWHC 2954 **9–76** (Ch); [2010] B.P.I.R. 138 at [27].

[27a] See *Holman v Howes* [2007] EWCA Civ 877; (2008–09) 10 I.T.E.L.R. 492 at [30]–[31].

Acquiring a share after the time of purchase

9-77 NOTE 50. AT THE END ADD: Where there is a change in common intention after the date of acquisition of the property, it is necessary to analyse whether there has been a disposition of a beneficial interest, or the enlargement of the extent of an indeterminate existing beneficial interest: *Chan Chui Mee v Mak Cho Chui* [2008] HKCFI 810; [2009] 1 H.K.L.R.D. 343 at [38]. This may be important in determining the effect of the change of common intention on any third parties with whom a beneficial owner has dealt.

NOTE 50. AT THE END ADD: In *Jones v Kernott* [2011] UKSC 53; [2011] 3 W.L.R. 1121, however, such an intention was inferred.

NOTE 53. AT THE END ADD: See *Aspden v Elvy* [2012] EWHC 1387 (Ch); [2012] 2 F.C.R. 435.

AT THE END OF THE TEXT ADD: In the absence of an express post-acquisition agreement, a court will be slow to infer from conduct alone that parties intended to vary existing beneficial interests established at the time of acquisition.[54a] Nevertheless, such an intention may be inferred, as where one party departs and acquires alternative accommodation and the party remaining in the property pays all the outgoings thereafter.[54b]

Relationship with the doctrine of proprietary estoppel

9-79 NOTE 57. FOR THE REFERENCE TO *Snell's Equity*, SEE NOW (32nd edn), §§ 12–016 *et seq.*

Alignment with the common intention principle

9-80 NOTE 66. FOR THE REFERENCE TO Underhill and Hayton, *Law of Trusts and Trustees*, SEE NOW (18th edn), §§ 30.45 to 30.49. ADD: *Thorner v Major* [2009] UKHL 18; [2009] 1 W.L.R. 776 at [20]; Etherton [2009] Conv. 104.

The need for a separate doctrine

9-81 NOTE 69. AT THE END ADD: But in such a case of agreement, especially in a commercial transaction, there must be certainty as to the interest that is to be acquired for the principles of constructive trusts or of proprietary estoppel to arise: *Herbert v Doyle* [2010] EWCA Civ 1095; [2010] All E.R. (D) 126 (Oct) at [56]–[57].

AT THE END OF THE TEXT ADD: In *Thorner v Major*, Lord Scott of Foscote suggested the following distinction:[78a]

[54a] *James v Thomas* [2007] EWCA Civ 1212; [2008] 1 F.L.R. 1598 at [24], *per* Sir John Chadwick; *Mirza v Mirza* [2009] EWHC 3 (Ch); [2009] 2 F.L.R. 115; *Williams v Lawrence* [2011] EWHC 2001 (Ch); [2011] W.T.L.R. 1455. The question to be asked is whether the person who acted to his detriment must have done so in the belief that he was acquiring an interest in the property: *Morris v Morris* [2008] EWCA Civ 257; [2008] Fam. Law 521 at [25]–[26] (where such a case was described, at [20], as a "rare bird").
[54b] *Jones v Kernott* [2011] UKSC 53; [2011] 3 W.L.R. 1121.
[78a] [2009] UKHL 18; [2009] 1 W.L.R. 776 at [20]. See § 7–23A.

"For my part I would prefer to keep proprietary estoppel and constructive trust as distinct and separate remedies, to confine proprietary estoppel to cases where the representation, whether express or implied, on which the claimant has acted is unconditional and to address the cases where the representations are of future benefits, and subject to qualification on account of unforeseen future events, via the principles of remedial constructive trusts."

Other jurisdictions

NOTE 79. AT THE END ADD: See now *Kerr v Babanow* [2011] SCC 10 at [12]– **9–82**
[29], holding that the common intention approach no longer has a useful role to play, in Canada, in resolving property and financial disputes in domestic cases.

Improvements to property

NOTE 86. FOR THE REFERENCE TO *Snell's Equity*, SEE NOW (32nd edn), §§ 12– **9–83**
016 *et seq.*

AT THE END OF TEXT ADD: It also applies in the case of engaged couples.[90a]

Joint venture arrangements

NOTE 92. AT THE END ADD: *Cobbe v Yeoman's Row Management Ltd* [2006] **9–84**
EWCA Civ 1139; [2006] 1 W.L.R. 2964 was reversed on appeal, *sub nom.*
Yeoman's Row Management Ltd v Cobbe [2008] UKHL 55; [2008] 1 W.L.R.
1752, on which see below in the text to 9–84 (Supplement). AT THE END OF
THE SECOND SENTENCE ADD: *Button v Phelps* [2006] EWHC 53 (Ch); [2006] All
E.R. (D) 33 (Feb); *Baynes Clarke v Corless* [2010] EWCA Civ 338; [2010]
W.T.L.R. 751; *White City Tennis Club Ltd v John Alexander's Clubs Pty Ltd*
[2010] HCA 19; (2010–11) 13 I.T.E.L.R. 85 at [64]–[74]. AT THE END OF THE
NOTE ADD: For a case where a claimant failed to invoke the equity, where an
acquisition agreement was entered into which precluded a claim based on an
alleged prior understanding, see *Benedetti v Sawaris* [2009] EWHC 1330
(Ch); [2009] All E.R. (D) 281 (Jun) at [504]–[526].

AT THE END OF THE TEXT ADD: It has been said that when such a constructive trust does arise, "[the defendant's] possession of the property is coloured from the first by the trust and confidence by means of which he obtained it, and his subsequent appropriation of the property to his own use is a breach of that trust."[92a] An equity may arise in relation to a proposed joint venture over property already owned by one party, but in such a case the

---

[90a] Law Reform (Miscellaneous Provisions) Act 1970, s.2(1). In *Dibble v Pfluger* [2010] EWCA Civ 1005; [2011] 1 F.L.R. 659, at first instance, this provision "did not cross the radar". See § 9–25.

[92a] *Paragon Finance plc v D.B. Thakerar & Co.* [1999] 1 All E.R. 400 at 408–409, *per* Millett L.J.

arrangement or understanding must be sufficiently certain to be capable of specific performance and reliance on the principles discussed in this paragraph is not required.[92b] In *Yeoman's Row Management Ltd v Cobbe*,[92c] the House of Lords refused to extend the scope of the principle, affirming that the unconscionable withdrawal from an inchoate agreement was not an adequate basis, by itself, to impose a constructive trust over property already owned by the defendant in order to give effect to the claimant's disappointed expectation. Therefore, where the claimant's acts were carried out in the knowledge that the defendant was not legally bound, no constructive trust arose to give effect to a *Pallant v Morgan* equity.[92d] Where the Court holds that such an equity has arisen, it acts so as to deprive the defendant of an unconscionable advantage obtained in breach of trust.[92e] The principles set out in this paragraph have long been seen to be analogous to those concerning proprietary estoppel.[92f] The Court of Appeal has, however, recently doubted the extent of the assimilation,[92g] citing the application of the doctrine of proprietary estoppel in the commercial context in *Yeoman's Row Management Ltd v Cobbe*.[92h] A constructive trust arising in order to give effect to a *Pallant v Morgan* equity is not a common intention constructive trust.[92i] Developments in the law have shown the two doctrines to be distinct.[92j] In considering whether a constructive trust should be imposed it is relevant for the court to take into account the impact of the imposition of such a trust on third parties, and it may be appropriate for a third party adversely affected by the remedy sought to be joined as a party.[92k]

[92b] *London and Regional Investments Ltd v TBI Ltd* [2002] EWCA Civ 355; [2002] All E.R. (D) 360 (Mar) at [48]; *Kilcarne Holdings Ltd v Targetfollow (Birmingham) Ltd* [2004] EWHC 2547 (Ch); [2005] 2 P. & C.R. 105 at [225], [230] (affirmed at [2005] EWCA Civ 1355; [2006] 1 P. & C.R. D55).

[92c] [2008] UKHL 55; [2008] 1 W.L.R. 1752 at [36].

[92d] *Yeoman's Row Management Ltd v Cobbe*, above, at [36]. The claimant was, however, awarded a quantum meruit in respect of the money and services he had provided.

[92e] *Crossco No.4 Unlimited v Jolan Ltd* [2011] EWCA Civ 1619; [2012] 2 All E.R. 754 at [95].

[92f] *Holiday Inns Inc v Broadhead* (1974) 232 E.G. 951; *Banner Homes Group plc v Luff Developments Ltd* [2000] Ch. 372, CA. See §§ 9–79 to 9–81.

[92g] *Crossco No.4 Unlimited v Jolan Ltd*, above at [80].

[92h] Above, at [78]. The Court in *Crossco* contrasted this treatment with its operation in the domestic context in *Thorner v Major* [2009] UKHL 18; [2009] 1 W.L.R. 776, see § 7–23A (Supplement).

[92i] Hence, no agreement is required that the claimant would acquire a proportionate interest in the land for the equity to arise: *Kearns Brothers Ltd v Hova Developments Ltd* [2012] EWHC 2968 (Ch); [2012] All E.R. (D) 291 (Oct).

[92j] *Crossco No.4 Unlimited v Jolan Ltd*, above at [85]–[92], where Etherton L.J. analyses the cases in detail. The special features normally accompanying a claim to a common intention constructive trust do not apply in a commercial context where it is expected that the parties will take legal advice, reduce their agreement to writing and not expect to be bound until a contract has been made, see at [87].

[92k] *White City Tennis Club Ltd v John Alexander's Clubs Pty Ltd*, above, at [126]–[138].

5. JOINT BANK ACCOUNTS

Joint bank accounts

One source of payments into the account

NOTE 94. AT THE END ADD: *Sillett v Meek* [2007] EWHC 1169 (Ch); (2008– **9–86**
09) 10 I.T.E.L.R. 617; *Northall v Northall* [2010] EWHC 1448 (Ch) at [8].

NOTE 96. AT THE END ADD: This presumption is to be abolished when the
Equality Act 2010 comes into force. See § 9–03A (Supplement).

NOTE 97. AT THE END ADD: The effect of a joint account held on these terms
was considered in *Drakeford v Cotton* [2012] EWHC 1414 (Ch); (2012–13) 15
I.T.E.L.R. 144 at [57]–[68]. See also *Russell v Scott* (1936) 55 C.L.R. 440,
HCA.

AT THE END OF THE TEXT ADD: Bank documents signed by the parties may, **9–87**
after an assessment of the totality of the evidence, be strong evidence of a
party's intention when considering whether the presumptions of resulting
trust and advancement are rebutted, but should not be assigned presumptive
value in themselves.[6a]

NOTE 6. AT THE END ADD: This statement was discussed in an *obiter* passage
in *Drakeford v Cotton* [2012] EWHC 1414 (Ch); (2012–13) 15 I.T.E.L.R. 144
at [53]. Where the beneficial interest in the account changes during its
existence, consideration must be given to the possible effect of Law of
Property Act, s.53(1)(*c*), see § 3–18 (Supplement).

[6a] *Saylor v Madsen Estate* (2005) 261 D.L.R. (4th) 597 at [27], Ont CA (affirmed [2007] SCC
18; [2007] 1 S.C.R. 838).

CHAPTER 10

CREATION OF TRUSTS BY CONTRACT

2. THE SELLER UNDER A SPECIFICALLY ENFORCEABLE CONTRACT

Sale of land

General principle

10–03 NOTE 3. AT THE END OF THE FIRST SENTENCE ADD: *Nelson v Greening & Sykes (Builders) Ltd* [2007] EWCA Civ 1358; (2007–08) 10 I.T.E.L.R. 689 AT [53]. THE CORRECT NEUTRAL CITATION OF *Englewood Properties Ltd v Patel* IS [2005] EWHC 188 (Ch) AND THE DECISION IS REPORTED AT [2005] 1 W.L.R. 1961.

10–04 NOTE 8. THE CORRECT NEUTRAL CITATION OF *Englewood Properties Ltd v Patel* IS [2005] EWHC 188 (Ch) AND THE DECISION IS REPORTED AT [2005] 1 W.L.R. 1961.

10–05 NOTE 20. AT THE END OF THE FIRST SENTENCE ADD: *First Laser Ltd v Fujian Enterprises (Holdings) Co. Ltd* [2011] HKCA 1; (2010–11) 13 I.T.E.L.R. 599 at [76.6]–[76.7] (land, approving this passage). The same applies to a contract to assign a lease when the assignment is subject to the lessor's consent: *Clarence House Ltd v National Westminster Bank plc* [2009] EWCA 1311; [2010] 1 W.L.R. 1216 at [45].

NOTE 21. AT THE END ADD: *First Laser Ltd v Fujian Enterprises (Holdings) Co. Ltd*, above, at [76.8]; *UBS Global Asset Management (UK) Ltd v Crown Estate Commissioners*, unreported, June 9, 2011, Ch D.

The qualified nature of the trust

10–06 NOTE 28. INSERT AT THE END: *Underwood v R.C.C.* [2008] EWCA Civ 1423; [2009] S.T.C. 239 at [38], citing this passage. A vesting order in favour of the purchaser may accordingly be made in a suitable case: *Re Purkiss* [1999] VSC 386, relying on legislation in terms similar to Trustee Act 1925, s.44, for which see §§ 18–04 *et seq.*

NOTE 33. THE CORRECT NEUTRAL CITATION OF *Englewood Properties Ltd v Patel* IS [2005] EWHC 188 (Ch) AND THE DECISION IS REPORTED AT [2005] 1 W.L.R. 1961.

The nature of the relationship

10–07 NOTE 40. FOR THE REFERENCE TO *Snell's Equity*, SEE NOW (32nd edn), § 24–003.

Sale of shares

NOTE 45: INSERT AT THE END: *Mills v Sportsdirect.com Retail Ltd* [2010] **10–09** EWHC 1072 (Ch); [2010] All E.R. (D) 111 (May) at [75].

NOTE 46: INSERT AT THE END: *Mills v Sportsdirect.com Retail Ltd*, above, *loc. cit.*

AT THE END OF THE TEXT ADD: The same is true even of quoted shares if the quantity of shares contracted for is not readily obtainable in the market.[46a] If the contracting seller of the shares wrongly sells the shares to a third party for a higher price, then as with land the purchase money received by the seller is held in trust for the original buyer, subject to an allowance for the price payable by the original buyer.[46b]

4. MUTUAL WILLS

General principle

Examples

DELETE gifts AND REPLACE BY: gift.   **10–36(1)**

Requirements

Need for agreement

NOTE 50: AT THE END ADD: *Fry v Densham-Smith* [2010] EWCA Civ 1410; **10–37** [2010] All E.R. (D) 136 (Dec) at [3]; *Webb v Smith* [2011] NZHC 1512.

NOTE 51: AT THE END ADD: *Charles v Fraser* [2010] EWHC 2154 (Ch); (2010–11) 13 I.T.E.L.R. 455; *Hussey v Bauer* [2011] QCA 91.

NOTE 55: AT THE END ADD: *Charles v Fraser*, above, at [66].   **10–38**

AT THE END OF THE LAST SENTENCE OF THE TEXT INSERT: where that is so.

[46a] *Mills v Sportsdirect.com Retail Ltd*, above, loc. cit., citing *Duncuft v Albrecht* (1841) 12 Sim. 189 at 198. In the case of shares held in uncertificated form, *i.e.* registered electronically, they are fungible, not being individually identifiable and not appropriated to a particular contract, so there may be some question whether those principles can apply to them: see Palmer's Company Law (25th edn), para.6.701 *et seq.* and Mills at [76]. We consider, however, that those principles ought to apply nonetheless; *cf. Hunter v Moss* [1994] 1 W.L.R. 452, CA (trust of undifferentiated shares), for which see § 3–06. Uncertificated shares attract the operation of Uncertificated Securities Regulations 2001 (SI 2001/3755, amended as stated in § 34–67), reg.31(2) of which provides that the transferor retains "title" to the shares until the transferee is entered as holder on the relevant issuer register of securities; but we consider that in context "title" means legal title. For uncertificated shares generally, see §§ 34–67 *et seq.*

[46b] *Luxe Holdings Ltd v Midland Resources Holdings Ltd* [2010] EWHC 1908 (Ch). Provided that the contract is governed by English law, it makes no difference that the shares are foreign shares indirectly owned through subsidiaries of the seller and that under the law of the country where the shares are situated an indirect sale of them is not permitted or trusts are not recognised: *ibid.*

No need for wills to follow agreement

10–41 AT THE END OF THE TEXT ADD: But in the former case it seems that the doctrine does not apply unless the wills are actually executed in accordance with the agreement.[62a]

Formalities required

10–43 NOTE 67. AT THE END ADD: *Walters v Olins* [2007] EWHC 3060 (Ch); [2008] W.T.L.R. 339 at [31] (point not taken on appeal, *sub nom. Olins v Walters* [2008] EWCA Civ 782; [2009] Ch. 212).

NOTE 68. DELETE THE REFERENCE TO *Williams on Wills*.

NOTE 72. AT THE END ADD: In *Walters v Olins*, above, at first instance, *Healey v Brown* was treated (*semble*) as deciding that a contract to make a will disposing of specific property had to comply with the formalities required by the 1989 Act, s.2, see [2007] EWHC 3060 (Ch) at [31] (point not taken on appeal, [2008] EWCA Civ 782).

AT THE END OF THE PENULTIMATE SENTENCE OF THE TEXT INSERT A NEW NOTE 74a: For a discussion of the extent to which s.2 of the 1989 Act precludes a constructive trust (or a proprietary estoppel) when there is an agreement between the parties, see *Whittaker v Kinnear* [2011] EWHC 1479 (QB).

DELETE THE FINAL SENTENCE OF THE TEXT AND REPLACE BY: Until it is, prudence dictates assuming that the 1989 Act may apply.

Obligations of testators—property affected

10–50 AT THE END OF THE FIRST SENTENCE OF THE TEXT INSERT A NEW NOTE 91a: *Walters v Olins* [2007] EWHC 3060 (Ch); [2008] W.T.L.R. 339 at [42], apparently accepted on appeal, *sub nom. Olins v Walters* [2008] EWCA Civ 782; [2009] Ch. 212 at [23], [44]; *Fazari v Cosentino* [2010] WASC 40 at [29]–[31].

AT THE END OF THE SECOND SENTENCE OF THE TEXT INSERT A NEW NOTE 91b: Note that the agreement may extend to T2's entire estate and not merely to that part of it (if any) derived from T1: see § 10–40 and the assumption made in *Walters v Olins* [2007] EWHC 3060 (Ch); [2008] W.T.L.R. 339 at [42], apparently accepted on appeal, *sub nom. Olins v Walters* [2008] EWCA Civ 782; [2009] Ch. 212 at [23], [44]; *Fazari v Cosentino*, above, at [31].

10–51 NOTE 98. AT THE END ADD: See the further the discussion of the effect of *Palmer v Bank of New South Wales* (1975) 133 C.L.R. 150, Aus. HC in *Fazari v Cosentino* [2010] WASC 40.

[62a] *Fry v Densham-Smith* [2010] EWCA Civ 1410; [2010] All E.R. (D) 136 (Dec) at [3]. We do not consider that the court intended in that decision to deal with a case in which the agreement was not to revoke existing wills.

Joint tenancies

NOTE 2: AFTER THE REFERENCE TO *Re Hagger* INSERT: *Szabo v Boros* (1967) 64 **10–52**
D.L.R. (2d) 48.

How mutual wills take effect

NOTE 6. INSERT AT THE END OF THE FIRST SENTENCE OF THE TEXT: *Olins v* **10–54**
Walters [2008] EWCA Civ 782; [2009] Ch. 212 at [37]–[39], [42].

NOTE 8. AT THE END ADD: See too *Russo v Russo* [2009] VSC 491.

NOTE 9. DELETE THE LAST SENTENCE AND REPLACE BY: In New Zealand, it has
been held that equivalent protection is available only where the agreement
for mutual wills identifies specific assets and not where it extends merely to
the residue of T2's estate: *Fisher v Mansfield* [1997] 2 N.Z.L.R. 320; *Bayer v
Wiltshier*, unreported, July 21, 1998; *Fundel v Wall* [2009] NZHC 1633,
summarising *Bayer v Wiltshier* at [35].

AT THE END OF THE LAST SENTENCE OF THE TEXT INSERT A NEW NOTE 9a: In *Olins
v Walters* [2008] EWCA Civ 782; [2009] Ch. 212, a claim was made for an
injunction *quia timet* against T2 (who was still alive) but abandoned because
of the difficulty in formulating it: see *ibid.* at [26] and, at first instance, [2007]
EWHC 3060 (Ch); [2008] W.T.L.R. 339 at [6].

NOTE 10. AT THE END ADD: A dispute as to the existence of mutual wills **10–55**
similarly attracts the ordinary rule that the loser is ordered to pay the costs
and not any special rule applicable in probate actions: *Shovelar v Lane*
[2011] EWCA Civ 802; [2012] 1 W.L.R. 637.

NOTE 13. *Barns v Barns* IS REPORTED AT (2003) 214 C.L.R. 169.   **10–56**

5. OTHER CONTRACTS AND COVENANTS TO MAKE A WILL

General

AT THE END OF THE TEXT INSERT A NEW NOTE 20a: Note, however, that assur- **10–58**
ances unsupported by consideration, or too imprecise to have contractual
effect, may nonetheless be significant in raising a proprietary estoppel; see,
for example, *Thorner v Major* [2009] UKHL 18; [2009] 1 W.L.R. 776;
Delaforce v Simpson-Cook [2010] NSWCA 84.

AT THE END OF THE FIRST SENTENCE OF THE TEXT INSERT A NEW NOTE 20b: **10–59**
Though a contract to leave a pecuniary legacy creates no trust, it will
nonetheless bind the estate and damages can be recovered for breach of it,
see *e.g. Soulsbury v Soulsbury* [2007] EWCA Civ 969; [2007] W.T.L.R. 1841.

NOTE 27. AT THE END ADD: *Thorner v Major* [2008] EWCA Civ 732; [2008] **10–61**
W.T.L.R. 1289 at [53], *obiter* (appeal allowed without adverting to this
point, [2009] UKHL 18; [2009] 1 W.L.R. 776).

NOTE 38. AT THE END ADD: *Thorner v Major* [2008] EWCA Civ 732; [2008] **10–65**
W.T.L.R. 1289 at [53], *obiter* (appeal allowed without adverting to this
point, [2009] UKHL 18; [2009] 1 W.L.R. 776).

CHAPTER 11

FOREIGN ELEMENTS

GENERAL NOTE: FOR THE REFERENCES IN THIS CHAPTER TO Dicey, Morris and Collins, *The Conflict of Laws* (14th edn), SEE NOW 15th edn (forthcoming at the time of writing).

2. THE JURISDICTION OF THE ENGLISH COURT

Jurisdiction at common law

General rule—person of defendant

11–06 NOTE 18. DELETE AND REPLACE BY: CPR, Pt 6, r.6.6(1).

NOTE 20. DELETE AND REPLACE BY: CPR, Pt 6, rr.6.3(2), 6.5(3)(*b*). 6.7, 6.8, 6.9 and the table following.

General rule—subject matter

AFTER §11–07 INSERT THE FOLLOWING NEW PARAGRAPH:

11–07A Similarly, a trustee may invoke the assistance of the English court to determine a question arising in the administration of the trust, even though the proper law of the trust is not English and the trustee himself is based abroad.[27a]

Jurisdiction clauses under the common law rules

Construction of jurisdiction clauses

11–10(2) NOTE 40. AT THE END OF THE FIRST SENTENCE ADD: approved *Helmsman Ltd v Bank of New York Trust Company (Cayman) Ltd* (2010–11) 13 I.T.E.L.R. 177 at [10], Cayman GC; cited with apparent approval *Representation of AA* [2010] JRC 164; (2010–11) 13 I.T.E.L.R. 690 at [26].

AT THE END OF THE TEXT ADD: But more recently the courts have favoured a narrower interpretation of the phrase so that it does not cover an action for breach of trust[42a] or other hostile proceedings[42b] against a former trustee.

[27a] *Berman v SPF CDO I Ltd* [2011] HKCFI 190; (2010–11) 13 I.T.E.L.R. 831, on Hong Kong rules equivalent to the English predecessor (R.S.C. O.85, r.2) of CPR Pt 64. For applications within CPR Pt 64, see §§ 27–05 *et seq.*
[42a] *Helmsman Ltd v Bank of New York Trust Company (Cayman) Ltd*, above.
[42b] *Representation of AA*, above.

NOTE 44. DELETE AND REPLACE BY: Briggs and Rees, *Civil Jurisdiction and* **11–10(3)**
Judgments (5th edn), § 4.45.

Effect of jurisdiction clauses

NOTE 49. DELETE THE SECOND SENTENCE AND REPLACE WITH: Contrast claims **11–11(1)**
about contracts, where a clause conferring jurisdiction on the English court
is a ground for service out of the jurisdiction: see Practice Direction 6B—
Service out of the Jurisdiction (supplementing Sec. IV of CPR, Pt 6), para.
3.1(6)(d).

NOTE 56. ADD: *Representation of AA* [2010] JRC 164 at [34].   **11–11(3)**

NOTE 57. FOR THE REFERENCE TO *Civil Procedure* (2007), Vol.1, 6.21.19,
SUBSTITUTE *Civil Procedure* (2011), Vol.1, 6.37.19.

NOTE 64. FOR THE REFERENCE TO *Civil Procedure* (2007), Vol.1, 6.21.19, **11–11(5)**
SUBSTITUTE *Civil Procedure* (2011), Vol.1, 6.37.19.

DELETE THE FIRST EIGHT WORDS AND REPLACE BY: In a case where there are **11–11(6)**
multiple defendants,

Variation of judicial forum

AT THE END OF THE FOURTH SENTENCE, INSERT A NEW NOTE 69a: *Cf. Oakley v* **11–12**
Osiris Trustees Ltd [2008] UKPC 2; (2008) 10 I.T.E.L.R. 789, where the
majority assumed and the minority expressly held (see at [44]) that a power
to change the proper law of a trust would be validly exercised only if
exercised in the interests of the beneficiaries.

AT THE END OF THE TEXT ADD: There is no objection to trustees exercising a
power to change the judicial forum so as to facilitate proceedings against
former trustees in what the trustees consider to be a more convenient
forum.[70a]

Appropriate forum under the common law rules

DELETE THE HEADING TO THIS PARAGRAPH AND REPLACE BY: **11–14**

Forum conveniens—*service of proceedings out of the jurisdiction with court's
permission*

NOTE 72. DELETE THE REFERENCE TO THE CPR AND REPLACE BY: CPR, Pt 6,
r.6.37(3).

NOTE 73. DELETE AND REPLACE BY: Briggs and Rees, *Civil Jurisdiction and
Judgments* (5th edn), § 4.80.

NOTE 74. FOR THE REFERENCE TO Briggs and Rees, *Civil Jurisdiction and
Judgments*, SEE NOW (5th edn), §§ 4.80 to 4.84. FOR THE REFERENCE TO *Civil
Procedure* (2007), Vol.1, 6.21.15(4), SUBSTITUTE *Civil Procedure* (2011),
Vol.1, 6.37.15(4).

[70a] *Helmsman Ltd v Bank of New York Trust Company (Cayman) Ltd* (2010–11) 13 I.T.E.L.R.
177 at [14], Cayman GC.

NOTE 77. DELETE THE SECOND SENTENCE AND REPLACE BY: The question whether there is an English governing law will, however, be decisive if the only potentially available ground for service out of the jurisdiction is that contained in Practice Direction 6B—Service out of the Jurisdiction (supplementing Sec. IV of CPR, Pt 6), para.3.1(12) (trusts), as to which see § 11–31.

NOTE 79. FOR THE REFERENCE TO Briggs and Rees, *Civil Jurisdiction and Judgments*, SEE NOW (5th edn), § 4.84.

Forum non conveniens—*stay of proceedings served within jurisdiction*

11–15 AT THE END OF THE THIRD SENTENCE OF THE TEXT INSERT A NEW NOTE 80a: See, *e.g.*, *Re A and MC Trust* 2007–08 G.L.R. N8, Guernsey RC (stay refused where proper law of trust was *lex fori*, few factual issues arose and decision of forum would be given much sooner than that of foreign court).

NOTE 81. DELETE AND REPLACE BY: *Spiliada Maritime Corp. v Cansulex* [1987] A.C. 460 at 464–465, 474–478, HL; Dicey, Morris and Collins, *The Conflict of Laws* (14th ed.), Vol.1, §§ 12R–001, 12–007 to 12–010 and 12–028 to 12–034; Briggs and Rees, *Civil Jurisdiction and Judgments* (5th edn), §§ 4.13 to 4.32; *Civil Procedure* (2011), Vol.1, 6.37.18.

NOTE 82. DELETE THE REFERENCE TO Briggs and Rees, *Civil Jurisdiction and Judgments* AND REPLACE BY: Briggs and Rees, *Civil Jurisdiction and Judgments* (5th edn), § 4.15 to 4.17.

Lis alibi pendens *and anti-suit injunctions*

11–16 NOTE 86. DELETE THE REFERENCE TO Briggs and Rees, *Civil Jurisdiction and Judgments* AND REPLACE BY: Briggs and Rees, *Civil Jurisdiction and Judgments* (5th edn), § 4.33.

NOTE 89. DELETE THE REFERENCE TO Briggs and Rees, *Civil Jurisdiction and Judgments* AND REPLACE BY: Briggs and Rees, *Civil Jurisdiction and Judgments* (5th edn), §§ 5.38 to 5.50.

European legislation

Three regimes

11–18 NOTE 98. AFTER Cyprus DELETE (Greek part). AT THE END ADD: The whole of Cyprus is part of the EU, the government of the southern, Greek, part being recognised by the other member states as the *de jure* government of Cyprus.

Domicile of defendant

11–20 NOTE 11. DELETE THE LAST SENTENCE AND REPLACE BY: That definition is adopted for CPR Pt 6 by r.6.31(1)(i).

DELETE HEADING TO § 11–21 AND REPLACE BY:

Claims involving trusts "domiciled" in England

DELETE THE LAST TWO SENTENCES AND NN. 18 AND 19 AND REPLACE BY: To **11–21** determine whether a trust is domiciled in a contracting state whose courts are seised of the matter, both the Conventions and the Judgments Regulation require those courts to apply their own rules of private international law.[18] In England, the relevant rules are provided by legislation: a trust is domiciled in the United Kingdom if it is domiciled in a part of the United Kingdom; and it is domiciled in a part of the United Kingdom if, and only if, the law of that part is the system of law with which the trust has its closest and most real connection.[18a] A trust governed by English law will be domiciled in England in all but extraordinary circumstances, even if the trust assets are abroad, the trustees and the beneficiaries reside abroad, and the trust is administered abroad.[18b] If the proper law of a trust has been changed by the exercise of a power in that behalf, it will be the later proper law, not the original one, which determines the domicile of the trust;[18c] and the relevant proper law is that governing when the proceedings are issued, not when the cause of action arose.[18d]

AFTER § 11–21 INSERT THE FOLLOWING NEW PARAGRAPHS:

To fall within the provision quoted in § 11–21, the trust must be created by **11–21A** the operation of a statute, or by written instrument, or be created orally and evidenced in writing. Express trusts created by declaration of trust or settlement to which trustees are a party plainly qualify. So do such statutory trusts as those created by the Administration of Estates Act 1925 on an intestacy.[18e] It is said, by contrast, that constructive trusts do not qualify;[18f] but that must mean only that the trust must be expressly created,[18g] since a trustee of an trust created by a written instrument who is sued to make him account for an unauthorised profit is sued as trustee of a trust within the provision even though he is a constructive trustee of the profit.[18h] (Moreover, certain claims asserting a constructive trust will fall within another special provision of the Conventions and the Judgments Regulation.[18i])

---

[18] Brussels Convention, art.53(2); Lugano Convention, art.53(2); Judgments Regulation, art.60(3).
[18a] Civil Jurisdiction and Judgments Act 1982, s.45 (as amended by Civil Jurisdiction and Judgments Act 1991, s.3 and Sch.2, para.20); Civil Jurisdiction and Judgments Order 2001 (SI 2001/3929), Sch.1, para.12.
[18b] *Gomez v Gomez-Monche Vives*, [2008] EWCA Civ 1065; [2009] 1 Ch. 245 at [58]–[64]. See too *Chellaram v Chellaram (No.2)* [2002] EWHC 632 (Ch); [2002] 3 All E.R. 17 at [141].
[18c] *Chellaram v Chellaram*, above, at [162].
[18d] *ibid.*, at [148]–[153].
[18e] Administration of Estates Act 1925, ss.46, 47.
[18f] *Chellaram v Chellaram (No.2)*, above, at [138], [162]. See too the report by Professor Schlosser on the accession of the United Kingdom to the Brussels Convention (OJ 1979 C 59, p. 71), para. 117. The Schlosser report is made authoritative for the construction of the Brussels Convention by Civil Jurisdiction and Judgments Act 1982, s.3(3).
[18g] The Schlosser report, at para. 117, gives as an instance of a trust outside the provision the trust which arises in favour of a purchaser on the making of a contract for the sale of land, for which see §§ 10–03 *et seq.* (though the contract of sale will ordinarily be a written instrument).
[18h] *Gomez v Gomez-Monche Vives* [2008] EWHC 259 (Ch); [2009] 1 Ch. 245 at [59]; point not taken on appeal, [2008] EWCA Civ 1065; [2009] 1 Ch. 274. For the trustee's liability as constructive trustee, see § 20–28.
[18i] See § 11–21C (Supplement).

11–21B It is not easy to say precisely what claims are within the provision quoted in § 11–21. Although the terms "settlor", "trustee" and "beneficiary" are of course familiar in English law, nothing in domestic law turns on characterising a claim as being (or not being) one in which a defendant is sued "as" settlor, trustee or beneficiary. The general intention is to distinguish between the internal relationships of a trust and its external relationships.[18j] The special jurisdiction over trusts is meant to apply to the former alone; but it does so imperfectly:

(1) As to suing a defendant as settlor, it seems obvious that where trustees sue the settlor on a covenant to settle further property he is sued "as" settlor; and the same is true where trustees or beneficiaries sue the settlor about the scope of reserved powers, including a power of revocation of the trust. We consider that the same is also true where trustees or beneficiaries sue the settlor to confirm the existence of a trust despite allegations of sham or undue influence or duress, even though the existence of the trust (and hence the existence of the settlor's role as such) is the very matter in issue.

(2) As to suing a defendant as trustee, a claim against a trustee for breach of trust plainly qualifies. Beneficiaries or other trustees who sue a trustee for making an unauthorised profit similarly sue the trustee as trustee.[18k] The same must be true of a claim, whether made by beneficiaries or other trustees, against a person whose appointment as trustee is of uncertain validity or whose removal as trustee under an express power is of uncertain validity,[18l] whether the claim is to resolve his status or to enforce a liability arising from his having acted in the trusts. It cannot in our view make a difference whether the claim asserts that the defendant is a trustee; or asks neutrally whether the defendant is a trustee; or asserts that the defendant, though claiming to be a trustee, is not in fact one. A settlor suing trustees who asserts that the trust is void because it is a will in disguise or is a sham or was executed under duress no doubt sues them as trustees, even if the claim is that the trust is void. Where the limitations of the trust instrument do not exhaust the beneficial interests, beneficiaries under the resulting trust who sue the trustees presumably also sue them as trustees.

[18j] See the Schlosser report at paras.109–113.

[18k] See § 11–21A (Supplement).

[18l] The Schlosser report at para.111 states that art.5(6) of the Brussels Convention was intended solve problems "between the trustees themselves, *between persons claiming the status of trustees* and, above all, between trustees on the one hand and the beneficiaries of a trust on the other. Disputes may occur among a number of persons as to who has been properly appointed as a trustee ...". (Emphasis added.)

(3) Trustees or beneficiaries suing a beneficiary to establish a point of construction of the trust instrument, *e.g.* the scope of a power of investment or the age of vesting, undoubtedly sue the defendant as beneficiary.[18m] Where they sue someone whose status as a beneficiary is uncertain, *e.g.* whether someone born outside wedlock is within the category of "children", it is less obvious that the defendant is sued as beneficiary, since his status as such is the very matter in issue; but as with doubtful trustees, it seems likely that the claim qualifies.[18n] A claim, whether made by trustees or beneficiaries, against a beneficiary who has been overpaid by the trustees, and whose only possible title to the payment was as a beneficiary of the trust, is a claim against the defendant as beneficiary.[18o]

(4) Claims concerning a power conferred by the trust instrument on a third party, such as a protector, where the donee is sued are not within the special jurisdiction as to trusts conferred by the Conventions and the Judgments Regulation: such claims arise out of the internal relationships of a the trust but the donee is not sued as settlor, trustee or beneficiary. Even when the power is, or is alleged to be, a fiduciary power and complaint is made of a breach of duty in its exercise, the donee will not be treated as a trustee for the purpose of the special jurisdiction.[18p]

Constructive trusts

The Conventions and the Judgments Regulation all provide in substance **11–21C** that a person domiciled in a member state may, in another member state, be sued:[19]

> "in matters relating to tort, delict or quasi-delict, in the courts for the place where the harmful event occurred or may occur".

The expression "matters relating to tort, delict or quasi-delict" embodies an autonomous concept independent of any particular domestic law.[19a] A claim based on dishonest assistance in a breach of trust and asserting that the defendant is liable as constructive trustee is within that provision, since the assistance is a harmful event in addition to the breach of trust.[19b] Whether a

---

[18m] The Schlosser report at para.111 states that art.5(6) of the Brussels Convention extends to "disputes between the trustees and the beneficiaries as to the rights of the latter to or in connection with the trust property, as to whether, for example, the trustee is obliged to hand over assets to a child beneficiary of the trust after the child has attained a certain age".

[18n] For claims against trustees whose status is uncertain, see § 11–21B(2) (Supplement).

[18o] *Gomez v Gomez-Monche Vives* [2008] EWCA Civ 1065; [2009] 1 Ch. 274.

[18p] *ibid.*, at [91], [97]–[99].

[19] Brussels Convention, art.5(3); Lugano Convention, art.5(3); Judgments Regulation, art.5.3.

[19a] *Kalfelis v Bankhaus Schröder, Munchmeyer, Hengst & Co.* [1988] E.C.R. 5565 at [16]–[17], E.C.J.

[19b] *Casio Computer Co. Ltd v Sayo* [2001] EWCA Civ 661; [2001] All E.R. (D) 147 (Apr).

claim based on knowing receipt of assets transferred in breach of trust is similarly within that provision is undecided.[19c] Restitutionary claims not presupposing a harmful event or a threatened wrong fall outside it.[19d]

Exclusive jurisdiction clauses under the European regimes

11–23 IN THE FIRST SENTENCE DELETE contracting state AND SUBSTITUTE member and contracting state.

AFTER § 11–23 INSERT THE FOLLOWING NEW PARAGRAPH:

11–23A Where a jurisdiction clause confers jurisdiction on the courts of a state other than a member or contracting state, it seems that the English court retains a discretion to give effect to the clause even though the defendant is domiciled in England, itself a member and a contracting state.[26a]

Defendants domiciled in more than one jurisdiction—effect of European rules

11–24 NOTE 27. ADD AT THE END: Note that those provisions presuppose that there is a claimant making connected claims against an English-domiciled defendant and a defendant domiciled elsewhere in Europe and do not enable a second claimant to join in bringing a claim against a defendant domiciled elsewhere, however closely connected, if he is not himself suing an English-domiciled defendant: *Madoff Securities International Ltd v Raven* [2011] EWHC 3102 (Comm).

NOTE 30. DELETE AND REPLACE BY: Practice Direction 6B – Service out of the Jurisdiction (supplementing Sec. IV of CPR, Pt 6), para.3.1(15).

NOTE 31. DELETE AND REPLACE BY: *ibid.*, para.3.1(3).

Stay of proceedings under European regimes

11–25 NOTE 33. DELETE *Osuwu* AND REPLACE BY: *Owusu*.

INSERT AFTER THE FIRST SENTENCE: That is so whether the ground on which the English court has jurisdiction is that the defendant is domiciled in England or is one of the special heads of jurisdiction provided for in the Conventions and the Judgments Regulation.[33a] But the English court is not precluded from staying proceedings to give effect to a jurisdiction clause

---

[19c] *ibid.*, at [22].
[19d] *Kleinwort Benson v Glasgow City Council* [1999] 1 A.C. 153, HL.
[26a] *Konkola Copper Mines plc v Coromin* [2005] EWHC 898 (Comm) (jurisdiction clause in contract); point not taken on appeal, see [2006] EWCA Civ 5; [2006] 1 Lloyd's Rep. 410 at [47], but cited with approval in *Lucasfilm Ltd v Ainsworth* [2009] EWCA Civ 1328; [2010] F.S.R. 270 at [133].
[33a] *Gomez v Gomez-Monche Vives* [2008] EWHC 259 (Ch); [2009] 1 Ch. 245 at [105]–[116] (jurisdiction over trusts under Judgments Regulation, art. 5(6)); point not taken on appeal, [2008] EWCA Civ 1065; [2009] 1 Ch. 274 at [22]. See too *Aiglon Ltd v Gau Shan Co. Ltd* [1993] B.C.L.C. 1321 (jurisdiction under equivalent of Judgments Regulation, art. 6(1) (domicile of co-defendant)); *Lafi Office and International Business SL v Meriden Animal Heal Ltd* [2001] 1 All E.R. (Comm.) 54 at 71–73 (jurisdiction under equivalent of Judgments Regulation, art. 23 (prorogation)).

where the clause confers jurisdiction on the courts of a state other than a contracting state.[33b]

Bringing the parties before the court

Defendant present in the jurisdiction and submission to the jurisdiction

NOTE 41. DELETE AND REPLACE BY: CPR, Pt 6, r.6.30 *et seq.* and Practice **11–26** Direction 6B – Service out of the Jurisdiction (supplementing Sec. IV of CPR, Pt 6).

Service out of the jurisdiction where the European rules apply

IN THE FIRST SENTENCE, DELETE Civil Procedure Rules, Part 6, rule 6.19 AND **11–27** REPLACE BY: Civil Procedure Rules, Part 6, rule 6.33.

NOTE 45. DELETE UP TO THE LAST SEMI-COLON AND REPLACE BY: See further the notes on CPR, Pt 6, rr.6.33 *et seq.* in *Civil Procedure* (2011), Vol.1.

NOTE 46. DELETE AND REPLACE BY: CPR, Pt 6, rr.6.33(1)(*a*), (2)(*b*).

Service out of the jurisdiction in non-European cases—grounds for service out

DELETE AND REPLACE BY: In all other cases the Civil Procedure Rules, Part 6, **11–28** rule 6.36 applies, requiring the permission of the court. Permission to serve out cannot be given except on one of the grounds specified in the associated Practice Direction.[46a] References to paragraphs in §§ 11–29 to 11–33 are to provisions of the Practice Direction.

Specific grounds concerning trusts

DELETE AND REPLACE BY: Paragraphs 3.1(12) to (16) apply to claims about **11–29** trusts. They provide that the court may grant permission to serve abroad in the following claims.

> "*Claims about trusts etc.*
>
> (12) A claim is made for any remedy which might be obtained in proceedings to execute the trusts of a written instrument where –
>
>> (a) the trusts ought to be executed according to English law; and
>> (b) the person on whom the claim form is to be served is a trustee of the trusts.
>
> (13) A claim is made for any remedy which might be obtained in proceedings for the administration of the estate of a person who died domiciled within the jurisdiction.
>
> (14) A probate claim or a claim for the rectification of a will.

[33b] See § 11–23A (Supplement).
[46a] Practice Direction 6B – Service out of the Jurisdiction (supplementing Sec. IV of CPR, Pt 6), para. 3.1.

(15) A claim is made for a remedy against the defendant as constructive trustee where the defendant's alleged liability arises out of acts committed within the jurisdiction.

(16) A claim is made for restitution where the defendant's alleged liability arises out of acts committed within the jurisdiction."

General grounds

11–30 AFTER three rules INSERT: (now contained in Practice Direction 6B)[47a].

11–30(1) IN THE FIRST SENTENCE, DELETE Rule 6.20(3) AND REPLACE BY: Paragraph 3.1(3).

NOTE 48. DELETE THE REFERENCE TO Briggs and Rees, *Civil Jurisdiction and Judgments* AND REPLACE BY: Briggs and Rees, *Civil Jurisdiction and Judgments* (5th edn), § 4.57.

11–30(2) IN THE FIRST SENTENCE, DELETE Rule 6.20(1) AND REPLACE BY: Paragraph 3.1(1).

NOTE 50. DELETE THE REFERENCE TO Briggs and Rees, *Civil Jurisdiction and Judgments* AND REPLACE BY: Briggs and Rees, *Civil Jurisdiction and Judgments* (5th edn), § 4.55.

11–30(3) IN THE FIRST, FOURTH AND FIFTH SENTENCES, DELETE Rule 6.20(10) AND REPLACE BY: Paragraph 3.1(11).

NOTE 51. DELETE THE REFERENCE TO Briggs and Rees, *Civil Jurisdiction and Judgments* AND REPLACE BY: Briggs and Rees, *Civil Jurisdiction and Judgments* (5th edn), § 4.67.

NOTE 53. AT THE END ADD: See too *Pakistan v Zardari* [2006] EWHC 2411 (Comm); [2006] All E.R. (D) 79 (Oct) at [157].

IN THE FOURTH SENTENCE OF THE TEXT DELETE rule 6.20(11) AND REPLACE BY: paragraph 3.1(12).

AT THE END OF THE TEXT ADD: Assets are often held through companies incorporated abroad, so that the immediate trust property is shares located overseas, even though the assets of the companies may be located within the jurisdiction. A claim may nonetheless be said to "relate" to assets within the jurisdiction if, *e.g.*, the complaint is that the trustees failed to supervise the conduct of the companies' affairs;[53a] and where a constructive trust is asserted over such assets it makes no difference that the wrongdoer holds them through overseas companies.[53b]

11–31 DELETE THE HEADING AND REPLACE BY:

[47a] Service out of the Jurisdiction (supplementing Sec. IV of CPR, Pt 6), see CPR Pt 6, r.6.36.
[53a] See §§ 34–49 *et seq.*
[53b] See *Pakistan v Zardari* [2006] EWHC 2411 (Comm) (assets alleged to be bought with proceeds of bribery).

Claims about express trusts—paragraph 3.1(12)

IN THE FIRST AND SECOND SENTENCES DELETE rule 6.20(11) AND REPLACE BY: paragraph 3.1(12).

IN THE SECOND SENTENCE DELETE rule 6.20(11) AND REPLACE BY: paragraph **11–31(1)** (12).

DELETE THE THIRD SENTENCE AND REPLACE BY: The limiting words "to execute" are enlarged by the previous words "any remedy which might be obtained in proceedings".

NOTE 57. DELETE AND REPLACE BY: In *Gomez v Gomez-Monche Vives*, [2008] EWCA Civ 1065; [2009] 1 Ch. 245 at [23] claims for breach of trust were held to be within what is now para. 3.1(12) (of Practice Direction 6B – Service out of the Jurisdiction (supplementing Sec. IV of CPR, Pt 6). See too *Chellaram v Chellaram (No.2)* [2002] EWHC 632 (Ch); [2002] 3 All E.R. 17 which was a claim for breach of trust but there was no suggestion that it fell outside the predecessor of para. 3.1(12) as not being a claim to execute the trusts.

IN THE SECOND AND THIRD SENTENCES DELETE rule 6.20(11) AND REPLACE BY: **11–31(2)** paragraph (12).

AT THE END OF THE THIRD SENTENCE ADD A NEW NOTE 60a: In the Cayman **11–31(4)** Islands a foreign beneficiary may be served out of the jurisdiction without the permission of the court in a trustee's application for directions (though not hostile litigation), but that favourable result turns on statutory provisions which have no English counterpart: *Merrill Lynch Bank and Trust Co. (Cayman) Ltd v Demirel* [2010] 2 C.I.L.R. 75, Cayman GC.

IN THE FIFTH, SEVENTH, NINTH AND THIRTEENTH SENTENCES DELETE rule 6.20(11) AND REPLACE BY: paragraph (12).

IN THE SIXTH SENTENCE DELETE rule 6.20(14) and (15) AND REPLACE BY: paragraph 3.1(15) and (16).

IN THE TWELFTH SENTENCE DELETE rule 6.20(14) AND REPLACE BY: paragraph 3.1(15).

DELETE THE HEADING AND REPLACE BY: **11–32**

Claims about constructive trustee liabilities—paragraphs 3.1(15) and (16)

IN THE FIRST SENTENCE DELETE rule 6.20(14), and rule 6.20(15) may also be relevant AND REPLACE BY: paragraph 3.1(15). Paragraph 3.1(16) will also be relevant, as it permits service out where a claim is made "for restitution" and the defendant's alleged liability arises out of acts committed within the jurisdiction.

IN THE SECOND SENTENCE DELETE rule 6.20(14) AND REPLACE BY: paragraph 3.1(15).

IN THE FIRST SENTENCE DELETE "as a constructive trustee" AND REPLACE BY: **11–32(1)** "as constructive trustee"

IN THE THIRD AND SEVENTH SENTENCES DELETE rule 6.20(14) AND REPLACE BY: paragraph 3.1(15).

NOTE 73. AT THE END ADD: *Pakistan v Zardari* [2006] EWHC 2411 (Comm) at [161]–[165].

IN THE FOURTH SENTENCE DELETE rule AND REPLACE BY: paragraph.

NOTE 76. DELETE As to whom see § 42–29 AND REPLACE BY: As to whom see §§ 41–40 *et seq.*

IN THE FIFTH AND SEVENTH SENTENCES DELETE rule 6.20(15) AND REPLACE BY: paragraph 3.1(16).

11–32(2) NOTE 81. DELETE CPR, Pt 6, r.6.20(15) AND REPLACE BY: paragraph 3.1(16).

IN THE SECOND SENTENCE DELETE The previous rule AND REPLACE BY: A previous rule.[81a]

IN THE THIRD SENTENCE DELETE rule 6.20(14) AND REPLACE BY: paragraph 3.1(15).

NOTE 82. AT THE END ADD: See too *Pakistan v Zardari* [2006] EWHC 2411 (Comm) at [166]–[170].

AFTER PARAGRAPH 11–32 INSERT THE FOLLOWING NEW PARAGRAPH AND HEADING:

Trusts created by contract

11–32A Paragraph 3.1(6)[82a] extends to claims "in respect of" a contract where the contract (i) was made within the jurisdiction or (ii) was made by or through an agent trading or residing within the jurisdiction or (iii) is governed by English law or (iv) contains a clause conferring jurisdiction on the English court. Hence a claim to enforce a covenant in a declaration of trust is covered.[82b] But in addition, because the claim need not be a claim to enforce the contract itself, the paragraph extends to a trust arising out of a contract. Hence a claim to enforce a trust founded on a common intention,[82c] a trust arising on a contract to sell land or unquoted shares,[82d] and other trusts arising from a contract[82e] will all be within the paragraph if the contract itself is within one of the four classes specified.[82f]

Injunctions

11–33 IN THE FIRST SENTENCE DELETE Civil Procedure Rules, Part 6, rule 6.20(2) AND REPLACE BY: paragraph 3.1(2).

[81a] R.S.C. O. 11 r. 1(1)(*t*) (revoked).
[82a] See generally Dicey, Morris and Collins, *The Conflict of Laws* (14th edn), Vol.1, §§ 11R–181 to 11–198; Briggs and Rees, *Civil Jurisdiction and Judgments* (5th edn), §§ 4.60 to 4.61.
[82b] *Official Solicitor v Stype Investments (Jersey) Ltd* [1983] 1 W.L.R. 214.
[82c] For such trusts, see §§ 9–66 *et seq.*
[82d] For such trusts, see §§ 10–03 *et seq.*
[82e] For other such trusts, see Chap. 10 *passim.*
[82f] *Cherney v Deripaska* [2008] EWHC 1530 (Comm); [2009] 1 All E.R. (Comm.) 333 at [137] (agreement to hold shares on trust for claimant); point not taken on appeal, [2009] EWCA Civ 849; [2009] N.J.L.R. 1138.

NOTE 83. FOR THE REFERENCE TO *Civil Procedure* (2007), Vol.1, 6.21.26, SUBSTITUTE *Civil Procedure* (2011), Vol.1, 6.37.27.

Service out of the jurisdiction in non-European cases—general requirements

IN THE FIRST SENTENCE DELETE paragraphs.   **11–34**

AT THE END OF THE SECOND SENTENCE INSERT A NEW NOTE 84a: See *AK Investment CJSG v Kyrgyz Mobil Tel Ltd* [2011] UKPC 7; [2011] All E.R. (D) 144 (Mar) at [71] for the first three of these requirements.

NOTE 84. DELETE AND REPLACE BY: CPR, Pt 6, r.6.37(1), (2).

NOTE 85. FOR THE REFERENCE TO Briggs and Rees, *Civil Jurisdiction and Judgments*, SEE NOW (5th edn), § 4.54. FOR THE REFERENCE TO *Civil Procedure* (2007), Vol.1, 6.21.15(1), SUBSTITUTE *Civil Procedure* (2011), Vol.1, 6.37.15.1.

DELETE rule 6.20 AND REPLACE BY: paragraph 3.1.   **11–34(1)**

NOTE 86. DELETE AND REPLACE BY: CPR, Pt 6, r.6.37(3).   **11–34(2)**

NOTE 88. FOR THE REFERENCE TO Briggs and Rees, *Civil Jurisdiction and* **11–34(3)** *Judgments*, SEE NOW (5th edn), § 4.85. FOR THE REFERENCE TO *Civil Procedure* (2007), Vol.1, 6.21.15(2), SUBSTITUTE *Civil Procedure* (2011), Vol.1, 6.37.15.2.

NOTE 89. DELETE AND REPLACE BY: CPR, Pt 6, r.6.37(1)(b).

NOTE 90. FOR THE REFERENCE TO *Civil Procedure* (2007), Vol.1, 6.21.15(2), SUBSTITUTE *Civil Procedure* (2011), Vol.1, 6.37.15.2.

NOTE 93. DELETE AND REPLACE BY: *Civil Procedure* (2011), Vol.1, 6.37.6 and **11–34(4)** cases there cited.

Challenging service

NOTE 96. FOR THE REFERENCE TO *Civil Procedure* (2007), Vol.1, 11.1.1, SUB- **11–35** STITUTE *Civil Procedure* (2011), Vol.1, 11.1.1.

Consequences of trustees submitting to a foreign jurisdiction

NOTE 3. FOR THE REFERENCE TO Briggs and Rees, *Civil Jurisdiction and* **11–37** *Judgments*, SEE NOW (5th edn), § 7.49.

NOTE 4. AT THE END ADD: *Re IMK Family Trust* [2008] JRC 136; (2008–09) 11 I.T.E.L.R. 580 (affirmed [2008] JCA 196; 2008 J.L.R. 430).

AFTER THE THIRD SENTENCE INSERT A NEW SENTENCE: It is now clear that in general Jersey trustees will be expected not to submit to the jurisdiction of the English court (or any other overseas court)[4a] unless, for example, the trust assets are within the jurisdiction of the English court, so that an English order will be enforceable without the trustees' co-operation,[4b] or it is

---

[4a]   See *e.g. Re M and L Trusts* [2003] JRC 002A; [2003] W.T.L.R. 491 (proceedings challenging trust in Illinois); *Re H Trust* [2006] JRC 057; [2007] W.T.L.R. 677 (divorce proceedings in England).

[4b]   *Re H Trust*, above, at [15]; *Re A and B Trusts* [2007] JRC 138; 2007 J.L.R. 444 at [31].

in the interests of the trust for the trustees to give evidence to the English court about the trust;[4c] and in the converse situation the English court will be likely to take the same view.[4d]

Supplementary—the *situs* rules

Choses in action

11–43 NOTE 34. DELETE CPR, Pt 6, r.19 AND REPLACE BY: CPR, Pt 6, r.33.

3. THE VALIDITY OF TRUSTS AND CHOICE OF LAW

Preliminary issues on lifetime trusts

11–49 AT THE END INSERT A NEW NOTE 66a: In other jurisdictions, the rule may be determined by legislation. In *CC Ltd v Apex Trust Ltd* [2012] JRC 071, for example, the court in Jersey held that Trusts (Jersey) Law 1984 (2007 rev.), art.9 required the application of Jersey law to the question whether a transfer of English realty and securities to a trust governed by Jersey law should be set aside for mistake. In a similar case in Guernsey, *Re Arun Estate Agencies Ltd Employee Benefit Trust* 2009–10 G.L.R. 437, the trust being governed by English law it was common ground (see [23]) that English law applied to that question but it is not clear why.

Contractual rights

11–52 NOTE 74. DELETE AND REPLACE BY: Regulation (EC) No.593/2008 of June 17, 2008 of the European Parliament and of the Council on the law applicable to contractual obligations (Rome I), art.14(1), (2).

Shares in companies

11–54 NOTE 76. AT THE END ADD: *Macmillan Inc. v Bishopsgate Investment Trust plc (No.3)* [1996] 1 W.L.R. 387.

AFTER § 11–54 INSERT THE FOLLOWING NEW PARAGRAPHS AND HEADINGS:

Preliminary issues on constructive trusts and similar liabilities

General

11–54A The Hague Convention applies by its terms only to trusts created by a settlor,[78a] and created voluntarily and evidenced in writing,[78b] but it permits

---

[4c] *C Trust Co. Ltd v Temple* [2009] JRC 048; [2010] W.T.L.R. 417. Note that it is possible for overseas trustees to participate in English proceedings by giving evidence without becoming parties (*B v B* [2009] EWHC 3422 (Fam); [2010] W.T.L.R. 1689 at [22]) but it is uncertain whether the Jersey court would treat such participation as warranting enforcement of an award in Jersey.

[4d] The same view has been taken in the Cayman Islands: *Re B Trust, RBS Coutts (Cayman) Ltd v W*, Cayman GC, December 10, 2010, unreported.

[78a] Art.2.

[78b] Art.3. See §§ 11–60, 11–61.

contracting states to extend its provisions to "trusts declared by judicial decisions".[78c] Section 1(2) of the Recognition of Trusts Act 1987 extends it to trusts "arising ... by virtue of a judicial decision". Although the latter wording is not wholly apt to cover constructive trusts existing before the judicial decision, the evident intention is to apply the provisions of the Convention to such trusts; and the same applies to implied and resulting trusts. But nothing in the Convention or the 1987 Act governs the pre-liminary issue whether such a trust has arisen at all.[78d] As with express testamentary and lifetime trusts, therefore, the English court has to apply its own rules of the conflict of laws to identify the law governing that issue. The Convention will apply only if that law (whether English or foreign) holds that such a trust has come into being.

There is little authority on the applicable rules.[78e] It has been pointed out **11–54B** that the terms "constructive trust" and "constructive trustee" are often imprecisely used and cover a range of dissimilar liabilities,[78f] so there is no reason why all claims which in a wholly domestic context would give rise to a constructive trust should be governed by the same rules. The question is now complicated by recent legislation, in the form of the European Union Regulation of 2007 on non-contractual obligations (the so-called Rome II Regulation).[78g] The rules introduced by the Regulation now apply in Eng-land generally, not merely to cases involving the law of another member state.[78h] The muddled provisions as to its commencement[78i] have been held to mean that events giving rise to damage occurring on and after January 11, 2009 will be subject to the Regulation (the date from which it is expressed to "apply"), even though it came into force before that date, and so earlier events are governed by the previous domestic law.[78j] It governs non-con-tractual obligations in civil and commercial matters[78k] but not "non-con-tractual obligations arising out of the relations between the settlors, trustees and beneficiaries of a trust created voluntarily"[78l] and certain other excluded cases.[78m] Two sets of rules created by the Regulation are material in this context:

[78c] Art.20 (not enacted as part of Recognition of Trusts Act 1987, Sch.).
[78d] The point, however, was left open in *Lightning v Lightning Electrical Contractors Ltd* [1998] N.P.C. 71, CA. The same seems to have happened in *Martin v Secretary of State for Work and Pensions* [2009] EWCA Civ 1289; [2010] W.T.L.R. 671 at [25], [35].
[78e] *Grupo Torras SA v Al-Sabah* [2000] EWCA Civ 273; [2001] C.L.C. 21 at [121].
[78f] *ibid.*, at [122].
[78g] Regulation (EC) No.864/2007 of July 11, 2007 of the European Parliament and of the Council on the law applicable to non-contractual obligations (Rome II).
[78h] The previous English legislation, Private International Law (Miscellaneous Provisions) Act 1995, has been modified (and largely superseded) to make it fit the Rome II Regulation by Law Applicable to Non-Contractual Obligations (England and Wales and Northern Ire-land) Regulations 2008 (SI 2008/2986), which also apply the Regulation so as to govern conflicts between the laws of different parts of the United Kingdom and between any of those parts and Gibraltar.
[78i] Rome II Regulation, arts.31, 32.
[78j] *Homawoo v GMF Assurances SA* Case C-412/10; *VTB Capital plc v Nutritek International Corp.* [2012] EWCA Civ 808. The previous domestic law is Private International Law (Miscellaneous Provisions) Act 1995 before its amendment as mentioned in the ante-penultimate footnote.
[78k] *ibid.*, art.1(1).
[78l] *ibid.*, art.1(2)(e).
[78m] *ibid.*, art.1(2)(a)–(d), (f)–(g).

(1) The general rules for "a non-contractual obligation arising out of a tort/delict" are that (i) the law applicable is the law of the country where the damage occurred (irrespective of the country where the event causing the damage occurred and irrespective of any country where the indirect consequences of the event occurred),[78n] although (ii) if both claimant and defendant were habitually resident in the same country when the damage occurred the law of that country applies[78o] and (iii) despite those rules if the tort/delict is "manifestly more closely connected" with another country then the law of that country applies. Such a close connection may be based on a pre-existing relationship between the parties that is closely connected with the tort/delict in question, such as a contract, says the Regulation,[78p] or, no doubt, an express trust.

(2) There are separate but similar rules for "a non-contractual obligation arising out of unjust enrichment" (including payment of amounts wrongly received) namely that (i) where the obligation concerns a relationship existing between the parties, such as one arising out of a contract or a tort/delict (or again, no doubt, an express trust), that is closely connected with that unjust enrichment, it is governed by the law that governs that relationship,[78q] (ii) where that is not so but the parties are habitually resident in the same country when the event giving rise to unjust enrichment occurs, the law of that country applies,[78r] (iii) absent both such a relationship and common habitual residence, the law of the country in which the unjust enrichment took place applies,[78s] but (iv) all of those rules may be displaced in favour of the law of another country where the non-contractual obligation arising out of unjust enrichment is manifestly more closely connected with that country.[78t]

Both sets of rules are expressed as if the relevant obligation has already arisen but it seems clear that the Regulation is meant to govern the question whether the obligation has arisen at all.[78u]

11–54C The absence of much domestic authority, and the loose terms of the Rome II Regulation, make it difficult to identify confidently the approach which the English court will take when the question is whether a constructive trust has arisen. We tentatively suggest the following answers to questions arising in connection with the commoner forms of liability under English law.

[78n] *ibid.*, art.4(1).
[78o] *ibid.*, art.4(2).
[78p] *ibid.*, art.4(3).
[78q] *ibid.*, art.10(1).
[78r] *ibid.*, art.10(2).
[78s] *ibid.*, art.10(3).
[78t] *ibid.*, art.10(4).
[78u] Under the Rome II Regulation, the applicable law governs such questions as the basis and extent of liability and the existence of the remedy claimed (art.15(*a*), (*c*)). Note also the recitals, requiring the concept of a non-contractual obligation to be treated as an autonomous concept (recital (11)), *i.e.* one independent of the domestic rules of any member state, a requirement difficult to reconcile with any expectation that the existence of the obligation would remain a matter for domestic law, and specifically requiring the applicable law to govern the question of capacity to incur a liability for tort/delict (recital (12)).

Express trust—obligations of settlor, trustee or beneficiary

Where there is an existing express trust, and the liability alleged (whether **11–54D**
personal or proprietary) is that of a settlor, trustee or beneficiary, the Rome
II Regulation will not apply: such liabilities are expressly excluded.[78v]
Instances are the liability of a trustee for an unauthorised profit[78w] and a
beneficiary's liability to refund an overpayment.[78x] Such liabilities are presumably governed by the proper law of the trust under the Recognition of
Trusts Act 1987, the personal liability of trustees being expressly referred to
the proper law.[78y] The same is probably true of one who is liable as a trustee
de son tort.[78z]

A resulting trust arises in favour of the settlor under English law when the **11–54E**
beneficial interests are not exhausted by the disposition on trust. The
question which law determines whether such a resulting trust arises is not
covered by the Rome II Regulation: the Regulation is concerned with
obligations, not property, and the exclusion just mentioned would in any
case apply. It seems clear that the proper law of the trust will determine that
question.[78aa]

Express trust—obligations of third parties

Where there is an existing express trust and the liability alleged is that of a **11–54F**
third party, *i.e.* not a settlor, trustee or beneficiary, the law is less clear. A
distinction has to be drawn between proprietary claims and personal claims.
We take proprietary claims first. Instances are those against an innocent
transferee of trust property who is a volunteer or who does not take a legal
estate and against one who knowingly receives trust property transferred in
breach of trust.[78ab] The Rome II Regulation is concerned with obligations,
not property, and so seemingly has no application. Disputes as to title
between a trustee or beneficiary and a third party recipient of trust property
have been held to be governed by the *lex situs* of the asset,[78ac] namely the law
of the place of incorporation in the case of shares,[78ad] and so on.[78ae]

Where there is an existing express trust and a personal liability is alleged **11–54G**
against a third party, the law is less clear. Instances are a liability for dishonest assistance in a breach of trust[78af] and the liability of one who
knowingly receives trust property transferred in breach of trust.[78ag] The

[78v] Rome II Regulation, art.1(1)(*e*).
[78w] See §§ 20–28 *et seq.*
[78x] *i.e.* the liability, whether personal or proprietary, of a "*Diplock* recipient", if a beneficiary;
see §§ 41–40, 4142, 42–04 *et seq.*
[78y] Hague Convention, art.8(*g*).
[78z] See §§ 42–74 *et seq.*
[78aa] *Cf.* § 11–62.
[78ab] See §§ 41–41 *et seq.*
[78ac] *Macmillan Inc. v Bishopsgate Investment Trust plc (No.3)* [1996] 1 W.L.R. 387, where
shares held on trust for the plaintiff were pledged, in breach of trust, to the main defendants as security for loans.
[78ad] *ibid.*; *cf.* § 11–54.
[78ae] See §§ 11–50 *et seq.* for the relevant rules as to situs.
[78af] See §§ 40–09 *et seq.*
[78ag] See §§ 42–22 *et seq.*

latter is a receipt-based liability and the former is not, and the applicable rules appear to be different:

(1) At common law, in cases of tort a rule of double actionability applied: the alleged wrong had to be actionable both by English law and by the law of the place where the act was committed. Although a liability for dishonest assistance is not a tort in English law,[78ah] it is plainly very like a tort; and it was held that even if the rule of double actionability did not apply, the court should take account of the presence or absence of liability by the law of the place where the act complained of occurred in deciding whether it would be equitable to hold the defendant liable.[78ai] For that purpose, it was irrelevant that the foreign law did not recognise the concept of proprietary rights arising under trusts.[78aj] The English legislation which abolished the rule of double actionability and replaced it with the rule applying the law of the country in which the events complained of occurred, the Private International Law (Miscellaneous Provisions) Act 1995,[78ak] may have applied only to tort in the English sense[78al] and if so did not affect that approach. Now, however, under the Rome II Regulation, a personal liability for dishonest assistance appears to be one of the non-contractual obligations within the Regulation, given that that category is to be treated as an autonomous concept,[78am] and specifically a liability for a "tort/delict". If that is correct, the primary rule is that the governing law determining the existence and incidents of the liability is that of the country where the damage occurred (not where the events complained of took place), though other rules may apply.[78an]

[78ah] *Metall & Rohstoff v Donaldson Lufkin & Jenrette Inc.* [1990] 1 Q.B. 391 at 474, CA.

[78ai] *Arab Monetary Fund v Hashim (No.9)*, The Times, October 11, 1994 (not a case of an express trust). The relevant passage was cited with approval in *Grupo Torras SA v Al-Sabah* [2000] EWCA Civ 273; [2001] C.L.C. 21 at [133]. It was held in *OJSC Oil Company Yugraneft v Abramovich* [2008] EWHC 2613 (Comm) that the rule of double actionability applied, see *ibid.* at [217].

[78aj] *Arab Monetary Fund*, above. It was sufficient that the foreign law imposed a right of recovery by civil action, whether or not the act or omission complained of was characterised by that law as a tort or delict: *Grupo Torras*, above, at [141].

[78ak] See s.10 (abolition of rule of double actionability), s.11(1) (new general rule). S.11(2) caters for cases in which elements of those events took place in different countries and s.12 provides for the application of a law which is "substantially more appropriate" than the law identified by s.11.

[78al] The term "tort" is a term of art in English law and it is used in Private International Law (Miscellaneous Provisions) Act 1995, ss.9–12 without any indication that it is to be understood in a wider sense. But it was said *obiter* in *Yugraneft*, above, at [223] that dishonest assistance in a breach of trust was probably a "tort" for the purpose of the 1995 Act and that view was adopted in *Fiona Trust & Holding Corpn v Privalov* [2010] EWHC 3199 (Comm); [2011] L.S. Gaz. R. 17 at [154].

[78am] Rome II Regulation, recital (11). *Cf. Kalfelis v Bankhaus Schröder, Munchmeyer, Hengst & Co.* [1988] E.C.R. 5565 at [16]–[17], E.C.J., holding that the term "tort/delict" in the Brussels Convention, art.5(3) was to be given an autonomous meaning; see § 11–21C (Supplement).

[78an] See § 11–54B(1). If the Rome II Regulation is held not to apply, the common law will continue to do so.

(2)   In the case of knowing receipt of trust property, however, the rule at common law was that the defendant's liability was ordinarily governed by the law of the country where the receipt took place,[78ao] seemingly the same thing as the *lex situs* of the asset at that time.[78ap] Under the Rome II Regulation, it seems clear that the liability will be treated as one of unjust enrichment and hence as governed by one of the rules applicable in such a case.[78aq] The primary rule, that the law governing any pre-existing relationship between the parties should govern the obligation arising out of an unjust enrichment where the two are closely connected, will tend to divorce the law applicable to the personal claim from the law applicable to the proprietary claim, *e.g.* if the English solicitor to offshore trustees is sought to be made liable for knowing receipt in both ways. The rule that a manifestly closer connection with another country will trump the other rules may then perhaps be invoked to ensure that both claims are governed by the same law.

Directors and other fiduciaries

Directors of companies are treated as if they are express trustees of the **11–54H** company's assets, since they have both fiduciary duties and a power of disposition over the assets, but they are not in fact trustees and the exclusion from the Rome II Regulation of non-contractual obligations arising between settlors, trustees and beneficiaries[78ar] will not apply to them. Under English domestic law directors may be made liable for dishonest assistance or knowing receipt and so may other fiduciaries, though there is no express trust. The common-law rules discussed above[78as] applied to such fiduciaries but now the question whether such liabilities arise we think is plainly within the Rome II Regulation.[78at]

[78ao] Dicey, Morris and Collins, *The Conflict of Laws* (14th edn), Vol.2, § 34R–001 (suggesting a different rule for contracts and immovables); *El Ajou Dollar Land Holdings plc* [1993] 3 All E.R. 717 at 736–737 (not a case of an express trust; reversed on another point [1994] 2 All E.R. 685), the latter passage cited with approval in *Grupo Torras*, above, at [131]. See too *Kuwait Oil Tanker Co. SAK v Al Bader* [2000] 2 All E.R. (Comm.) 271 at [190], CA; *Christopher v Zimmerman* (2001) 192 D.L.R. (4th) 476 at [14], BC CA. In *OJSC Oil Company Yugraneft v Abramovich* [2008] EWHC 2613 (Comm), however, it was held that at common law the applicable law was the law which had the closest connection with the obligation to make restitution, see at [246].

[78ap] See § 11–54F (Supplement).

[78aq] See § 11–54B(2) (Supplement).

[78ar] See §§ 11–54B, 11–54D (Supplement).

[78as] See §§ 11–54F, 11–54G (Supplement). The authorities there cited are mainly decisions on claims against directors.

[78at] Note that at common law, where the question arose whether a person was to be regarded as a fiduciary but the duties to which a relationship gave rise were determined by a foreign law, the question for the foreign law was what was the nature of those duties; but it was for the English court to decide whether duties of that nature were to be regarded as fiduciary: *Arab Monetary Fund v Hashim* (No.9), *The Times*, October 11, 1994 in a passage approved in *Kuwait Oil Tanker Co. SAK v Al Bader* (2000) *The Times*, May 30, 2000 at [192] and in *Grupo Torras SA v Al-Sabah* [2000] EWCA Civ 273; [2001] C.L.C. 21 at [125], CA. It is not easy to see that that approach, relevant under a rule of double actionability, can have survived the Rome II Regulation.

Trusts arising under contracts

11–54I Where a trust is treated by English law as arising under a contract, such as the trust which arises in favour of a purchaser under a contract to sell land or unquoted shares[78au] or the trust which arises under an agreement for mutual wills,[78av] we do not consider that the Rome II Regulation can have any application. The trust is not ordinarily regarded as an express trust but it seems to have been created voluntarily within the terms of the exclusion of trusts so created from the Rome II Regulation.[78aw]

11–54J The question whether such a trust has arisen is presumably governed by the proper law of the contract. Until recently the law determining the proper law of most contracts was to be found in the Contracts (Applicable Law) Act 1990, giving effect to the Rome Convention of 1981 on the law applicable to contractual obligations.[78ax] From December 17, 2009, however, it is to be found in the European Union Regulation of 2008 on the law applicable to contractual obligations (the so-called Rome I Regulation),[78ay] the 1990 Act having been modified so that it is inapplicable wherever the Rome I Regulation applies.[78az] Both the Rome Convention and the Rome I Regulation exclude "the constitution of trusts and the relationship between settlers, trustees and beneficiaries".[78ba] It seems unlikely, however, that contracts were meant to be excluded merely because under domestic law they are of a kind held to give rise to a trust; and indeed contracts governing immovables are especially mentioned in both.[78bb] The basic rule in both the Convention and the Regulation is that the parties to a contract have complete freedom to choose the law applicable to the contract, either expressly or impliedly.[78bc] Absent such a choice, the two instruments diverge. Under the Rome Convention the contract is governed by the law of the country with which it is most closely connected,[78bd] though certain presumptions are imposed, one of which is that a contract affecting immovables is most closely connected with the *lex situs*;[78be] under the Rome I Regulation, there

---

[78au] See §§ 10–03 *et seq.*
[78av] See §§ 10–35 *et seq.*
[78aw] Art.1(1)(*e*). See § 11–54B (Supplement).
[78ax] The Rome Convention is scheduled to Contracts (Applicable Law) Act 1990 (in Sch.1). It applied to contracts made after April 1, 1991: art.17 and Contracts (Applicable Law) Act 1990 (Commencement No.1) Order 1991 (SI 1991/707).
[78ay] Regulation (EC) No.593/2008 of June 17, 2008 of the European Parliament and of the Council on the law applicable to contractual obligations (Rome I). Art.29 provides that it is to apply from December 17, 2009, which has been taken to mean that it applies to contracts concluded on or after that date.
[78az] By Law Applicable to Contractual Obligations (England and Wales and Northern Ireland) Regulations 2009 (SI 2009/3064), which (by reg.2) insert a new s.4A into Contracts (Applicable Law) Act 1990 having that effect. The 2009 Regulations also (by reg.5) apply the Rome I Regulation to conflicts between the laws of different parts of the United Kingdom.
[78ba] Rome Convention, art.1(2)(*g*); Rome I Regulation, art.1(2)(*h*).
[78bb] Rome Convention, art.4(3); Rome I Regulation, art.4(1)(*c*).
[78bc] Rome Convention, art.3(1); Rome I Regulation, art.3(1). In both cases, where all the connecting factors point to a different country from that whose law has been chosen, the parties cannot opt out of rules of that law which have overriding force, see art.3(3) of both instruments.
[78bd] Rome Convention, art.4(1); Rome I Regulation, art.3(1).
[78be] Rome Convention, art.4(3). But not if there is a closer connection with another country: art.4(5).

are binding rules for certain particular contracts,[78bf] one of which is to the same effect as to contracts affecting immovables,[78bg] though a close connection governs where the case falls outside the rules[78bh] and a manifestly closer connection will override the rules.[78bi]

Hence the question whether a contract for the sale of land creates a trust, if **11–54K** determined by the proper law of the contract, will be governed by the law expressly or impliedly chosen by the parties or, if none is chosen, ordinarily by the *lex situs*; that is so for such contracts made both before and after December 17, 2009. The question whether a contract for mutual wills creates a trust receives a slightly different answer, since the Rome Convention expressly excludes contractual obligations relating to wills and succession[78bj] but the Rome I Regulation does not. The latter will therefore apply only to such contracts made on or after December 17, 2009 and earlier contracts will be governed by the common law, which allowed the parties to choose the proper law of the contract, expressly or impliedly, and in the absence of such a choice looked to the law with which the contract was most closely connected.[78bk]

Trusts arising in relation to the acquisition of property

In the case of a resulting trust which, under English domestic law, would **11–54L** arise on the payment of the purchase price of property followed by a purchase in the name of another,[78bl] and the similar trust arising where contributions have been made to the purchase price,[78bm] it has been held that the law determining whether such a trust arises depends on the law governing the relationship or arrangement between the parties. If the property happens to be abroad but everything else to do with the arrangement is English, then the trust will arise.[78bn] But if the arrangement was made by reference to some other system of law, as where a purchase funded by A was taken in B's name so as to avoid the impact of a provision of French succession law which would have applied if A had been the purchaser, then French law governed the arrangement, with the result that no trust arose.[78bo] Those decisions did not depend on the proper law of the contract between the parties, if there was one, and the suggestion that the Contracts (Applicable Law) Act 1990 governed the question was rejected.[78bp] Hence it seems that the Rome I Regulation will also be inapplicable.

[78bf] Rome I Regulation, art.4(1), (2).
[78bg] *ibid.*, art.4(1)(c).
[78bh] *ibid.*, art.4(3).
[78bi] *ibid.*, art.4(4).
[78bj] Rome Convention, art.1(2)(b).
[78bk] Dicey and Morris, *The Conflict of Laws* (14th edn), §§ 32–005 to 32–006.
[78bl] See §§ 9–16 *et seq.*
[78bm] See §§ 9–57 *et seq.*
[78bn] *Lightning v Lightning Electrical Contractors Ltd* [1998] N.P.C. 71, CA (property in Scotland). See too *Webb v Webb* [1991] 1 W.L.R. 1410.
[78bo] *Martin v Secretary of State for Work and Pensions* [2009] EWCA Civ 1289; [2010] W.T.L.R. 671.
[78bp] See *Lightning*, above, where the contract would probably have been governed by Scots law.

11–54M In the light of those authorities, it is not wholly clear what law will apply to the question whether a "common intention" trust arises on the acquisition of property[78br] but a similar approach would seem to be warranted.

11–54N Special considerations apply in the common case when the acquisition is by husband and wife. In jurisdictions with a special regime for matrimonial property, the rights obtained by the spouses in each other's movables depend on the law of the matrimonial domicile at the time of the marriage. Where the parties are domiciled in the same country at the time of the marriage, that country is ordinarily the matrimonial domicile. The rule applies whether the property was already owned at the time of the marriage or was acquired later and is not affected by a change of domicile. As to immovables, the law is less clear but it has been held that the same rule applies, at least where the law of the matrimonial domicile permits a contrary agreement but the parties have made none; it is possible that in other cases the *lex situs* applies.[78bs]

The Recognition of Trusts Act 1987, the Hague Convention and the von Overbeck Report

11–56 NOTE 81. INSERT IN THE LIST IN THE FIRST SENTENCE: Manitoba, Malta, Monaco, and the Turks and Caicos Islands.

NOTE 83. THE CORRECT NEUTRAL CITATION FOR *Tod v Barton* IS [2002] EWHC 264 (Ch).

Timing

11–59 NOTE 91. FOR THE REFERENCE TO Underhill and Hayton, *Law of Trusts and Trustees*, SEE NOW (18th edn), § 100.49.

Involuntary trusts

11–60 NOTE 91. FOR THE REFERENCE TO Underhill and Hayton, *Law of Trusts and Trustees*, SEE NOW (18th edn), § 100.83.

Writing

11–61 AT THE END OF THE SECOND SENTENCE, INSERT A NEW NOTE 98a: *Berezovsky v Abramovitch* [2010] EWHC 647 (Comm); [2010] All E.R. (D) 2 (Apr) at [176] (where "Article 2" is a slip for "section 1(2)").

Constructive and resulting trusts

11–62 NOTE 5. DELETE THE SECOND SENTENCE.

DELETE THE LAST SENTENCE OF THE TEXT AND N.6 AND REPLACE BY: The preliminary question whether a constructive or resulting trust arises at all falls

---

[78br] See §§ 9–66 *et seq.*
[78bs] For the law stated in this paragraph, see the discussion in *Slutsker v Haron Investments Ltd* [2012] EWHC 2539 (Ch), citing *Welch v Tennent* [1891] A.C. 639, HL; *Chiwell v Carlyon*, unreported; *De Nicols v Curlier* [1900] A.C. 21, HL; *Re De Nicols (No.2)* [1900] 2 Ch. 410; *Callwood v Callwood* [1960] A.C. 659, PC; *Murakami v Wiryadi* [2010] NSWCA 7.

outside the Convention. That is governed by rules already discussed.[6] It is only if the law identified by those rules holds that a constructive or resulting trust arises that the Convention can apply, and then only if the liability is proprietary and not merely personal.

Trusts declared without transfers

DELETE THE LAST TWO SENTENCES (AND NOTE 8) AND REPLACE BY: The declaration **11–63** must therefore be taken to be the "placing" within Article 2 of the Convention and the references in the Report to a transfer to the trustee as a condition of the creation of a trust must be taken to embrace the change in the capacity in which the owner holds the property upon making the declaration. Indeed, elsewhere in the von Overbeck Report (paragraph 57) that view is expressed.

AFTER §§ 11–63 INSERT A NEW PARAGRAPH AS FOLLOWS:

Given that trusts created by a declaration of trust are within the Conven- **11–63A** tion, it is a separate question whether there is any preliminary issue to be decided, not governed by the Convention, as to the validity of the declaration. It seems that there is and that the law pointed out by the forum will govern the formal and substantive validity of the declaration, so that, for example, in the case of realty or chattels the intending settlor would not be able by making a declaration to defeat a rule of the *lex situs* preventing the alienation of the property.[8]

The settlor's choice of governing law

INSERT AT THE END OF THE FIRST SENTENCE AFTER THE QUOTATION: Where the **11–65** trust is wholly oral, the reference to the terms of the instrument or writing has to be understood as meaning the words spoken in the course of creating the trust.[9a]

NOTE 13. THE CORRECT NEUTRAL CITATION FOR *Tod v Barton* IS [2002] EWHC 264 (Ch).

NOTE 16. DELETE AND REPLACE BY: Compare Regulation (EC) No.593/2008 of June 17, 2008 of the European Parliament and of the Council on the law applicable to contractual obligations (Rome I), art.3(3), applicable where there is only one connected law and preserving its mandatory rules.

INSERT AT THE END OF THE TENTH SENTENCE AFTER THE QUOTATION: before its repeal.[18a]

INSERT AFTER of the very strong kind IN THE THIRTEENTH SENTENCE AFTER THE QUOTATION: (especially given the repeal of the former).

---

[6] See §§ 11–54A to 11–54M (Supplement).

[8] *Clark & Whitehouse (Joint Administrators of Rangers Football Club plc), Re Directions* [2012] ScotCS CSOH 55 at [19] to [26], approving Underhill and Hayton, *Law of Trusts and Trustees* (18th edn), § 100.122, and Harris, *The Hague Trusts Convention*, at 19 and disapproving the view previously expressed in this work.

[9a] *Berezovsky v Abramovitch* [2010] EWHC 647 (Comm) at [177]–[178].

[18a] For which see § 5–100A (Supplement).

Governing law in default of choice

11–67 NOTE 23. AT THE END ADD: *Tod v Barton* [2002] EWHC 264 (Ch); (2001–02) 4 I.T.E.L.R. 715.

NOTE 26. DELETE AND REPLACE BY: Von Overbeck, para. 61; Parker & Mellows, *The Modern Law of Trusts* (9th edn), § 23–053; Underhill and Hayton, *Law of Trusts and Trustees* (18th edn), § 100.156. But the contrary view has also been expressed, that the invalidity of the trust under the law with which it is most closely connected is irrelevant: Harris, *The Hague Trusts Convention*, at pp.226–227, supported *obiter* by *Berezovsky v Abramovitch* [2010] EWHC 647 (Comm) at [121], [183].

Governing effects of the applicable law

11–70 NOTE 33. THE CORRECT NEUTRAL CITATION FOR *Tod v Barton* is [2002] EWHC 264 (Ch).

AFTER PARAGRAPH 11–70 INSERT THE FOLLOWING NEW PARAGRAPH AND HEADING:

Validity of trusts

11–70A Article 8 provides that the proper law governs, amongst other things, the validity of the trust. That rule, however, is subject to the qualification that the Convention does not apply to the validity of wills or other acts by which assets are transferred to the trustee. Hence it does not extend to, *e.g.*, questions of the settlor's capacity. But it seems that the proper law does govern questions as to whether a trust, or a transfer into trust, may be set aside for mistake.[36a]

Variation of trusts

11–71 NOTE 37. THE CORRECT NEUTRAL CITATION FOR *Tod v Barton* IS [2002] EWHC 264 (Ch).

Variation under matrimonial legislation

NOTE 40. DELETE AND REPLACE BY: See Matrimonial Causes Act 1973, s.24 (prospectively replaced by Family Law Act 1996, s.15, Sch.2, para.6) and (after a foreign decree) Matrimonial and Family Proceedings Act 1984, s.17 (as amended by Welfare Reform and Pensions Act 1999, s.84(1), Sch.12, Pt I, paras.2, 3 and prospectively by Family Law Act 1996, s.66(1), Sch.8, Pt I, para.32(2) and Welfare Reform and Pensions Act 1999, s.84(1), Sch.12, Pt I, paras.64, 66(1), (14)).

[36a] *Re DSL Remuneration Trust* [2007] JRC 251; [2009] W.T.L.R. 373: the Jersey court applied English law to the question whether a trust should be set aside for mistake, as the trust was governed by English law; but no reference was made to the Hague Convention.

Changing the proper law

AT THE END OF THE THIRD SENTENCE INSERT A NEW NOTE 50a: In *Oakley v*   **11–74**
Osiris Trustees Ltd [2008] UKPC 2; (2008) 10 I.T.E.L.R. 789, the PC took it
for granted that such a provision was valid. Powers to change the proper law
are almost universal in offshore trusts. In *Oakley*, the majority assumed and
the minority expressly held (see at [44]) that a power to change the proper
law of a trust would be validly exercised only if exercised in the interests of
the beneficiaries. If the trustees exercise it ignoring relevant considerations
or taking into account irrelevant considerations, then in common with other
powers the exercise may be set aside: *Re Green GLG Trust* 2002 J.L.R. 57
and §§ 29–238 *et seq.*

Recognition

Third parties

NOTE 58. FOR THE REFERENCE TO Underhill and Hayton, *Law of Trusts and*   **11–76**
Trustees, SEE NOW (18th edn), §§ 100.215 to 100.218.

Registration

IN THE LAST SENTENCE DELETE by s.360 of the Companies Act 1985 AND N.62   **11–79**
AND REPLACE BY: by section 126 of the Companies Act 2006.[62]

Mandatory rules

NOTE 63. THE CORRECT NEUTRAL CITATION FOR *Tod v Barton* IS [2002] EWHC   **11–80**
264 (Ch).

Overriding rules

NOTE 71. DELETE AND REPLACE BY: Also (and somewhat confusingly)   **11–82**
described as "overriding mandatory provisions" in Regulation (EC)
No.593/2008 of June 17, 2008 of the European Parliament and of the
Council on the law applicable to contractual obligations (Rome I), art.9. *Cf.*
§ 11–80.

Public policy

Trusts invalid under English law

NOTE 82. FOR THE REFERENCE TO Cayman Islands Trust Law, SEE NOW (2011   **11–84**
Revision), Pt VIII (STAR Trusts).

---

[62]   Replacing Companies Act 1985, s.360. Companies Act 2006, s.126 came into force on
October 1, 2009: Companies Act 2006 (Commencement No.8, Transitional Provisions and
Savings) Order 2008 (SI 2008/2860).

Apart from the Convention

Lifetime settlements of foreign movables

11–88   DELETE THE THIRD SENTENCE AND REPLACE BY: For instance, it may well be that an English settlor of English movables with English trustees, and beneficiaries residing in England and Wales, would not have been allowed to avoid the former rule against excessive accumulations in section 164 of the Law of Property Act 1925 (now repealed)[91a] simply by choosing a law, such as the law of the Bahamas, which has no such rule at all.

5. FOREIGN INCAPACITIES

DELETE THE HEADING TO PARAGRAPH 11–99 AND THE ENTIRE PARAGRAPH AND N.32 AND REPLACE BY:

Foreign rules as to minority

11–99   References in a trust instrument to the age of majority and the like are construed, by virtue of the Recognition of Trusts Act 1987, in accordance with the proper law of the trust.[32]

AFTER § 11–99 INSERT THE FOLLOWING THREE NEW PARAGRAPHS:

11–99A   Trustees are concerned from time to time with the ability of a beneficiary who is domiciled abroad to give them a good receipt when the beneficiary is of age by the law of his domicile but a minor by the proper law of the trust or (if different) by English law; or when the beneficiary is a minor by the law of his domicile but of age by the proper law or by English law. It has been held that a legatee under a will may give a good receipt if of age either by the law of his own domicile or by the law of the testator's domicile.[32a] Apart from the Recognition of Trusts Act 1987, it should follow that a beneficiary who is of age by the law of his domicile, though not by the proper law of the trust or by English law, can give a good receipt to the trustees; and presumably also that a beneficiary who is a minor by the law of his domicile or by English law can nonetheless give a good receipt to the trustees if of age by the proper law of the trust. The 1987 Act, however, refers to the proper law the relationship between the trustees and the beneficiaries, and the distribution of the trust assets,[32b] and if those provisions are apt to deal with questions of minority it will follow that a beneficiary cannot give a good receipt if under age by the proper law, even if of age by the law of his domicile, though conversely that a beneficiary of age by the proper law can give a good receipt even if under age by the law of his domicile. The 1987

[91a]   See § 5–100A (Supplement).

[32]   *Re Jagos* [2007] ABQB 56, Alberta Ct of QB, referring to Art. 8(i) of the Hague Convention, enacted in England by Recognition of Trusts Act 1987, Sch. and printed at § 11–70.

[32a]   *Re Hellmann's Will* (1866) L.R. 2 Eq. 363; *Re Schnapper* [1928] Ch. 420; *Re Fargus* 1997 J.L.R. 89, Jersey RC. All those cases concerned beneficiaries who were of age by the law of their domicile but not by the law of the testator's domicile.

[32b]   Recognition of Trusts Act 1987, Sch., Art. 8(g), (i), printed at § 11–70.

Act permits the *lex fori* to apply the law designated by its conflicts rules "in so far as [it] cannot be derogated from by voluntary act" where it relates to the protection of minors;[32c] but since English law has not insisted on applying restrictive rules of the beneficiary's domicile where the alternative was more relaxed[32d] it seems that in an English court that permission will have no operation.

It is common nowadays to provide that should moneys be payable to a beneficiary under age, or assets transferable to such a beneficiary, the trustees are discharged if they pay the money or transfer the assets to the parent or guardian of the beneficiary.[32e] Trustees may also be authorised to pay money or transfer assets to a beneficiary at a given age even though he is then under the age of majority.[32f] There is no reason to doubt the efficacy of such provisions even when the beneficiary is domiciled abroad. Absent such provisions, and apart from the Recognition of Trusts Act 1987, a parent or guardian of a minor domiciled abroad may give a good receipt for trust income or capital if so authorised by the law of that domicile.[32g] Where, however, the fund is in court, the court may decline to pay it out to the father or guardian entitled to call for it under the law of the domicile and may instead consider in its discretion whether the payment is properly required for the benefit of the minor, acting for the protection of the minor accordingly.[32h] We think it unlikely that the 1987 Act has altered those rules. **11–99B**

When the court is considering an application under the Variation of Trusts Act 1958,[32i] it has jurisdiction to give consent to an arrangement on behalf of any beneficiary who "by reason of infancy" cannot consent for himself.[32j] It seems likely that in that context infancy refers solely to a person under the age of eighteen years in accordance with English law[32k] and that accordingly the court can consent (and its consent is required) even if the beneficiary is of full age by the law of his domicile.[32l] If the beneficiary is of full age by English law, then on that construction the English court has no power to consent for him, even though he is a minor by the law of his domicile or the proper law of the trust; but if we are right as to the ability of such a beneficiary to give a good receipt to the trustees,[32m] his consent will be binding under the 1958 Act unless the 1987 Act requires the application of the proper law of the trust.[32n] **11–99C**

[32c] *ibid.*, Art. 15(a).
[32d] See text to n.32a and following.
[32e] The Standard Provisions of the Society of Trust and Estate Practitioners (1st edn), para. 6, confer such a power.
[32f] *ibid.*
[32g] *Re Chatard's Settlement* [1899] 1 Ch. 712 at 716 ("the trustee would have had a legal discharge if he had paid the money of the infants to their guardian").
[32h] *Re Chatard's Settlement*, above. See too Children Act 1989, s.1 (child's welfare to be the paramount consideration when court makes order as to child's property).
[32i] See §§ 45–31 *et seq.*
[32j] Variation of Trusts Act 1958, ss.1(1)(*a*), printed at § 45–34.
[32k] Family Law Reform Act 1969, s.1(1), (2).
[32l] *Cf. Re Representation of N and N* 1999 J.L.R. 86, Jersey RC, seemingly reaching the same conclusion on comparable Jersey legislation.
[32m] § 11–99A (Supplement).
[32n] *ibid.*

CHAPTER 12

BECOMING A TRUSTEE

4. DUTIES OF A NEW TRUSTEE ON ACCEPTANCE OF A TRUST

Trust provisions

12–35   AT THE END OF THE FIRST SENTENCE INSERT A NEW NOTE 96a: *Nestle v National Westminster Bank plc* [1993] 1 W.L.R. 1260 at 1265, CA (as to powers); *Prudential Staff Pensions Ltd v The Prudential Assurance Co. Ltd* [2011] EWHC 960 (Ch); [2011] N.J.L.R. 597 at [232] (citing this sentence), [235].

AT THE END OF THE TEXT INSERT: But a trustee need not be aware of every possibility inherent in his powers and the extent to which he should go to understand them depends on the duty to exercise reasonable care and skill, and varies according to the circumstances.[98a]

Trust papers and information

12–41   NOTE 10. DELETE AND REPLACE BY: See §§ 23–97 to 23–100, in particular as to the duty of a new trustee to investigate breaches of trust committed by his predecessors.

AFTER § 12–41 ADD THE FOLLOWING NEW PARAGRAPH AND HEADING:

Indemnities to outgoing trustees

12–42   An incoming trustee may be called on to grant indemnities to an outgoing trustee. The extent of the power to grant such indemnities is considered elsewhere.[11]

[98a]   *Prudential Staff Pensions Ltd v The Prudential Assurance Co. Ltd*, above, at [235].
[11]   §§ 14–61 to 14–62.

CHAPTER 13

DEATH, RETIREMENT AND REMOVAL OF TRUSTEES

1. DEATH OF TRUSTEE

NOTE 2. DELETE THE CROSS-REFERENCE TO CHAP.29 AND REPLACE BY: §§ 29–54 **13–02** to 29–56.

2. VOLUNTARY RETIREMENT OF TRUSTEE

Retirement under the Trustee Act 1925

AT THE END ADD: It has been held in Jersey, on the basis of expert evidence as **13–07** to English law, that the requirement for consent by the person empowered to appoint new trustees will be satisfied if such consent is given by a separate deed.[18a]

3. COMPULSORY RETIREMENT OF TRUSTEE

Directions relating to retirement

Enforcement

NOTE 67. Supreme Court Act 1981 is renamed Senior Courts Act 1981 from **13–35** October 1 2009, see Constitutional Reform Act 2005, Sch.11, para.1 and Constitutional Reform Act 2005 (Commencement No.11) Order 2009 (SI 2009/1604).

Vesting of trusts following retirement or appointment

FOURTH AND FIFTH SENTENCES. DELETE section 40(3) of the Trustee Act 1925 **13–42** AND REPLACE BY: section 40(4) of the Trustee Act 1925. LAST SENTENCE. DELETE section 40(3)(c) of the Trustee Act 1925 AND REPLACE BY: section 40(4)(c) of the Trustee Act 1925.

[18a] *Re T 1998 Discretionary Settlement* [2008] JRC 062; [2009] W.T.L.R. 87.

4. REMOVAL OF TRUSTEE

Under an express power or provision

13–44 NOTE 96. DELETE THE CROSS-REFERENCE TO CHAP.29 AND REPLACE BY: §§ 29–16 and 29–17.

NOTE 98. AT THE END INSERT: In later Australian decisions it has been held that a power of removal not conferred on a beneficiary will ordinarily be a fiduciary power: *Hillcrest (Ilford) Pty Ltd v Kingsford (Ilford) Pty Ltd (No.2)* [2010] NSWSC 285 at [38] (citing this paragraph); *Berger v Lysteron Pty Ltd* [2012] VSC 95.

NOTE 2. DELETE THE CROSS-REFERENCE TO CHAP.29 AND REPLACE BY: §§ 29–139 *et seq.*

NOTE 8. DELETE THE CROSS-REFERENCE TO CHAP.29 AND REPLACE BY: §§ 29–149 to 29–152.

By the court under its inherent jurisdiction

13–47 AT THE END OF THE TEXT ADD: or other appropriate arrangements are in place for the ongoing administration of the trust, for example where the trust is being administered by the court.[24a]

Principle guiding court in exercise of its inherent jurisdiction

13–49 NOTE 26. ADD: *Critchley v Critchley* [2006] NSSC 219; [2008] W.T.LR. 1563; *Dobson v Heyman* [2007] EWHC 3503 (Ch); [2010] W.T.L.R. 1151 (removal of executors under statutory jurisdiction on similar principles to removal of trustees under inherent jurisdiction).

NOTE 27. AT THE END ADD: And see *Isaac v Isaac* [2005] EWHC 435 (Ch); [2009] W.T.L.R. 265 at [65]–[73] (citing this paragraph with comments on the welfare of the beneficiaries); *Jones v Firkin-Flood* [2008] EWHC 2417 (Ch); [2008] All E.R. (D) 175 (Oct) (citing with approval this paragraph and § 13–50).

13–50 NOTE 28. AT THE END ADD: *Re Steel* [2010] EWHC 154 (Ch); [2010] W.T.L.R. 531 (removal of executors under statutory jurisdiction on similar principles to removal of trustees under inherent jurisdiction).

AT THE END OF THE TEXT ADD: In assessing the significance of friction or hostility between original trustees or executors and a beneficiary, it is relevant to have regard to the fact that they were chosen by the settlor or testator and evidence as to his reasons for that choice.[28a]

[24a] *Gonder v Gonder Estate* [2010] ONCA 172; (2010–11) 13 I.T.E.L.R. 44.
[28a] *Alkin v Raymond* [2010] W.T.L.R. 1117 at [29]–[39], Ch D.

Reasons for which a trustee may be removed

AFTER THE TEXT TO N.38 ADD: where the trustee acted in the administration of **13–54** the trust for his own benefit and in breach of the self dealing rule;[38a] where the trustee acted as trustee of two sets of trusts owning shares in the same company and found itself in a plain position of conflict in relation to a dispute which arose between the beneficiaries of the two sets of trusts concerning the company;[38b]

AFTER THE TEXT TO N.40 ADD: where the trustee has exhibited irrational hostility to a co-trustee;[40a]

Trustee will not be removed without reasonable cause

NOTE 53. ADD: *Kershaw v Micklethwaite* [2010] EWHC 506 (Ch); [2011] **13–56** W.T.L.R. 413 (executors).

[38a] *Walker v Walker* [2007] EWHC 597 (Ch); [2010] W.T.L.R. 1617 at [228]–[259].
[38b] *Re E, L, O and R Trusts* [2008] JRC 150; (2009–10) 12 I.T.E.L.R. 1.
[40a] *Scott v Scott* [2012] EWHC 2397 (Ch). The former trustee was removed and the latter left in office even though they were both principal beneficiaries.

CHAPTER 14

APPOINTMENT OF NEW TRUSTEES OUT OF COURT

1. EXPRESS POWERS

Compliance with terms of express power

14–03 AFTER THE ELEVENTH SENTENCE (ENDING ... restrictions on numbers) INSERT: Beneficiaries may be disqualified for appointment as trustees.[8a]

3. GENERAL CONSIDERATIONS

Fiduciary character of the power

14–40 DELETE THE LAST SENTENCE OF THE TEXT AND NN.34 AND 35 AND REPLACE BY: Appointments of new trustees under section 36 of the Trustee Act 1925 have in the past not been held invalid on the ground of a failure to take into account relevant considerations[34] under what was then considered to be the principle in *Hastings-Bass*.[35] It is now clear that such appointments would not be held invalid on this ground, though they might be set aside on the ground of breach of fiduciary duty by the appointor if the failure amounted to a breach of fiduciary duty,[35a] or remedied in appropriate circumstances under the court's powers of removal and appointment of trustees.[35b]

[8a] It has been held in Australia (on the construction of the particular trust instrument) that such a disqualification does not preclude the appointment of a company of which the beneficiary is sole shareholder and director: *Montevento Holdings Pty Ltd v Scaffidi* [2012] HCA 48. For the appointment of beneficiaries generally, see § 14–43.

[34] *Re Duxbury's Settlement Trusts* [1995] 1 W.L.R. 425 at 427–428, CA (appointment of trust corporation as sole trustee not rendered invalid by reason of fact that appointor failed to take account of provision in trust instrument that powers conferred on trustees not to be exercised at any time when there were less than two trustees; no appeal on this point); *Re Osiris Trustees Ltd and Goodways Ltd* (1999–00) 2 I.T.E.L.R. 404, Manx HC.

[35] [1975] Ch. 25, CA. See §§ 29–238 et seq. (Supplement).

[35a] *Pitt v Holt* [2011] EWCA Civ 197; [2012] Ch. 132 especially at [126]–[131]. See §§ 29–238 et seq. (Supplement). It is thought that the fiduciary nature of the power of appointment of new trustees is sufficient, especially when vested in trustees, for the donee to have a duty to take into account relevant considerations and disregard irrelevant considerations, so as to come within the principles of *Pitt v Holt*.

[35b] See §§ 13–47 et seq. This would be the better remedy in cases where it is appropriate for the remedy to have prospective effect only and not interfere with previous decisions of the new trustee whose appointment is sought to be set aside.

Appointment of persons resident abroad

NOTE 69. FOR THE REFERENCE TO *Whiteman on Income Tax*, SEE NOW **14–49** *Whiteman & Sherry on Income Tax* (4th edn), §§ 20.013 *et seq.*

NOTE 70. DELETE AND REPLACE BY: Income Tax Act 2007, ss.714 *et seq.*

Retirement in contemplation of breach of trust

NOTE 75. Supreme Court Act 1981 is renamed Senior Courts Act 1981 from **14–52** October 1, 2009, see Constitutional Reform Act 2005, Sch.11, para.1 and Constitutional Reform Act 2005 (Commencement No.11) Order 2009 (SI 2009/1604).

Indemnity of former trustees upon appointment of new trustees

Continuance of former trustee's right of indemnity after appointment of new trustees

AT THE END OF THE FIRST SENTENCE INSERT A NEW NOTE 95a: This paragraph was **14–59** cited with approval in *Oakhurst Property Developments Ltd v Blackstar (Isle of Man) Ltd* [2012] EWHC 1131 (Ch) at [36]–[37].

NOTE 98. AT THE END OF THE FIRST SENTENCE ADD: *Commissioner of Taxation v Bruton Holdings Pty Ltd* [2007] FCA 1643; (2008) 244 A.L.R. 177 at [62]; *Lemery Holdings Pty Ltd v Reliance Financial Services Pty Ltd* [2008] NSWSC 1344; (2008–09) 74 N.S.W.L.R. 550.

AFTER THE TEXT TO N.99 ADD: It has further been held in Australia that a former trustee does not have a right to retain, as against a new trustee, the trust assets as security for an accrued right of indemnity, though the former trustee is entitled to ensure that the new trustee does not take steps which will destroy, diminish or jeopardise the former trustee's rights of indemnity in the trust assets after they have been transferred to the new trustee.[99a]

Express covenants for indemnity of former trustees

NOTE 9. ADD: See too *Jones v Firkin-Flood* [2008] EWHC 2417 (Ch); [2008] **14–61** All E.R. (D) 175 (Oct) at [207]–[217] (retention provisions in respect of sale of shares).

[99a] *Lemery Holdings Pty Ltd v Reliance Financial Services Pty Ltd*, above, at [50].

CHAPTER 15

APPOINTMENT OF NEW TRUSTEES BY THE COURT

Mode of application

15–04 NOTE 11. DELETE AND REPLACE BY: CPR, Pt 8, r.8.1(2)(b) and (6); Practice Direction, Pt 8, Section B.

NOTE 12. DELETE AND REPLACE BY: *ibid.*

Appointment in place of personal representative

15–15 NOTE 68. Supreme Court Act 1981 is renamed Senior Courts Act 1981 from October 1, 2009, see Constitutional Reform Act 2005, Sch.11, para.1 and Constitutional Reform Act 2005 (Commencement No.11) Order 2009 (SI 2009/1604).

CHAPTER 16

APPOINTMENT OF NEW TRUSTEES IN PLACE OF TRUSTEES LACKING MENTAL CAPACITY

1. INTRODUCTION

Agent acting on behalf of trustee lacking capacity

NOTE 1. FOR THE REFERENCE TO *Chitty on Contracts*, SEE NOW (30th edn), **16–02** Vol.2, § 31–164.

Lack of capacity

Statutory definitions concerning lack of capacity

NOTE 22. Mental Health Act 1983, s.1 is amended by Mental Health Act **16–08** 2007, s.1 with effect from November 3, 2008: Mental Health Act 2007 (Commencement No.7 and Transitional Provisions) Order 2008 (SI 2008/ 1900). For the reference to Heywood and Massey, *Court of Protection Practice*, see now Chap.4.

2. APPOINTMENT UNDER STATUTORY AND EXPRESS POWERS

Statutory power

Nominated person lacking capacity

NOTE 42. FOR THE REFERENCE TO Heywood and Massey, *Court of Protection* **16–12** *Practice*, SEE NOW §§ 22–010 and 22–011.

Trustee lacks capacity: nominated person available to act

THIRD SENTENCE. Delete the reference to section 40(3) of the Trustee Act **16–15** 1925 and replace by a reference to section 40(4) of the Trustee Act 1925.

Trustee lacks capacity, no available nominated person but another trustee available to act

NOTE 71. FOR THE REFERENCE TO Heywood and Massey, *Court of Protection* **16–16** *Practice*, SEE NOW §§ 22–013 and 22–014.

3. Appointment at the Instance of Beneficiaries

Directions by beneficiaries

16–24   Note 94. For the reference to Heywood and Massey, *Court of Protection Practice*, see now § 22–021.

Vesting of trust assets

16–25   Second sentence. Delete section 40(3) of the Trustee Act 1925 and replace by: section 40(4) of the Trustee Act 1925.

4. Appointment by the Court

Concurrent jurisdiction of Court of Protection

16–28   Note 16. For the reference to Heywood and Massey, *Court of Protection Practice*, see now § 22–016.

5. Retirement or Removal Without New Appointment

Retirement under section 39 of the Trustee Act 1925 or under express power

16–31   Notes 27, 30 and 32. For the reference to Heywood and Massey, *Court of Protection Practice*, see now §§ 22–010 and 22–011.

CHAPTER 17

VESTING TRUST PROPERTY OUT OF COURT ON CHANGE OF TRUSTEES

DELETE § 17–01 AND REPLACE BY:

Obligations to vest trust property

Statutory obligations

On the appointment or retirement of a trustee most trust property vests in **17–01** the new or continuing trustees by virtue of an implied vesting declaration operating under section 40 of the Trustee Act 1925.[1] But that does not mean that the obligation of an outgoing trustee to vest the trust property in the new or continuing trustees is unimportant since section 40 does not cover all kinds of property and applies only to an appointment by deed. Further, an implied vesting declaration will not cover all steps that need to be taken on, or are incidental to, the vesting of the trust property on a change of trusteeship.[1a] Section 37(1)(*d*) of the Trustee Act 1925[1b] provides that:

> "(1) On the appointment of a trustee for the whole or any part of trust property—
>
> ...
>
> (*d*) any assurance or thing or thing requisite for vesting the trust property, or any part thereof, in a sole trustee, or jointly in the persons who are the trustees, shall be executed or done."

There are two further statutory obligations to vest trust property on the retirement of trustees, namely section 39(2) of the Trustee Act 1925,[1c] concerned with retirement of trustees under the statutory power in section 39(1) of the 1925 Act, and section 19(4) of the Trusts of Land and Appointment of Trustees Act 1996,[1d] concerned with compulsory retirement of trustees under section 19(2) of the 1996 Act. Sections 37(1)(*d*) and 39(2) of the 1925 Act differ from section 19(4) of the 1996 Act in that no express reference is made to protection of the rights of the outgoing trustee, but we do not consider that that the terms of sections 37(1)(*d*) prejudice in any way the

---

[1]   See §§ 17–02 *et seq.*
[1a] On which see *Re Essel Trust* [2008] JRC 065; 2008 J.L.R. N.18.
[1b] Referred to in § 14–36.
[1c] Referred to in § 13–08.
[1d] Set out and considered in § 13–42.

rights of indemnity to which a an outgoing trustee is entitled under the general law.[1e]

Obligations under general law

17–01A The statutory provision in section 37(1)(*d*) of the Trustee Act 1925 is not in terms limited to appointments under the statutory power in section 36 of the 1925 Act, and probably covers an appointment under an express power. Section 39(2) appears to be ancillary to section 39(2) and may not cover a retirement under an express power. None of the statutory provisions cover the case of removal without appointment of a new trustee under an express power. It cannot, however, be doubted that, to the extent that the statutory provisions do not apply, an outgoing trustee has an obligation, subject to reasonable protection in respect of liabilities in accordance with his rights of indemnity, to do everything on his part that is needed to vest the trust property in the persons who are the trustees after a change in the trustee-ship, that being consequential upon the change of trusteeship.[1f]

Trust papers and information

17–01B The position as to trust papers and information is considered in §§ 23–97 to 23–100.

[1e]   As to which see §§ 14–58 to 14–63.
[1f]   *Noble v Meymott* (1851) 14 Beav. 471; *Re Essel Trust*, above.

CHAPTER 18

VESTING AND SIMILAR ORDERS

Introduction

NOTE 2. FOR THE REFERENCE TO *Halsbury's Laws of England*, SEE NOW (5th **18–01** edn), Vol.13 (2009), § 707. FOR THE REFERENCE TO Scottish as well as English assets, SEE NOW *Chancery Guide* (6th edn, 2009), paras.25.21 and 25.22.

Vesting orders of land

NOTE 4. DELETE THE FIRST TWO SENTENCES AND REPLACE BY: CPR, Pt 8, **18–04** r.8.1(2)(b) and (6); Practice Direction 8A—Alternative Procedure for Claims, Section B.

When a vesting order of land may be made

NOTE 20. FOR THE REFERENCE TO Underhill and Hayton, *Law of Trusts and* **18–05** *Trustees*, SEE NOW (18th edn), § 73.16.

PENULTIMATE SENTENCE. Supreme Court Act 1981 is renamed Senior Courts Act 1981 from October 1, 2009, see Constitutional Reform Act 2005, Sch.11, para.1 and Constitutional Reform Act 2005 (Commencement No.11) Order 2009 (SI 2009/1604).

Orders for specific performance—consequential vesting

NOTE 30. Supreme Court Act 1981 is renamed Senior Courts Act 1981 from **18–09** October 1, 2009, see Constitutional Reform Act 2005, Sch.11, para.1 and Constitutional Reform Act 2005 (Commencement No.11) Order 2009 (SI 2009/1604).

Orders relating to stock and things in action

Effect of order

IN THE FIRST QUOTATION DELETE Bank of England and all other companies AND **18–15** REPLACE BY: Registrar of Government Stock or any company[50a].

[50a] The words "Registrar of Government Stock or any company" were substituted for "Bank of England and all other companies" by Government Stock (Consequential and Transitional Provision) (No.2) Order 2004 (SI 2004/1662), Sch.1(2), para.10(2)(*a*).

IN THE SECOND QUOTATION DELETE Bank of England or any other company AND REPLACE BY: Registrar of Government Stock or any company[50b].

[50b] The words "Registrar of Government Stock or any company" were substituted for "Bank of England or any other company" by Government Stock (Consequential and Transitional Provision) (No.2) Order 2004 (SI 2004/1662), Sch.1(2), para.10(2)(b).

CHAPTER 19

PARTICULAR TRUSTEES

1. JUDICIAL TRUSTEES

Creation of judicial trustees

NOTE 2. DELETE printed AND FOR THE REFERENCE TO *Civil Procedure* (2005), **19–01**
Vol.2, Section 6D, SUBSTITUTE *Civil Procedure* (2012), Vol.2, Section 6D
(CD).

The application

AT THE END OF THE SECOND SENTENCE ADD: (or, if made in an existing claim, **19–04**
then by application notice in that claim).

NOTE 15. DELETE AND REPLACE BY: *Chancery Guide* (6th edn, 2009),
para.25.32. This is consistent with CPR, Pt 8, r.8.1(b) and (6) since,
although Practice Direction, Pt 8, Section B contains no reference to the
1896 Act, Judicial Trustees Rules 1983, r.3(1) provides for the application to
be made by originating summons (or by summons or motion in a pending
cause or matter) and so it follows that the Pt 8 procedure should be used, see
Practice Direction 8A—Alternative Procedure for Claims, para.3.3.

Who may be appointed a judicial trustee

NOTE 26. AT THE END ADD: Where it is proposed to appoint the Official **19–05**
Solicitor inquiries should first be made to his office for confirmation that he
is prepared to act if appointed: *Chancery Guide* (6th edn, 2009), para.25.33.

Terms of appointment and remuneration

NOTE 32. AT THE END ADD: See too *Chancery Guide* (6th edn, 2009), **19–06**
para.25.33.

NOTE 37. AT THE END ADD: See too *Chancery Guide* (6th edn, 2009),
para.25.34.

Administration by a judicial trustee

NOTE 39. DELETE THE REFERENCE TO Judicial Trustees Act 1896. **19–07**

NOTE 40. AT THE BEGINNING INSERT: Judicial Trustees Act 1896, s.1(4).

AT THE END ADD: See too *Chancery Guide* (6th edn, 2009), para.25.32. For an instance, see *Official Solicitor to the Senior Courts v Yemoh* [2010] EWHC 3727 (Ch).

2. THE PUBLIC TRUSTEE

The Public Trustee

19–08 NOTE 44. DELETE printed AND FOR THE REFERENCE TO *Civil Procedure* (2007), Vol.2, Section 6D, SUBSTITUTE *Civil Procedure* (2012), Vol.2, Section 6D (CD).

FIRST PARAGRAPH. DELETE THE FIFTH AND SIXTH SENTENCE AND REPLACE BY: The Public Trustee and the Official Solicitor to the Senior Courts have the same office, though they have independent statutory functions and the Public Trustee and the Official Solicitor are presently different persons (but the Public Trustee also heads the Court Funds Office which shares some corporate services with the office of the Public Trustee and Official Solicitor). The Public Trustee now accepts new trusts only on a "last resort" basis, broadly where there is no one else willing and able to act and an injustice to a vulnerable person would be caused if he did not act. In recent years the Public Trustee has retired from a large number of trusts and the role of the Public Trustee is significantly smaller than was formerly the case.

SECOND PARAGRAPH: DELETE THE FIRST AND SECOND SENTENCES AND REPLACE BY: The Public Trustee may exercise the functions of a deputy appointed by the Court of Protection.[48] This topic is outside the scope of this work.

General powers

19–09 NOTE 51. DELETE AND REPLACE BY: The present Public Trustee is Mr Eddie Bloomfield.

Trusts for religious or charitable purposes and security trusts

19–12 NOTE 66. FOR THE REFERENCE TO *Civil Procedure* (2007), Vol.2, para.6D–47, SUBSTITUTE *Civil Procedure* (2012), Vol.2, para.6D–50 (CD).

Direction that Public Trustee not to be appointed

Notice of appointment

19–18 NOTE 80. DELETE THE FIRST TWO SENTENCES AND REPLACE BY: CPR, Pt 8, r.8.1(2)(b) and (6); Practice Direction 8A—Alternative Procedure for Claims, Section B.

NOTE 81. DELETE AND REPLACE BY: CPR, Pt 8, r.8.1(2)(b) and (6); Practice Direction 8A—Alternative Procedure for Claims, Section B. Since the Public Trustee will not accept appointment except where an injustice to a

[48] Public Trustee and Administration of Funds Act 1986, s.3(1), as substituted by Mental Capacity Act 2005, s.67(1) and Sch.6, para.33.

vulnerable person is involved (see § 19–08), it will be normally be appropriate for the hearing to be in private.

General provisions

Application to Court

NOTE 1. AT THE BEGINNING INSERT: Public Trustee Act 1906, s.10(1).   **19–29**

NOTE 2. DELETE THE FIRST SENTENCE AND REPLACE BY: Public Trustee Act 1906, s.10(2); and CPR, Pt 8, r.8.1(2)(b) and (6); Practice Direction 8A—Alternative Procedure for Claims, Section B.

Investments

NOTE 11. AT THE END ADD: Court Funds (Amendment) Rules 2000 (SI 2000/ **19–36**
2918); Court Funds (Amendment) Rules 2001 (SI 2001/703); Court Funds (Amendment) Rules 2003 (SI 2003/375); Court Funds (Amendment No.2) Rules 2003 (SI 2003/720); Court Funds (Amendment) Rules 2007 (SI 2007/729); Court Funds (Amendment No.2) Rules 2007 (SI 2007/2617); Court Funds (Amendment) Rules 2010 (SI 2010/172).

Fees and expenses

NOTE 26. DELETE THE FIRST SENTENCE AND REPLACE BY: Public Trustee (Fees) **19–45**
Order 2008 (SI 2008/611).

3. CUSTODIAN TRUSTEES

Who may be appointed a custodian trustee

NOTE 35. DELETE AND REPLACE BY: It is thought that this includes a reference **19–47**
to the Companies Act 1985 and the Companies Act 2006: see Interpretation Act 1978, ss.17 and 23, Companies Consolidation (Consequential Provisions) Act 1985, s.31 and Companies Act 2006, s.1297.

4. TRUST CORPORATIONS

Meaning of trust corporation

NOTE 53. Supreme Court Act 1981 is renamed Senior Courts Act 1981 from **19–52**
October 1, 2009, see Constitutional Reform Act 2005, Sch.11, para.1 and Constitutional Reform Act 2005 (Commencement No.11) Order 2009 (SI 2009/1604).

CHAPTER 20

UNAUTHORISED PROFITS AND CONFLICTS OF INTEREST

2. RENEWALS OF LEASES AND PURCHASES OF REVERSIONS BY TRUSTEES

Renewal of leases by trustees—*Keech v Sandford*

Keech v Sandford

20–03   NOTE 5. ADD: For a critical view see Hicks (2010) 69 C.L.J. 287.

Extension of the rule to purchase of the reversion

20–07   AT THE END OF THE SECOND SENTENCE ADD: in circumstances such that the beneficiary can properly be considered to have given a fully informed consent to the purchase.

NOTE 32. AT THE END OF THE FIRST SENTENCE ADD: *Foreman v King* [2008] EWHC 592 (Ch) at [41]–[44].

Purchase of property associated with trust property

20–09   NOTE 39. ADD: But see § 20–28B (Supplement).

Application of the rule to other fiduciaries and persons interested in lease

Partners

20–16   NOTE 61. ADD: *Foreman v King* [2008] EWHC 592 (Ch).

NOTE 62. INSERT AT THE END: *Barber v Rasco International Ltd* [2012] EWHC 269 (QB).

AFTER § 20–16 INSERT A NEW PARAGRAPH:

20–16A   Where a tenancy is partnership property and is the subject of statutory protection conferring a right of succession when the tenant dies on a person who fulfils the statutory criteria for succession only by virtue of being a partner, then that person will hold the tenancy on trust for the partnership.[67a]

[67a]   *Shirt v Shirt* [2012] EWCA Civ 1029 at [43], [72] (agricultural tenancy within Agricultural Holdings Act 1986).

The remedy

AT THE END OF THE FIRST SENTENCE INSERT A NEW NOTE 70a: We do not **20–19** consider that the remedy of constructive trust under the rule is affected by *Sinclair Investments (UK) Ltd v Versailles Trade Finance Ltd* [2011] EWCA Civ 347; [2011] 4 All E.R. 335, see §§ 20–28A and 20–28B (Supplement).

3. PROFITS FROM TRANSACTIONS WITH THIRD PARTIES

The remedy—general principles

AFTER § 20–28 INSERT THE FOLLOWING NEW PARAGRAPHS:

What is said in the previous paragraph must be read subject to *Sinclair* **20–28A** *Investments (UK) Ltd v Versailles Trade Finance Ltd*,[16a] a case concerned with the liability of a company director rather than the liability of the trustee of a trust in the strict sense. In that case it was held that a constructive trust of the profit is imposed only where the money or asset constituting the profit is or has been beneficially the property of the beneficiary, or is property which the trustee acquired by taking advantage of an opportunity or right which was properly that of the beneficiary, and in other cases the remedy is limited to a personal liability to account.[16b] The decision in *Sinclair* was based on a number of Court of Appeal decisions (all concerned with companies, none with trusts in the strict sense)[16c] which prevailed[16d] over the Privy Council decision in *Att.-Gen. for Hong Kong v Reid*,[16e] the leading modern authority in favour of the imposition of a constructive trust on profits made by fiduciaries, the soundness of which was doubted by the Court of Appeal in *Sinclair*.[16f] And so it was decided in *Sinclair* that no constructive trust is imposed on the profitable proceeds of a sale by director of shares in a company owned by him in circumstances where the value of his own shares has been inflated in consequence of breaches by him of his fiduciary duties to the company and manipulation of the assets of the company assets.[16g]

Under the law stated in *Sinclair Investments (UK) Ltd v Versailles Trade* **20–28B** *Finance Ltd*[16h] there are three categories of case where a proprietary remedy is available:

[16a] [2011] EWCA Civ 347; [2011] 3 W.L.R. 1153; affirming [2010] EWHC 1614 (Ch); [2011] 1 B.C.L.C. 202. See Hayton (2011) 25 Tru.L.I. 3.

[16b] See at [88].

[16c] Principally *Metropolitan Bank v Heiron* (1880) L.R. 5 Ex. D. 319, CA; *Lister & Co. v Stubbs* (1890) 45 Ch.D. 1, CA; *Gwembe Valley Development Co. Ltd v Koshy* [2003] EWCA Civ 1478; [2004] 1 B.C.L.C. 131 and *Halton International Inc. v Guernroy Ltd* [2006] EWCA Civ 801; [2006] W.T.L.R. 1241. Reliance was also placed on *Tyrrell v Bank of London* (1862) 10 H.L. Cas. 26, HL. For a review of the authorities by the CA, see [57]–[71], [77], [84]–[87]. For a mere detailed review of the authorities at first instance, see [2010] EWHC 1614 (Ch); [2011] 1 B.C.L.C. 202 at [35]–[79].

[16d] See at [73]–[74].

[16e] [1994] 1 A.C. 324, PC.

[16f] See at [80]–[83].

[16g] See at [49]–[56] and [92], approving the first instance decision [2010] EWHC 1614 (Ch); [2011] 1 B.C.L.C. 202 at [81].

[16h] [2011] EWCA Civ 347; [2011] 3 W.L.R. 1153. See (2011) 70 C.L.J. 502 (Virgo).

(1) The first is where the money or asset is beneficially the property of the beneficiary, as where it is the traceable product of trust assets, for example where the trustee speculates with property taken from the trust fund.[16i] This category is no more than an application of the proprietary remedy considered elsewhere.[16j] It does not involve the imposition of a constructive trust upon property acquired by the trustees but rather the vindication of the beneficiary's continuing beneficial interest in the property which represents trust property wrongly applied by the trustee in making the profit.[16k]

(2) The second is where the asset or money constituting the profit has in the past been trust property but has ceased to be trust property before the profit has been made by the trustee. An example of such a case is where money is validly and without impropriety advanced out of the trust to a beneficiary who then uses part of the money to bribe the trustee to make a further and improper advance to the beneficiary. The rationale for imposition of a constructive trust on property which is not trust property but has in the past been trust property is not clear, and perhaps the explanation for this category is that it explains[16l] a case[16m] which might be thought to support a wider view of the circumstances in which a constructive trust is imposed.[16n]

(3) The third is where the trustee acquired the asset or money by taking advantage of an opportunity or right which was properly that of the beneficiary. It is the third category which is of particular importance in the present context since it covers cases which cannot be explained solely in terms of a vindication of beneficial ownership in the traceable product of trust property. What distinguishes this category from cases where there is a personal remedy only is that the trustee enriches himself by depriving the beneficiary of an asset, rather than by simply doing a wrong to the beneficiary.[16o] The wording of this category[16p] is somewhat vague and it remains to be seen whether it will be narrowly interpreted, or widely applied so as to cover most of the cases which before *Sinclair* were regarded as giving rise to a proprietary remedy. This category covers cases[16q] within the rule in *Keech v Sandford*,[16r] and

[16i] See § 20–33.
[16j] See Chap.41.
[16k] See § 41–05.
[16l] *Sinclair Investments (UK) Ltd v Versailles Trade Finance Ltd*, above, at [63]–[64].
[16m] *Re Caerphilly Colliery Company, Pearson's Case* (1877) 5 Ch.D. 336, CA.
[16n] *Re Caerphilly Colliery Company, Pearson's Case*, above, at 339–340, cited in *Sinclair Investments (UK) Ltd v Versailles Trade Finance Ltd*, above, at [63]. This second category was said to be non-existent in *Cadogan Petroleum plc v Tolley* [2011] EWHC 2286 (Ch) at [36].
[16o] *Sinclair Investments (UK) Ltd v Versailles Trade Finance Ltd*, above, at [80].
[16p] *ibid*, at [88].
[16q] *ibid*, at [58].
[16r] (1726) Sel. Cas. T. King 61. See §§ 20–02 *et seq.* (including Supplement).

covers cases[16s] where a trustee purchases property from a third party which the trust has an interest in acquiring and sells it on to the trust at a profit, so that the trustee cannot be heard to say that he acquired the property for himself rather than for the trust.[16t] This category would appear to cover cases where the profit is acquired through the exercise (or non-exercise) of a pre-existing right conferred on the trustee or other fiduciary as legal owner of pre-existing property subject to the trust or fiduciary relationship,[16u] as where a trustee obtains remunerative employment with a company owned by the trust,[16v] and may cover cases where the opportunity and knowledge gained from that position enable the trustee to make a profit, as in *Phipps v Boardman*[16w] and similar cases.[16x]

The consequences of limitation of the remedy to a personal remedy in cases **20–28C** where a proprietary remedy is not available are these:

(1) The beneficiaries are unprotected in the event of the trustee's insolvency and compete along with the trustee's other unsecured creditors.

(2) There may be no recovery in respect of any increase after the profit is made in the value of the asset or money constituting the profit or the property from time to time representing the same,[16y] though the

---

[16s] *Sinclair Investments (UK) Ltd v Versailles Trade Finance Ltd*, above, at [58].

[16t] *Tyrrell v Bank of London* (1862) 10 H.L. Cas. 26, HL; *Re Cape Breton Company* (1885) 29 Ch.D. 795 at 803–806, CA.

[16u] Though this would appear to come clearly within the third category, a doubt may arise from observations made at first instance in *Sinclair*, see [2010] EWHC 1614 (Ch); [2011] 1 B.C.L.C. 202 at [76]–[79], in relation to *Halton International Inc. v Guernroy Ltd* [2006] EWCA Civ 801; [2006] W.T.L.R. 1241, echoed to some extent by the CA in *Sinclair* at [87].

[16v] See §§ 20–39 to 20–41 (including Supplement).

[16w] [1967] 2 A.C. 46, HL. In *Sinclair* the CA (see [2011] EWCA Civ 347; [2011] 4 All E.R. 335 at [70]) agreed with view expressed at first instance (see [2010] EWHC 1614 (Ch); [2011] 1 B.C.L.C. 202 at [42]–[47]) that *Phipps v Boardman* is not binding authority for the proposition that a constructive trust is imposed in this kind of case. On the other hand, the CA did not say that *Phipps v Boardman* was authority against that proposition, or that the matter was concluded one way or the other by authority. The view at first instance in *Sinclair* supported the same judge's earlier view in *Ultraframe (UK) Ltd v Fielding* [2005] EWHC 1638 (Ch); [2007] W.T.L.R. 835 at [1546]; and contrasted with the different views expressed by a different judge in *Sinclair Investment Holdings SA v Versailles Trade Finance Ltd* [2007] EWHC 915 (Ch); [2007] 2 All E.R. (Comm.) 993 at [105]; and contrasted with the view subsequently expressed in *Dyson Technology Ltd v Curtis* [2010] EWHC 3289 (Ch) at [187]. Sir Peter Millett in [1993] R.L.R. 7 at 12 (writing before the PC decision in *Att.-Gen. for Hong Kong v Reid* [1994] 1 A.C. 324, PC) considered that it was "obviously appropriate" that the remedy in *Phipps v Boardman* was a constructive trust. A reading of the first instance order ([1964] 1 W.L.R. 993 at 1018) suggests that Wilberforce J. was ready to order a transfer of the shares, but this was stood over, perhaps because on the facts personal accountability (something flowing from imposition of a constructive trust—see § 20–29) gave the successful plaintiffs a better remedy. That perhaps explains why the appellate courts focused on personal accountability while also referring to constructive trusteeship. As to whether information is property and whether property acquired through use of confidential information is the traceable product of the information, see §§ 20–45 and 20–53.

[16x] See §§ 20–44 to 20–46.

[16y] *Lister & Co. v Stubbs* (1890) 45 Ch.D. 1 at 15, CA.

Court of Appeal in *Sinclair* has left to the door open, with limited enthusiasm, to the possibility of a personal remedy in respect of such profits.[16z]

(3) The remedies of dishonest assistance and knowing receipt are not available against third parties who assist in the disposal of the profit after it is made or receive it from the trustee.[16aa]

Consequences of constructive trusteeship—the proprietary remedy and consequential personal remedies

20–29 DELETE THE FIRST SENTENCE AND REPLACE BY: In cases where a profit is held on a constructive trust in accordance with the principles stated in §§ 20–28 to 20–28C (including Supplement), it follows that the trustee will, subject to his lien, and like in cases where there is no constructive trust, be personally accountable for the amount or value of the profit, just as he is personally accountable for other assets of the trust.

Allowance for skill and labour

20–30 NOTE 23. AT THE END ADD: *Estate Realties Ltd v Wignall* [1992] 2 NZLR 615, NZ HC; *Chirnside v Fay* [2006] NZSC 68; (2007–08) 10 I.T.E.L.R. 226 reversing in part [2004] 3 N.Z.L.R. 637, NZ CA.

AT THE END OF THE TEXT ADD. It has been doubted whether an allowance for skill and labour is available where the profit consists of property forming part of the trust property, rather than property obtained from a third party, on the ground that this would involve an impermissible discretionary interference by the court with the property rights of the beneficiaries.[33a]

Bribes and commissions

Remedies against a trustee who takes a bribe or commission

20–36 DELETE THE LAST SENTENCE AND N.56 AND REPLACE BY: Later the constructive trust remedy was broadened by the Privy Council so as to be available in all

---

[16z]   *Sinclair Investments (UK) Ltd v Versailles Trade Finance Ltd* [2011] EWCA Civ 347; [2011] 4 All E.R. 335 at [89]–[91]. The concept of surviving enrichment referred to in § 20–28, n.13 was not considered by the CA.

[16aa]   See § 20–53.

[33a]   *Ultraframe (UK) Ltd v Fielding* [2005] EWHC 1638 (Ch); [2007] W.T.L.R. 835 at [1542]–[1545]. This part of the decision in *Ultraframe* should be approached with some caution. The court has a discretionary jurisdiction to authorise payment of remuneration out of the trust property for the past services of the trustee, and though that jurisdiction concerns retrospective authorisation of remuneration for authorised work done, rather than allowances for work done in making unauthorised profits, there are elements in that jurisdiction which overlap with the jurisdiction here under consideration, see § 20–176. The court also has a discretionary jurisdiction to authorise retention of fees made from a remunerative employment with a third party, see § 20–41. The court does not have discretion to determine whether property rights should be conferred or confiscated, but that does not mean that the court can have no discretion in relation to the manner in which relief is granted in relation to equitable proprietary rights see § 41–36.

cases.[56] But the Court of Appeal has narrowed the constructive trust remedy so that it is now available in England only where the bribe or commission derives from the trust property,[56a] or where it can be said that the trustee has taken advantage of an opportunity or right which was properly that of the beneficiary.[56b]

Remedies against the other party to the transaction

NOTE 64. FOR THE REFERENCE TO *Clerk and Lindsell on Torts*, SEE NOW (20th **20–38** edn), §§ 18–55 and 18–56.

NOTE 68. AT THE END OF THE FIRST SENTENCE ADD: considered in *Murad v al-Saraj* [2005] EWCA Civ 959; [2005] W.T.L.R. 1573 at [69]; *Ultraframe UK Ltd v Fielding* [2005] EWHC 1638 (Ch); [2007] W.T.L.R. 835 at [1589]–[1584]; *Sinclair Investment Holdings SA v Versailles Trade Finance Ltd* [2007] EWHC 915 (Ch); [2007] 2 All E.R. (Comm.) 993 at [131]–[134].

AT THE END ADD: On the question whether the briber can be made accountable in equity (rather than at common law) for the bribe paid or profit made by the trustee as distinct from the briber's own profit, see § 20–53.

Remunerative employment with third party

NOTE 70. DELETE AND REPLACE BY: See §§ 20–28 to 20–29 (including Sup- **20–39** plement), especially 20–28B(3). In view of *Sinclair Investments (UK) Ltd v Versailles Trade Finance Ltd* [2011] EWCA Civ 347; [2011] W.T.L.R. 1043, mere misuse of a fiduciary position in order to obtain remunerative employment would not be enough for a proprietary as distinct from personal remedy. But different considerations apply where the employment is obtained through the exercise (or non-exercise) of pre-existing voting rights attached to company shares comprised in the trust property, though even here there may be a doubt whether a constructive trust remedy is available, see § 20–28B, n.16u.

---

[56] *Att.-Gen. for Hong Kong v Reid* [1994] 1 A.C. 324, PC; *Corporacion Nacional del Cobre de Chile v Interglobal Inc* (2002–03) 5 I.T.E.L.R. 744, Cayman GC; *Daraydan Holdings Ltd v Solland International Ltd* [2004] EWHC 622 (Ch); [2005] Ch. 119; *Ultraframe (UK) Ltd v Fielding* [2005] EWHC 1638 (Ch); [2007] W.T.L.R. 835 at [1490]; *Dyson Technology Ltd v Curtis* [2010] EWHC 3289 (Ch) at [170]–[191].

[56a] *Sinclair Investments (UK) Ltd v Versailles Trade Finance Ltd* [2011] EWCA Civ 347; [2011] 4 All E.R. 335 at [64]; and see § 20–28B(2) (Supplement). Note that in *Williams v Barton* [1927] 2 Ch. 9 the commission derived from the trust property (though that was not the reason why a trust was imposed in that case) and in most cases of open commissions, the commission derives, at least indirectly, from the trust property. See too *Cadogan Petroleum plc v Tolley* [2011] EWHC 2286 (Ch) at [14]–[39].

[56b] *Sinclair Investments (UK) Ltd v Versailles Trade Finance Ltd*, above, at [88]; and see § 20–28B(3) (Supplement). Where the trustee as seller of trust property is entitled to brokerage in respect of the sale, it may be said that the right to obtain brokerage is properly that of the beneficiary so that the trustee cannot be heard to say that he obtained the brokerage on his own account rather than for the trust. Trust instruments often permit professional trustees to retain brokerage. See too *Cadogan Petroleum plc v Tolley*, above.

Profit obtained by third party

Claim based on connection between third party and trustee

20–49   NOTE 8. AT THE END ADD: *Ultraframe UK Ltd v Fielding* [2005] EWHC 1638 (Ch); [2007] W.T.L.R. 835 at [1561]–[1564]. The parenthetical statement in the text to this footnote should not be read out of context. It is not suggested in the text that it is enough to establish a substantial interest. The purpose of the parenthetical statement is to make it clear that a company in which the defendant's interest is less than 100 per cent. can (but not necessarily will) be one which is a cloak or alter ego, as for example where some shares in the company are owned by persons connected with the defendant so as to give an (incorrect) appearance of autonomy. See too § 42–43 (concerned with receipt in the context of knowing receipt).

NOTE 9. AT THE END ADD: critically considered in *Ultraframe UK Ltd v Fielding*, above, at [1565]–[1576], [1584]–[1585].

AT THE END OF THE FIRST SENTENCE ADD: or which could have been taken by the trustee but which is arranged by him to be taken by a company.[9a]

NOTE 10. AT THE END ADD: *Ultraframe UK Ltd v Fielding*, above, at [1588].

NOTE 11. AFTER THE REFERENCE TO *Timber Engineering Co. Pty Ltd v Anderson* INSERT: (considered in *Ultraframe UK Ltd v Fielding*, above, at [1536]–[1542]). AT THE END ADD: As to the circumstances in which a trust (as distinct from mere personal liability to account) will be imposed, see §§ 20–28 to 20–28C (including Supplement).

Claim based on participation in breach of fiduciary duty

20–53   NOTE 26. AT THE END OF THE FIRST SENTENCE ADD: *Warman International Ltd v Dwyer* (1995) 182 C.L.R. 544 at 564–565, Aus. HC; *Ultraframe UK Ltd v Fielding* [2005] EWHC 1638 (Ch); [2007] W.T.L.R. 835 at [1589]–[1594]; but see *Sinclair Investment Holdings SA v Versailles Trade Finance Ltd* [2007] EWHC 915 (Ch); [2007] 2 All E.R. (Comm.) 993 at [109]–[135] in which the proposition in the text was not treated as conclusively settled in English law. AFTER THE SECOND SENTENCE INSERT: The remedy is a personal one and the third party does not become a constructive trustee of the profit made by him so as to enable the claimant to pursue a proprietary remedy in respect of the profit, see *Sinclair Investment Holdings SA v Versailles Trade Finance Ltd*, above.

AT THE BEGINNING OF THE SENTENCE WHICH IS THE TEXT TO N.29 INSERT: It has been held in Canada that

AFTER THE TEXT TO N.29 INSERT: But this wide principle has not been accepted in England: a dishonest assistant is liable to pay compensation in respect of the loss to the trust fund resulting from the trustee's breach of trust and is liable to account for his own profit, but is not liable to account

---

[9a]   *Comax Secure Business Services Ltd v Wilson* [2001] All E.R. (D) 222 (Jun), considered in *Ultraframe UK Ltd v Fielding* [2005] EWHC 1638 (Ch); [2007] W.T.L.R. 835 at [1598]–[1599]; see too at [1576].

for a profit made by the trustee or another dishonest assistant which has caused no corresponding loss to the beneficiaries.[29a] The dishonest assistant may, however, be accountable for a profit which he could have made for himself but which he arranges to be taken by a company.[29b]

NOTE 31. ADD: In *Ultraframe UK Ltd v Fielding* [2005] EWHC 1638 (Ch); [2007] W.T.L.R. 835 at [1489] it was considered that property which becomes trust property under the profit rule counts as trust property for the purpose of knowing receipt. But a profit made by a trustee is not necessarily subject to a trust in favour of the beneficiaries and may give rise to no more than a personal remedy to account against the trustee, see *Sinclair Investments (UK) Ltd v Versailles Trade Finance Ltd* [2011] EWCA Civ 347; [2011] W.T.L.R. 1043 and §§ 20–28A to 20–28C (Supplement). In cases where there is no trust, the remedy of knowing receipt is not available (nor is any remedy of dishonest assistance available in relation to the disposal of the profit after it has been made), see *Apcoa Parking (UK) Ltd v Perera*, unreported, October 14, 2010, Ch D. But if there is a trust, both remedies are available, see *Dyson Technology Ltd v Curtis* [2010] EWHC 3289 (Ch) at [170]–[211].

NOTE 34. ADD: *Ultraframe UK Ltd v Fielding* [2005] EWHC 1638 (Ch); [2007] W.T.L.R. 835 at [1482], [1574], agreeing with the statement in the text.

4. PURCHASE OF TRUST PROPERTY BY TRUSTEES AND OTHER SELF DEALING TRANSACTIONS

The self dealing rule

NOTE 88. AT THE END INSERT: This sentence of the text was cited with **20–63** approval in *Earl of Cardigan v Moore* [2012] EWHC 1024 (Ch); (2012) 14 I.T.E.L.R. 967 at [41].

NOTE 89. AT THE END ADD: As to the scope of *Holder v Holder* [1968] Ch. 353, CA and whether it confers any discretion on the court to disapply the self-dealing rule, see *Re Thompson's Settlement* [1986] Ch. 99 at 115; *Re One.Tel Networks Holdings Pty Ltd* [2001] NSWSC 1065; (2001) 40 A.C.S.R. 83 at [54]; *Re Carrington* [2008] NZHC 2126; (2008–09) 11 I.T.E.L.R. 693; *Calvo v Sweeney* [2009] NSWSC 719 at [230]–[242], where the rule was held to be mandatory, and the court had no power to disapply the rule in its discretion.

NOTE 93. AT THE END INSERT: This sentence of the text was cited with approval in *Earl of Cardigan v Moore* [2012] EWHC 1024 (Ch); (2012) 14 I.T.E.L.R. 967 at [41].

[29a] *Ultraframe UK Ltd v Fielding* [2005] EWHC 1638 (Ch); [2007] W.T.L.R. 835 at [1595]–[1601].

[29b] *Comax Secure Business Services Ltd v Wilson* [2001] All E.R. (D) 222 (Jun), considered in *Ultraframe UK Ltd v Fielding*, above, at [1598]–[1599] (and compare § 20–49).

20–64 NOTE 1. AT THE END ADD: Where a trustee is expressly authorised to act notwithstanding a conflict of interest, there is no such burden on the trustee: *McNulty v McNulty* [2011] NZHC 1173; (2011-12) 14 I.T.E.L.R. 361 at [108]–[109].

Application of the self dealing rule to transactions other than purchase of trust property

Leases of trust property

20–66 NOTE 6. ADD: *Walker v Walker* [2007] EWHC 597 (Ch); [2010] W.T.L.R. 1617 at [232]–[237]; *Earl of Cardigan v Moore* [2012] EWHC 1024 (Ch); (2012) 14 I.T.E.L.R. 967 at [41].

Indirect purchase by trustee and purchase by former trustee

Purchase by former trustee

20–75 NOTE 34. AT THE END ADD: See too *Holder v Holder* [1968] Ch. 353 at 398, CA, *per* Harman L.J; *Spincode Pty Ltd v Look Software Pty Ltd* [2001] VSCA 248 at [56].

Trustee not placing himself in a position of conflict of interest and duty

20–97 AFTER THE FIRST SENTENCE INSERT: Hence a person appointed as a successor trustee at a time when he has a personal interest capable of conflicting with those of the trust is not thereby impliedly authorised to act.[14a]

Purchase with concurrence of beneficiaries

20–98 AT THE END ADD: In relation to requirement (7), concurrence by one or more of a class of beneficiaries may have the consequence that the concurring beneficiaries have any accretion to their entitlement arising from the defaulting trustee being held to account impounded, leaving the non-concurring beneficiaries free to benefit, in proportion to their share of the fund which is augmented.[29a]

Purchase with the sanction of the court

Non-concurring or opposing adult beneficiaries

20–102 NOTE 37. AT THE END ADD: *Holder v Holder* [1968] Ch. 353, CA was not followed in *Re Carrington* [2008] NZHC 2126; (2008–09) 11 I.T.E.L.R. 693, though the question whether the purchasing trustee might be authorised by the court to repurchase the property was not considered.

[14a] *Earl of Cardigan v Moore* [2012] EWHC 1024 (Ch); (2012) 14 I.T.E.L.R. 967 at [47].
[29a] *Jones v Firkin-Flood* [2008] EWHC 2417 (Ch); [2008] All E.R. (D) 175 (Oct) at [224], *per* Briggs J.

5. INTEREST OF TRUSTEES IN EXERCISE OF DISPOSITIVE POWERS

The problem with trustees' powers

NOTE 8. AT THE END ADD: *Royal Bank of Scotland plc v Chandra* [2011] **20–124**
EWCA Civ 192 at [24].

Construction of the power and role of the self dealing rule

NOTE 30. AT THE END OF THE FIRST SENTENCE ADD: *Breakspear v Ackland* **20–129**
[2008] EWHC 220; [2009] Ch. 32 at [114]; *Rafferty v Philp* [2011] EWHC 709
(Ch) at [34]–[35], [69] (statement in text approved).

AT THE END ADD: See too *Dever v Knobloch* [2009] NZHC 2013 at [37]–[54] as
to the position in New Zealand.

Exclusion of the rule where the trustee does not place himself in a position of conflict

NOTE 41. AT THE BEGINNING INSERT: *Breakspear v Ackland* [2008] EWHC 220; **20–131**
[2009] Ch. 32 at [122].

NOTE 42. AT THE END ADD: Nor was the exception applied to a successor
trustee in *Breakspear v Ackland*, above, see at [122].

Express and implied exclusion of the rule by the terms of the trust

AFTER THE SECOND SENTENCE INSERT: It is clear that the self dealing rule can **20–132**
be excluded by the terms of the trust.[47a]

AFTER THE FOURTH SENTENCE INSERT: A provision conferring power on the
trustees to enter into any transaction concerning the trust fund notwithstanding that any of the trustees is interested in the transaction other than as
one of the trustees has, in the context of the terms of the settlement as a
whole and admissible evidence as to the background of the settlement, been
broadly construed so as to encompass an addition of a trustee to the class of
beneficiaries under a power of addition and a subsequent appointment to
that trustee under a power of appointment in favour of the beneficiaries.[47b]

AFTER § 20–132 INSERT THE FOLLOWING NEW PARAGRAPH AND HEADING:

No rescue for bad timing

If neither of the exceptions considered in §§ 20–131 and 20–132 is available, **20–132A**
the self dealing rule might needlessly be engaged as a result of bad timing,
but the court will not rescue the trustee from the application of the self
dealing rule for that reason.[50a] If it is contemplated that a beneficiary will
both benefit under a power of appointment conferred on the trustees and be
appointed as one of the trustees, the appointment under the power of

---

[47a] *Breakspear v Ackland* [2008] EWHC 220; [2009] Ch. 32 at [114] and [117]–[125]; *McNulty v McNulty* [2011] NZHC 1173; (2011–12) 14 I.T.E.L.R. 361 at [40]–[73].
[47b] *Breakspear v Ackland*, above, at [114] and [117]–[125].
[50a] *Breakspear v Ackland* [2008] EWHC 220; [2009] Ch. 32 at [115], [127]–[128], *per* Briggs J.

appointment will not be impugned if the existing trustees make the appointment in favour of the beneficiary and subsequently the beneficiary is appointed as a trustee. But if the appointment in favour of the beneficiary is made after the beneficiary's appointment as a trustee then it will be caught by the self dealing rule. The difference between the two cases is one of substance, and the court cannot approach the matter as though the relevant deeds had been executed in a different order from the order in which they were actually executed or formed a single composite deed when they did not. In the first case the beneficiary has no fiduciary functions in relation to the exercise of the power of appointment even if it is contemplated that the beneficiary will become a trustee subsequently. In the second case the beneficiary, having already become a trustee, even though for a short time, does have fiduciary functions in relation to the exercise of the power of appointment and cannot say that those functions were not performed since that would, if correct, itself taint the exercise of the power of appointment.

6. Purchase of Beneficial Interest from Beneficiary

The fair dealing rule

20–136   At the end add: It has been held in Australia that the fair dealing rule does not apply to the purchase by one partner from another of his partnership share in circumstances where title to the partnership property is vested in the purchasing partner on trust for the partners. In such a case the relevant obligations are those arising between partners under partnership law, not the more extensive obligations imposed by the fair dealing rule on a trustee buying a beneficial interest from a beneficiary of the trust.[59a]

7. Remuneration of Trustees

Remuneration authorised by order of the court

The inherent jurisdiction

20–175   Note 25. Add: *Regent Trust Co. Ltd v RJD* [2009] JRC 117.

After the text to n.25 add: And the court may be persuaded to do so even where the application is opposed by the beneficiaries and the trustee is an unlicensed trust company which inadvertently failed to transfer the trusteeship to another trust company which acted as though the trusteeship had been transferred.[25a]

Remuneration for work already done

20–176   Note 37. At the beginning insert: *Regent Trust Co. Ltd v RJD* [2009] JRC 117 (where a trust company charged fees for 37 years in accordance with its scale in force from time to time having overlooked the terms of the charging

---

[59a] *Beale v Trinkler* [2009] NSWCA 30; (2008–09) 11 I.T.E.L.R. 862.
[25a] *Landau v Anburn Trustees Ltd* [2007] JRC 084; [2008] W.T.L.R. 487.

clause which authorised only the scale applicable at the date of the settlement).

8. BONA VACANTIA; ADVERSE TITLE; JUS TERTII

Total failure of beneficiaries

NOTE 59. DELETE Companies Act 1985, s.654 AND REPLACE BY Companies Act 2006, s.1012. **20–183**

CHAPTER 21

INDEMNITY OF TRUSTEES

2. INDEMNITY OUT OF TRUST PROPERTY IN RESPECT OF ADMINISTRATION EXPENSES

The general principle

Excluding, restricting or enhancing the statutory right of indemnity

21–08 NOTE 25. DELETE AND REPLACE BY: See § 39–138.

The liabilities of trustees and their rights of indemnity

Liability in contract

21–11 NOTE 38. AT THE END ADD: A provision in a mortgage of trust property limiting the personal liability of the trustee under the mortgage to that property does not give the trustee priority against the mortgagee to payment out of the proceeds of the property of third party liabilities incurred by the trustee in respect of the property, see *Dominion Corporate Trustees Ltd v Capmark Bank Europe plc* [2010] EWHC 1605 (Ch); (2010–11) 13 I.T.E.L.R. 154.

NOTE 41. Trusts (Guernsey) Law 1989, s.37 has been replaced by Trusts (Guernsey) Law 2007, s.42 with effect from March 17, 2008.

UK and foreign fiscal liabilities

21–18 NOTE 68. For the reference to *Whiteman on Capital Gains Tax*, see now *Whiteman & Sherry on Capital Gains Tax* (5th edn), §§ 34.142 to 34.156.

NOTE 69. ADD: Mere personal inconvenience to a trustee's travel arrangements is not, however, enough, see *Sutton v England* [2009] EWHC 3270 (Ch); [2010] W.T.L.R. 335 at [53]–[54] (reversed on appeal on other grounds *sub nom. Southgate v Sutton* [2011] EWCA Civ 637; [2011] W.T.L.R. 1235).

AT THE END ADD: Moreover, under recent legislation implementing Directives of the European Union or international convention many foreign fiscal liabilities have become enforceable in the United Kingdom.[71a] In those cases

---

[71a] Finance Act 2002, s.134 and Sch.39; Finance Act 2006, s.173; and Finance Act 2011, s.87 and Sch.25. The 2002 and 2011 Acts provide for enforcement within the European Union and the 2006 Act provides for other international arrangements to be given effect by order in council. Numerous orders in council have been made under the 2006 Act; for the question how far the legislation is retrospective, see *HMRC v Ben Nevis (Holdings) Ltd* [2012] EWHC 1807 (Ch).

there can be no doubt that as a matter of English law a trustee will be justified in discharging such liabilities out of the trust property. But the legislation permits enforcement only as specifically provided in those arrangements: it has not abrogated the general rule that foreign fiscal liabilities are not enforceable in the English courts.[71b]

Indemnity of particular trustees

Constructive trustees

NOTE 7. AT THE END ADD: *Provident Capital Ltd v Agusta Pty Ltd* [2011] **21–28** NSWSC 258 at [47], citing this passage.

Mode of satisfaction of the right to indemnity

A trustee's charge or lien on the trust property

NOTE 35. ADD: *McKnight v Ice Skating Queensland Inc.* [2007] QSC 273; **21–33** (2007–08) 10 I.T.E.L.R. 570.

NOTE 41. DELETE AND REPLACE BY: *Re Knox's Trusts* [1895] 2 Ch. 483, CA.

AT THE END OF § 21–33(3) ADD: A trustee must make proper inquiries as to what the contingent or future liabilities consist of and the extent of his potential liability at the time that he asserts a right of retention.[44a]

Property or income subject to the charge or lien

NOTE 55. AT THE END ADD: See too *White v Williams (No.2)* [2011] EWHC **21–34** 494 (Ch); [2011] W.T.L.R. 899 at [66] (charity).

Rights of creditors and other claimants against the trust property— subrogation

NOTE 68. ADD: *Official Assignee of Bainbridge v Menzies* [2011] NZHC 87 at **21–38** [41]–[43] and Australian cases there cited.

Right of subrogation not co-extensive with right of indemnity

NOTE 93. AT THE END ADD: *Re Pumfrey* (1882) 22 Ch.D. 255 at 263; *Re* **21–41** *Wilson* [1942] V.L.R. 177 at 183; *Deancrest Nominees Pty Ltd v Nixon* [2007] WASC 304; (2007) A.C.L.C. 1681 at [49]; *Zen Ridgeway Pty Ltd v Adams* [2009] QSC 117; (2009) 3 A.S.T.L.R. 44 at [13]; but see *Re Geary* [1939] N.1. 152 at 162.

Interest

NOTE 98. DELETE AND REPLACE BY: CPR, Practice Direction, Pt 40A— **21–43** Accounts & Inquiries, para.14.

[71b] See *Ben Nevis*, above, at [53].
[44a] *Wester v Borland* [2007] EWHC 2484 (Ch); [2007] All E.R. (D) 204 (Oct).

4. Costs of Third Party Proceedings

The position as between the trustee and the third party

21–51   NOTE 29. Supreme Court Act 1981 is renamed Senior Courts Act 1981 from October 1, 2009, see Constitutional Reform Act 2005, Sch.11, para.1 and Constitutional Reform Act 2005 (Commencement No.11) Order 2009 (SI 2009/1604).

5. Costs of Trust Proceedings

Trustee's costs—effect of statute and rules of court

Statutory provisions

21–71   TEXT TO N.26. Supreme Court Act 1981 is renamed Senior Courts Act 1981 from October 1, 2009, see Constitutional Reform Act 2005, Sch.11, para.1 and Constitutional Reform Act 2005 (Commencement No.11) Order 2009 (SI 2009/1604).

The Civil Procedure Rules

21–75   NOTE 37. AT THE END ADD: The title to CPR, Pt 48, r.48(4) is now misleading. It should be read with Practice Direction Pts 43 to 48—The Costs Practice Direction, paras.50A.1 to 50A.3.

Assessment of costs under the Civil Procedure Rules

21–76   NOTE 43. AT THE END ADD: In the Cayman Islands there is no requirement for trustees' costs on the indemnity basis to be subject to a process of taxation or agreement, see *Re Ojjeh Trust* [1994–95] C.I.L.R. 118 at 124, 125, Cayman GC.

Beneficiaries' costs

21–77   NOTE 48. For the reference to *The Chancery Guide* (2005), see now *The Chancery Guide* (6th edn, 2009), para.25.8.

Basis of assessment of costs in favour of beneficiaries and against trustees

21–78   TEXT TO N.51. For the reference to *The Chancery Guide* (2005), see now *The Chancery Guide* (6th edn, 2009), para.25.8.

        NOTE 52. For the reference to *Civil Procedure* (2007), Vol.1, 44.4.3 substitute *Civil Procedure* (2011), Vol.1, 44.4.3.

Construction proceedings

21–79   NOTE 54. AT THE END OF THE LAST SENTENCE ADD: *Singapore Airlines Ltd v Buck Consultants Ltd* [2011] EWCA Civ 1542 at [64]–[78], approving the statement of the *Buckton* principles in this paragraph at [67].

AT THE END OF THE TEXT ADD: The determination of the category into which a particular case falls is a question of law, not an exercise of discretion on the facts, and so may be appealed.[61a]

A fourth category?

AT THE BEGINNING INSERT: The categories of proceedings enumerated in *Re* **21–80** *Buckton*[61b] are not closed.[61c] A further category is where an issue of construction is pursued by a third party acting in dual capacity in part for the benefit of beneficiaries (whom he is ordered to represent for the purpose of the issue) and in part for his own benefit by way of defence to a hostile claim against him. This category falls neither within *Buckton* category (2) nor within *Buckton* category (3).[61d] The appropriate order for a case within this category is for a proportion of the costs that would have been borne by the fund had the case fallen within *Buckton* category (2), *prima facie* a half share, to be paid out of the trust fund.[61e]

The role of the trustee and his costs

AT THE END OF THE FIFTH SENTENCE ADD: and likewise where there is a class of **21–81** beneficiaries with an opposing interest none of whom is willing to participate in the proceedings.[68a]

NOTE 69. INSERT AT THE BEGINNING: *Re Hemming* [2008] EWHC 8565 (Ch); [2008] W.T.L.R. 1833 at [40].

Beneficiaries' costs

AFTER THE FOURTH SENTENCE ADD: Beneficiaries who have used construction **21–82** proceedings as a vehicle for raising issues not germane to the proceedings have not only been deprived of costs, but also been ordered to pay the costs of the trustees in reading and responding to their evidence, the costs being assessed on the indemnity basis in view of those beneficiaries' disgraceful conduct.[75a]

Prospective costs orders for beneficiaries

AFTER THE TEXT TO N.80 ADD: A prospective costs order may similarly be **21–83** made in a case within *Buckton* category (2).[80a] Such an order will not be made in a case within *Buckton* category (3) unless the case is one analogous to a minority shareholder's action, in which the beneficiaries have given consideration for their interests (typically in a pension trust) and the claimant beneficiary is seeking restitution on behalf of the whole fund,

---

[61a]   *Singapore Airlines Ltd v Buck Consultants Ltd*, above, at [73].
[61b]   [1907] 2 Ch. 406.
[61c]   *Singapore Airlines Ltd v Buck Consultants Ltd*, above, at [75], citing this paragraph.
[61d]   *ibid.* at [71]–[75].
[61e]   *ibid.* at [76]–[77].
[68a]   *State Street Bank and Trust Co. v Sompo Japan Insurance Inc.* [2010] EWHC 1461 (Ch) at [28]–[30].
[75a]   *Grender v Dresden* [2009] EWHC 500 (Ch); [2010] W.T.L.R. 1163.
[80a]   *IBM United Kingdom Pensions Trust Ltd v Metcalfe* [2012] EWHC 125 (Ch) at [19].

sometimes called the *McDonald v Horn* exception, or unless the case is otherwise exceptional.[80b] Prospective costs orders in favour of beneficiaries will usually be made only where the court is satisfied that the proceedings fall within *Buckton* category (1) or (2), and so where the court considers that it is unclear whether the proceedings are of that character or that the proceedings might turn into a *Buckton* category (3) case, a prospective costs order will not generally be made.[80c] Nor will a prospective costs order be made in a case within *Buckton* category (1) or (2) unless the judge at trial would inevitably, or almost inevitably, make an order for costs in favour of the beneficiary seeking the order;[80d] but it has been held that that test need not be satisfied in a case within the *McDonald v Horn* exception.[80e]

NOTE 81. ADD: A model form of order is contained in the appendix to this practice direction.

Costs of appeal

21–84 NOTE 88. AT THE END ADD: but see the authority cited in the next footnote (Supplement).

AFTER THE TEXT TO N.88 ADD: Further, where there is an appeal by another party, unless a trustee has good reason to think that its actions will be subject to criticism or there is some other special reason, it should normally be unnecessary for a trustee to make representations or be represented at the hearing of an appeal (save for instructing a note-taker), where the trustee's stance on the issues dividing the other parties is neutral; and directions can be sought at a relatively early stage in the appeal to enable the trustee to make submissions (possibly in writing) if the trustee's assistance is required or on which the trustee desires to have a say.[88a]

NOTE 89. AT THE END OF THE FIRST SENTENCE ADD: *Re IMG Pension Plan* [2010] EWHC 321 (Ch); [2010] P.L.R. 131 (application granted). DELETE THE THIRD TO SIXTH SENTENCES AND REPLACE BY: The application for a prospective costs order for an appeal on a construction question by a beneficiary who lost in the HC may be based on two alternative grounds. One ground is that the beneficiary's costs of the appeal will be payable out of the trust fund whatever the outcome (see § 21–120). Normally an application based on that ground will fail, see *Chessels v British Telecommunications plc* [2002] P.L.R. 141 and *Re IMG Pension Plan*, above. That is because, even though the case falls within *Buckton* category (1) or (2) (see § 21–79 referring to *Re Buckton* [1907] 2 Ch. 406), the principle that costs should be paid from the trust fund whatever the outcome applies at first instance (see § 21–83) but not on appeal (see text to n.86 in § 21–84). The alternative ground is that the

---

[80b] *HR Trustees Ltd v German* [2010] EWHC 321 (Ch); [2010] Pens. L.R. 131; *IBM United Kingdom Pensions Trust Ltd*, above, at [19]–[20], relying on *McDonald v Horn*, above.

[80c] *International Committee of the Red Cross v Thommessen* 2009–10 G.L.R. 377. See too § 21–120.

[80d] *McDonald v Horn*, above, at 971–972; *IBM United Kingdom Pensions Trust Ltd*, above, at [19].

[80e] *HR Trustees Ltd v German*, above.

[88a] *BNY Corporate Trustee Services Ltd v Eurosail-UK 2007-3BL plc* [2011] EWCA Civ 227 at [102]–[105].

application satisfies the special principle applicable to pension schemes and other trusts where the beneficiaries are not volunteers, formulated in *McDonald v Horn* [1995] 1 All E.R. 961 at 973–975 (see § 21–100). The alternative ground is not restricted to hostile litigation and so may be relied upon, where appropriate (as in the context of an appeal), in cases coming within *Buckton* categories (1) and (2), see *Re IMG Pension Plan*, above, at [41]–[52].

NOTE 90. AT THE END ADD: There is no express provision on this matter in the UKSC Practice Directions, but it would normally be appropriate to follow the former practice pursuant to UKSC Practice Direction 5.1.1.

Directions sought for the guidance or proper protection of the trustee on administration questions

NOTE 94. FOR THE REFERENCE TO *The Chancery Guide* (2005), SEE NOW *The* **21–85** *Chancery Guide* (6th edn, 2009), para.25.8.

Proceedings seeking the assistance of the court under statutory provisions

Section 203(5) of the Law of Property Act 1925

LAST SENTENCE. Supreme Court Act 1981 is renamed Senior Courts Act **21–89** 1981 from October 1, 2009, see Constitutional Reform Act 2005, Sch.11, para.1 and Constitutional Reform Act 2005 (Commencement No.11) Order 2009 (SI 2009/1604).

Proceedings for the enforcement of rights of beneficiaries against the trustee

Claims for production of accounts or information by the trustee

NOTE 34. DELETE AND REPLACE BY: *Wingate v Butterfield Trust (Bermuda) Ltd* **21–91** *(Costs)* [2008] SC (Bda) 6; [2008] W.T.L.R. 593. See §§ 23–23, 23–28 and 23–30 as to when there is no reasonable doubt about provision of information.

NOTE 35. DELETE AND REPLACE BY: See § 23–05.

Breach of trust proceedings

Successful defence by trustee

NOTE 75. ADD: *Hayman v Equity Trustees Ltd* [2003] VSC 353; (2003) V.R. **21–98** 548; *Close Trustees (Switzerland) SA v Vildósola* [2008] EWHC 1267 (Ch); (2007–08) 10 I.T.E.L.R. 1135 at [19].

DELETE NN.79 AND 80 AND THE TEXT TO THEM AND REPLACE BY: As between the beneficiaries, the costs of the successful trustee may be ordered to be borne primarily by the unsuccessful claimant's share of the trust fund.[79] But it is an oversimplification to say that the costs will necessarily be borne in this way and it is relevant to have regard to whether other beneficiaries would have

---

[79]   *National Trustees Executors and Agency Co. of Australasia Ltd v Barnes* (1941) 64 C.L.R. 268 at 276, Aus. HC.

benefited had the action succeeded.[80] The trustee's unrecovered costs of an unsuccessful claim by an income beneficiary have been ordered to be paid out of the beneficiary's income held by the trustees at the time when the right of indemnity becomes exercisable[80a] and out of future income,[80b] but they have also been ordered to be paid out of capital of a share of the trust fund in which the income beneficiary is interested.[80c] In a case where the income beneficiary's unsuccessful claim relates to the income of the trust fund, it is reasonable to expect that the unrecovered costs will be primarily borne by income, but where the claim relates to the capital of the trust fund, and would if successful have resulted in an augmentation of capital, it is doubtful whether such costs, which have a capital character, will be liable to be borne by income.[80d]

AT THE END OF THE TEXT ADD: The trustee is entitled to retain capital to cover his contingent indemnity pending the resolution of the beneficiary's claim, even if the capital would apart from the claim be distributable and the beneficiary wishes to have access to capital to fund his claim.[81a] However, the court, while accepting that income may in general terms be retained by a trustee if a contingent liability, if it becomes payable, will or may be liable to be borne by income, has refused an application by trustees to retain part of an income beneficiary's income pending resolution of a claim by that beneficiary against the trustees and others which if successful would result in an augmentation of the capital of the trust fund which was sufficient without any augmentation to cover the trustee's costs.[81b]

Proceedings for or concerning the removal of trustees

21–102 FOURTH SENTENCE. AFTER THE WORDS the court might normally be expected to make an order for costs against the trustee, INSERT A NEW NOTE 95a: *Re E, L, O and R Trusts* [2008] JRC 150; (2009–10) 12 I.T.E.L.R. 1.

AFTER THE TEXT TO N.98 INSERT: A beneficiary who unsuccessfully seeks the removal of a trustee will normally be ordered to pay costs.[98a]

6. COSTS OF PROCEEDINGS AGAINST THE TRUST OR THE TRUST PROPERTY

Claims by settlor's creditors or trustee in bankruptcy under the insolvency legislation

21–107 NOTE 44. ADD: *Re Hemming* [2008] EWHC 8565 (Ch); [2008] W.T.L.R. 1833.

---

[80]   *Close Trustees (Switzerland) SA v Vildósola* [2008] EWHC 1267 (Ch); (2007–08) 10 I.T.E.L.R. 1135 at [19] at [45]–[59].
[80a] *D'Oechsner v Scott* (1857) 24 Beav. 239.
[80b] *Re Andrews* (1885) 30 Ch.D. 159 at 161.
[80c] *Thompson v Clive* (1848) 11 Beav. 475.
[80d] *Close Trustees (Switzerland) SA v Vildósola*, above, at [2], [31], [45]–[45].
[81a] *Hayman v Equity Trustees Ltd* [2003] VSC 353; (2003) V.R. 548.
[81b] *Close Trustees (Switzerland) SA v Vildósola*, above.
[98a] *Isaac v Isaac* [2005] EWHC 435 (Ch); [2009] W.T.L.R. 265 at [96]–[97].

Claims based on an adverse equitable proprietary claim binding the trust property

NOTE 50. AT THE END ADD: See too *Chan Gordon v Lee Wai Hing* [2011] **21–108** HKCFI 273.

AT THE END OF THE TEXT ADD: In a case where the question of an adverse proprietary claim to company assets arises in a liquidation, and the costs of determination of the question would be disproportionate to the value of the assets concerned, the court may protect the liquidator by authorising him to act on counsel's opinion (on matters of law as well as fact), subject to notice being given to potential claimants.[52a]

Claims based on money laundering

AT THE END ADD: For the position as to a trustee's costs in civil recovery **21–109** proceedings, see *Serious Organised Crime Agency v Szepietowski*[53a] and § 46–143 (Supplement).

7. *BEDDOE* APPLICATIONS

Procedure on *Beddoe* applications

NOTE 15. DELETE AND REPLACE BY: ACD Direction, para.4.3. Permission to **21–124** issue the claim form under CPR, Pt 8, r.8.2A is required: *The Chancery Guide* (6th edn, 2009), para.25.4.

NOTE 16. DELETE THE REFERENCE TO *The Chancery Guide.*

NOTE 19. DELETE THE REFERENCE TO *The Chancery Guide.*

NOTE 21. AT THE END ADD: With effect from October 1, 2011 the ACD is amended to provide that *Beddoe* applications will be disposed of without an oral hearing in the first instance; and that any request for an oral hearing must be stated in evidence giving the reasons why.

The evidence

NOTE 24. DELETE THE REFERENCE TO *The Chancery Guide.*   **21–125**

NOTE 26. DELETE THE REFERENCE TO *The Chancery Guide.*

NOTE 28. AT THE END ADD: *Kleanthous v Paphitis* [2011] EWHC 2287 (Ch) at [44].

Procedure where the other party to the main action is a beneficiary

NOTE 34. *Three Individual Present Professional Trustees of Two Trusts v An* **21–126** *Infant Prospective Beneficiary of one Trust* IS REPORTED AT [2007] W.T.L.R. 1631.

[52a] *Re Equilift Ltd* [2009] EWHC 3104 (Ch); [2010] B.P.I.R. 116. And see § 27–17A (Supplement).
[53a] [2009] EWHC 344 (Ch); [2009] 4 All E.R. 393.

AT THE END ADD: The modern tendency is to allow those with whom trustees are in litigation to participate as fully as possible in *Beddoe* applications: *Kleanthous v Paphitis* [2011] EWHC 2287 (Ch) at [44].

NOTE 36. DELETE THE REFERENCE TO *The Chancery Guide*.

NOTE 37. DELETE THE REFERENCE TO *The Chancery Guide*.

Consultation with beneficiaries

21–130 FIRST SENTENCE. DELETE THE REFERENCE TO *The Chancery Guide*.

Urgent applications

21–132 NOTE 46. DELETE THE REFERENCE TO *The Chancery Guide*.

CHAPTER 22

INSOLVENCY OF A TRUSTEE

1. TRUSTEESHIP

Exercise of trusteeship

AT THE END OF THE SECOND SENTENCE, INSERT A NEW NOTE 3a: It is assumed **22–02** here that the insolvent corporate trustee is subject to a winding-up, an administration or an administrative receivership; until it becomes subject to one of those procedures, the trusteeship is conducted by its directors and other proper officers, see §§ 29–80, 29–81. It has been held that an insolvent trust company should almost invariably be put into liquidation: *Commissioner of Inland Revenue v Newmarket Trustees Ltd* [2012] NZCA 351 at [75].

Liquidator

NOTE 6. INSERT AT THE BEGINNING: See the discussions of material factors in **22–03** *Irvine Australia Shareholding and Underwriting Ltd* (1996) 22 ACSR 765 (VSC) at 783 and 785–786; *Wells v Wily* [2004] NSWSC 607; (2004) 183 F.L.R. 284 at [24]–[31]; *Kardiasmenos v Pioneer Management Pty Ltd* [2005] NSWSC 770 at [36]–[38]; *Dreiberg v Bettles* [2007] NSWSC 1204 at [4]; *Austec Wagga Wagga Pty Ltd v Rarebreed Wagga Ltd* [2012] NSWSC 343 at [90]–[98]; *Commissioner of Inland Revenue v Newmarket Trustees Ltd*, above, at [71].

NOTE 7. DELETE AND REPLACE BY: *Chirkinian v Arnfield* [2006] EWHC 1917 (Ch); [2006] B.P.I.R. 1363 at [18] (liquidator can make appointment if in pursuit of statutory functions but must act in interests of beneficiaries). Compare *Re Crest Realty Pty* Ltd [1977] 1 N.S.W.L.R. 664 (power of liquidator to apply to court for appointment); but contrast *Sjoquist v Rock Eisteddfod Productions Pty Ltd* (1996) 19 A.C.S.R. 339 at 342. In the context of pension trusts, see Pensions Act 1995, ss.22–23, 25 (as amended or substituted by Pensions Act 2004, ss.36(1), (2), (3), (4), 319(1), 320, Sch.12, paras.34, 40, 41, Sch.13, Pt 1 and Companies Act 2006 (Consequential Amendments, Transitional Provisions and Savings) Order 2009 (SI 2009/ 1941), art.2(1), Sch.1, para.155(1), (3)).

Administrators

NOTE 10. DELETE AND REPLACE BY: Under Insolvency Act 1986, s.8 and **22–04** Sch.B1, substituted and inserted by Enterprise Act 2002, s.248 and Sch.16.

Note 11. Delete under Insolvency Act 1986, s.8 and replace by: under what is now Insolvency Act 1986, Sch.B1 (inserted by Enterprise Act 2002, s.248 and Sch.16).

At the end add: Decisions so holding were given at a time when only the court could appoint administrators; now both a chargee and the company itself or its directors may do so[12a] but there seems no reason to doubt that they apply equally to an administrator so appointed.

Administrative receivers

22–05 Note 14. Delete the first sentence and replace by: The powers of an administrator are conferred by statute (Insolvency Act 1986, Sch.B1 (inserted by Enterprise Act 2002, s.248 and Sch.16), paras.59–61) and in particular he may remove and replace directors (*ibid.*, para.61, a point relied on in *Denny v Yeldon* [1995] 3 All E.R. 624).

Costs and expenses of insolvency practitioner

22–06 Note 16. Delete in the first sentence Insolvency Rules 1986, r.4.218 and replace by: Insolvency Rules 1986, r.4.218 (as amended by Insolvency (Amendment) Rules 1987 (SI 1987/1919), r.3(1), Sch., Pt 1, para.79; Insolvency (Amendment) Rules 1995 (SI 1995/586), r.3, Sch.; Insolvency (Amendment) (No.2) Rules 2002 (SI 2002/2712), r.4(1), Sch., Pt 2, para.23(*b*), (*c*), (*d*); Insolvency (Amendment) Rules 2005 (SI 2005/527), rr.1(2), 3(2), Insolvency (Amendment) Rules 2008 (SI 2008/737), rr.3, 4).

Delete the second sentence and replace by: See too Insolvency Rules 1986, r.4.127 (as amended by Insolvency (Amendment) Rules 2004 (SI 2004/584), r.14; Insolvency (Amendment) Rules 2010 (SI 2010/686), r.2, Sch.1, para.217).

Note 18. Delete Insolvency Rules 1986, r.2.47(1) and replace by: Insolvency Rules 1986, r.2.106(1) (as substituted by Insolvency (Amendment) Rules 2003 (SI 2003/1730), r.5(1), Sch.1, Pt 2, para.9 and amended by Insolvency (Amendment) Rules 2005 (SI 2005/527), r.5.15; Insolvency (Amendment) Rules 2010 (SI 2010/686), r.2, Sch.1, para.90).

22–07 Note 20. At the end add: *13 Coromandel Place Pty Ltd v CL Custodians Pty Ltd* (1999) 30 A.C.S.R. 377.

After the first sentence insert: The same applies to an administrator.[20a]

[12a] Insolvency Act 1986, Sch.B1, paras.14, 22.
[20a] *Re Sports Betting Media Ltd* [2007] EWHC 2085 (Ch); [2008] 2 B.C.L.C. 89.

2. EFFECT ON TRUST PROPERTY

General

Individual trustees

NOTE 24. DELETE THE FIRST SENTENCE AND REPLACE BY: Defined in Insolvency **22–08**
Act 1986, s.283 (as amended by Housing Act 1988, s.117(1)).

NOTE 26. DELETE AND REPLACE BY: Insolvency Act 1986, ss.305(2), 302 and
330 (the last as amended by Insolvency Act 1986 (Amendment) (No.2)
Regulations 2002 (SI 2002/1240), regs.3, 15).

AT THE END ADD: A power vested in an individual trustee as such does not
pass to his trustee in bankruptcy; the point is considered elsewhere.[27a]

AT THE END ADD: But where trust money is misapplied when it should have **22–09**
been paid into a client account, the beneficiary has no proprietary claim
against the funds in the client account even if there is a surplus on that
account after satisfying all other proprietary claims.[33a]

AT THE END ADD: Nor is a prior disposition in favour of beneficiaries of **22–10**
property held on trust by a bankrupt liable to be set aside as a transaction at
an undervalue under the insolvency legislation:[35a] the element of gift or
provision of consideration on the part of the bankrupt, which the legislation
assumes, is missing.[35b]

Corporate trustees

AT THE END ADD: A power vested in a corporate trustee as such will continue **22–11**
to be exercisable, along with the trusteeship generally, by its liquidator or
administrator; the point is considered elsewhere.[38a]

NOTE 39: AFTER Insolvency Act 1986, s.129 INSERT: (as amended by Enter- **22–12**
prise Act 2002, s.248(3), Sch.17, paras.9, 16).

NOTE 40: AFTER Insolvency Act 1986, s.127 INSERT: (as amended by Enterprise Act 2002, s.248(3), Sch.17, paras.9, 15).

AT THE END OF THE TEXT ADD: As in the case of individual insolvency, a prior
disposition in favour of beneficiaries of property held on trust by a company
is not liable to be set aside as a transaction at an undervalue under the
insolvency legislation.[40a]

AFTER PARAGRAPH 22–12 INSERT THE FOLLOWING NEW PARAGRAPH AND
HEADING:

[27a] § 29–78.
[33a] *Re BA Peters plc* [2008] EWCA Civ 1604; [2010] 1 B.C.L.C. 142 (trader's client account
rather than solicitor's).
[35a] Under Insolvency Act 1986, s.339 (as amended by Civil Partnership Act 2004, s.261(1),
Sch.27, para.119).
[35b] *Cf. Levin v Ikiua* [2010] NZCA 509; [2011] 1 N.Z.L.R. 678, on comparable New Zealand
insolvency legislation.
[38a] § 29–81.
[40a] Insolvency Act 1986, s. 238 (as amended by Enterprise Act 2002, s.248(3), Sch.17, paras.9,
25); *cf.* § 22–10.

Arrangements

22–12A The insolvency legislation makes provision for individual voluntary arrangements and company voluntary arrangements as alternatives to bankruptcy or winding-up.[40b] Where the arrangement is approved by the requisite majority,[40c] it become binding on every "creditor" of the individual or the company.[40d] Beneficiaries of property held on trust by the individual or the company, however, are not creditors and so will not be bound by such voluntary arrangements without their individual consents. Similarly, the court has no jurisdiction to bind such beneficiaries by means of its power to sanction a compromise or arrangement between a company and its creditors under Part 26 of the Companies Act 2006.[40e]

Trustee with a beneficial interest

22–15 NOTE 50. AFTER Insolvency Act 1986, s.335A INSERT: (as inserted by Trusts of Land and Appointment of Trustees Act 1996, s.25(1), Sch.3, para.23 and amended by Civil Partnership Act 2004, s.261(1), Sch.27, para.118).

NOTE 52. DELETE AND REPLACE BY: Law of Property Act 1925, s.36(2) (as amended by Trusts of Land and Appointment of Trustees Act 1996, s.5, Sch.2, para.4).

3. TRUSTEE'S RIGHT OF INDEMNITY

Nature of right

22–20 NOTE 74. DELETE Companies Act 1985, s.360 AND REPLACE BY: Companies Act 2006, s.126, replacing Companies Act 1985, s.360.

Effect of insolvency on right of indemnity

22–22 NOTE 80. AT THE END ADD: *Official Assignee of Bainbridge v Menzies* [2011] NZHC 87 at [22]–[25].

NOTE 82. AT THE END OF THE FIRST SENTENCE ADD: *Agusta Pty Ltd v The Official Trustee in Bankruptcy* [2008] NSWSC 685 at [35]; *Re OPC Managed Rehab Ltd* (2009–10) 12 I.T.E.L.R. 405 at [118], NZ HC.

[40b] Insolvency Act 1986, Pt I, Pt VIII.
[40c] For which see Insolvency Rules 1986, r.1.19 (as amended by Insolvency (Amendment) (No.2) Rules 2002 (SI 2002/2712), r.3(1), Sch., Pt 1, para.10 and Insolvency (Amendment) Rules 2010 (SI 2010/686), r.2, Sch.1, para.13(1), (2)), r.1.20 (as amended by Insolvency (Amendment) Rules 1987 (SI 1987/1919), r.3(1), Sch., Pt 1, para.5 and Insolvency (Amendment) (No.2) Rules 2002 (SI 2002/2712), r.3(1), Sch., Pt 1, para.110) and r.5.23 (as substituted by Insolvency (Amendment) (No.2) Rules 2002 (SI 2002/2712), r.5(1), Sch. Pt 3, para.24 and amended by Insolvency (Amendment) Rules 2010, above, r.2, Sch.1, para.273).
[40d] See § 22–35.
[40e] *Re Lehman Brothers International (Europe)* [2009] EWCA Civ 1161; [2010] B.C.C. 272.

Creditors benefiting

NOTE 87. AT THE END OF THE FIRST SENTENCE ADD: *Juratowitch v Iannotti* **22–24**
[2009] FMCA 1133 at [48]–[49]. AT THE END ADD: See too *Commissioner of
Taxation v Bruton Holdings Pty Ltd* [2008] FCAFC 184; (2008) 244 A.L.R.
177 at [47]–[58], Aus FC.

Duration of right

NOTE 88. DELETE AND REPLACE BY: *Coates v McInerney* (1992) 7 W.A.R. 537; **22–25**
Lemery Holdings Pty Ltd v Reliance Financial Services Pty Ltd [2008]
NSWSC 1344; (2008–09) 74 N.S.W.L.R. 550. Compare §§ 14–59 and 14–60
(retirement) and see those paragraphs (including Supplement) as to whether
the trustee ceasing to hold office is entitled to retain, as against a new
trustee, the trust assets as security for an accrued right of indemnity.

Priorities between creditors

NOTE 93. DELETE AND REPLACE BY: See Insolvency Act 1986, ss.175, 328 and **22–29**
386–387 (the last as amended by Insolvency Act 2000, ss.1, 3, Sch.1, paras.1,
9, Sch. 3, paras.1, 15; Enterprise Act 2002, ss.248(3), 251(3), Sch.17, paras.9,
34; Insolvency Act 1986 (Amendment) (No 2) Regulations 2002 (SI 2002/
1240), regs.3, 16).

NOTE 2. DELETE AND REPLACE BY: Insolvency Rules 1986, r.4.75(1)(*e*) (as **22–31**
substituted by Insolvency (Amendment) Rules 2004 (SI 2004/584), r.10) and
r.6.98(1)(*e*) (as substituted by *ibid.*, r.2).

NOTE 3. DELETE AND REPLACE BY: Insolvency Rules 1986, r.4.96(1) (as
amended by Insolvency (Amendment) Rules 2010 (SI 2010/686), r.2, Sch.1,
para.196) and r.6.116(1).

Recoupment from beneficiaries

IN THE SECOND SENTENCE DELETE authority AND REPLACE BY: English **22–32**
authority.

AT THE END OF THE SECOND SENTENCE INSERT A NEW NOTE 5a: See *Marginson v
Ian Potter & Co.* (1976) 136 C.L.R. 161 at 175–176, Aus HC; *Ron Kingham
Real Estate Pty Ltd v Edgar* [1999] 2 Qd. R. 439, Qd. CA.

NOTE 6. DELETE FIRST SENTENCE AND REPLACE BY: Insolvency Act 1986, s.238 **22–33**
(as amended by Enterprise Act 2002, s.248(3), Sch.17, paras.9, 25) and s.339
(as amended by Civil Partnership Act 2004, s.261(1), Sch.27, para.119).

NOTE 7. DELETE FIRST SENTENCE AND REPLACE BY: Insolvency Act 1986, s.240
(as amended by Enterprise Act 2002, ss.248(3), 278(2), Sch.17, paras.9, 26,
Sch.26) and s.341 (as prospectively amended by Criminal Justice Act 1988,
s.170(2), Sch.16).

NOTE 8. DELETE SECOND SENTENCE AND REPLACE BY: There is no corresponding provision for companies in liquidation; *cf.* Insolvency Act 1986,
s.241 (as amended by Insolvency (No.2) Act 1994, s.1 and Enterprise Act
2002, s.248(3), Sch.17, paras.9, 27).

4. BREACH OF TRUST

Voluntary arrangements

22–35 NOTE 11. AFTER s.260(2) INSERT: (as amended by Insolvency Act 2000, s.3, Sch.3, paras.1, 10). AFTER s.382(1) INSERT: (as prospectively amended by Criminal Justice Act 1988, s.170(2), Sch.16). DELETE ss.5(2) and (3) AND REPLACE BY: ss.3(3) and 5(2) (as amended by Insolvency Act 2000, ss.2(*a*), 15(1), Sch.2, Pt I, paras.1, 6).

Proof for liability for breach of trust

22–36 NOTE 15. IN THE FIRST SENTENCE AFTER s.382(1) INSERT: (as prospectively amended by Criminal Justice Act 1988, s.170(2), Sch.16). IN THE THIRD SENTENCE DELETE Insolvency Rules 1986, rr.4.73 and 4.180 AND REPLACE BY: Insolvency Rules 1986, r.4.73 (as amended by Insolvency (Amendment) Rules 2003 (SI 2003/1730), r.7, Sch.1, Pt 4, para.18. and Insolvency (Amendment) Rules 2010 (SI 2010/686), r.2, Sch.1, paras.1, 191) and r.4.180.

Quantum of proof

22–39 NOTE 21. AFTER r.4.93(1) INSERT: (as amended by Insolvency (Amendment) Rules 2010 (SI 2010/686), r.2, Sch.1, para.195(1), (3)). AFTER r.6.113 INSERT: (as amended by Insolvency (Amendment) Rules 1987 (SI 1987/1919), r.3(1), Sch., Pt 1, para.112).

Secured creditors

22–48 NOTE 52. DELETE AND REPLACE BY: Insolvency Rules 1986, r.4.75(1)(*e*) (as substituted by Insolvency (Amendment) Rules 2004 (SI 2004/584), r.10) and r.6.98(1)(*e*) (as substituted by *ibid.*, r.2).

NOTE 54. DELETE FIRST SENTENCE AND REPLACE BY: Insolvency Rules 1986, r.4.96(1) (as amended by Insolvency (Amendment) Rules 2010 (SI 2010/686), r.2, Sch.1, para.196) and r.6.116(1).

Preferences

22–50 NOTE 55. AT THE END OF THE SECOND SENTENCE INSERT AFTER s.435(5): (as amended by Companies Act 2006 (Consequential Amendments, Transitional Provisions and Savings) Order 2009 (SI 2009/1941), art.2(1), Sch.1, para.82).

CHAPTER 23

DISCLOSURE TO PERSONS INTERESTED UNDER THE TRUST

1. INTRODUCTION

Potentially controversial nature of issues concerning disclosure to beneficiaries on demand

NOTE 1. AFTER THE THIRD SENTENCE ADD: For a case where a trustee failed to **23–05** apply for directions and suffered an adverse costs order in proceedings commenced by a beneficiary, see *Wingate v Butterfield Trust (Bermuda) Ltd (Costs)* [2008] SC (Bda) 6; [2008] W.T.L.R. 593.

Sources of law about disclosure under trust law

NOTE 2. FOR THE REFERENCE TO Cayman Islands Trust Law, SEE NOW (2011 **23–06** Revision), s.102. Trusts (Guernsey) Law 1989, ss.21, 22 and 33 HAVE BEEN REPLACED WITH AMENDMENTS BY Trusts (Guernsey) Law 2007, ss.25, 26 and 38 with effect from March 17, 2008.

2. TRUSTEES' DUTY TO NOTIFY BENEFICIARIES OF THEIR INTERESTS

Adult beneficiaries of lifetime settlement with future interests

NOTE 8. FOR THE REFERENCE TO Underhill and Hayton, *Law of Trusts and* **23–08** *Trustees*, SEE NOW (18th edn), §§ 50.2 and 56.9–56.10.

NOTE 10. ADD: In *Breakspear v Ackland* [2008] EWHC 220 (Ch); [2009] Ch. 32 the omission of trustees to notify adult beneficiaries with defeasible reversionary vested interests of the existence of the settlement until ten years after its creation was relied upon by them as demonstrating a wrong-headed and unfair tight-fistedness with regard to disclosure of information, but the court declined to consider whether the trustees had good reason for their past attitude to disclosure of information, see at [81] and [89].

Modification of the duty of disclosure by the terms of the trust

23–14 AT THE END OF THE TEXT ADD: A clause in a discretionary trust that the trustees are not bound to disclose the existence of the trust to any beneficiary who has not taken an absolute and indefeasible interest under the trust does not render the trust as a whole invalid, though it remains unclear whether such a clause is in itself invalid.[41a]

3. DISCLOSURE BY TRUSTEES TO BENEFICIARIES ON DEMAND

Schmidt v Rosewood Trust Ltd—the general principles

23–18 AT THE END ADD: Following *Schmidt v Rosewood Trust Ltd*[79a] it is now settled in English law that the court should approach a request by a beneficiary for disclosure of a document in the possession of the trustees in their capacity as such as one calling for the exercise of discretion rather than the adjudication upon a proprietary right.[79b]

The role of the court and the trustees

23–20 DELETE THE TEXT FROM THE THIRD SENTENCE TO THE END AND REPLACE BY: The court does have an original jurisdiction to intervene in the administration of the trust, but if a trustee's refusal to make disclosure to a beneficiary cannot be successfully challenged on those limited grounds, the court may not be persuaded, merely because of the trustee's refusal to make disclosure, to intervene at all in the administration of the trust under its supervisory jurisdiction, so leaving the trustees' refusal to stand.[86a] The trustees therefore have a central role in the decision making process on disclosure. Disclosure will, in the first place, be sought by beneficiaries from trustees. Normally applications for disclosure will be dealt with by trustees and the court will not be involved. In many circumstances, for example in relation to disclosure of trust instruments and accounts to principal beneficiaries with vested interests, trustees have no real choice to refuse disclosure save in special circumstances.[86b] But trustees need to have a discretion for the same reasons as the court needs to have a discretion. And so in the context of disclosure of confidential information the trustees have a discretion to determine whether, what and how disclosure should be made and, unless they make an application to the court seeking to surrender their discretion, the decision will be that of the trustees and the decision will stand in the

---

[41a] *Tam Mei Kam v HSBC International Trustee Ltd* [2011] HKCFA 34 at [41]–[47]; affirming sub nom. *Re Estate of Mui Yim Fong* [2010] HKCA 197; [2010] 4 H.K.L.R.D. 69. The HK CA decided in favour of the validity of the clause, see [2010] HKCA 197 at [62], but the HK CFA did not decide the point though acknowledged that "it may be void", see [2011] HKCFA 34 at [45].

[79a] [2003] UKPC 26; [2003] 2 A.C. 709.

[79b] *Breakspear v Ackland* [2008] EWHC 220 (Ch); [2009] Ch. 32 at [52] (though note that *Schmidt v Rosewood Trust Ltd*, above, has not received universal acclaim abroad, see *McDonald v Ellis* [2007] NSWSC 1068; (2008–09) 72 N.S.W.L.R. 605 for a critical view).

[86a] *Breakspear v Ackland* [2008] EWHC 220 (Ch); [2009] Ch. 32 at [69]–[71].

[86b] See § 23–24.

absence of a successful challenge to the decision or successful invocation of the supervisory jurisdiction.[86c]

AFTER § 23–20 INSERT THE FOLLOWING NEW PARAGRAPH AND HEADING:

Disclosure under the court's supervisory jurisdiction as a precursor to hostile litigation

The court's jurisdiction to supervise and where necessary intervene in the **23–20A** administration of a trust by ordering disclosure of documents or information is limited to cases where disclosure is sought by a beneficiary (or other person interested under the trust) in his capacity as such and does not enable a stranger to the trust to obtain disclosure as a form of pre-action disclosure for the purpose of hostile proceedings against the trustees[87] or indeed enable trustees to obtain to obtain disclosure against a person otherwise than in his capacity as a beneficiary (or other person interested under the trust) as a form of pre-action disclosure.[88] In such a case disclosure may be obtained only if a proper case is made for pre-action disclosure under a quite different jurisdiction from that now under consideration.[89] There is, however, a different kind of case where a beneficiary seeks disclosure against a background of hostility between him and the trustees, and it is obvious that the application for disclosure is being made in anticipation that disclosure, if made, will be followed by a breach of trust claim by the beneficiary against the trustees. Though beneficiaries rarely help themselves by adopting a rude or excessively aggressive attitude in seeking disclosure from trustees, we do not consider that the fact that the beneficiary's purpose in seeking disclosure is to assess the prospects of a breach of trust action is a reason why disclosure should not be ordered, That is because the jurisdiction is based on the accountability of trustees[89a] and beneficiaries have a legitimate interest in seeking disclosure so that they are in a position to assess whether the trustees have properly accounted for their conduct of the trusteeship, and if not to seek an appropriate remedy. Nor do we think that fear a breach of trust claim could ever be a good reason for trustees refusing disclosure, and so if that was the only reason for declining or limiting disclosure, the duty of the trustees in making disclosure would be clear. There may, of course, be other circumstances which militate against disclosure, and so the fact that the trustees fear a breach of trust action does not mean that disclosure must be made. Nevertheless, in a case where the beneficiary does appear to have a real grievance or potential grievance, and is not merely a time-wasting troublemaker intent on disrupting the sound administration of the trust to the detriment of other beneficiaries, it may be easier than otherwise would be the case for the beneficiary to persuade the court to intervene under the supervisory jurisdiction, having regard to the conflict between the trustee's

---

[86c] *Breakspear v Ackland*, above, at [67] and [73]; and on the trustees' discretion see too *Rouse v IOOF Australia Trustees Ltd* [1999] SASC 181; [2000] W.T.L.R. 111 at [105].

[87] *Re C.A. Settlement* 2002 J.L.R. 312, Jersey RC; *Re Internine Trust and Azali Trust* [2006] JCA 093; 2006 J.L.R. 195 at [25].

[88] *Re A Settlement* [2010] JCA 231 at [34(ii)].

[89] See §§ 23–93 to 23–94.

[89a] See § 23–16.

duty to give proper consideration to an application for disclosure and his personal interest in not being sued for breach of trust.[89b]

AFTER § 23–21 INSERT THE FOLLOWING NEW PARAGRAPH AND HEADING:

Trusts and estates in administration

23–21A We consider that generally similar principles apply in relation to disclosure to beneficiaries by personal representatives of an unadministered estate as apply to disclosure by trustees to beneficiaries of a trust. Beneficiaries of an unadministered estate do not have a proprietary interest in particular assets of the estate,[96a] but since the right to seek disclosure is not founded on the existence of a proprietary interest, the focus on the absence of such an interest is liable to lead one astray.[96b] Personal representatives of an unadministered estate are trustees for many purposes,[96c] are accountable to their beneficiaries,[96d] and have a duty to their beneficiaries of due administration.[96e] The court has jurisdiction, in administration proceedings, to supervise and where appropriate intervene in the administration of an estate.[96f] These matters are a sufficient basis, in our view, for the application of the *Schmidt* principles to an unadministered estate. Rights for beneficiaries of unadministered estate to seek disclosure of information in relation to the estate have been accepted in Canada,[96g] though not in New Zealand.[96h] In our view, in English law, beneficiaries of an unadministered estate have a right to seek disclosure in relation to matters concerning the estate, such as what assets are comprised in the estate and whether or not assets have in which the deceased was interested were subject to a beneficial joint tenancy and so passed by survivorship, but not (save in the context of a probate action) disclosure of previous wills of the deceased since that does not relate to the will proved by the personal representatives under which the rights of the beneficiaries seeking disclosure arise.[96i]

[89b] Compare *Re A Settlement* [2011] JRC 109 at [7]–[15].

[96a] *Commissioner of Stamp Duties v Livingston* [1965] A.C. 694, PC.

[96b] *Att.-Gen. of Ontario v Stavro* (1994) 119 D.L.R. (4th) 750 at 756, Ontario.

[96c] *Bernstein v Jacobson* [2008] EWHC 3454; [2010] W.T.L.R. 559.

[96d] See generally Williams, Mortimer and Sunnucks, *Executors, Administrators and Probate* (19th edn), § 61–23.

[96e] See *e.g. Re Leigh's Will Trusts* [1970] Ch. 277 at 281, cited with approval in *Marshall v Kerr* [1995] 1 A.C. 148 at 157, HL.

[96f] On administration proceedings concerning estates, see generally Williams, Mortimer and Sunnucks, *Executors, Administrators and Probate* (19th edn), Chap.60.

[96g] *Att.-Gen. of Ontario v Stavro*, above, considered in *Schmidt v Rosewood Trust Ltd* [2003] UKPC 26; [2002] 2 A.C. 709 at [62].

[96h] *Re Maguire* (2010–11) 13 I.T.E.L.R. 139, NZ HC. *Att.-Gen. of Ontario v Stavro*, above, was not cited in this case, though *Schmidt v Rosewood Trust Ltd*, above, which did discuss the *Stavro* case as a case about unadministered estate, was cited.

[96i] In *Re Maguire*, above, the court rejected claims for disclosure of (i) documents relating to a property in which the deceased was interested and which was said to have passed by survivorship and (ii) claims for disclosure of former wills of the deceased. We consider that, so far as English law is concerned, the decision is incorrect as to (i) but correct as to (ii).

Accounts and information about the state of the trust

Duty to keep accounts

NOTE 99. ADD: *Jones v Firkin-Flood* [2008] EWHC 2417 (Ch) at [216]. **23–22**

Disclosure of trust accounts to beneficiaries

NOTE 4. AT THE END ADD: In *McDonald v Ellis* [2007] NSWSC 1068; (2008– **23–23**
09) 72 N.S.W.L.R. 605 a beneficiary with a fixed interest was considered to
have an entitlement to inspect trusts accounts on the basis of a proprietary
right, that being preferred as the basis for the rights of a beneficiary with a
fixed interest to inspection over the principles of *Schmidt v Rosewood Trust
Ltd* [2003] UKPC 26, [2003] 2 A.C. 709. Contrast the earlier case *Avanes v
Marshall* [2007] NSWSC 191; (2007) 68 N.S.W.L.R. 595 where the *Schmidt*
principles were accepted as applicable to a beneficiary with a fixed interest.

Remedies for default

AT THE END OF THE TEXT ADD: The court may decline to order an account **23–27**
where an order for disclosure of documents and information by the trustee
to the beneficiary is an adequate and more cost-efficient remedy.[25a]

Information about the state of the trust

AFTER THE TEXT TO N.31 ADD: Ordinarily a beneficiary may seek reasonable **23–28**
information and supporting documents about transactions concerning the
trust property and property owned by companies owned by the trust entered
into by or with the authority of the trustees.[31a]

AFTER § 23–28 INSERT THE FOLLOWING NEW SUB-HEADING AND PARAGRAPH:

Information about trustee charges

Ordinarily a beneficiary may seek reasonable breakdowns and supporting **23–28A**
documents in relation to fees and expenses of the trustees, including fees and
expenses charged to companies owned by the trust.[32a]

*Information about discretionary distributions to or for the benefit of
beneficiaries*

NOTE 33. AT THE END ADD: *Wingate v Butterfield Trust (Bermuda) Ltd* [2007] **23–29**
SC (Bda) 67; [2008] W.T.L.R. 357 at [37]. Contrast *Re A Settlement* [2011]
JRC 109 at [32]–[35] where the court directed disclosure of a schedule of
distributions specifying the dates and amounts of distributions but with
redaction of the identity of the beneficiaries receiving the distributions,

---

[25a] *Wingate v Butterfield Trust (Bermuda) Ltd* [2007] SC (Bda) 67; [2008] W.T.L.R. 357 at [42].
[31a] *Wingate v Butterfield Trust (Bermuda) Ltd* [2007] SC (Bda) 67; [2008] W.T.L.R. 357 at
[38]–[41]. As to disclosure in relation to companies, see §§ 23–62 to 23–64.
[32a] *Walker v Cherry*, July 15, 1994, Ch D (Rich J.), unreported; *Wingate v Butterfield Trust
(Bermuda) Ltd* [2007] SC (Bda) 67; [2008] W.T.L.R. 357 at [10], [11] and [36]. As to
disclosure in relation to companies, see §§ 23–62 to 23–64. As to questioning trustee
charges, see § 20–163.

though the circumstances of that case were unusual in that a number of settlements were involved, and what was important in the context of that case was what distributions had been made from the various settlements involved rather than which particular beneficiaries had received the distributions.

Documents relating to reasons for the exercise of powers or discretions by trustees

23–37   NOTE 61. REPLACE THE REFERENCES TO n.57 and n.61 BY REFERENCES TO n.58 and n.62.

NOTE 64. ADD: *Breakspear v Ackland* [2008] EWHC 220 (Ch); [2009] Ch. 32 at [53]–[57].

Judicial discretion as to disclosure of documents relating to trustees' reasons

23–40   AT THE END ADD: In *Breakspear v Ackland*,[81a] concerned with disclosure of a settlor's letter of wishes which was determined[81b] to fall within the principle of *Re Londonderry's Settlement*,[81c] the principle was based, not on an absolute right, but rather on a discretion conferred on the trustees in the interests of the beneficiaries and the sound administration of the trust, and it was recognised that the court had a discretion to override the trustees' confidentiality.[81d]

23–41   NOTE 83. Trusts (Guernsey) Law 1989, s.33 HAS BEEN REPLACED WITH AMENDMENTS BY Trusts (Guernsey) Law 2007, s.38 with effect from March 17, 2008.

Internal trust correspondence and records, *etc.* during administration

Protection of confidentiality of other beneficiaries

23–43   NOTE 98. ADD: See too *Representation of Y* [2010] JRC 154; *Re A Settlement* [2011] JRC 109 at [20].

Legal advice and communications with lawyers

23–45   NOTE 6. ADD: *Schreuder v Murray (No.2)* [2009] WASCA 145; (2009) 260 A.L.R. 139.

AT THE END OF THE TEXT ADD: A beneficiary should, of course, seek disclosure from the trustee, or if necessary in proceedings to which the trustee is a party, and not directly from the lawyer who gave the advice since the lawyer is bound by privilege and is in no position to waive it at the instance of a beneficiary.[6a]

[81a] [2008] EWHC 220 (Ch); [2009] Ch. 32.
[81b] See § 23–53A.
[81c] [1965] Ch. 918, CA.
[81d] *Breakspear v Ackland*, above, at [54], [56] and [62]–[63].
[6a] *Cunningham v Cunningham* [2010] JRC 074.

Legal advice relating to exercise of powers

IN THE SECOND SENTENCE AFTER trustees' INSERT reasons.   **23–46**

Communications between the trustees and their lawyers

AFTER THE FIRST SENTENCE OF THE TEXT ADD: Where, however, in the context   **23–48**
of an application by the trustees for directions, extensive disclosure is sought
of communications between the trustees and their lawyers in relation to
those proceedings, the court may limit disclosure both so as to ensure that
the trustees are not inhibited in their communications with their lawyers by
the fear that all with have to be disclosed to beneficiaries involved in the
application, and to ensure that the application does not become sidetracked
into a mini investigation which will not assist the substantive hearing of the
application.[16a]

Legal advice and communications with lawyers in breach of trust actions

NOTE 18. AT THE END ADD: See too *Thommesen v Butterfield Trust (Guern-*   **23–49**
sey) Ltd 2009–10 G.L.R. 102 (hostile action by settlor for removal of
trustee).

The settlor's letter of wishes

The case for disclosure

NOTE 31. FOR THE REFERENCE TO Underhill and Hayton, *Law of Trusts and*   **23–53**
Trustees, SEE NOW (18th edn), §§ 56.51. AT THE END ADD: criticised in
Breakspear v Ackland [2008] EWHC 220 (Ch); [2009] Ch. 32 at [46]–[47] and
see [60].

DELETE THE THIRD SENTENCE, THE WORD "But" IN THE FOURTH SENTENCE, AND
THE LAST THREE SENTENCES.

AFTER § 23–53 INSERT THE FOLLOWING NEW PARAGRAPH AND HEADING:

General rule in England—no compulsory disclosure

The case for disclosure of a settlor's letter of wishes was rejected in   **23–53A**
Breakspear v Ackland,[37a] in the context of a family discretionary trust. The
basis for the rejection was this. The defining characteristic of a settlor's letter
of wishes is that it contains material which the settlor desires that the
trustees should take into account in exercising their powers. Having been
brought into existence for the purpose of serving and facilitating an inherently confidential process, the settlor's letter of wishes is properly to be
regarded as confidential, to substantially the same extent and effect as the
process which it is intended to serve. The settlor's letter of wishes is different
in character from the trust instrument. The trust instrument confers and
identifies the trustees' powers. By contrast the settlor's letter of wishes
operates exclusively within the boundaries set by the trust instrument and

---

[16a] *Re A Settlement* [2011] JRC 109 at [15] and [22]–[24].
[37a] [2008] EWHC 220 (Ch); [2009] Ch. 32, see especially at [5]–[14] and [58]–[62].

purely in furtherance of the trustees' exercise of discretionary powers, and so may properly be afforded a status of confidentiality which the trust instrument itself entirely lacks. Consequently, the trustees are in general not bound to disclose the settlor's letter of wishes and may keep it confidential from the beneficiaries, unless, in their view, disclosure is in the interests of the sound administration of the trust and the discharge of their powers and discretions.

Objections to disclosure based on the Londonderry *case*

23–54 NOTE 42. AT THE END ADD: *Bathurst (Countess) v Kleinwort Benson (Channel Islands) Trustees Ltd* [2007] W.T.L.R. 959 was effectively reversed by Trusts (Guernsey) Law 2007, s.38(1)(*b*) and (2), which expressly bring letters of wishes within the categories of documents generally excluded from disclosure.

AT THE END OF THE TEXT ADD: In England, what is crucial is not whether letters of wishes come within any particular excluded category in *Re Londonderry's Settlement*.[42a] The categories do not appear to have been formulated with letters of wishes in mind. What is crucial is that letters of wishes come within the *Londonderry* principle that documents forming part of the decision making process on the exercise of discretionary powers are protected by confidentiality. If asked, the Court of Appeal might have put letters of wishes into a separate category of documents protected by confidentiality.[42b]

23–55 DELETE THE FIRST NINE SENTENCES AND REPLACE BY: The confidentiality afforded to letters of wishes and the question whether disclosure should be refused by the trustees or the court does not in general turn on the context in which the beneficiary's demand for disclosure arises or the subjective purpose for which disclosure is sought, but rather on the objective consequences of disclosure. Even if disclosure is not sought in the context of dissatisfaction with a particular decision of the trustees, but for the purpose of evaluating a beneficiary's prospective entitlement under the trust, the disclosure sought may too easily, once obtained, be used for the purposes of challenging the subsequent exercise by the trustees of their dispositive discretion on grounds of rationality.[43] Nevertheless, despite that criticism, it is striking that the purpose for which disclosure of a letter of wishes is sought is a matter apparently to be generally disregarded as irrelevant. For instance, a beneficiary, having inherited the estate of the settlor or another relative, may wish to consider re-directing the inheritance in whole or in part to his children within two years of the death, something that is likely to have tax advantages for him and his family, and for that purpose wish to know whether the trust fund in the family discretionary trust is earmarked under the settlor's letter of wishes for him or for them. But it seems that this is a matter to be disregarded by the trustees (and the court) in deciding whether

---

[42a] [1965] Ch. 918, CA.
[42b] *Breakspear v Ackland* [2008] EWHC 220 (Ch); [2009] Ch. 32 at [24] and [65].
[43] *Breakspear v Ackland* [2008] EWHC 220 (Ch); [2009] Ch. 32 at [50]–[51], taking a critical approach to observations made in the deleted text of § 23–55.

or not to make disclosure, a restrictive approach which does not fit easily with what is said in § 23–56 which was broadly accepted in *Breakspear v Ackland*[44] subject to a qualification about the role of the settlor in asserting confidentiality.[45] The only circumstances in which the purpose for which disclosure is sought for an evaluation of a beneficiary's future prospects is relevant is where disclosure of a letter of wishes is sought for the purpose of an evaluation of the beneficiary's prospects in the context of divorce proceedings. And so trustees (and the court), though they apparently cannot assist an harmonious family which wishes to regulate its financial affairs for sound tax planning reasons, can assist a divided family where the disclosure is sought in the context of divorce proceedings.

THIS PARAGRAPH, WHICH WAS FOR THE MOST PART ENDORSED IN *Breakspear v Ackland* [2008] EWHC 220 (Ch); [2009] Ch. 32 at [62] SHOULD BE READ SUBJECT TO WHAT IS SAID IN THE REPLACEMENT TEXT OF § 23–55. **23–56**

DELETE THIS PARAGRAPH (NOT CONSIDERED IN *Breakspear v Ackland* [2008] EWHC 220 (Ch); [2009] Ch. 32) AND REPLACE BY: Where the confidentiality is of the limited character referred to in § 23–56, trustees may in a proper case make disclosure (and the court may in its discretion order disclosure if the trustees do not), but disclosure should not be made on slight grounds. For instance, an application for disclosure by a young adult beneficiary is likely to be refused if the beneficiary wants access to the settlor's letter of wishes so that he can tell whether there is no need for him to pursue his studies or training since he can expect to be able, in view of the letters of wishes, to lead a life of idleness and live off the trust. Different considerations might be thought to apply where disclosure was sought in a tax planning context[50a] or, for example, if the beneficiary was thinking of buying a house and wished to ascertain his expectations, having regard to the letter of wishes, of obtaining money for a deposit from the trust, or of obtaining support under an income discretionary trust to help pay mortgage instalments or interest. Nevertheless, it seems that such a purpose falls to be disregarded in deciding whether or not disclosure should be made.[50b] The only circumstance in which the purpose for seeking disclosure has been recognised as material is when disclosure is sought in the context of divorce proceedings.[50c] **23–57**

DELETE THE THIRD SENTENCE AND REPLACE BY: It is doubtful whether it is appropriate for the trustees to be greatly influenced by the subsequent giving or withholding of consent to disclosure by the settlor. In the absence of special terms, the confidentiality in which a letter of wishes is enfolded is something given to the trustees for them to use, in accordance with their best judgment as to the interests of the beneficiaries and the sound administration of the trust. Once the settlor has completely constituted the trust, and sent his letter of wishes, the preservation, judicious relaxation or **23–58**

---

[44] Above.
[45] *Breakspear v Ackland*, above, at [62] and see § 23–58.
[50a] See replacement text of § 23–55.
[50b] See *Breakspear v Ackland*, above, at [50]–[51] and the replacement text of § 23–55.
[50c] See § 23–55.

abandonment of that confidence is a matter for the trustees or, in an appropriate case, the court.[52a] It follows that the settlor is bound by the confidentiality and so may be unable to disclose the letter of wishes to beneficiaries without the trustees' consent. Further, it is doubtful whether it is either appropriate or legitimate for a settlor to fetter the trustees' discretion in that respect, either by the inclusion of special terms as to confidentiality in the letter of wishes itself or, still less, on any subsequent occasion.[52b]

NOTE 55. AT THE END OF THE SECOND SENTENCE ADD: (not repeated in 18th edn).

23–60   NOTE 58. ADD: See *Breakspear v Ackland* [2008] EWHC 220 (Ch); [2009] Ch. 32 at [68].

AFTER THE TEXT TO N.58 ADD: Further, if the trustees seek directions from the court blessing a refusal to disclose a letter of wishes, they will, under their duty of disclosure in such applications,[58a] need to disclose their reasons for the proposed refusal.[58b] And where the trustees make no such application, but in an application by beneficiaries for disclosure of the settlor's letter of wishes, indicate that they intend to make an application to the court for approval of a decision on the exercise of their dispositive powers which will involve a disclosure of that letter, the court may, despite opposition from the trustees, decide to exercise its supervisory jurisdiction by ordering disclosure of the settlor's letter of wishes. And so, despite the general theme of protection of the confidentiality of a settlor's letter of wishes pervading *Breakspear v Ackland*, above, disclosure of the settlor's letter of wishes was ordered in that case, as sought by the beneficiaries, because it would be disclosed anyway in the trustees' intended application, and there were in the circumstances sound reasons for disclosure sooner rather than later.[58c]

DELETE THE LAST TWO SENTENCES AND NN.59 AND 60 AND REPLACE BY: And so in *Breakspear v Ackland*[59] the judge did read the settlor's letter of wishes before reaching his decision.[60]

Company documents

AFTER § 23–64 INSERT THE FOLLOWING NEW PARAGRAPH:

[52a]   *Breakspear v Ackland* [2008] EWHC 220 (Ch); [2009] Ch. 32 at [62].
[52b]   *Breakspear v Ackland*, above, at [63]–[64].
[58a]   See § 29–299.
[58b]   *Breakspear v Ackland* [2008] EWHC 220 (Ch); [2009] Ch. 32 at [70].
[58c]   *Breakspear v Ackland*, above, at [90]–[101].
[59]   Above.
[60]   See at [95]–[97]. An order for such disclosure was refused in *Hartigan Nominees Pty Ltd v Rydge* (1992) 29 NSWLR 405 at 409, NSW CA, but largely because there was no ground for introducing new evidence in the CA. In that case, the first instance judge felt able to decide the issue of disclosure without examining the letter of wishes which remained in a sealed envelope throughout the trial, see *ibid*. Note that this procedure cannot be utilised in an application for pre-action disclosure under rules of court, compare *BSW Ltd v Balltec Ltd* [2006] EWHC 822 (Ch); [2006] All E.R. (D) 142 (Apr) at [84]–[86] (which rejects a procedure based on use of a court appointed expert), but that is a quite different kind of application, see §§ 23–90 *et seq.*, see *ibid*.

Where none of the trustees is a director of the company concerned, a ben- **23–64A** eficiary seeking disclosure under the court's supervisory jurisdiction should seek an order requiring the trustees to assert such rights as they have under company law to obtain disclosure from the directors, if necessary by separate company law proceedings. It is not a permissible exercise of the court's powers under the supervisory jurisdiction to make disclosure orders in the trust proceedings directly against the directors, even if they are also beneficiaries and before the court in their capacity as beneficiaries.[75a]

Particular beneficiaries

Objects and donees of particular powers

NOTE 89. FOR THE REFERENCE TO Thomas and Hudson, *The Law of Trusts,* **23–72** SEE NOW (2nd edn), §§ 19.07 to 19.11.

5. DISCLOSURE IN TRUST LITIGATION

Disclosure after commencement of proceedings

NOTE 50. FOR THE REFERENCE TO *Civil Procedure* (2007), Vol.1, 31.3.5 to **23–91** 31.3.30, SUBSTITUTE *Civil Procedure* (2011), Vol.1, 31.3.5 to 31.3.30.1.

Confidentiality and reasons for exercise of powers or discretions

NOTE 55. AT THE END OF THE FIRST SENTENCE ADD: *Breakspear v Ackland* **23–92** [2008] EWHC 220 (Ch); [2009] Ch. 32 at [17].

Pre-action disclosure

NOTE 61. Supreme Court Act 1981 is renamed Senior Courts Act 1981 from **23–93** October 1, 2009, see Constitutional Reform Act 2005, Sch.11, para.1 and Constitutional Reform Act 2005 (Commencement No.11) Order 2009 (SI 2009/1604).

AFTER § 23–96 INSERT THE FOLLOWING NEW PARAGRAPH AND HEADING:

Disclosure by beneficiary of trust documents held by non-party trustees

Disclosure by a party to litigation is limited to documents which are or have **23–96A** been in the control of the party to the litigation, and for this purpose the party has or has had a document in his control if he is or was in physical possession of it, or has or has had a right to possession of it, or has or has had a right to inspect or take copies of it.[77a] Under the principles of *Schmidt v Rosewood Trust Ltd*[77b] a beneficiary does not have an automatic right to disclosure of trust documents.[77c] Accordingly,[77d] in many, perhaps most

---

[75a] *Re A Settlement* [2010] JCA 231.
[77a] CPR, Pt 31, r.31.8.
[77b] [2003] UKPC 26; [2003] 2 A.C. 709.
[77c] *Schmidt v Rosewood Trust Ltd*, above, at [67]. See §§ 23–18 to 23–21.
[77d] *North Shore Ventures Ltd v Anstead Holdings Inc.* [2012] EWCA Civ 11 at [43]–[45].

cases, a disclosure order against a beneficiary of a document held by the trustee of the trust concerned would not be proper, since production by the beneficiary would depend upon the exercise of consent by a party over whom the beneficiary had no control or the exercise of discretion by the court.[77e] But it would go too far to say that an order might never be made against a beneficiary in respect of a trust document not in his physical possession, as in circumstances in which the trustee would have no ground upon which to oppose production of a document at the instance of the beneficiary.[77f] In special circumstances, a beneficiary (or settlor) may be taken as being in control of trust documents under principles unrelated to those of *Schmidt v Rosewood Trust Ltd*, as where the beneficiary settled his assets into an offshore trust at the time when he received notice of a claim against him and the evidence indicates that the true nature of the relationship between the beneficiary and the trustee is that the beneficiary (or settlor) is the puppet master in the handling of money entrusted to the trustee for the purpose of defeating the creditor's claim.[77g] Questions of disclosure by a beneficiary of trust documents not in his possession may sometimes be circumvented by a third party disclosure order[77h] against the trustees, but there are limitations on the availability of a third party disclosure order[77i] and such an order may be of no practical use in the case of offshore trusts and trustees.

6. DISCLOSURE BY OUTGOING TRUSTEES TO THEIR SUCCESSORS

Transfer of trust papers on change of trusteeship

23–97   NOTE 78. AT THE END ADD: The statement of the law in this and the next two paragraphs was approved in *Equity Trust (Bahamas) Ltd v Basel Trust Corp. (Channel Islands) Ltd* [2012] JRC 006 at [26].

7. DISCLOSURE BY AND TO SETTLORS AND PROTECTORS

Disclosure by trustees to settlor

23–103   NOTE 83. Trusts (Guernsey) Law 1989, s.22(1) has in relation to a settlor been replaced with amendments by Trusts (Guernsey) Law 2007, s.26(1)(*b*)(iii) and (2) with effect from March 17, 2008.

[77e]   *North Shore Ventures Ltd v Anstead Holdings Inc.*, above, at [45].
[77f]   *ibid.* For a case where that may be so, see § 23–24.
[77g]   *North Shore Ventures Ltd v Anstead Holdings Inc*, above, at [24]–[41]. Note that there was no requirement, for the purpose of obtaining a disclosure order, for the creditor either to obtain an order under Insolvency Act 1986, s.423 setting aside dispositions into the trust or to establish that the trust was a sham.
[77h]   CPR, Pt 31, r.31.17.
[77i]   See § 23–95.

CHAPTER 24

THE RIGHT TO CALL FOR THE TRUST PROPERTY

1. DISTRIBUTION AT THE END OF THE TRUST

Undivided shares

Generally

AFTER THE THIRD SENTENCE, INSERT A NEW NOTE 15a: Membership rights in a **24–03** company limited by guarantee may also be divided, if need be by admitting new members of the company: *Walbrook Trustees (Jersey) Ltd v Fattal* [2010] EWCA Civ 408; [2011] 1 All E.R. (Comm) 647 at [18]–[19], [29].

Trust shareholdings

NOTE 42. AT THE END ADD: See § 9–84.   **24–05**

2. BRINGING THE TRUST TO AN END

Conversion of special trust into simple trust—the rule in *Saunders v Vautier*

NOTE 52. AFTER THE SECOND SENTENCE ADD: *Austin v Wells* [2008] NSWSC **24–07(3)** 1266 at [12].

AFTER THE FIRST SENTENCE OF THE TEXT ADD: If a fund is held in trust for a **24–07(6)** beneficiary absolutely subject to a discretion of the trustee as to the mode of its application for the beneficiary, the beneficiary is entitled to the transfer to him of the whole of the fund.[58a]

NOTE 62. AT THE END ADD: *Hughes v Bourne* [2012] EWHC 2232 (Ch) **24–07(9)** (separate fund within a trust).

NOTE 66. FOR THE REFERENCE TO Scott, *The Law of Trusts*, SEE NOW Scott and **24–08** Ascher, *The Law of Trusts* (5th edn), Vol.V, §§ 34.1 *et seq.* AT THE END ADD: In connection with the rule in *Saunders v Vautier* generally, see Matthews (2006) 122 L.Q.R. 266.

Position of trustee

NOTE 67. AT THE END OF THE FIRST SENTENCE ADD: *McKnight v Ice Skating* **24–09** *Queensland Inc.* [2007] QSC 273; (2007–08) 10 I.T.E.L.R. 570 at [35].

[58a] *Webb v Oldfield* [2010] EWHC 3469 (Ch).

Likewise, a trustee in whom a lease is vested cannot be compelled by the beneficiaries to act in such a way as to put him in breach of his obligations to his landlord under the lease: *Clarence House Ltd v National Westminster Bank plc* [2009] EWCA Civ 1311; [2010] 1 W.L.R. 1216 at [45].

When the principle does not apply

Persons interested

24–12 NOTE 72. ADD: *Thorpe v R.C.C.* [2009] EWHC 611 (Ch); [2009] S.T.C. 2107 at [45] (affirmed [2010] EWCA Civ 339; [2010] S.T.C. 964) (rule has no application where there are future beneficiaries not yet in existence, however unlikely it may be that they will come into existence). *Cf.* §§ 5–59, 26–44 to 26–54.

AFTER THE FIRST SENTENCE OF THE TEXT INSERT: A requisite consent may be given either by the beneficiary concerned joining in an agreed termination of the trust with the other beneficiaries, or by way of irrevocable unilateral direction by that beneficiary to the trustees.[72a]

Objects of dispositive powers

24–13 NOTE 76. AT THE END ADD: For the objects to terminate the trust in this way, it is necessary that they (together with beneficiaries with fixed interests) are the only persons who are or may become entitled to due administration of the trust, but there is no requirement for their rights to be indefeasible: *Miskelly v Arnheim* [2008] NSWSC 1075; (2008–09) 11 I.T.E.L.R. 381 at [38]–[39].

NOTE 82. AT THE END ADD: See too *Re IMK Family Trust* [2008] JCA 196; [2008] J.L.R. 430 at [41], [109]–[115] where the Jersey CA took the view (in the context of variation of trust proceedings) that an effective variation could be made even though the trust contained a wide power of addition of beneficiaries conferred on a beneficiary (who was taken as having consented to the variation) during his lifetime and after his death on the trustees (who appear to have had no power to release this power).

Capacity

24–15 NOTE 84. DELETE THE LAST SENTENCE AND REPLACE BY: Mental Health Act 1983, s.1(2) is amended by Mental Health Act 2007, s.1 with effect from November 3, 2008: Mental Health Act 2007 (Commencement No.7 and Transitional Provisions) Order 2008 (SI 2008/1900).

24–16 NOTE 88. AT THE END ADD: *Cf.*, in Canada, *Drescher v Drescher's Estate* [2007] NSSC 352; (2007–08) 10 I.T.E.L.R. 679.

[72a] Compare § 45–89 (Supplement). For a case where a beneficiary was held to have consented by way of irrevocable unilateral direction to the trustees, see *Re IMK Family Trust* [2008] JCA 196; [2008] J.L.R. 430 at [116]–[124].

Special cases

AT THE END OF THE TEXT ADD: In theory, the rule applies to pension trusts, **24–17** but subject to the terms of the trust and to the rules according to which the fund is held.[95a]

Controlling trustees' discretions—declaring new trusts

NOTE 14. FOR THE REFERENCE TO Underhill and Hayton, *Law of Trusts and* **24–20** *Trustees*, SEE NOW (18th edn), § 66.25.

NOTE 15. ADD: *Nelson v Greening & Sykes (Builders) Ltd* [2007] EWCA Civ **24–21** 1358; (2007–08) 10 I.T.E.L.R. 689 at [55]–[56].

IN THE SECOND SENTENCE, AFTER accept new trusts, INSERT A NEW NOTE 15a: *Westpac Banking Corp. v The Bell Group Ltd* [2012] WASCA 157 at [2495], citing this passage.

[95a] *Thorpe v R.C.C.* [2010] EWCA Civ 339; [2010] S.T.C. 964 at [25]. In Canada, it has been said that the rule in *Saunders v Vautier* does not apply to pension trusts there, see *Buschau v Rogers Communications Inc* [2006] SCC 28; (2006–07) 9 I.T.E.L.R. 73, not considered in *Thorpe*. As an absolute rule, however, this was doubted in *Kidd v Canada Life* [2010] ONSC 1097, although the point was not there decided. In practice, there are likely to be contingent benefits payable which will prevent the rule from being used in the context of a pension trust, and so in practice the position in England and Canada is likely to be the same.

CHAPTER 25

CAPITAL AND INCOME

1. SCOPE OF CHAPTER

General

25–01 AT THE END ADD: And though a charitable trust does not give rise to successive interests, where the charity has a permanent endowment, the trustees must know which receipts are income and which are capital, since the latter cannot in general be spent on its purposes.

Reform

25–03 DELETE THE ENTIRE PARAGRAPH AND NN.4–11 AND REPLACE BY: Proposals have been made by the Law Commission for reform of the law stated in this chapter.[4] The proposals, which to some considerable extent depart from the prior consultation paper,[5] include the following:

> (1) Distributions from corporations to trustees holding shares, if tax-exempt, would be treated as capital. The practical effect would be that shares received in consequence of direct and indirect demergers would be treated as capital, making a change in the former but not the latter case.[6] There would be a provision to allow further categories of distribution to be so treated by delegated legislation if they became tax-exempt. The proposal would apply to existing and not merely to new trusts. That is the remnant of earlier proposals (i) to treat most distributions from corporations as capital and (ii) to give trustees a power to allocate all trust receipts between capital and income as a matter of discretion, so that the rules for classifying trust receipts (both existing and new) would have become default rules only. The reason for abandoning those proposals is that the reform would have effectively abolished the 'income in possession' trust so far as concerned the income taxation of corporate distributions; hence the restriction of the current proposal to tax-exempt distributions.

---

[4]   Law Commission Report *Capital and Income in Trusts: Classification and Apportionment* (LC No.315, 2009).

[5]   Law Commission Consultation Paper No.175 *Capital and Income in Trusts: Classification and Apportionment* (2004). See too the Trust Law Committee's Report *Capital and Income of Trusts* (1999).

[6]   For direct demergers, see §§ 25–30 *et seq.*; for indirect demergers, see § 25–34.

(2) No change is now proposed to the existing rules for classifying other corporate distributions or any other trust receipts.[7]

(3) No change is now proposed to the existing rules for classifying trust expenses.[8] The earlier proposal to give trustees a power to allocate all trust expenses (like trust receipts) between capital and income as a matter of discretion has been abandoned.

(4) The existing equitable rules of apportionment would all be abolished, including both branches of the rule in *Howe v Lord Dartmouth*,[9] subject to any contrary provision in the trust instrument. That reform would apply only to new trusts.

(5) The statutory provision for apportionment by time[10] would likewise become inapplicable to new trusts.

Much of this chapter would be obsolete in relation to new trusts if those proposals were implemented. At the time of writing, a Bill is before Parliament to implement them, though it would also introduce a new power for trustees to compensate an income beneficiary for the loss of income caused by the making of a distribution treated as capital.[11]

2. WHAT RECEIPTS ARE CAPITAL AND WHAT ARE INCOME

General

NOTE 13. AT THE END OF THE FIRST SENTENCE INSERT: *cf. Aribisala v St James* **25–05** *Homes (Grosvenor Dock) Ltd* [2007] EWHC 1694 (Ch); [2007] 3 E.G.L.R. 39.

AT THE END OF THE FOURTH SENTENCE INSERT A NEW NOTE 14a: As in *Cunard's Trustees v I.R.C.* [1946] 1 All E.R. 159, CA.

NOTE 15. FOR THE REFERENCE TO the Standard Provisions of the Society of Trust and Estate Practitioners, SEE NOW (2nd edn), para.21.2.

DELETE THE LAST SENTENCE AND N.17 AND REPLACE BY: But a direction or power to treat income as capital, having the effect that the income would be retained, had formerly to be confined so as to be compatible with the statutory restrictions on accumulations, now repealed (for most instruments taking effect on or after April 6, 2010).[17]

---

[7] For the existing rules as to distributions from corporations, see §§ 25–21 *et seq.*; for the existing rules as to receipts from land, see §§ 25–06 *et seq.*; and for the existing rules as to other receipts, see §§ 25–41 *et seq.*

[8] For the existing rules as to trust expenses, see §§ 25–52 *et seq.*

[9] For the first branch of the rule in *Howe v Lord Dartmouth*, see §§ 25–70 *et seq.*; for the second branch, see §§ 25–97 *et seq.*; for the other equitable rules of apportionment, see §§ 25–88 *et seq.*, §§ 25–116 *et seq.* and §§ 25–123 *et seq.*

[10] For which see §§ 25–129 *et seq.*

[11] See cl. 3 of the Bill.

[17] See §§ 5–100 to 5–100B (including Supplement), § 5–107.

Land

Leases

25–13 Note 37. Delete the second sentence and replace by: In *Re Medows* [1898] 1 Ch. 300 the tenant for life of a manor was held solely entitled to fines paid by tenants for the renewal of leases of copyhold land when he was under no obligation to renew but the receipt of a fine on renewal was the customary mode of enjoyment of the manor.

Shares, debentures and other securities

Ordinary dividends

25–23 Note 98. Add: A special dividend out of distributable profits has been treated as income in the hands of trustees even though it amounted to substantially the whole of the current market value of the shares and even though the rights of those shares to participate in capital was reduced at the same time as the dividend was authorised: *Trustees of the Bessie Taube Discretionary Settlement Trust v R.C.C.* [2010] UKFTT 473 (TC).

Enhanced scrip dividends

25–29 At the end of the third sentence insert a new note 14a: For example, in *Howell v Trippier* [2004] EWCA Civ 885; [2004] S.T.C. 1245 the cash dividend was £700 and the bonus shares offered in the alternative were worth over £15 million.

After the fifth sentence of the text insert: Legislation apart, the treatment of the shares distributed is as follows.

At the end of the text add: It has been held, however, that the effect of the income tax legislation is to deem the scrip to be income not merely for the purposes of income tax[18a] but also for trust purposes.[18b]

Distributions of shares in other companies—direct demergers

25–31 Note 25. In the second sentence delete *Re Rudd's Settlement Trusts* and replace by *Re Rudd's Will Trusts*.

25–32 Note 33. For the reference to the Standard Provisions of the Society of Trust and Estate Practitioners, see now (2nd edn), para.21.1.

Trustees controlling company

25–40 Note 51. For the reference to the Standard Provisions of the Society of Trust and Estate Practitioners, see now (2nd edn), para.21.1.2.

[18a] See *Howell v Trippier* [2004] EWCA Civ 885; [2004] S.T.C. 1245, a decision on Income and Corporation Taxes Act 1988, s.249(6) (repealed and replaced by Income Tax (Trading and Other Income) Act 2005, s.410).

[18b] *Pierce v Wood* [2009] EWHC 3225 (Ch); [2010] W.T.L.R. 253, holding that to be the effect of *Howell v Trippier*, above; *sed quaere*.

AT THE END OF THE PARAGRAPH ADD: Where the terms of a trust require minimum annual distributions to be made to income beneficiaries determined by reference to the total return of trust assets, the trustees may cause a company controlled by them to pay sufficient income to the trustees to enable those distributions to be made.[51a]

AFTER § 25–44 INSERT THE FOLLOWING NEW PARAGRAPH AND HEADING:

National Savings Certificates

The nature of returns (to use a neutral expression) on National Savings **25–44A** Certificates depends on the terms and conditions of the particular issue. The index-linked growth, and not merely the interest, has been held to be income.[59a]

Damages and equitable compensation

AFTER THE FIFTH SENTENCE INSERT: Where the income beneficiary is precluded **25–47** from complaining of a loss of income by laches or acquiescence but the capital beneficiary is not, compensation for the loss will be payable only after the termination of the income interest and will go solely to the capital beneficiary.[66a]

3. USUAL INCIDENCE OF EXPENSES

Generally

NOTE 86. FOR THE REFERENCE TO the Standard Provisions of the Society of **25–52** Trust and Estate Practitioners, SEE NOW (2nd edn), para.21.2.

DELETE THE PENULTIMATE SENTENCE AND N.92 AND REPLACE BY: Otherwise, the test is the benefit of the whole trust estate, so that expenses incurred for the benefit of both the income and capital beneficiaries must be charged against capital alone; it is only those expenses which are incurred exclusively for the benefit of the income beneficiaries that may be charged against income.[92]

NOTE 93. DELETE AND REPLACE BY: *ibid.*, at [17], [30]–[33], [37].

NOTE 96. AFTER THE SECOND SENTENCE INSERT: (For later proceedings, see **25–53** *Page v West* [2010] EWHC 504 (Ch); [2010] W.T.L.R. 1811, citing this passage of the text at [42]).

[51a] *Canada Trust Co. v Browne* [2010] ONSC 4118; (2010–11) 13 I.T.E.L.R. 648 at [44]–[59].
[59a] *Martin v Triggs Turner Barton* [2009] EWHC 1920 (Ch); [2009] All E.R. (D) 12 (Aug) at [101]–[105]. *Cf. Re Holder* [1953] Ch. 468.
[66a] *Sinclair v Sinclair* [2009] EWHC 926 (Ch) at [74]–[75]. See too §§ 44–38.
[92] *R.C.C. v Trustees of the Peter Clay Discretionary Trust* [2008] EWCA Civ 1441; [2009] Ch. 296 at [29].

Loss on business

25–60 NOTE 29. AFTER THE REFERENCE TO *Upton v Brown* INSERT: *Raftland Pty Ltd v Commissioner of Taxation* [2008] HCA 21 at [66]–[69], citing this paragraph of the text.

Trust administration

Trustee's remuneration

25–61 NOTE 33. DELETE THE FIRST SENTENCE AND REPLACE BY: Public Trustee (Fees) Order 2008 (SI 2008/611), art.3.

25–62 DELETE THE EIGHTH SENTENCE AND N.38 AND REPLACE BY: Time charges should be apportioned according to the work actually done, so that capital bears the general costs of administering the trust but income bears the costs of work which is exclusively for the benefit of income beneficiaries, *e.g.* time spent in considering to whom and in what amounts income should be distributed where there is a discretionary trust of income;[38] and the same treatment should be given to a fixed fee.[38a]

Other general administration costs

25–63 NOTE 44. DELETE THE SECOND SENTENCE AND INSERT AT THE END OF THE FIRST: (point not considered on appeal in the HC or the CA, see [2007] EWHC 2661 (Ch); [2008] Ch. 291 and [2008] EWCA Civ 1441; [2009] Ch. 296, but Special Commissioners' ruling consistent with the CA's decision).

NOTE 46. DELETE AND REPLACE BY: *R.C.C. v Trustees of the Peter Clay Discretionary Trust*, above, at [40]–[41].

NOTE 49. AT THE END ADD: (point not taken on appeal in the HC or the CA, see [2007] EWHC 2661 (Ch) at [37] and [2008] EWCA Civ 1441; [2009] Ch. 296 at [6]).

Accounts and audit

25–64 NOTE 50. AFTER THE FIRST SENTENCE INSERT: The Special Commissioners' decision on that point was not appealed either to the HC or to the CA, see [2008] EWCA Civ 1441; [2009] Ch. 296 at [6]–[7], [17]; but the judgment of the CA seems to be at least consistent with it, at [32]–[33].

DELETE THE LAST TWO SENTENCES OF THE TEXT AND REPLACE BY: But even though it is part of the purpose of the accounts to identify the trust income, that function is as much for the benefit of the capital beneficiaries as for that of the income beneficiaries, unless there is accountancy work concerning the income beneficiaries alone (*e.g.* where there are concurrent income interests);

---

[38] *R.C.C. v Trustees of the Peter Clay Discretionary Trust* [2008] EWCA Civ 1441; [2009] Ch. 296 at [30]–[33], [38].
[38a] *ibid.*

and except in such a case it seems difficult to justify any course except that of debiting the whole cost to capital.[54-55]

NOTE 58. DELETE.   **25–65**

DELETE THE LAST SENTENCE AND N.59 AND REPLACE BY: Nonetheless, the decision has recently been treated as standing for the proposition that where work is done for the benefit of both tenant for life and remainderman it is done for the estate as a whole and should therefore fall entirely on capital, the income beneficiary contributing by his loss of income on the amount expended;[58-59] and so it seems that the cost of the audit should be so borne.

Legal costs

NOTE 65. AT THE END ADD: For the incidence of the costs of an unsuccessful **25–66** claim for breach of trust, to the extent that they are ultimately borne by the trust fund, see § 21–98 (including Supplement).

A general discretion under the Trustee Act 2000?

NOTE 76. FOR THE REFERENCE TO Kessler, *Drafting Trusts and Will Trusts*, SEE **25–67** NOW (9th edn), § 21–28. FOR THE REFERENCE TO Underhill and Hayton, *Law of Trusts and Trustees*, SEE NOW (18th) edn, §§ 47.2 to 47.4. FOR THE REFERENCE TO Thomas and Hudson, *Law of Trusts*, SEE NOW (2nd edn), § 10.70.

Time of obligation and time apportionment

NOTE 80. DELETE AND REPLACE BY: *Cf. R.C.C. v Trustees of the Peter Clay* **25–69** *Discretionary Trust* [2007] EWHC 2661 (Ch); [2008] Ch. 291 at [50]–[56], holding that expenses could properly be deducted from income on either an accruals basis or a cash basis for the purpose of income tax, if done consistently (point not taken on appeal, [2008] EWCA Civ 1441; [2009] Ch. 296).

4. IMPLIED DUTY TO CONVERT RESIDUARY PERSONALTY—FIRST BRANCH OF THE RULE IN *HOWE V LORD DARTMOUTH*

Where the first branch of the rule does not apply

Express exclusion—authorised investments

NOTE 89. FOR THE REFERENCE TO the Standard Provisions of the Society of **25–74** Trust and Estate Practitioners, SEE NOW (2nd edn), para.21.1.1(i).

[54-55] In *Trustees of the Peter Clay Discretionary Trust v. R.C.C.* [2007] SPC 595; [2007] S.T.C. (S.C.D.) 362 the Special Commissioners approved the debiting of the costs of the income accounts to income and the costs of the balance sheet and capital account to capital; but although that part of their decision was not the subject of the appeal to the CA, the judgment of that court is not readily reconcilable with it, see [2008] EWCA Civ 1441; [2009] Ch. 296. *Cf.* the treatment of the cost of auditing trust accounts, see § 25–65.

[58-59] *Trustees of the Peter Clay Discretionary Trust v. R.C.C.*, above, at [22]–[24], [28].

NOTE 91. FOR THE REFERENCE TO the Standard Provisions of the Society of Trust and Estate Practitioners, SEE NOW (2nd edn), para.4.1.

5. INCOME OF PARTS OF ESTATE LATER APPLIED TO DEBTS AND LEGACIES – *ALLHUSEN V WHITTELL*

The rule in *Allhusen v Whittell*

25–88 NOTE 40. DELETE THE REFERENCE IN THE SECOND SENTENCE TO Income and Corporation Taxes Act 1988 AND REPLACE BY Corporation Tax Act 2009.

When the rule in *Allhusen v Whittell* does not apply

25–93 NOTE 57. FOR THE REFERENCE TO *Williams on Wills*, SEE NOW (9th edn), Vol.2, §§ 214.19, 214.43 to 214.47. FOR THE REFERENCE TO Kessler, *Drafting Trusts and Will Trusts*, SEE NOW (9th edn), § 21–32. FOR THE REFERENCE TO the Standard Provisions of the Society of Trust and Estate Practitioners, SEE NOW (2nd edn).

NOTE 63. DELETE THE REFERENCE IN THE SECOND SENTENCE TO Income and Corporation Taxes Act 1988 AND REPLACE BY Corporation Tax Act 2009.

6. APPORTIONMENT OF INCOME PENDING CONVERSION – SECOND BRANCH OF THE RULE IN *HOWE V LORD DARTMOUTH*

Where the second branch of the rule does not apply

25–99 NOTE 84. FOR THE REFERENCE TO *Williams on Wills*, SEE NOW (9th edn), Vol.2, §§ 214.19, 214.35 to 214.42. FOR THE REFERENCE TO Kessler, *Drafting Trusts and Will Trusts*, SEE NOW (9th edn), § 21–32.

Power to postpone sale or retain investments

25–102 NOTE 97. FOR THE REFERENCE TO Underhill and Hayton, *Law of Trusts and Trustees*, SEE NOW (18th) edn, § 46.11.

7. LIFE TENANT'S RIGHTS IN REVERSIONARY INTERESTS – *RE EARL OF CHESTERFIELD'S TRUSTS*

Where the rule does not apply

25–121 NOTE 52. FOR THE REFERENCE TO *Williams on Wills*, SEE NOW (9th edn), Vol.2, §§ 214.19, 214.35 to 214.42. FOR THE REFERENCE TO Kessler, *Drafting Trusts and Will Trusts*, SEE NOW (9th edn), § 21–32.

25–122 NOTE 60. FOR THE REFERENCE TO the Standard Provisions of the Society of Trust and Estate Practitioners, SEE NOW (2nd edn), para.21.1.1(ii).

9. TIME APPORTIONMENT

The Apportionment Act 1870

Interest

NOTE 96. DELETE AND REPLACE BY: Under Inheritance Tax Act 1984, s.235 (as **25–132** amended by Finance Act 1989, s.180(4), (7) and Finance Act 2009, s.105(4)(b)).

Excluding apportionment

NOTE 24. FOR THE REFERENCE TO *Williams on Wills*, SEE NOW (9th edn), Vol.2, **25–142** §§ 214.19, 214.48 to 214.54. FOR THE REFERENCE TO Kessler, *Drafting Trusts and Will Trusts*, SEE NOW (9th edn), § 21–54. FOR THE REFERENCE TO the Standard Provisions of the Society of Trust and Estate Practitioners, SEE NOW (2nd edn), para.8.

CHAPTER 26

DISTRIBUTION OF THE TRUST FUND WITHOUT THE INTERVENTION OF THE COURT

2. GENERAL DUTY OF TRUSTEE

The trustee must distribute correctly

Proof of entitlement

26–03 NOTE 3. FOR THE REFERENCE TO *Snell's Equity*, SEE NOW (32nd edn), §§ 4–017 *et seq.*

Liability for incorrect distribution

AFTER § 26–04 INSERT THE FOLLOWING NEW PARAGRAPH:

26–04A Trustees may be uncertain that they have identified all the beneficiaries, a difficulty most likely to arise where the beneficiaries are numerous, as in the case of pension funds. There may be beneficiaries known to the trustees whom they cannot trace, beneficiaries known to them who decline to accept benefits and beneficiaries unknown to them. Various courses are open to the trustees. They may make inquiries to trace beneficiaries[15a] and they may protect themselves by advertising.[15b] They may make a retainer, if they can estimate the fund required, though doing so will prevent them from winding up the trust. In some cases they may effect insurance and distribute only to the known beneficiaries.[15c] Where they have a power to exclude beneficiaries, it may well be a proper exercise of the power to exclude such beneficiaries.[15d] They may ask the court to make a *Benjamin* order, an order authorising them to distribute on a specified footing, *e.g.* that a given person is dead.[15e] As a last resort, they may pay the trust fund into court.[15f]

Insurance

26–06 DELETE THE SECOND SENTENCE AND N.19 AND REPLACE BY: Such insurance will necessarily benefit the trustee by protecting him, to some extent at least, from a claim for breach of trust. But a trustee is not entitled to effect

---

[15a] See §§ 26–22 to 26–24.
[15b] See §§ 26–08 to 26–18.
[15c] See § 26–06.
[15d] *NBPF Pension Trustees Ltd. v Warnock-Smith* [2008] EWHC 455 (Ch); [2008] 2 All ER (Comm) 740 (where it is not wholly clear, see [38], how the power had arisen).
[15e] See §§ 27–15 *et seq.*, together with §§ 26–45, 26–50.
[15f] See §§ 27–42 *et seq.*

insurance with a view to his own benefit, whether against a liability for a failure to distribute correctly or for other breach of trust,[19] unless so authorised by the trust instrument; the test is whether the insurance will be for the benefit of the beneficiaries,[19a] as it often will be where the alternative is for the trustee to make a retainer against a possible claim.[19b]

NOTE 22. DELETE AND REPLACE BY: Charities Act 2011, s.189.

3. ADVERTISEMENT, SEARCHES AND INQUIRIES FOR THOSE ENTITLED

Advertisement for claims

Effect of advertisement

NOTE 39. AT THE END ADD: *MCP Pension Trustees Ltd v AON Pension* 26–14 *Trustees Ltd* [2010] EWCA Civ 377; [2010] All E.R. (D) 48 (Aug).

AT THE END OF THE TEXT ADD: For that purpose a trustee has notice of claims of which he had at any time been aware, even though he later overlooked or forgot them;[39a] and notice to the trustee's agent is notice to the trustee.[39b]

Inquiries

NOTE 57. IN THE FIRST SENTENCE DELETE THE REFERENCE TO THE PRACTICE 26–23 DIRECTION AND REPLACE BY: CPR, Practice Direction Pt 40A—Accounts & Inquiries, para.7. DELETE penultimate AND REPLACE BY: ante-penultimate.

4. DISTRIBUTION NOTWITHSTANDING THIRD PARTY CLAIMS

Upsetting the trust

NOTE 65. AT THE BEGINNING INSERT *Representation of BNP Paribas Jersey* 26–26 *Trust Corp. Ltd* [2010] JRC 199; (2010–11) 13 I.T.E.L.R 867.

Liabilities and trustee's rights of indemnity

NOTE 88. AT THE END ADD: *ATC (Cayman) Ltd v Rothschild Trust Cayman* 26–29 *Ltd* (2010) 14 I.T.E.L.R. 523, Cay GC.

---

[19] *Kemble v Hicks* [1999] P.L.R. 287, not cited in *Leadenhall Independent Trustees Ltd v Welham* [2004] EWHC 740 (Ch); [2004] O.P.L.R. 115.
[19a] *NBPF Pension Trustees Ltd. v Warnock-Smith* [2009] EWHC 455 (Ch); [2008] 2 All ER (Comm) 740; see in particular [54], [57]. Note that if the trustee is protected by an exoneration clause, it will be necessary to consider effecting the insurance on terms that the insurer will not seek to rely on the clause; *cf. ibid.*, at [37].
[19b] *ibid.*, at [50].
[39a] *MCP Pension Trustees Ltd v AON Pension Trustees Ltd*, above (incorrect deletion of members from records of pension scheme). How far constructive notice sufficed was left open.
[39b] *ibid.* See the decision at first instance [2009] EWHC 1351 (Ch); [2010] 2 W.L.R. 268.

INSERT AT THE END OF THE SEVENTH SENTENCE: including a claim for breach of trust (since the trustees may become entitled to take their costs out of the trust fund).[89a]

NOTE 90. AT THE END ADD: See too *Hayman v Equity Trustees Ltd*, above, at [65].

26–31 NOTE 1. FOR THE REFERENCE TO *Snell's Equity*, SEE NOW (32nd edn), § 33–027.

5. CIRCUMSTANCES AFFECTING DISTRIBUTION

Incapacity of childbearing

26–47 NOTE 62. AT THE END ADD: *Simpson v Trust Co. Fiduciary Services Ltd* [2009] NSWSC 912.

26–51 NOTE 83. INSERT AT THE END OF THE SECOND SENTENCE: and in *Simpson v Trust Co. Fiduciary Services Ltd* [2009] NSWSC 912.

Identifying children and other issue

26–52 NOTE 90. DELETE ENTIRE NOTE AND REPLACE BY: The Standard Provisions of the Society of Trust and Estate Practitioners (2nd edn), para.23, contain a provision permitting trustees to make a distribution without having ascertained that there is anyone entitled by virtue of a relationship unknown to the trustees.

8. FINAL DISTRIBUTION—SETTLING ACCOUNTS: RELEASE

Release of trustee

26–72 NOTE 33. DELETE THE LAST SENTENCE AND REPLACE BY: Nor has he an unrestricted power to apply trust money in effecting insurance against his own breach of duty: see § 26–06 (including Supplement).

[89a] *Hayman v Equity Trustees Ltd* [2003] VSC 353; (2003) 8 V.R. 548 at [62]–[63]; *ATC (Cayman) Ltd v Rothschild Trust Cayman Ltd*, above. For such orders, see § 21–98.

CHAPTER 27

DISTRIBUTION OF THE TRUST FUND WITH THE INTERVENTION OF THE COURT

I. INTRODUCTION

Scope of chapter

AFTER THE LAST SENTENCE INSERT: For that reason we also deal in this chapter **27–01**
with arbitration in connexion with trusts.[2a]

2. APPLICATION TO COURT

Administration questions and remedies

NOTE 12. DELETE THE SECOND SENTENCE AND REPLACE BY: Assistance with **27–05**
practice and procedure is also to be found in *The Chancery Guide* (6th edn,
2009), paras.25.1 *et seq.*

Particular administration remedies

NOTE 45. INSERT AT THE END: , and in particular, § 29–309.   **27–12**

Nature of relief which may be granted

Benjamin *orders*

NOTE 53. INSERT AT THE END: where the trustees are faced with an adverse **27–16**
claim to the trust assets which the claimant will not pursue, they may be
authorised to administer the trust on the footing that the assets are free of
his claim: § 27–34 and *Representation of BNP Paribas Jersey Trust Corp. Ltd*
[2010] JRC 199; (2010–11) 13 I.T.E.L.R 867 (where the claimant was given
six months in which to issue proceedings before the order took effect). For
lost trust instruments, see too § 26–54.

NOTE 56. DELETE THE SECOND SENTENCE AND REPLACE BY: The court was not
so satisfied in *Gonzales v Claridades* [2003] NSWSC 508; (2003) 58
N.S.W.L.R. 188 (affirmed [2003] NSWCA 227; (2003) 58 N.S.W.L.R. 211).

AFTER § 27–17 INSERT THE FOLLOWING NEW PARAGRAPH:

The court's power to authorise trustees to distribute on a given footing **27–17A**

[2a]   See §§ 27–56 *et seq.*

extends not merely to questions of fact but also permits it to authorise them to act on a legal opinion that certain assets are or are not held on trust and, if so, what the beneficial interests are; and it will do so where the difficulty and expense of actually deciding the relevant questions are out of proportion to the value of the fund.[60a]

Directions as to trustees' powers

27–19 AT THE END OF THE LAST SENTENCE INSERT A NEW NOTE 66a: See § 29–299.

Future questions

27–21 NOTE 71. AFTER THE REFERENCE TO *Re Staples* INSERT: *Re Earl of Strafford* [1980] Ch. 28 at 39, CA, *per* Goff L.J. *arguendo*.

Practice

27–22 NOTE 73. FOR THE REFERENCE TO *The Chancery Guide* (5th edn, 2005), SEE NOW (6th edn, 2009), paras.25.1 *et seq*.

Parties

27–23 NOTE 80. FOR THE REFERENCE TO *The Chancery Guide* (5th edn, 2005), SEE NOW (6th edn, 2009), para.25.4.

DELETE THE SECOND AND THIRD SENTENCES AND N.81 AND REPLACE BY: The trustees do not need permission to issue such a claim form if they are seeking the approval of a sale, purchase, compromise or other transaction, including a case in which the approval is sought because of a conflict of interest or duties;[81] and since in such cases the application will typically be disposed of without a hearing,[81a] it will be cheaper to make and hence useful, especially when the trustees are inhibited by a conflict. An application under section 48 of the Administration of Justice Act 1985 not naming defendants may also be issued without the permission of the court.[81b] In the previous edition of *The Chancery Guide* it was said that the procedure of not naming defendant might enable trustees to obtain directions where the expense and delay associated with an application naming defendants might not be in the

---

[60a] *Re Equilift Ltd* [2009] EWHC 3104 (Ch); [2010] B.P.I.R. 116. (The authority to distribute was not to take effect until persons who might have been beneficiaries had been given an opportunity to contend that a distribution in a different way ought to be made.) The trustees may also be authorised to act on a legal opinion either by a suitable provision in the trust instrument or, on a discrete point, by a power conferred under Trustee Act 1925, s.57: see *Sutton v England* [2009] EWHC 3270 (Ch); [2010] W.T.L.R. 335 at [22] (reversed on appeal on other grounds *sub nom. Southgate v Sutton* [2011] EWCA Civ 637; [2011] W.T.L.R. 1235) and § 45–16(11).

[81] ETC Direction, paras.1A.1, 1A.2; *The Chancery Guide* (6th edn, 2009), para.25.4. The procedural requirements are stated in the ETC Direction, para.1A.3. For trustees seeking approval of such administrative decisions, see §§ 29–296 *et seq*. It is unlikely that the ability to apply without naming defendants extends to an application under Trustee Act 1925, s.57 (for which see §§ 45–12 *et seq*.). Nor is it clear whether that ability extends to an application for a *Benjamin* order to permit a distribution on a given footing (for which see §§ 27–15 *et seq*.), since it is doubtful whether the distribution can count as a "transaction" within the ETC Direction.

[81a] See § 27–29 (including Supplement).

[81b] See § 27–37.

interests of beneficiaries.[81c] That somewhat general guidance suggests, if still applicable, that the procedure is primarily useful (cases of seeking approval and under section 48 apart) where the fund is small, or where the principal beneficiaries are adult and agreeable to the course proposed and the other beneficiaries are unborn, unascertained or cannot be found. It has certainly been used where the beneficiaries all had the same interest and had over-whelmingly expressed approval of the course proposed.[81d]

AFTER THE SECOND SENTENCE INSERT: It suffices if the representative has the **27–24** same interest in a given answer to a question as those whom he is appointed to represent and it is not necessary that he should have a like beneficial interest.[86a] The order can be made at any stage of the proceedings.[86b] The representative appointed is not a spokesman for the class and continues free to act in his own interests, *e.g.* by compromising the claim (unless, perhaps, he has sought the making of a prospective costs order in his favour[86c]), but if he ceases to be suitable as a representative the order will be discharged.[86d]

AFTER THE THIRD SENTENCE INSERT: Conversely, the court has jurisdiction to make a representation order against the opposition of one or more of the persons to be represented, and to refuse an application by such a person to be joined in his own right, where that is necessary for effective case man-agement.[87a] Ordinarily it is necessary to ensure that each separate interest is represented but where the separate interests are numerous and it would be unwieldy or disproportionately expensive to insist on such representation, as may happen with pension trusts in particular,[87b] the court will modify the procedure,[87c] as by permitting a single team of lawyers to present conten-tions on behalf of beneficiaries with conflicting interests.[87d]

NOTE 88. FOR THE REFERENCE TO *The Chancery Guide* (5th edn, 2005), SEE NOW (6th edn, 2009), para.25.7.

Mode of commencing claim

NOTE 90. DELETE THE REFERENCE TO Practice Direction – Alternative Pro- **27–26** cedure for Claims.

[81c] (5th edn, 2005), para. 26.7.
[81d] *Re SMP Trustees Ltd* [2012] EWHC 772 (Ch) at [20] (amending terms of failing investment scheme, where bondholders as beneficiaries had voted in favour of amendment).
[86a] *Capita ATL Pension Trustees Ltd v Zurkinskas* [2010] EWHC 3365 (Ch); [2010] All E.R. (D) 285 (Dec) at [9]–[13].
[86b] *IBM United Kingdom Pensions Trusts Ltd v Metcalfe* [2012] EWHC 125 (Ch) at [24].
[86c] See § 21–83.
[86d] See the discussion in *IBM United Kingdom Pensions Trusts Ltd v Metcalfe*, above.
[87a] *PNPF Trust Co. Ltd v Taylor* [2009] EWHC 1693 (Ch); [2009] All E.R. (D) 119 (Jul).
[87b] In *NBPF Pension Trustees Ltd v Warnock-Smith* [2008] EWHC 455 (Ch), it was possible to identify over 200 categories of potential recipients of pension benefits.
[87c] *Bestrustees v Stuart* [2001] EWHC 549 (Ch); [2001] P.L.R. 283 at [27]; *NBPF Pension Trustees Ltd*, above; *Walker Morris Trustees Ltd v Masterson* [2009] EWHC 1955 (Ch); [2009] P.L.R. 307 at [11]–[12].
[87d] *NBPF Pension Trustees Ltd*, above, at [15].

IN THE SECOND SENTENCE AFTER brought by Part 8 claim form INSERT: as are certain other claims concerning trusts,[92]

NOTE 92. DELETE.

NOTE 95. DELETE THE REFERENCE TO Practice Direction – Alternative Procedure for Claims AND REPLACE BY: Practice Direction 8 – Alternative Procedure for Claims, paras.3.4, 3.5.

27–27   NOTE 99. DELETE THE REFERENCE TO Practice Direction – Alternative Procedure for Claims AND REPLACE BY: Practice Direction 8 – Alternative Procedure for Claims, paras.3.4, 3.5.

Management, hearing and order

27–29   NOTE 12. AT THE END ADD: *The Chancery Guide* (6th edn, 2009), para.25.5.

AFTER THE THIRD SENTENCE INSERT: Where a claim form not naming defendants seeking approval of a transaction is made without the permission of the court, as is now possible,[13a] the court will consider the claim on the papers and make the order sought if it thinks that no oral hearing is needed but if it thinks that a hearing is needed it will give appropriate directions.[13b]

27–30   DELETE AND REPLACE BY: The order, unless it was made in public, will not be open to inspection by a non-party without the court's permission; and the same applies to the other documents on the court file in a Part 8 claim other than the claim form.[24] The court may further restrict a non-party's right of inspection.[24a]

Distribution

27–31   NOTE 25. DELETE THE REFERENCE TO Directions Relating to Part 48, para.50A.1 to 50A.3 AND REPLACE BY: CPR, Practice Direction Pts 43 to 48, paras.50A1–50A.3.

Upsetting the trust—generally

27–34   NOTE 34. AT THE END OF THE FIRST SENTENCE ADD: *Representation of BNP Paribas Jersey Trust Corp. Ltd* [2010] JRC 199; (2010–11) 13 I.T.E.L.R 867 (where the claimant was given six months in which to issue proceedings before the order took effect).

---

[92]   See Practice Direction 8—Alternative Procedure for Claims, paras.3.2(1), 9.1 and Table to Sec. B, mentioning applications under Trustee Act 1925 and Public Trustee Act 1906 (and see paras.12.1, 12.2).

[13a]   See § 27–23 (Supplement).

[13b]   ETC Direction, paras.1A.4, 1A.5, 1A.6.

[24]   Practice Direction 5A—Court Documents, para.5.4C(1), allowing access without the court's permission to a statement of case (of which the claim form in a Pt 8 claim will be the sole instance) and a judgment or order given or made in public. Certain other restrictions apply: see *ibid.*, para.5.4C(3). Different rules govern access to statements of case filed before October 2, 2006: see *ibid.*, para.5.4C(1A).

[24a]   Practice Direction 5A—Court Documents, para.5.4C(4).

Ordinary personal liabilities

NOTE 46. FOR THE REFERENCE TO *The Chancery Guide* (5th edn, 2005), SEE **27–36** NOW (6th edn, 2009), paras.25.6, 25.26 *et seq.*

3. APPROVAL OF LEGAL OPINION

The statutory power

NOTE 55. AT THE END INSERT: *The Chancery Guide* (6th edn, 2009), **27–39** para.25.15 now provides (though without explanation) that the claim form "should not seek a decision of the court on the construction of any instrument".

Practice

NOTE 57. DELETE AND REPLACE BY: See *The Chancery Guide* (6th edn, 2009), **27–41** paras.25.15 *et seq.*

DELETE AND REPLACE BY: The witness statement or affidavit (or the exhibits) **27–41(2)** should state:

(a) the reason for the application;

(b) the names of all persons who are, or may be, affected by the order sought;

(c) all surrounding circumstances admissible and relevant in construing the document;[58]

(d) the date of qualification of the qualified person and his or her experience in the construction of trust documents;

(e) the approximate value of the fund or property in question;

(f) whether it is known to the applicant that a dispute exists and, if so, details of the dispute; and

(g) what steps are proposed to be taken in reliance on the opinion.

4. PAYMENT INTO COURT

Power to pay in

NOTE 63. DELETE AND REPLACE BY: For the procedure, see Court Funds Rules **27–42** 2011 (SI 2011/1734), rr.6 to 10 (especially r.6(6)); CPR, Pt 37, r.37.4; Practice Direction 37—Miscellaneous Provisions about Payments into

---

[58]   As to which, see §§ 6–03 *et seq.*

Court (supplementing CPR, Pt 37), para.6. For mortgagees wishing to pay into court surplus proceeds of sale, see in addition *The Chancery Guide* (6th edn, 2009), para.25.25.

Effect of payment in

AFTER § 27–43 INSERT THE FOLLOWING NEW PARAGRAPH:

27–43A The payment of trust moneys or securities into court does not, of itself, alter the beneficial rights in those assets, which remain subject to the prior trusts.[73a]

When payment into court is justifiable

27–46 DELETE THE LAST SENTENCE AND NN.81–82.

27–47 DELETE AND REPLACE BY: It may sometimes be more convenient to apply to the court for a *Benjamin* order[81] or alternatively an order for payment in under Part 64 of the Civil Procedure Rules,[82] for then the payment in has the approval of the court.

Payment out of court

27–49 NOTE 84. DELETE AND REPLACE BY: The procedure upon application for payment out is not within the scope of this work. See, however, Court Funds Rules 2011 (SI 2011/1734), rr.22 *et seq.*; CPR, Pt 37, r.37.4; Practice Direction 37—Miscellaneous Provisions about Payments into Court (supplementing CPR, Pt 37), paras.3, 7; *The Chancery Guide* (2009 edn), paras.5.56, 5.57.

AFTER § 27–49 INSERT THE FOLLOWING NEW PARAGRAPH:

27–49A The rules do not lay down what has to be proved on making an application for payment out but we consider that it will be necessary for the applicant to establish the following:[85a]

> (1) The identity of the person who is primarily entitled to any funds paid into court and the basis of that entitlement;
>
> (2) The fact that the applicant has a beneficial interest in the funds and is not merely an unsecured creditor; and
>
> (3) The identity of any other claimants to the funds, coupled with proof that those persons have had notice of the application and

---

[73a] *Harmer v Federal Commissioner of Taxation* (1991) 173 C.L.R. 264 at [9], Aus HC; *Vertical Australia Pty Ltd v Air Company Vertical-T LLC* [2012] NSWSC 719 at [66], both on Australian legislation in much the same terms as Trustee Act 1925, s.63.

[81] See §§ 27–15 *et seq.*

[82] Read with the ETC Direction, para.1(2)(*a*)(ii); see § 27–10.

[85a] Taken from *Commonwealth Bank v Estate of late Slieman* [2010] NSWSC 661 at [8] to [11]; *Chong v Super Equity Invests Pty Ltd* [2012] NSWSC 27 at [14], both on Australian rules comparable to Practice Direction 37—Miscellaneous Provisions about Payments into Court (supplementing CPR, Pt 37), paras.6, 7.

either that they consent or else that the applicant has priority over any claims that they have.

The court may direct notice of the application to be served on any person.[85b]

AFTER § 27–56 ADD THE FOLLOWING NEW SECTION:

5. ARBITRATION

Arbitration generally

When a question has arisen between those interested in the trust they may **27–57** submit the question to arbitration. A determination by that method may resolve a difficulty in the way of a distribution, which is the primary concern of this chapter, such as a question of construction, but it is equally suited to resolving a dispute about, say, an alleged breach of trust.

The usefulness of arbitration in trust matters is limited by practical con- **27–58** siderations. If arbitration is undertaken by agreement made once a question has arisen, it is only if all those concerned in the question to be determined are of full age and capacity that there can be an effective decision. Minor, unborn and incapable beneficiaries cannot join in by contract and there is no means of binding them. Hence if relief is sought which requires all those interested in the trust to be bound, such as the determination of a question of construction or reconstitution of a trust fund in consequence of a breach of trust, an agreement to arbitrate cannot be made if such beneficiaries are interested. Moreover, an arbitrator lacks the powers conferred on the court by statute, such as the power to make a vesting order and similarly lacks the court's jurisdiction to give directions to trustees.

Arbitration clauses

On occasion, however, trust instruments include a provision designed to **27–59** compel arbitration of questions arising between those interested in the trust. Arbitration offers advantages of privacy and confidentiality, often matters significant in family trusts, and a choice of arbitrator.

There seems no doubt that a provision for arbitration is valid as between the **27–60** original parties to the trust instrument (when there is more than one, *i.e.* when it does not take the form of a unilateral declaration of trust). Under the Arbitration Act 1996 if proceedings in court are brought against a party to an arbitration agreement in respect of a matter which, under the agreement, is to be referred to arbitration, the court is bound to stay the proceedings on the application of that party unless the arbitration agreement is null and void, inoperative or incapable of being performed.[1] The arbitration

---

[85b] Practice Direction 37—Miscellaneous Provisions about Payments into Court (supplementing CPR, Pt 37), para.7.2.

[1] Arbitration Act 1996, s.9(1), (4). A statutory exception for "domestic" arbitration agreements, giving the court instead a discretion to stay, has not been brought into force; see *ibid.*, ss.85–87.

agreement must be in writing.[2] A trust instrument is not primarily a contract but a suitable provision in it would undoubtedly constitute an arbitration agreement between the parties within the 1996 Act.[3] Hence the settlor and the original trustees, if different, could bind themselves to arbitrate. Such an obligation would extend, for example, to a covenant on the part of the settlor to settle additional property, though such covenants are now uncommon, and even to a challenge to the validity of the settlement itself based on, say, duress, if the provision for arbitration is wide enough to embrace such a challenge, since the rule is that an arbitration agreement has to be treated as a distinct agreement[4] and so is vitiated only by factors which directly concern the arbitration agreement itself and is not automatically brought into question by a challenge to the transaction of which it forms a part.[5]

27–61 It is less obvious that an obligation to arbitrate or an entitlement to arbitrate can be imposed or conferred on successor trustees or on beneficiaries, as neither will ordinarily be parties to the trust instrument. Under the 1996 Act, however, it is a party to the arbitration agreement who can demand a stay of proceedings in court; and the term "party to an arbitration agreement" extends to persons "claiming under or through" an actual party to the agreement.[6] Though the 1996 Act is not in terms confined to cases in which the *claimant* is also a party to the arbitration agreement, such a restriction is implied, so that a stay is available only against such a party;[7] but it is likely that the statutory extension of the term applies also to a claimant.[8] It is therefore material to know whether successor trustees or beneficiaries claim under or through a party to the arbitration agreement, so that, for example, when a beneficiary sues successor trustees for breach of trust, either side can insist on arbitration. The claim in question is not the claim being asserted in the proceedings, since it is the defendant who invokes the provision for a stay, but seems rather to be the entitlement to which the arbitration agreement is ancillary. Arbitration agreements are primarily found in contracts and the entitlements of successor trustees and beneficiaries are proprietary, not contractual. Nonetheless, while the expression "claiming under or through a party" is certainly apt to refer to a contractual entitlement, so that an assignee of contractual rights is entitled or bound to arbitrate, there appears to be no reason why a proprietary entitlement should not suffice. Beneficiaries may rationally be regarded as claiming under the settlor, since they take their beneficial interests by way of grant from him, and successor trustees may similarly be regarded as claiming under him, as their legal title to the trust assets ultimately derives from him. If so, and if the obligation to arbitrate extends to a claimant who claims

---

2   *ibid.*, s.5.
3   For the definition of "arbitration agreement", see *ibid.*, s.9.
4   *ibid.*, s.7.
5   *El Nasharty v J Sainsbury plc* [2007] EWHC 2618 (Comm); [2007] All E.R. (D) 200 (Nov) (duress), relying on *Premium Nafta Products Limited v Fili Shipping Company Limited* [2007] UKHL 40; [2007] 4 All ER 951 (bribery or want of authority of agent to enter into main transaction does not vitiate arbitration agreement; forgery does so).
6   Arbitration Act 1996, s.82(2).
7   *City of London v Sancheti* [2008] EWCA Civ 1283; [2009] Bus. L.R. 996.
8   *Cf. ibid.* at [29].

under or through a party to the arbitration agreement, then the statutory regime will extend to trust disputes between such persons.

It must be acknowledged, however, that that conclusion entails difficulties **27–62** similar to those which arise where the trust instrument has no arbitration clause. First, neither the 1996 Act nor the general law of arbitration contains provision for representation orders or for permitting the representation of minor beneficiaries. The court appears to have no jurisdiction to assist an arbitration by appointing a person to represent such interests in the arbitration.[9] Hence, as before, if relief is sought which requires all those interested in the trust to be bound, it may be necessary to treat the arbitration as incapable of being performed within the terms of the 1996 Act, so that a stay is not available.[10] Secondly, an arbitrator again lacks the powers conferred on the court by statute, such as the power to approve a variation of the trusts[11] or to appoint a new trustee,[12] and lacks the court's jurisdiction to give directions to trustees.[13] Claims for such relief cannot fall within an arbitration agreement. Thirdly, the application of the 1996 Act depends on the existence of an arbitration agreement, which can be found only in a trust instrument to which more than one person is a party, so that an attempt to provide for arbitration in a unilateral declaration of trust would necessarily fall outside the Act.

We consider that those difficulties can be overcome by suitable provisions in **27–63** the trust instrument. The settlor is free to frame the beneficial interests as he sees fit. It is open to him to confer suitable powers and impose suitable duties on the trustees, or on a third party, such as a protector, to re-mould them in accordance with the decision of an arbitrator and to provide within the trust instrument for the appointment of persons to represent the interests of those not of full age and capacity in the course of arbitral proceedings. If the provision for arbitration constitutes an arbitration agreement within the 1996 Act, proceedings in court brought by any of those bound by it can be stayed under that Act;[14] and if it is not (as when it is included in a unilateral declaration of trust) or if the claimant in the proceedings in court is not contractually bound by it, the defendants may invoke the inherent jurisdiction of the court.[15] Moreover the fact that an arbitrator cannot grant particular relief does not of itself preclude a reference of the underlying dispute to arbitration and court proceedings for suitable relief may follow after an arbitrator has determined the dispute.[16]

---

[9] Arbitration Act 1996, s.44 (court powers exercisable in support of arbitral proceedings) confers no relevant power.
[10] Arbitration Act 1996, s.9.
[11] Under Variation of Trusts Act 1958; see §§ 45–31 *et seq.*
[12] Under Trustee Act 1925, s.41; see §§ 15–01 *et seq.*
[13] See §§ 29–291 *et seq.*
[14] See § 26–61.
[15] Recognised in *Al-Naimi v Islamic Press Agency Inc.* [2000] EWCA Civ 17; [2000] 1 Lloyd's Rep. 522 and now to be found in CPR, Pt 3, r.3.1(2)(e).
[16] *Fulham Football Club (1987) Ltd v Richards* [2011] EWCA Civ 855, staying a petition for relief from unfair prejudice under Companies Act 2006, s.994 in favour of arbitration; see especially [83].

CHAPTER 28

HOTCHPOT

When hotchpot applies

28–02 NOTE 4. FOR THE REFERENCE TO *Snell's Equity*, SEE NOW (32nd edn), §§ 6–068 *et seq.*

Property subject to inheritance tax

28–07 AT THE END DELETE : AND REPLACE BY: .

AFTER § 28–10 INSERT THE FOLLOWING NEW PARAGRAPH AND HEADING:

Before distribution date

28–10A It may happen that hotchpotting has to be considered by reason of inheritance tax before the date fixed for distribution. Where, for example, an undivided fund is held to pay the income to more than one beneficiary in fixed shares, inheritance tax may be payable on the death of one of the income beneficiaries. It then has to be decided how the reduction in the fund affects the interests of the surviving income beneficiary or beneficiaries (whether the share of the deceased beneficiary continues subject to an income interest or is distributable). Two alternative methods for doing so are available, corresponding to the two methods for bringing interest into account on the final distribution of the fund, which is discussed shortly.[27a] One is to treat the tax paid as an advance in anticipation of the final distribution. Hence while income remains payable on any part of the fund, interest on the advance is calculated (at a rate of 4 per cent.) and is added to the income actually available for distribution;[27b] the fixed shares are applied to that aggregated (and partly notional) sum, and income distributed accordingly. On the final distribution, the advances are added back, the division is performed, and then the advances are debited from each share before it is paid. The other method treats the inheritance tax as having reduced the share of the deceased beneficiary from the date when it was paid, and hence as having increased the other shares, though in a smaller fund. The adjusted shares are then applied both while income remains to be paid and on the final distribution. The existence of the two methods has

---

[27a] §§ 28–11 *et seq.*
[27b] An adjustment for income tax may be required: see § 28–15.

been acknowledged but there is no authority on the criterion for choosing between them.[27c]

[27c] *Sutton v England* [2009] EWHC 3270 (Ch); [2010] W.T.L.R. 335 at [11]–[22] (reversed on appeal on other grounds *sub nom. Southgate v Sutton* [2011] EWCA Civ 637; [2011] W.T.L.R. 1235). *Cf.*, however, § 28–14.

CHAPTER 29

POWERS GENERALLY

1. SCOPE OF CHAPTER

General

29–01 NOTE 3. FOR THE REFERENCE TO *Thomas on Powers*, SEE NOW (2nd edn, 2012).

2. CLASSIFICATION AND TERMINOLOGY OF POWERS

Legal powers and equitable powers

29–06 NOTE 7. DELETE AND REPLACE BY: *Donaldson v Smith* [2006] EWHC B9 (Ch); [2007] W.T.L.R. 421 at [12].

Beneficial powers, limited powers and fiduciary powers

Fiduciary powers

29–17 AT THE END OF THE SIXTH SENTENCE INSERT: Such a power remains fiduciary but subject to the qualification that the donee is not debarred from exercising it in a way which confers some benefit on himself; the precise constraints on the donee depend on the particular trust instrument.[32a]

Imperative powers and permissive powers—trust powers and mere powers

29–22 DELETE THE LAST SENTENCE AND REPLACE BY: The donee is under a duty to exercise the power—he holds the property on trust to exercise it—with the consequence that if he does not exercise it in due time[57] either he will be permitted to do so late[57a] or else the court will do so for him, by directing an equal or unequal division amongst the objects or some of them.[57b]

[32a] *Re Z Trust* [1997] C.I.L.R. 248 at 265, Cayman GC; *Re Internine Trust and Intertraders Trust* [2005] JRC 072; [2010] W.T.L.R. 443 at [56].
[57] For the time for exercising powers, see §§ 29–196 *et seq.*
[57a] §§ 29–197, 29–202 to 29–203.
[57b] For the execution of trust powers by the court, see §§ 30–25 *et seq.*

3. CREATION OF POWERS

Creation by or under trust instrument

Creation by reference

NOTE 77. DELETE AND REPLACE BY: The current edition is the 2nd. Note that **29–31**
there are special provisions (paras.13 *et seq.*) which are not incorporated
unless express reference is made to them; see para.1, especially para.1.4.

NOTE 79. FOR THE REFERENCE TO *Thomas on Powers*, SEE NOW (2nd edn, **29–32**
2012), paras.3.16 *et seq.*

4. THIRD PARTY POWERS AND CONSENTS

Third parties generally

AT THE END OF THE FOURTH SENTENCE, INSERT A NEW NOTE 90a: A requirement **29–35**
of a third party's consent is treated as a power of veto, so as to be subject to
the rules about powers: see, *e.g.*, *Scully v Coley* [2009] UKPC 29; [2009] All
E.R. (D) 10 (Nov) at [47]–[49].

NOTE 92. AT THE END ADD: For a case in which the person whose consent was
required was also the trustee, see *Bestrustees v Stuart* [2001] EWHC 549
(Ch); [2001] P.L.R. 283.

Classification of third party powers—general factors

Express terms of settlement

AT THE END OF THE SECOND SENTENCE INSERT A NEW NOTE 95a: See, *e.g.*, *Centre* **29–37**
Trustees Ltd v Pabst [2009] JRC 109; (2009–10) 12 I.T.E.L.R. 720.

NOTE 96. FOR THE REFERENCE TO the Standard Provisions of the Society of
Trust and Estate Practitioners, SEE NOW (2nd edn), para.9.

Nature of donee

AT THE END ADD: The power of an income beneficiary (whether conferred by **29–40**
the trust instrument or by statute[2a]) to withhold consent to the exercise of a
power of advancement of capital is plainly likewise given for the beneficiary's own protection and so is a beneficial power.[2b]

NOTE 4. THE CORRECT CITATION OF *Re Papadimitriou* IS [2004] W.T.L.R. 1141, **29–41**
Manx HC. AT THE END ADD: *Centre Trustees Ltd v Pabst* [2009] JRC 109;
(2009–10) 12 I.T.E.L.R. 720.

NOTE 6. AT THE END ADD: *Re Bird Charitable Trust* [2008] JRC 013; (2008)
11 I.T.E.L.R. 157.

[2a] Trustee Act 1925, s.32, for which see Chap.32.
[2b] *PJC v ADC* [2009] EWHC 1491 (Fam); [2009] W.T.L.R. 1419 at [15].

Third party powers requiring consent of trustees

29–49   AT THE END ADD: Where a power of appointment or any other power is exercisable only with the consent of the trustees, the consent of all of them is required.[28a]

Dispensing with consent

29–50   NOTE 32. AT THE END ADD: But a requirement of consent was dispensed with in *Page v West* [2010] EWHC 504 (Ch); [2010] W.T.L.R. 1811.

AFTER § 29–50, INSERT A NEW PARAGRAPH:

29–50A   A requirement of consent is a power of veto[34a] and so, in common with all powers other than beneficial powers, it is subject to the limitation that it can be used only for the purpose for which it was conferred.[34b] It appears to follow that if there are no circumstances in which the power can properly be exercised, the requirement of consent can be ignored.[34c] But it will seldom be safe for trustees to act without the consent until the court has confirmed that it is not required.

5. WHO CAN EXERCISE A POWER

Whether all donees must act

Trust a joint office

29–61   IN THE THIRD SENTENCE, AFTER is known to the law, INSERT A NEW NOTE 60a: *Ponniah v Palmer* [2012] NZHC 1574 at [26].

Unanimity

29–62   NOTE 65. IN THE FIRST SENTENCE, AFTER THE REFERENCE TO *Cowan v Scargill*, INSERT *Rodney Aero Club Inc. v Moore* [1998] 2 N.Z.L.R. 192 AND AT THE END ADD: *Ponniah v Palmer*, above.

AFTER § 29–62 INSERT THE FOLLOWING NEW PARAGRAPH:

29–62A   The act of one trustee done with the sanction and approval of a co-trustee will be regarded as the act of both,[70a] so that a contract entered into by one trustee as such will bind a co-trustee who sanctions his doing so.[70b] We deal elsewhere with the question how far trustees exercising a power need to do so simultaneously.[70c] It is not necessary that the actual implementation of any exercise of a power should be effected by all of the trustees, unless that is

---

[28a]   See § 29–70.
[34a]   See § 29–35.
[34b]   See §§ 29–255 et seq.
[34c]   *Scully v Coley* [2009] UKPC 29; [2009] All E.R. (D) 10 (Nov) at [47]–[49].
[70a]   *Messeena v Carr* (1870) L.R. 9 Eq. 260; *Edwards v Proprius Holdings Ltd* [2009] NZHC 597; and see *Brazier v Camp* (1894) 63 L.J.Q.B. 257.
[70b]   *Edwards v Proprius Holdings Ltd*, above.
[70c]   § 29–209. See too § 29–166 (how far all trustees must comply with legal formalities).

required (as, *e.g.*, in the case of a transfer of land) by the nature of the act to be done.

DELETE THE FIRST SENTENCE AND REPLACE BY: The general rule requiring **29–63** unanimity in the exercise of a power has exceptions.

NOTE 74. IN THE SECOND SENTENCE, DELETE THE TEXT AFTER THE COLON AND REPLACE BY: Charities Act 2011, s.275(5).

Landlord and tenant

AT THE END ADD: A secure tenancy within the Housing Act 1988 in favour of **29–69** two or more joint tenants, if determined by notice given by only one of them, will be succeeded by a statutory periodic tenancy in favour of all of them as long as, when the notice took effect, any one of them occupied the property as his sole or principal home.[92a]

Capacity

IN THE LAST SENTENCE DELETE and so an enduring power of attorney AND **29–74** REPLACE BY: and so an attorney holding a lasting or an enduring power.

Bankruptcy of donee

INSERT AFTER THE FOURTH SENTENCE: A power of revocation of settlement **29–79** vested in the settlor, being a beneficial power, will also do so.[36a]

INSERT AFTER THE FIFTH SENTENCE: Nor does a power to remove or appoint new trustees of the trust, even when the bankrupt is himself a discretionary beneficiary, since such powers are fiduciary.[37a]

No one capable of exercising a power

AT THE END OF THE LAST SENTENCE INSERT A NEW NOTE 48a: A view adopted in **29–82** *Bridge Trustees Ltd v Noel Penny (Turbines) Ltd* [2008] EWHC 2054 (Ch) (where the power was imperative).

6. DELEGATION OF POWERS

Delegation to co-trustee

NOTE 65. AT THE END ADD: *Commissioner of Inland Revenue v Newmarket* **29–88** *Trustees Ltd* [2012] NZCA 351 at [49].

[92a] Housing Act 1988, ss.1(1), 5(2), (3), 45(3).
[36a] *Cf. Tasarruf Mevduati Sigorta Fonu v Merrill Lynch Bank and Trust Co. (Cayman) Ltd* [2011] UKPC 17; (2011–12) 14 I.T.E.L.R. 102, on appeal from the Cayman Islands, where the settlor was not bankrupt in that jurisdiction and it was held that the court could appoint a receiver over the power to exercise it for the benefit of a judgment creditor.
[37a] *Wily v Burton* [1994] FCA 1146; (1994) 126 A.L.R. 557 on comparable Australian legislation.

Delegation distinguished from consultation

29–89 Note 68. In the first sentence, delete §§ 37–52 *et seq.* and replace by: §§ 37–55 *et seq.*

After the third sentence, insert: The trust instrument may specifically provide that the trustees are under no duty to consult the beneficiaries.[69a]

7. Duties of Donees—Preliminary Matters

Judgment as to state of facts

29–122 Note 6: At the end add: It is a matter of construction, not always easy to resolve, whether a given provision merely requires a judgment as to a state of facts or confers a genuine discretion on the trustees; see, *e.g.*, *Entrust Pension Ltd v Prospect Hospice Ltd* [2012] EWHC 1666 (Ch) at [49] *et seq.*

Duty of consideration

29–123 Note 12. Add: *Stuart v Armourguard Security Ltd* [1996] 1 N.Z.L.R. 484, NZ HC; *McNulty v McNulty* [2011] NZHC 1173; (2011–12) 14 I.T.E.L.R. 361 at [97], [105].

Duty (4)—Taking matters into account

29–130 In the fifth sentence delete cat and replace by: act.

8. Duties of Donees—Considering Exercise of Powers

Duty (1)—To act responsibly and in good faith

29–140 Note 52. Insert at the end (within the final bracket): and [2008] NZSC 61.

29–141 Note 54. Insert at the end (within the final bracket): and [2008] NZSC 61.

29–143 Note 63. After the first sentence insert: Reference to principles of public law in the context of trusts was deprecated in *Pitt v Holt* [2011] EWCA Civ 197; [2012] Ch. 132 at [77].

At the end add: See too *Dever v Knobloch* [2009] NZHC 2013 at [55]–[64]; *McNulty v McNulty* [2011] NZHC 1173; (2011–12) 14 I.T.E.L.R. 361 at [115]–[116].

[69a] The Standard Provisions of the Society of Trust and Estate Practitioners (2nd edn), at para.19, so provide. The statutory obligation of trustees of land to consult the beneficiaries may effectively be excluded in that way, see § 37–56.

Duty (2)—To take only relevant matters into account

General

AFTER THE LAST SENTENCE INSERT: Time and quantum may play a part, in the **29–146** sense that a decision to release a modest part of the trust fund to meet an urgent need of one of several beneficiaries may not require the same degree of enquiry and examination as would be required if there was no urgency or the proposed distribution affected a large part of the trust fund.[81a]

AT THE END OF THE FIRST SENTENCE INSERT A NEW NOTE 81a: For fraud on the **29–147** power, see §§ 29–255 *et seq.*

IN THE SECOND SENTENCE AFTER when exercising a power INSERT: or that they wrongly took account of an irrelevant matter when making only a provisional decision to exercise the power, for which they are seeking the approval of the court.[81b]

AT THE END OF THE FIRST SENTENCE INSERT A NEW NOTE 81c: *Pitt v Holt* [2011] **29–148** EWCA Civ 197; [2012] Ch. 132 at [114]; and *cf.* the argument in *Independent Trustee Services Ltd v Hope* [2009] EWHC 2810 (Ch); [2009] All E.R. (D) 234 (Nov) at [108(1)].

INSERT AFTER THE SIXTH SENTENCE: Public policy may place constraints on the matters which the trustees may take into account.[83a]

Settlor's wishes

AT THE END OF THE FIRST SENTENCE, INSERT A NEW NOTE 83a: The settlor's **29–150** wishes are a material consideration for trustees even when the wishes are not recorded in a formal letter of wishes: *Re A Trust, Investec Co-Trustees Ltd v Kidd* [2012] JRC 066 at [62]–[63]; *Slutsker v Haron Investments Ltd* [2012] EWHC 2539 (Ch) at [37].

NOTE 85. DELETE THE REFERENCE TO *Kain v Hutton* AND INSERT: *Kain v Hutton* [2005] W.T.L.R. 1024 at [301], NZ HC; on appeal [2007] NZCA 199; (2007) 10 I.T.E.L.R. 287 at [272]; and on further appeal [2008] NZSC 61.

NOTE 86. INSERT AFTER THE REFERENCE TO *Schmidt v Rosewood Trustees Ltd*: *Pitt v Holt* [2011] EWCA Civ 197; [2012] Ch. 132 at [114] ("may well be one thing that trustees should take into account").

NOTE 87. FOR THE REFERENCE TO Underhill and Hayton, *Law of Trusts and Trustees*, SEE NOW (18th edn), §§ 56.49, 56.57.

NOTE 88. DELETE AND REPLACE BY: *Kain v Hutton* [2007] NZCA 199; (2007) 10 I.T.E.L.R. 287 at [272] (on further appeal [2008] NZSC 61).

NOTE 90. INSERT AT THE END: Approved on this point in *Pitt v Holt*, above, at [114].

AFTER § 29–150 INSERT A NEW PARAGRAPH AS FOLLOWS:

[81a] *Pitt v Holt* [2011] EWCA Civ 197; [2012] Ch. 132, at [117].
[81b] As in *Jones v Firkin-Flood* [2008] EWHC 2417 (Ch); [2008] All E.R. (D) 175 (Oct) at [280].
[83a] *Independent Trustee Services Ltd v Hope*, above, at [118]–[120].

29–150A When the trust is a charitable trust, it seems that the trustees should likewise give weight to the settlor's wishes. Authorities make it clear that the court itself, when giving directions to charity trustees, will treat the settlor's wishes as important.[90a] From that principle, and from the rule applicable to private trusts, it must follow that the trustees themselves should do so.

29–151 NOTE 93. INSERT AT THE END (WITHIN THE FINAL BRACKET): and [2008] NZSC 61.

NOTE 94. DELETE AND REPLACE BY: *Power v Ekstein* [2000] NSWSC 905.

Beneficiaries' wishes and needs

29–153 NOTE 97. AT THE END ADD: *Pitt v Holt* [2011] EWCA Civ 197; [2012] Ch. 132 at [114] ("so far as made known to the trustees"); *Whaley v Whaley* [2011] EWCA Civ 617; (2011–12) 14 I.T.E.L.R. 1 at [112] (citing this passage).

29–155 NOTE 6. AT THE END ADD: *Stuart v Armourguard Security Ltd* [1996] 1 N.Z.L.R. 484, NZ HC; *McNulty v McNulty* [2011] NZHC 1173; (2011–12) 14 I.T.E.L.R. 361 at [97], [105]; *Re Y Trust* [2011] JRC 135 at [55] *et seq.*, quoting this paragraph.

IN THE LAST SENTENCE DELETE any previous indications that have given AND REPLACE BY: any previous indications that they have given.

NOTE 9. AT THE END ADD: Hence even clear indications that they will decide in a particular way are not binding on them: *Re Y Trust*, above.

AT THE END OF THE TEXT ADD: It is at least arguable that trustees may need on the particular facts of a given case to make enquiries as to the respective positions of the class of beneficiaries.[9a]

"Judicious encouragement"

29–157 IN THE SECOND SENTENCE DELETE not they might like them AND REPLACE BY: not as they might like them.

IN THE FOURTH SENTENCE DELETE to give ancillary relief to a spouse on a divorce AND REPLACE BY to make a financial order in favour of a spouse on a divorce.

NOTE 16. ADD AT THE END: and Family Procedure Rules 2010 (SI 2010/2955), rr.9.1 *et seq.*

IN THE FIFTH SENTENCE DELETE in giving ancillary relief AND REPLACE BY: in making a financial order.

NOTE 20. AT THE END ADD: *SR v CR* [2008] EWHC 2329 (Fam); (2008–09) 11

[90a] *Att.-Gen. v Dedham School* (1857) 23 Beav. 350 at 355 ("What this Court looks at, in all charities, is the original intention of the founder, and ... this Court carries into effect the wishes and intentions of the founder of the charity"); *Re J.W. Laing Trust* [1984] Ch. 143 at 154 ("The court should always be slow to thwart a donor's wishes"). See too *Re Hampton Fuel Allotment Charity* [1989] Ch. 484, CA, where the court held that the settlor could be a "person interested" for the purpose of what is now Charities Act 2011, s.115(1) and hence eligible to apply to the court for directions concerning the charity.

[9a] *McNulty v McNulty* [2011] NZHC 1173; (2011–12) 14 I.T.E.L.R. 361 at [118]–[128].

I.T.E.L.R. 395. But where the beneficial interests under the trust are fixed, or the trustees have no relevant power which they can exercise without the consent of someone unlikely to give it, there is no scope for judicious encouragement: *PJC v ADC* [2009] EWHC 1491 (Fam); [2009] W.T.L.R. 1419.

NOTE 23. AT THE END ADD: (a passage approved in *A v A* [2007] EWHC 99 (Fam); [2007] 2 F.L.R. 467 at [91]).

NOTE 24. AT THE END ADD: *BJ v MJ* [2011] EWHC 2708 (Fam). Where a dispositive power is exercisable by the trustees only with the consent of a third party, the court has to consider what the third party would be likely to do: *Whaley v Whaley* [2011] EWCA Civ 617; (2011–12) 14 I.T.E.L.R. 1 (where the court inferred that the trustees would be likely to make the assets of the trust available to the husband, though to do so they would have first to add him as a beneficiary and then to resolve to distribute capital to him, both steps for which they would require the consent of protectors).

IN THE LAST SENTENCE, AFTER commonly it will be decisive; INSERT A NEW NOTE 24a: This sentence was cited with approval in *Whaley v Whaley*, above, at [114].

INSERT AT THE END OF THE LAST SENTENCE A NEW NOTE 24b: *A v A*, above, at [97]. See too *Whaley v Whaley*, above.

AFTER § 29–159 INSERT THE FOLLOWING NEW PARAGRAPH AND HEADING:

Facts disputed

A source of difficulty for trustees from time to time is that matters material **29–159A** for them to take into account are disputed in point of fact. It is when the exercise of dispositive powers is under consideration that the difficulty usually arises, particularly if the beneficiaries are already at loggerheads. The extent of the means of a given beneficiary, or his financial responsibility, are frequent subjects of controversy; but there may be other disputes, such as the nature of the settlor's wishes, sometimes left in a state of uncertainty at his death, or the source of funds put into settlement.[24a] Though trustees are expected to make enquiries and not to act merely on the information to hand,[24b] they are not detectives and they lack the resources to resolve such differences; beneficiaries do not have the right to a hearing from them.[24c] Nor can the trustees be expected to approach the court whenever such a controversy exists, since the costs of doing so would be prohibitive, though there is no doubt that they may do so if the proposed exercise of their discretionary power will be sufficiently momentous;[24d] indeed, it is not clear that the court can make declarations of fact which do not determine legal rights, merely because trustees would find it convenient to have an authoritative decision to take into account, though it seems that

---

[24a] As in *S v L* [2005] JRC 109.
[24b] See §§ 29–130, 29–146.
[24c] See § 29–155.
[24d] See §§ 29–296 *et seq.* for applying to the court for the court's blessing for a provisional decision taken by trustees and for surrendering their discretion.

applications for such a determination as part of an application for directions have been entertained.[24e] We consider that, where the matter is not sufficiently momentous to warrant an application to the court, the trustees will have done their duty if they seek the comments of any antagonists and do their best on the material so disclosed. A beneficiary then alleging that the trustees based themselves on a view of the facts which was incorrect will have to establish that they were mistaken as to a fact which was "basic to the transaction", the test for setting aside a voluntary disposition,[24f] the principle in *Re Hastings-Bass*[24g] being unavailable in the absence of a breach of duty on the part of the trustees.[24h]

Duty (3)—To act impartially

29–164 NOTE 38. FOR THE REFERENCE TO the Standard Provisions of the Society of Trust and Estate Practitioners, SEE NOW (2nd edn), para.21.

Other fiduciaries

29–165 IN THE THIRD SENTENCE DELETE he remains under to consider AND REPLACE BY: he remains under a duty to consider.

9. MANNER OF EXERCISE OF POWERS

Formalities

Formalities required by statute

29–168 NOTE 45. For the reference to Megarry and Wade, *The Law of Real Property*, see now (7th edn), § 11–047 and n.286.

NOTE 48. DELETE *ibid.* AND REPLACE BY: Wills Act 1837.

Formalities required by settlor

29–170 NOTE 54. INSERT AT THE END: *HR Trustees Ltd v Wembley plc* [2011] EWHC 2974 (Ch).

NOTE 57. INSERT AT THE END (WITHIN THE FINAL BRACKET): and [2008] NZSC 61.

[24e] *S v L*, above (where the trustees acknowledged that their decision on a distribution would be influenced by the answer to the question whether one of the beneficiaries was the source of some of the settled funds). In *X v A* [2005] EWHC 2706 (Ch); [2006] 1 W.L.R. 741 at [30], [50] the court said that where trustees applied for the court's blessing, cross-examination and disclosure were not usual, but did not rule them out. Both took place in *Jones v Firkin-Flood* [2008] EWHC 2417 (Ch) but there the trustees' application for the court's blessing had been met with a counterclaim from two of the beneficiaries for a variety of other relief, including the removal of the trustees. The Jersey court in *Re A Settlement* [2010] JRC 085 asserted a jurisdiction (relying on Jersey legislation) to require a beneficiary to make disclosure material to a decision to be taken by trustees (reversed [2010] JCA 231); see § 23–64A (Supplement).
[24f] As stated in *Pitt v Holt* [2011] EWCA Civ 197; [2012] Ch. 132, see §§ 29–231, 29–232.
[24g] [1975] Ch. 25, CA.
[24h] See §§ 29–239, 29–242, 29–243.

Administrative powers

In the last sentence delete If the power is exercisable and replace by: If **29–171** the power is a power of appointment and is exercisable.

After § 29–171 insert a new heading and paragraph:

Preconditions to exercise

The donor of a power may impose preconditions on its exercise. Cases in **29–171A** which the donee must first form a judgment as to a given state of facts have already been mentioned,[60a] as have cases in which the consent of another person to the exercise is required.[60b] Other preconditions may be imposed, such as the obtaining of professional advice before the power is exercised. If such a precondition is imposed, any purported exercise of the power without obtaining the advice is void;[60c] and it makes no difference that the advice would necessarily have been in favour of the proposed exercise.[60d]

Intention to exercise

Other indications—implied exercise

After the sixth sentence insert: Even if the exercise of the power is not **29–176** necessary for the given transaction to take effect, it may be that a mere recital that the power has been previously exercised will itself suffice as an exercise of the power.[84a]

At the end of the penultimate sentence insert: Nor will trustees be treated as having exercised a power of accumulation over a given receipt when they incorrectly thought that it already was capital[85a] or as having exercised a power of appointment when they set out to exercise a power of advancement.[85b]

Note 86. At the end add: But a rather narrower view was taken in *Kain v Hutton*, above.

Note 87. The correct neutral citation of *Betafence Ltd v Veys* is [2006] **29–177** EWHC 999 (Ch).

Note 89. Insert at the end (within the final bracket): on further appeal [2008] NZSC 61.

10. Defective Execution of Powers

Entitlement of beneficiaries of trust to a formal exercise

At the end of the fifth sentence, insert a new Note 12a: In *HR Trustees* **29–182** *Ltd v Wembley plc* [2011] EWHC 2974 (Ch) at [66], in the context of a

---

[60a] See §§ 29–122 *et seq.*
[60b] See §§ 29–35 *et seq.*
[60c] *Walker Morris Trustees Ltd v Masterson* [2009] EWHC 1955 (Ch); [2009] P.L.R. 307 (power to amend pension trust subject to written actuarial advice that existing rights not prejudiced).
[60d] *ibid.*, at [38], [54].
[84a] *Lees v Lees* (1871) I.R. 5 Eq. 549; *Re Shinorvic Trust* [2012] JRC 081.
[85a] *Pierce v Wood* [2009] EWHC 325 (Ch); [2010] W.T.L.R. 253.
[85b] *Kain v Hutton* [2008] NZSC 61; (2008) 11 I.T.E.L.R. 130. See § 32–22A (Supplement).

pension trust, it was said that the members, not being volunteers, could have obtained specific performance against the trustee of "their exercise of the power", meaning compliance with the specified formalities once the trustees had decided on an exercise.

29–183 NOTE 16. INSERT AT THE END (WITHIN THE FINAL BRACKET): and [2008] NZSC 61 AND CONTINUE But in *HR Trustees Ltd v Wembley plc*, above, where the beneficiaries were not volunteers, the court treated a purely discretionary power as having been exercised.

Prerequisites for exercise of jurisdiction

Formal defects only

29–186 NOTE 20. INSERT AT THE END: *Re Shinorvic Trust* [2012] JRC 081 (non-compliance with requirement for witnessing donee's signature).

Persons able to invoke the jurisdiction

29–188 NOTE 34. INSERT AT THE END (WITHIN THE FINAL BRACKET): and [2008] NZSC 61.

Children and other dependants

29–189 NOTE 40. INSERT AT THE END (WITHIN THE MISSING FINAL BRACKET): and [2008] NZSC 61.

INSERT AFTER THE THIRD SENTENCE: Despite those authorities, however, it has been held in Jersey that the principle may be invoked by any person for whom the donee is under a natural or moral obligation to provide, including therefore a former cohabitant.[40a]

11. TIME FOR EXERCISE OF POWERS

Time limits

29–196 INSERT AFTER THE THIRD SENTENCE: But where a power of appointment is expressed to be exercisable during a prescribed time, the power may be exercised within that time so as to override the trusts in default of appointment even after the vesting, expressed to be "absolutely", of an interest under those trusts.[61a]

Exercise within a reasonable time

29–202 INSERT AFTER THE FIRST SENTENCE: A similar obligation may apply, as a matter of construction, to other discretions, such as a power vested in pension trustees to award a share of a surplus to a member of the pension scheme on his retirement.[77a]

AT THE END OF THE PARAGRAPH ADD: But in the context of a pension scheme the same rule has not been applied and it has been held that trustees remain

---

[40a] *Re Shinorvic Trust* [2012] JRC 081.
[61a] *Howell v Lees-Millais* [2009] EWHC 1754 (Ch); [2009] W.T.L.R. 1163.
[77a] *Entrust Pension Ltd v Prospect Hospice Ltd* [2012] EWHC 1666 (Ch).

bound to consider the exercise of a fiduciary mere power in favour of members of the scheme even though a reasonable time for its exercise has expired.[83a]

Fettering the exercise of a power

Fiduciary power

NOTE 87. AT THE END OF THE FIRST SENTENCE ADD: *Re Y Trust* [2011] JRC 135 **29–204** at [54].

AT THE END OF THE THIRD SENTENCE INSERT: Similarly, trustees selling shares **29–205** which give a controlling interest in a company may, if necessary to obtain the best price, give warranties common in such agreements and contract not to distribute the consideration within the period of the warranties (not least because in the absence of such a restriction they would have been entitled to retain part or all of the trust fund[95a] to protect their entitlement to be indemnified in respect of the liability on the warranties).[95b]

AT THE END ADD: Note that if an agreement alleged to be a fetter is made **29–206** with a third party, and the agreement is said to be ineffective (and not merely a breach of trust), it is necessary to join the third party to any proceedings in which its effectiveness is challenged.[98a]

More than one donee—simultaneous exercise

NOTE 7. AT THE END ADD: and [2008] NZSC 61. **29–209**

12. GIVING REASONS FOR DECISIONS

No general duty to give reasons

NOTE 15. INSERT AT THE END OF THE FIRST SENTENCE: *Breakspear v Ackland* **29–210** [2008] EWHC 220; [2009] Ch. 32.

NOTE 22. DELETE THE LAST SENTENCE.

13. EXCESSIVE EXECUTION

General

AFTER THE PENULTIMATE SENTENCE INSERT: Severance is possible if, as a **29–217** conceptual matter, it is possible to distinguish the boundary between the valid and the invalid; but in the case of a fiduciary power it is also material to enquire whether the trustees would not have exercised the power at all, or would have exercised it differently, if they had been properly instructed as to the limits on the power, for otherwise the principle in *Re Hastings-Bass*[38a] would vitiate the exercise.[38b]

[83a] *Entrust Pension Ltd v Prospect Hospice Ltd*, above.
[95a] For trustees' entitlement to an indemnity against contractual liabilities, see § 21–13.
[95b] *Jones v Firkin-Flood* [2008] EWHC 2417 (Ch); [2008] All E.R. (D) 175 (Oct) at [213].
[98a] *Jones v Firkin-Flood*, above, at [216].
[38a] [1975] Ch. 25, CA. For the principle in *Re Hastings-Bass*, see §§ 29–238 *et seq.*
[38b] *Bestrustees v Stuart* [2001] EWHC 549 (Ch); [2001] O.P.L.R. 341.

Appointment to non-objects

29–221 NOTE 55. FOR THE REFERENCE TO *Thomas on Powers*, SEE NOW (2nd edn, 2012), paras.8.23 *et seq.*

14. MISTAKE, MISAPPREHENSION AND INADVERTENCE

General

DELETE §§ 29–229 AND 29–230 AND REPLACE BY THE FOLLOWING:

29–229 Trustees and other donees may exercise a power while labouring to some extent under a mistake or misapprehension, whether as to the nature of the exercise or the facts on which their decision is based or the effect of what they are doing. Relief is available in various circumstances which are described here. The grounds on which relief is available may be divided into those dependent on the duties owed by fiduciaries and those not so dependent. The primary point of distinction is that in the latter case it is necessary to show that the mistake was a mistake as to the nature or legal effect of the transaction and not merely as to its consequences;[80] in the former that is not necessary and relief may be available in wider circumstances.

29–230 In the former class of case, the jurisdiction of the court became prominent in recent years, especially when the fiscal treatment of a proposed exercise had been misunderstood. Decisions of trustees who had exercised a power in a way which proved expensive in tax came to be set aside on the ground that they had not understood the consequences of what they were doing, under what became known as the principle in *Re Hastings-Bass*.[81] Other taxpayers did not have the benefit of revisiting their decisions to the same extent and disquiet was expressed that the principles on which the court was acting was unduly indulgent.[82] The disquiet was shared by the revenue authorities,[83] which began to take part in and oppose applications for relief under that principle, both in England and elsewhere.[83a] The Court of Appeal, in *Pitt v Holt*,[83b] has now re-stated the relevant principles in both classes of case, that is, those dependent on the duties owed by fiduciaries and those not so dependent. We begin with the latter.

---

[80] See § 29–232.

[81] [1975] Ch. 25, CA.

[82] Walker, 'The Limits of the Principle in *In Re Hastings-Bass*' [2002] P.C.B. 226 (an extra-judicial view expressed by Lord Walker of Gestingthorpe). Neuberger, *Aspects of the law of mistake: Re Hastings-Bass* (2009) Trusts & Trustees, Vol.15(4), 189 (an extra-judicial view expressed by Lord Neuberger of Abbotsbury, M.R.).

[83] H.M. Revenue & Customs' *Tax Bulletin*, issue 83, at 1292–1294 (June 2006), setting out criticisms of decisions developing the principle in *Re Hastings-Bass*, for which see §§ 29–238 *et seq.*

[83a] See, in England, *Pitt v Holt* [2010] EWHC 236 (Ch); [2010] S.T.C. 901 and *Re Futter* [2010] EWHC 449 (Ch); [2010] S.T.C. 982, appeals in which were heard together, [2011] EWCA Civ 197; [2012] Ch. 132. H.M.R.C. successfully sought to be joined in proceedings in Guernsey in *H.M.R.C. v Gresh* [2010] W.T.L.R. 1303, Guernsey CA.

[83b] Above.

Circumstances not dependent on duties owed by fiduciaries

Rescission

NOTE 84. INSERT AT THE END: and in *Pitt v Holt* [2011] EWCA Civ 197; [2012] **29–231**
Ch. 132 at [165]–[210].

NOTE 85. DELETE AND REPLACE BY: See §§ 4–56 *et seq.* (including
Supplement).

AFTER THE END OF THE PARAGRAPH INSERT: In summary, there must be a
mistake on the part of the disponor either as to the legal effect of the
disposition or as to an existing fact which is basic to the transaction.[92a]

DELETE THE WHOLE PARAGRAPH AND THE ASSOCIATED FOOTNOTES AND REPLACE **29–232**
BY: The seriousness of the mistake is an additional element in the jurisdiction. There is the authority of the House of Lords for saying (in the case of a
gift) that a donor "can only obtain back property which he has given away
by showing that he was under some mistake of so serious a character as to
render it unjust on the part of the donee to retain the property given to
him".[93] Before the jurisdiction can be invoked, the mistake must both satisfy
that test and must be a mistake as to the legal effect of the disposition or as
to a basic existing fact.[94]

INSERT AT THE END OF THE THIRD SENTENCE OF THE TEXT: and it has recently **29–233**
been confirmed that the unforeseen fiscal effects of a transaction will not
bring the jurisdiction into play.[96a] DELETE THE REMAINING SENTENCES OF THE
TEXT AND THE ASSOCIATED FOOTNOTES.

Circumstances dependent on duties owed by fiduciaries—*Re Hastings-Bass*[20]

DELETE §§ 29–238 TO 29–254 AND REPLACE BY THE FOLLOWING:

General

A principle has been developed dependent on the duty of trustees (or, see- **29–238**
mingly, other fiduciary donees) to have regard to relevant considerations,
and only relevant considerations, when exercising powers vested in them.
The duty extends to considering the consequences of a proposed exercise of
a power in a particular way and not merely its nature or legal effect. If the
exercise has effects or consequences not apprehended by the trustees, when
they ought to have been, it may be vitiated. This is the so-called principle in
Re Hastings-Bass;[21] and though, as will appear, the name has become
inapposite it is likely to continue in use.

[92a] *Pitt v Holt* [2011] EWCA Civ 197; [2012] Ch. 132, at [210]. See § 4–58 (Supplement).
[93] *Ogilvie v Littleboy* (1897) 13 T.L.R. 399 at 400, CA, *per* Lindley L.J.; approved in HL *sub
    nom. Ogilvie v Allen* (1899) 15 T.L.R. 294 *per* Lord Halsbury L.C. and Lord Macnaghten.
[94] *Pitt v Holt*, above, at [167], [203], [210].
[96a] *Pitt v Holt*, above, at [210].
[20] [1975] Ch. 25, CA.
[21] Above.

29–239 As it now stands, the principle takes the form enunciated by the Court of Appeal in *Pitt v Holt*[22] in 2011, when the authorities were exhaustively discussed. Its main features are as follows:[23]

(1) Trustees are bound to take relevant matters into account and to ignore irrelevant matters when exercising a discretionary power.

(2) Relevant matters include the fiscal consequences, if any, of any proposed exercise.

(3) If there is a breach of their fiduciary duty in failing to take into account relevant matters, or to ignore irrelevant matters, but only if there is such a breach, then the exercise of the power will be open to challenge,

(4) In such a case the exercise is not void but voidable and relief is both discretionary and subject to any available equitable defences.

(5) The exercise is not open to challenge in the absence of fault on the part of the trustees, as where their failure to take a given matter into account (for instance, adverse tax consequences) was the result of incorrect professional advice.

The Supreme Court, however, has given permission to appeal against the decision of the Court of Appeal and so the exposition of the principle in this work must be treated as provisional until the Supreme Court has given judgment.

History of the principle

29–240 In decisions preceding *Pitt v Holt*, the principle had been thought to take a different and much wider form, by which any decision of trustees was vitiated if taken in ignorance of material considerations or taking into account immaterial considerations, the general view, though not the universal view, being that that was so whether or not the trustees had been at fault and that the exercise was then void rather than voidable.[24] The

---

[22] [2011] EWCA Civ 197; [2012] Ch. 132, CA. The decision disposed of two appeals, heard together, that in *Pitt v Holt* and another in *Re Futter*.

[23] *ibid.*, at [126]–[131], especially [127].

[24] English decisions before *Pitt v Holt* included *Green v Cobham* [2000] W.T.L.R. 1101; *Abacus Trust Co. (Isle of Man) Ltd v National Society for the Prevention of Cruelty to Children* [2001] S.T.C. 1344; *AMP (UK) Ltd v Barker* [2001] P.L.R. 77 (*obiter*); *Hearn v Younger* [2002] EWHC 963 (Ch); [2002] All E.R. (D) 223 (May); *Abacus Trust Co. (Isle of Man) Ltd v Barr* [2003] EWHC 114 (Ch); [2003] Ch. 409; *Sieff v Fox* [2005] EWHC 1312 (Ch); [2005] 1 W.L.R. 3811; *Gallaher Ltd v Gallaher Pensions Ltd* [2005] EWHC 42 (Ch); [2005] O.P.L.R. 57 (*obiter*); *Burrell v Burrell* [2005] EWHC 245 (Ch); [2005] S.T.C. 569; *Smithson v Hamilton* [2007] EWHC 2900 (Ch); [2008] 1 W.L.R. 1453; *Jiggens v Low* [2010] EWHC 1566 (Ch); [2010] S.T.C. 1899; *Wyantt v Tyrrell* [2010] EWHC 3633 (Ch), together with the decisions at first instance reversed in *Pitt v Holt* itself, namely *Pitt v Holt* [2010] EWHC 236 (Ch); [2010] S.T.C. 901 and *Re Futter* [2010] EWHC 449 (Ch); [2010] S.T.C. 982. *Abacus Trust Co. (Isle of Man) Ltd v Barr* was alone in holding (i) that there had to be a breach of duty on the part of the trustees and (ii) that the exercise was then voidable, not void, though other decisions left one or other point open.

principle was attributed to the decision of the Court of Appeal in 1975 in *Re Hasting-Bass*, as understood and applied in *Mettoy Pension Trustees Ltd v Evans*[25] in 1989, and so went under the name 'the principle in *Re Hastings-Bass*'. In *Pitt v Holt*, however, it was held that *Re Hasting-Bass* had been misinterpreted in *Mettoy* and was not authority for the wide principle until then attributed to it.[26]

The problem in *Re Hastings-Bass* arose out of the exercise of a power of **29–241** advancement by way of sub-settlement, effected by a transfer to another settlement for the benefit of the object of the power. A life interest so created in favour of the object did not breach the rule against perpetuities but the remaining trusts did so and hence were void.[27] The question arose whether the whole advancement was ineffective.[28] The Court of Appeal upheld the life interest, holding that the exercise of the power could be upset only if the exercise could not reasonably be regarded as being for the benefit of the beneficiary intended to be advanced.[29] In words much quoted in later decisions, however, the court said,[30]

> "... [W]here by the terms of a trust ... a trustee is given a discretion as to some matter under which he acts in good faith, the court should not interfere with his action notwithstanding that it does not have the full effect which he intended, unless (1) what he has achieved is unauthorised by the power conferred upon him, or (2) it is clear that he would not have acted as he did (a) had he not taken into account considerations which he should not have taken into account, or (b) had he not failed to take into account considerations which he ought to have taken into account."

That passage was relied on in *Mettoy* and later decisions to support a principle expressed in positive terms, to the effect that where a trustee acts under a discretion given to him by the terms of the trust but the effect of the exercise is different from that which he intended, the court will interfere if he would not have acted as he did but for failing to take into account considerations which he ought to have taken into account or taking into account considerations which he ought not to have taken into account.[31] The wording quoted from *Re Hastings-Bass* is in fact to the effect that the court will not interfere in the absence of certain circumstances and it does not follow that it will interfere wherever those circumstances are present.

---

[25]   [1990] 1 W.L.R. 1587 at 1621.
[26]   *Pitt v Holt* [2011] EWCA Civ 197; [2012] Ch. 132 at [72], [131].
[27]   Under the rule that the exercise of a power of advancement had to be read back into the original settlement for the purpose of the rule against perpetuities, see § 5–90 (including Supplement).
[28]   The question arose between the trustees and the Inland Revenue, the Inland Revenue contending that the purported advancement was entirely void; no beneficiary sought to set the advancement aside.
[29]   [1975] Ch. 25 at 41B–C. See § 32–21.
[30]   [1975] Ch. 25 at 41F–H.
[31]   The formulation in *Mettoy Pension Trustees Ltd v Evans* [1990] 1 W.L.R. 1587 at 1621H, as modified and adopted in *Sieff v Fox* [2005] EWHC 1312; [2005] 1 W.L.R. 3811 at [46]–[49], [114], [119].

Indeed, in *Re Hastings-Bass* the court expressly rejected a submission that the trustees could not have exercised their power validly unless they had had a proper understanding of the effect of the sub-settlement.[32]

29–242 The court in *Pitt v Holt* drew attention to that rejection and held that the passage quoted had to be understood consistently with it: the fact that the trustees had misunderstood the effect of the advancement did not make it void.[33] *Mettoy* and the later authorities following it were wrong in holding that a misapprehension or similar failing on the part of trustees would do so.[34] It was only if the exercise of the power, once its effects were examined, could not reasonably have been regarded as being for the benefit of the beneficiary being advanced that the exercise would have been void, for then it would have been outside the scope of the power.[35] Otherwise the exercise might be voidable at the instance of a beneficiary but it would be valid until set aside; and it would be voidable only if the trustees had been in breach of duty.[36] No such question had arisen in *Re Hastings-Bass*, for no beneficiary had sought to set the decision aside and the contest was between the Inland Revenue, concerned to argue that the exercise was wholly void, and the trustees.

29–243 In future, therefore, attention will usually focus on the question whether the trustees were in breach of duty in exercising the power as they did and, if so, whether it should be avoided at the instance of a beneficiary. That is so at least in England. In a number of jurisdictions abroad the principle in *Re Hastings-Bass* in its wider form was adopted before *Pitt v Holt*.[37] Whether those jurisdictions will now adopt the narrowing of the principle effected in *Pitt v Holt* remains to be seen.[38]

Examples

29–244 Examples of the application of the principle in its re-stated form may be given as follows:

---

[32] [1975] Ch. 25 at 41E, referring to a submission summarised at 35G–H.
[33] *Pitt v Holt* [2011] EWCA Civ 197; [2012] Ch. 132 at [58], [62], [63]–[67].
[34] *Ibid.*, at [72], [94], [122].
[35] *Re Hastings-Bass*, above, at 41B–C; *Pitt v Holt*, above, at [58], [66], [96], [222].
[36] *Pitt v Holt*, above, at [99], [222].
[37] *Re Green GLG Trust* [2002] JRC 235; (2002–03) 5 I.T.E.L.R. 590; *Barclays Private Bank & Trust (Cayman) Ltd v Chamberlain* (2006–07) 9 I.T.E.L.R. 302, Cayman GC; *Irish Pensions Trust Ltd v Central Remedial Clinic* [2005] O.P.L.R. 137, Ir HC; *A v Rothschild Trust Cayman Ltd* (2006–07) 9 I.T.E.L.R. 307, Cayman GC; *Re RAS I Trust* [2006] JRC 187; (2006–07) 9 I.T.E.L.R. 798; *Re Winton Investment Trust* [2007] JRC 206; [2008] W.T.L.R. 553; *Re Howe Family No.1 Trust* [2007] JRC 248; *Re Seaton Trustees Ltd* [2009] JRC 050; [2010] W.T.L.R. 105; *Re Ta-Ming Wang Trust* (2010–11) 13 I.T.E.L.R. 854, Cayman GC; *Re R Trust* [2011] JRC 85.
[38] In *Re S Trust* [2011] JRC 117 the Jersey RC declined to follow *Pitt v Holt* in so far as it re-stated in a narrow form the grounds on which a gift into trust could be set aside so as to exclude a misapprehension of the consequences of the gift (notably the fiscal consequences), for which see § 4–58 (including Supplement). The Jersey RC did not consider the *Hastings-Bass* principle in that case, though it is notable that, in considering *Pitt v Holt*, the Jersey RC took a less sympathetic view of the weight to be attached to the interests of the tax authority than did the CA in *Pitt v Holt*, see [2011] JRC 117 at [39] ("Leviathan can look after itself").

(1) Where the rule against perpetuities rendered void much of an exercise of a power of advancement but the residue could still be regarded as being for the benefit of the object of the power, the exercise was not void but might be voidable at the instance of a beneficiary.[39]

(2) Where the trustees of a pension scheme did not properly inform themselves as to the value of the fund and the consequences of that value when exercising an imperative power to fix an amount to be transferred to another scheme on a sale by the employer of part of its business, their decision fixing the amount was held to be flawed.[40]

(3) Where trustees were held to be at fault in exercising a power of appointment as to 60 per cent. of the fund, under the impression that in so doing they were acting in accordance with the settlor's wishes, when in fact his wishes were that they should exercise the power as to 40 per cent. of the fund only, the exercise was liable to be avoided.[41]

(4) Where the trustees executed a lease (held also to be vitiated by the self-dealing rule[41a]) without giving any consideration to the interests of the beneficiaries.[41b]

Cases of voidability and voidness

Since it is now clear that the application of the narrowed principle in *Re*   **29–245** *Hastings-Bass* leaves the exercise of a power voidable and not void, it will be necessary to draw a sharp distinction between cases within the principle and cases within other rules which may render the exercise void, particularly rules having some resemblance to the principle:

(1) Where the misapprehension on the part of the trustees is such that the exercise cannot properly be regarded as being for the benefit of the beneficiary intended to be benefited, as where the limitations have been largely struck down by the rule against perpetuities, the exercise is void. (The test is an objective one, not requiring an investigation of what the trustees would have done if they had

---

[39]   *Re Hastings-Bass*, above, itself, as explained in *Pitt v Holt* [2011] EWCA Civ 197; [2012] Ch. 132, see §§ 29–241, 29–242.

[40]   *Stannard v Fisons Pensions Trust Ltd* [1992] I.R.L.R. 27, CA, as commented on in *Pitt v Holt*, above, at [73]–[74]. It is not in fact clear from the report of *Stannard* what relief was sought or whether the decision was treated only as voidable.

[41]   *Abacus Trust Co. (Isle of Man) v Barr* [2003] Ch. 409, as commented on in *Pitt v Holt*, above, at [81]–[89], [129]. The decision anticipated *Pitt v Holt* in that it was held that under the principle in *Re Hastings-Bass* the exercise of a power was voidable rather than void. The case was adjourned for consideration whether the exercise should be avoided.

[41a]   See §§ 20–58, 20–63 *et seq.*

[41b]   *Earl of Cardigan v Moore* [2012] EWHC 1024 (Ch); [2012] W.T.L.R. 931 at [51].

known of the problem.[42]) In such a case, the exercise is not within the terms of the power at all.[43] But such cases will be infrequent.

(2) A somewhat different failure to take relevant matters into account occurs where trustees have given no independent consideration to an exercise of their powers but have merely acted on the prompting of others. Appointments have been held void where the trustees executed documents prepared on the instructions of the settlor and never applied their minds at all to the exercise of the discretion entrusted to them.[44] In such cases there is undoubtedly a breach of the duty recognised in *Re Hastings-Bass* to take relevant matters into account and that authority has been relied on when holding the purported exercise void;[45] but they turn rather on the absence of any real decision by the trustees than on the taking of a decision vitiated by mistake or misapprehension.[46] *Pitt v Holt* does not suggest that they should be subsumed into the narrow principle that it recognises or that such a purported exercise should be treated as only voidable.[47] Hence they are considered elsewhere.[48]

(3) Where there is a fraud on the power, the exercise is also void and not voidable,[49] a rule acknowledged in *Pitt v Holt*.[50]

(4) There are other defects in the exercise of a power rendering the exercise void, some of them mentioned in *Pitt v Holt*,[51] such as the want of a requisite formality,[52] the failure to obtain a necessary prior consent,[53] an unauthorised delegation[54] and an excessive appointment.[55]

Scope of trustees' duty

29-246 The decision in *Pitt v Holt* that there must be a breach of the trustees' fiduciary duty before the exercise of a power can be avoided will necessarily focus attention on the precise scope of the trustees' duty to have regard to relevant matters and to disregard irrelevant matters. As the principal judgment acknowledges, however, the decisions do not give a great deal of

---

[42] *Pitt v Holt* [2011] EWCA Civ 197; [2012] Ch. 132 at [66].
[43] *Re Abrahams' Will Trusts* [1969] 1 Ch. 463, as explained in *Re Hastings-Bass*, above, at 41; *Pitt v Holt*, above, at [57]–[58], [96], [222]. See §§ 5–90, 32–21 (including Supplement).
[44] *Turner v Turner* [1984] Ch. 100. See too *Betafence Ltd v Veys* [2006] EWHC 999 (Ch); [2006] W.T.L.R. 941 at [73]–[74].
[45] *Turner v Turner*, above, at 111A–C.
[46] *Mettoy Pension Trustees Ltd v Evans* [1990] 1 W.L.R. 1587 at 1624G–H.
[47] See *Pitt v Holt*, above, at [88], citing *Turner v Turner*, above, and the comment on it in *Abacus Trust Co. (Isle of Man) Ltd v Barr* [2003] EWHC 114 (Ch); [2003] Ch. 409 at [32]–[33], to the effect that in such cases the purported exercise is void.
[48] § 29–144.
[49] See §§ 29–277 to 29–279.
[50] See *Pitt v Holt*, above, at [97]–[98].
[51] Above, at [96].
[52] See §§ 29–166 to 29–171.
[53] See §§ 29–35 *et seq.*, especially § 29–50.
[54] See §§ 29–90, 29–225.
[55] See §§ 29–216 *et seq.*

guidance in detail as to what ought to be taken into account in the case of ordinary discretionary trusts.[56] We have tried to expound what are and what are not relevant matters elsewhere.[57]

It is clear, however, that the fiscal consequences of a proposed exercise of a **29–247** power are matters which the trustees are bound to take into account.[58] If they fail to do so, then they will be in breach of their duty and it will be open to a beneficiary to seek the setting-aside of the exercise. It seems that, in general, if a voidable exercise of a power is in fact avoided on an application to the court the exercise will be treated for tax purposes as if it had not occurred; that is specifically provided for inheritance tax[59] and the same appears to apply to other taxes.[60] Hence a beneficiary can be expected to challenge the exercise if, through the fault of the trustees, there are unforeseen fiscal consequences which are adverse for the trust as a whole or for himself. On such a challenge the revenue authorities will seemingly have no standing to appear and so none to object.[61] Before *Pitt v Holt*, applications under the principle in *Re Hastings-Bass* were commonly, though not invariably, prompted by the adverse fiscal consequences of an exercise of the trustees' powers[62] and the decision in *Pitt v Holt* has not closed the door on challenges to such an exercise.

Nonetheless, in one common set of circumstances no challenge will be **29–248** possible. The trustees will have performed their duty if they take apparently competent professional advice even when the advice is wrong. Put another way, if it is said that the trustees failed to have regard to a relevant matter but the reason why they did not do so is that they obtained and acted on such advice, which turned out to be incorrect, there will be no breach of duty on their part and hence no ground for challenging the exercise of the powers based on it.[63] The remedy, if any, will lie against the professional advisers. This was the actual decision in *Pitt v Holt* itself and in the appeal heard with it, in both of which professional advice had been taken that was incorrect; the exercise of the powers had unfavourable fiscal consequences which were overlooked by the advisers. It was held that there was no breach of fiduciary duty and so the exercise in each case could not be avoided.[64]

If the trustees take no professional advice but it was reasonable for them not **29–249** to do so, then likewise they will not have failed in their duty and any decision taken cannot be impugned.[64a] There will be other situations in which the trustees fail to take a relevant matter into account without fault on their part. An instance is an appointment of quoted shares to a particular

---

[56] *Pitt v Holt* [2011] EWCA Civ 197; [2012] Ch. 132 at [114]–[118].
[57] §§ 29–146 *et seq.*
[58] *Pitt v Holt*, above, at [115]–[116], [222].
[59] Inheritance Tax Act 1984, s.150.
[60] *Pitt v Holt* [2011] EWCA Civ 197; [2012] Ch. 132 at [91].
[61] *Cf. ibid.*, at [92].
[62] As in *Green v Cobham* [2000] W.T.L.R. 1101.
[63] *Pitt v Holt*, above, at [119]–[125], [222].
[64] *ibid.*, at [139], [143]–[144], [162]–[163]. It made no difference that in one case one of the trustees was a partner in the firm of solicitors giving the advice: *ibid.*, at [140]–[142].
[64a] *Prudential Staff Pensions Ltd v The Prudential Assurance Co. Ltd* [2011] EWHC 960 (Ch); [2011] N.J.L.R. 597 at [228] *et seq.*

value to a beneficiary when the shares subsequently turn out at the date of
the appointment to have been markedly more or less valuable than their
quoted price by reason of a fact not reasonably ascertainable at the time,
such as an imminent take-over bid or a massive fraud perpetrated on the
quoted company.[65] In such cases there will be no breach of duty on the part
of the trustees and no jurisdiction to avoid the appointment.

Nature and seriousness of mistake or misapprehension

29–250 The distinction between the legal effect of the transaction, or an existing fact
basic to it, on the one hand and its consequences on the other, though
important under the general jurisdiction to relieve against the consequences
of a mistake,[66] are without significance for the purpose of the principle re-
stated in *Pitt v Holt*. A mistake as to consequences only, leading to a failure
to take them into account, will suffice. That follows from the fact that fiscal
consequences were recognised in *Pitt v Holt* as capable of attracting the
operation of the principle.[67]

29–250A Before *Pitt v Holt* there had been some controversy whether it was necessary
to show that the trustees would have taken a different decision if properly
apprised of the relevant considerations or whether it was sufficient merely
that they might have done so. The authorities were largely reconciled by a
decision that the test was indeed whether the trustees would have acted
differently where the power was wholly discretionary; but where the trustees
were bound to act, the power being what we have called an imperative
power[68] and any discretion being confined to the manner or timing of the
exercise, then the test was only whether they might have acted differently.[69]
It is not clear whether that distinction has any role to play in the principle
re-stated in *Pitt v Holt*; the point is not discussed. A complaining beneficiary
who establishes only that the trustees might have acted differently will not
have established any loss caused by the breach of duty; but that is not
conclusive for present purposes, as the question is whether the challenged
exercise of the power is to be avoided, not whether compensation should be
paid. It may be that the answer is to be found in the fact that the court's
intervention is now discretionary; an exercise is unlikely to be set aside
unless the trustees' decision would have been different.

---

[65] An instance given in *Abacus Trust Co. (Isle of Man) Ltd v Barr* [2003] EWHC 114 (Ch);
[2003] Ch. 409 at [23], the only decision before *Pitt v Holt* to require a breach of duty on the
part of the trustees.
[66] See §§ 29–231 *et seq.*
[67] See § 29–247.
[68] See §§ 29–22, 29–112 to 29–116.
[69] *Sieff v Fox* [2005] EWHC 1312 (Ch); [2005] 1 W.L.R. 3811 at [50]–[56], [77], adopted obiter
in *St Mary and St Michael Parish Advisory Co. Ltd. v The Westminster Roman Catholic
Diocese Trustee* [2006] EWHC 762 (Ch); [2006] W.T.L.R. 881 at [167].

Standing to challenge

Since it is now necessary to prove a breach of duty on the part of the trustees **29–250B**
in order to invoke the principle re-stated in *Pitt v Holt*, it will usually be a
beneficiary who does so.[70] Previously it was not uncommon for the trustees
to approach the court to overturn a decision of their own once it was
realised that it had unintended consequences.[71] The trustees at fault will not
generally wish to acknowledge a breach of duty; nor is it obvious that they,
or indeed successor trustees, can invoke the jurisdiction of the court to avoid
the exercise of the power. But it was recognised in *Pitt v Holt* that trustees
might seek directions from the court if a beneficiary alleged a breach of trust
but did not bring his own proceedings;[72] and when trustees identify a problem promptly it would be unfair not to allow them go to court themselves,
if need be, since delay might increase the adverse financial consequences for
which they would be liable.

Discretion and equitable defences

Where there is a case for challenging the exercise of a power, the court's **29–250C**
intervention is discretionary and is subject to available equitable defences.[73]
How far the discretion adds to the available defences is not yet clear. We
have already suggested that the seriousness of the mistake or other failing on
the part of the trustees will be a material factor.[74]

As between those interested in the trust, the principal equitable defence **29–250D**
likely to be invoked is laches. A beneficiary who stands by once he knows of
the possibility of a challenge is unlikely to succeed in upsetting the exercise
of a power.[75] Supervening equitable interests created by later exercises of
dispositive powers will not have an automatic priority, even though the right
to seek an avoidance of the prior exercise of the power is a mere equity, but
will be an important factor in the exercise of the court's discretion.

As to third parties, they may have dealings either with a beneficiary or with **29–250E**
the trustees. In the former case, a gratuitous assignee of a supervening
equitable interest will be in the same position as the assignor. But if the third
party gives value for the assignment, and has no notice of the defect in the
prior exercise of the trustees' discretion, his interest, though equitable, will
on ordinary principles have priority over the right to seek an avoidance of
the prior exercise.[76] If the third party deals with the trustees and the subject

---

[70] *Pitt v Holt* [2011] EWCA Civ 197; [2012] Ch. 132 at [130], saying also that proceedings
ought to be by a Part 7 claim form, since there may be a substantial dispute of fact to be
resolved.
[71] See, *e.g.*, *Abacus Trust Co. (Isle of Man) Ltd v National Society for the Prevention of
Cruelty to Children* [2001] S.T.C. 1344.
[72] *Pitt v Holt*, above, *loc. cit.*
[73] *Pitt v Holt*, above, at [127], [222].
[74] See § 29–250A (Supplement).
[75] For laches generally, see §§ 44–15 to 44–16. In *Abacus Trust Co. (Isle of Man) Ltd v Barr*
[2003] EWHC 114 (Ch); [2003] Ch. 409, the only decision before *Pitt v Holt* to hold that the
exercise was voidable rather than void, the life tenant (and settlor) had known of the
problem for nearly ten years before proceedings were issued and the case was adjourned for
consideration whether the exercise should be avoided.
[76] *Snell's Equity* (32nd edn), § 4–023.

of the assignment is the trust property itself, of which he takes a legal assignment, for value and without notice, then again on ordinary principles he will take free of the right to seek an avoidance, though the right will attach to the proceeds of sale.[77]

Relief

29–250F The relief to be sought when invoking the principle re-stated in *Pitt v Holt* will ordinarily be the setting-aside of the whole exercise of the power under challenge and the consequent reversal of any steps taken under it, such as the transfer of trust funds. Under the broader principle that was understood to exist before that decision, the question arose whether only part of the exercise could be treated as bad; and it was held that it could.[78] Hence, so it was said, if on a proper consideration of relevant matters trustees would still have executed the deed they did execute but with the omission of a particular provision, the court might declare only that provision ineffective;[79] similarly, if trustees given proper tax advice would have omitted some assets from an appointment but not others, the appointment might be held ineffective only as to the assets which would have been omitted.[80] But a single provision in an instrument could not be omitted if the omission would leave the remainder unworkable or would amount to rectification of the instrument rather than a partial undoing of the exercise of a power.[81] Whether a partial avoidance remains possible after *Pitt v Holt* was left open in that case[82] but there seems to be no reason why not: it must be easier to avoid part of the exercise of a power if the exercise is only voidable.

29–251 Since an application to avoid the exercise of a power must now be based on a breach of duty on the part of trustees, it will be common to combine it with a claim for compensation to the extent that an order avoiding the exercise is refused or such an order does not fully restore the trust fund. Consequential orders may also be claimed against the recipients of dispositions sought to be avoided. Where trustees exercised a power to pay to a widow "generous and appropriate sums" out of both income and capital without making any enquiry as to her other means, though directed by the trust instrument to do so, her estate was held liable to refund the entirety of the sums so paid.[83]

---

[77] *Pitt v Holt* [2011] EWCA Civ 197; [2012] Ch. 132 at [99]. The same applies to a contract with a third party: *Donaldson v Smith* [2007] W.T.L.R. 421 at [51]–[55]. (The passage is omitted in [2006] EWHC B9 (Ch).) It may perhaps be different where the third party is agreeable to the setting-aside of the contract or disposition: *Re Winton Investment Trust* [2007] JRC 206; [2008] W.T.L.R. 553 at [12], [19].

[78] *Mettoy Pension Trustees Ltd v Evans* [1990] 1 W.L.R. 1587 at 1624H–1625B; *Burrell v Burrell* [2005] EWHC 245 (Ch); [2005] S.T.C. 569 at [25].

[79] *Mettoy Pension Trustees Ltd v Evans*, above, *loc. cit.*

[80] *Burrell v Burrell*, above, at [25].

[81] *Smithson v Hamilton* [2007] EWHC 2900 (Ch); [2008] 1 W.L.R. 1453.

[82] *Pitt v Holt*, above, at [72].

[83] *Sinclair v Moss* [2006] VSC 130. The trustees' decisions were held void in consequence of the failure to make enquiries. It was held on the facts that the trustees would have made different decisions if they had made those enquiries.

No positive effect of principle

The principle re-stated in *Pitt v Holt* is negative only. It is invoked where the **29–252** trustees have not given proper consideration to relevant matters and if in consequence the exercise of a power is avoided the power is treated as not having been exercised. It does not apply in the converse case, so as to permit the court to treat the trustees as having exercised a power which they have not in fact exercised on the ground that the failure to exercise it was caused by a misapprehension and that they would have done so if properly informed.[83a] Hence if trustees fail to exercise a power before it has expired there can be no recourse to the principle.[83b]

Third parties

The cases of a power vested in trustees but subject to the consent of a third **29–253** party and of a power vested in a third party but vested in trustees have already been mentioned in the discussion of the general jurisdiction to give relief for mistake.[83c] We consider that if the trustees have exercised the power under a mistake which would otherwise attract the operation of the principle re-stated in *Pitt v Holt*, the fact that a requisite consent is forthcoming from a third party who is not mistaken should not be a bar to relief; and that if the trustees have consented to an exercise under such a mistake, that similarly should ground relief even though the donee was not mistaken.[83d]

Other fiduciaries

The principle re-stated in *Pitt v Holt* may apply to other fiduciaries, at any **29–254** rate those holding a discretionary power which obliges them to consider relevant matters and ignore irrelevant ones. The Court of Appeal was prepared to assume in that case that the principle did apply to a receiver of another's property appointed under the Mental Health Act 1983 (now a deputy appointed under the Mental Capacity Act 2005).[83e] In Jersey the former principle in *Re Hastings-Bass* has been applied to a protector when deciding on the appointment of new trustees.[83f] Directors have been said to fall within the principle.[83g] We consider that such fiduciaries should be treated as being on the same footing as trustees.

[83a] *Breadner v Granville-Grossman* [2001] Ch. 523, decided before *Pitt v Holt* but there can be no doubt that it remains good law.

[83b] *ibid.* As to the possibility of a claim for damages by a disappointed beneficiary, see § 43–09.

[83c] See § 29–236.

[83d] But in *Smithson v Hamilton* [2007] EWHC 2900 (Ch); [2008] 1 W.L.R. 1453 relief was refused where a definitive pension deed had been entered into under a misapprehension, on the ground that it had been devised by the employer, though accepted by the trustees, and so the adoption of the deed was "essentially", "predominantly" or "overwhelmingly" the act of the employer, not the trustees (*ibid.*, at [81], [92]). An appeal was compromised: see [2008] EWCA Civ 996.

[83e] *Pitt v Holt* [2011] EWCA Civ 197; [2012] Ch. 132 at [162]. The court at first instance had decided that a receiver did attract the operation of the former principle in *Re Hastings-Bass*, see [2010] EWHC 236 (Ch); [2010] S.T.C. 901.

[83f] *Re R Trust* [2011] JRC 085.

[83g] *Re Ta-Ming Wang Trust* (2010) 13 I.T.E.L.R. 854, Cayman GC. See too *Hunter v Senate Support Services Ltd* [2004] EWHC 1085 (Ch); [2005] 1 B.C.L.C. 175 at [172] *et seq.*

15. Fraud on a Power—Ulterior Purposes

General principle

29–256 Note 85. At the end add: *Kain v Hutton* [2008] NZSC 61 at [18].

Categories of fraud on a power

Division (2)—Bargain to benefit non-object

29–260 In the fourth sentence delete to make him liable and replace by: to make the donee liable.

29–261 Note 5. At the end add: (on appeal at [2008] NZSC 61).

29–262 Note 7. Insert at the end (within the final bracket): and [2008] NZSC 61.

29–263 Note 8. At the end add: (and see on appeal [2008] NZSC 61).

Note 10. At the end add: *Kain v Hutton* [2008] NZSC 61; (2001) 11 I.T.E.L.R. 130 at [21], [52]–[53].

Division (3)—Other foreign purpose

29–264 Note 13. After the reference to *Re Cohen* insert: *Jones v Firkin-Flood* [2008] EWHC 2417 (Ch) at [262]–[264], [280].

Who can complain

Powers of appointment and other dispositive powers

29–269 In the first sentence delete any those interested and replace by: any of those interested.

Powers within the principle

29–272 Note 43. At the end add: Seemingly it applies also to a power to change the proper law of a trust (for which see § 11–74): see *Oakley v Osiris Trustees Ltd* [2008] UKPC 2; (2007–08) 10 I.T.E.L.R. 789.

Note 44. The correct citation of *Re Papadimitriou* is [2004] W.T.L.R. 1141, Manx HC. At the end add: *Re Bird Charitable Trust* [2008] JRC 013; (2008) 11 I.T.E.L.R. 157 at [75]; *Austec Wagga Wagga Pty Ltd v Rarebreed Wagga Pty Ltd* [2012] NSWSC 343.

Re Nicholson's Settlement

29–274 Note 50. For the reference to *Thomas on Powers*, see now (2nd edn, 2012), paras.9.29 to 9.34.

Consequences where exercise is a fraud on a power

29–277 Note 56. Insert at the end of the first sentence: *Pitt v Holt* [2011] EWCA Civ 197; [2012] Ch. 132 at [97]–[98] (expressed with some reservation). Delete the second sentence and replace by: Contrast the consequences of an exercise of a power vitiated by the principle of *Re Hastings-Bass* [1975] Ch. 25, CA restated in *Pitt v Holt*; see §§ 29–239 *et seq.* (Supplement).

16. DISCLAIMER AND RELEASE OF POWERS

Release

NOTE 86. DELETE THE FIRST FIVE WORDS AND REPLACE BY: See cases cited in **29–285** n.83.

NOTE 95. DELETE AND REPLACE BY: See cases cited in n.92.   **29–287**

17. CONTROL BY THE COURT

Category (1)—Extent of trustees' powers

IN THE SECOND SENTENCE DELETE rely on AND REPLACE BY: ascertain.   **29–293**

Category (2) and (3)—"Blessing" and surrender of discretion

Application without surrendering discretion

NOTE 28. AT THE END ADD: See too *Investec Co-Trustees (Jersey) Ltd v Kidd* **29–298** [2012] JRC 066.

AFTER THE SECOND SENTENCE, INSERT: An application may be suitable where a third party, such as a foreign court, has to be satisfied that a power has been properly exercised.[28a]

NOTE 30. IN THE SECOND SENTENCE, DELETE in not appropriate AND REPLACE BY: is not appropriate.

NOTE 32. AT THE END ADD: *Re V Settlement* [2007–08] G.L.R. 240; (2009–10) **29–299** 12 I.T.E.L.R. 360; *NBPF Pension Trustees Ltd v Warnock-Smith* [2008] EWHC 455 (Ch); [2008] 2 All E.R. (Comm) 740.

NOTE 33. AT THE END OF THE FIRST SENTENCE INSERT: *NBPF Pension Trustees Ltd v Warnock-Smith*, above, at [21]; *A Trustees Ltd v W* [2008] JRC 097 at [18].

IN THE SECOND SENTENCE AFTER or the trust estate INSERT: that the proposed exercise of their powers is untainted by any collateral purpose such as might amount to a fraud on the power,[31a]

AT THE END OF THE FIFTH SENTENCE INSERT A NEW NOTE 35a: But it has been held in Jersey that if the court refuses approval of a decision taken by trustees as being unreasonable it may direct a different exercise of the trustees' powers: *A Trustees Ltd v W*, above (where, however, the trustee was also affected by a conflict with its duty as trustee of a separate fund).

[28a] *Re SMP Trustees Ltd* [2012] EWHC 772 (Ch).
[31a] *Tamlin v Edgar*, *The Times*, February 23, 2012.

Insert after the fifth sentence: The court may also withhold approval where the trustees have demonstrated a general unfitness to act, by conduct before the taking of the decision in question.[35b]

Note 37: Insert at the beginning of the note: *Thommessen v Butterfield Trust (Guernsey) Ltd* 2009–10 G.L.R. 102, Guernsey RC; *Tamlin v Edgar*, above.

At the end of the last sentence of the text insert a new Note 38a: This paragraph was quoted with approval in *Jones v Firkin-Flood* [2008] EWHC 2417 (Ch); [2008] All E.R. (D) 175 (Oct) at [257] and *Re Y Trust* [2011] JRC 135 at [40]. It was criticised in *Tamlin v Edgar*, above, perhaps for under-stating the court's role, but in the absence of a full report of the judgment that is not clear.

At the end of the text add: The trustees must also demonstrate that they have concluded how best to exercise their discretion and that they intend, subject to the approval of the court, forthwith to act on that conclusion, since they are not entitled to raise hypothetical questions.[38b]

Application surrendering discretion

29–300   Note 49. Insert at the end: *Jones v Firkin-Flood* [2008] EWHC 2417 (Ch) at [254]–[255], approving what was said in *Public Trustee v Cooper* about managing conflicts of interest.

Category (4)—Attack on actual exercise

29–302   Note 54. At the end of the first sentence add: *McNulty v McNulty* [2011] NZHC 1173; (2011–12) 14 I.T.E.L.R. 361 at [108]–[112].

29–302(5) Note 61. Delete the second sentence and replace by: See §§ 29–238 *et seq.*

29–303   Note 70. Insert a stop at the end and add: But as to applications under the principle in *Re Hastings-Bass*, as re-stated in *Pitt v Holt* [2011] EWCA Civ 197; [2012] Ch. 132, see now § 29–250B (Supplement).

Principle of non-intervention

Where power permissive

29–305   Note 72. At the end add: *Pitt v Holt* [2011] EWCA Civ 197; [2012] Ch. 132 at [108]–[113].

In the first sentence after the quotation, after a particular exercise of the power insert a new Note 73a: *Foo v Foo* (2011) 14 I.T.E.L.R. 708, HC Sing.

29–306   At the end add. The court has refused to overturn a trustee's reasonable decision to sell the sole asset of the trust, even when the settlor was opposed

---

[35b] *Jones v Firkin-Flood* [2008] EWHC 2417 (Ch) at [281].
[38b] *Berman v SPF CDO I Ltd* (2011) 13 I.T.E.L.R. 831, HK CFI. For hypothetical questions, see § 27–21.

to the decision.[78a] Decisions in the exercise of administrative powers, such as a decision not to commence proceedings, are similarly left to the discretion of the trustees.[78b]

AFTER THE THIRD SENTENCE INSERT: Charitable trusts have to satisfy the **29–307** statutory requirement of "public benefit", now stated in the Charities Act 2011,[80a] but the manner in which that obligation is fulfilled is a matter for the trustees and not the Charity Commission or the court.[80b]

NOTE 85. FOR THE REFERENCE TO the Standard Provisions of the Society of **29–308** Trust and Estate Practitioners, SEE NOW (2nd edn), para.19.1.

AT THE END ADD: *AN v Barclays Private Bank and Trust (Cayman) Ltd* (2006–07) 9 I.T.E.L.R. 630 at [19], Cayman GC.

Exceptions to principle of non-intervention

Disclosure to beneficiaries

DELETE THE LAST THREE SENTENCES AND N.3 AND REPLACE BY: The trustees' **29–314** decision to withhold disclosure may no doubt be impugned on one of the conventional grounds for challenging their decisions; such a decision may not be the exercise of a power in the ordinary sense but the trustees cannot be under a duty to give disclosure in response to every request and hence, except in circumstances where they have no real choice,[3] they must have a discretion to withhold disclosure. The court, however, may also intervene in the exercise of its supervisory jurisdiction, though if not persuaded to do so only the conventional grounds of challenge will be available.[3a]

Appointment of trustees

NOTE 8. AT THE END ADD: (and on further appeal [2008] NZSC 61).   **29–315**

[78a] *MM v S.G. Hambros Trust Co. (Channel Islands) Ltd* [2010] JRC 037.
[78b] *Satinland Finance SARL v BNP Paribas Trust Corp UK Ltd* [2010] EWHC 3062 (Ch); [2010] All E.R. (D) 287 (Nov) at [50]–[57].
[80a] See s.4, replacing Charities Act 2006, s.3.
[80b] *R. (Independent Schools Council) v Charity Commission for England and Wales* [2011] UKUT 421 (TCC); [2012] 1 Ch. 214 at [220], [233].
[3]   See § 23–24.
[3a] See § 23–20 (Supplement).

CHAPTER 30

POWERS OF APPOINTMENT, AMENDMENT AND LIKE POWERS

2. GENERAL POWERS OF APPOINTMENT

Creation of general power

30–06 NOTE 11. THE CORRECT REFERENCE FOR *Gregory v Hudson* IS [1997] NSWSC 140; (1997) 41 N.S.W.L.R. 573; affirmed [1998] NSWSC 582; (1998) 45 N.S.W.L.R. 300, NSW CA. AT THE END ADD: See further § 4–36 (including Supplement).

Characteristics of a general power

Perpetuities

30–10 DELETE THE SECOND AND THIRD SENTENCES AND N.15 AND REPLACE BY: The Perpetuities and Accumulations Acts 1964 and 2009 have not altered the rule in substance but have refined what counts as a general power for that purpose. A general power exercisable by will alone, however, was void if it might be exercised outside the perpetuity period; but now, under section 3(3) of the 1964 Act and section 7(5) and (6) of the 2009 Act,[15] if the testator dies after the commencement of the relevant Act, it is valid as to any exercise within the period.

3. SPECIAL POWERS OF APPOINTMENT

General

30–16(3) IN THE FIRST SENTENCE DELETE The Perpetuities and Accumulations Act 1964 provides AND REPLACE BY: The Perpetuities and Accumulations Acts 1964 and 2009 provide.

30–16(7) DELETE the corresponding principle of equity prescribe that AND REPLACE BY: the corresponding principle of equity so prescribe only in the case of a general power.

---

[15] Respectively July 16, 1964, the date of royal assent, and April 6, 2010.

Trust power and mere power

Note 51. At the end add: *Law Shuk Hoi v Lok Fung Kenneth* [2010] **30–21**
HKCFI 641; (2010–11) 13 I.T.E.L.R. 436.

Note 58. At the end add: *Re Bose* [2012] EWHC 858 (Ch). See too *Law Shuk Hoi v Lok Fung Kenneth*, above.

Whether power fiduciary

In the third sentence delete It will be necessarily be and replace by: It **30–22**
will necessarily be.

Where power not exercised

Trust power

Note 80. At the end add: *Bridge Trustees Ltd v Noel Penny (Turbines) Ltd* **30–25**
[2008] EWHC 2054 (Ch).

Note 84. At the end add: *Bridge Trustees Ltd v Noel Penny (Turbines) Ltd* **30–26**
[2008] EWHC 2054 (Ch) (a case on a trust power not vested in a trustee).

Mere power

Note 96. Delete and replace by: § 29–137. **30–27**

Construction of trust powers

Meaning of "relations" and "family"

Delete the second sentence and replace by: Such a power is not inherently **30–33**
uncertain[18a] but the class so pointed out is obviously indeterminate.

4. Intermediate Powers of Appointment

Characteristics of intermediate power

Perpetuities

In the last sentence delete Now the Perpetuities and Accumulations Act **30–39**
1964 treats and replace by: Now the Perpetuities and Accumulations Acts
1964 and 2009 treat.

5. Powers of Addition and Exclusion

Power of addition

Creation

Note 60. At the end add: See too §§ 4–32 and 4–36. **30–46**

[18a] *Re Bose* [2012] EWHC 858 (Ch) at [18], citing this paragraph.

AT THE END OF THE PARAGRAPH ADD: Such a power is akin to a dispositive power and so cannot be conferred on trustees under section 57 of the Trustee Act 1925.[60a]

Effect of existence of power

30–47   INSERT AFTER THE FIRST SENTENCE: The duty cannot be owed to the existing beneficiaries of the trust, as most of the trustees' duties are owed, for if that were so it is hard to see how it could be exercised at all, and it must be owed more widely.[60b]

NOTE 62. INSERT AT THE END: In *Investec Co-Trustees (Jersey) Ltd v Kidd* [2012] JRC 066, the wishes of the settlors were considered critical and in *Tam Mei Kam v HSBC International Trustee Ltd*, above, at [247] in identifying matters for the trustee to consider the court mentioned the named beneficiaries, their relationships to the settlor, the settlor's wishes as expressed in any letter of wishes, the general purposes of creating the trust in the first place and the sources of the trust assets.

Power of exclusion

30–51   INSERT AT THE END: Nor may it be used for the benefit of the trustee himself (or for any other purpose which would constitute a fraud on the power), such as stifling a claim against the trustee[65a] or denying a beneficiary access to information.[65b]

6. POWERS OF AMENDMENT

Validity of power of amendment

30–55   NOTE 74. INSERT AT THE END: The period is now 125 years for settlements created after April 6, 2010, the date on which Perpetuities and Accumulations Act 2009 came into force; see §§ 5–35 *et seq.* (including Supplement).

Scope of power of amendment

30–59   INSERT AFTER THE FIRST SENTENCE: It may be expressly confined in some way; for example, it may be restricted to amendments which do not materially prejudice the interests of the beneficiaries[85a] and a power to change the proper law of a settlement[85b] is often accompanied by a power to make such

---

[60a] *Re Representation of A and B, DDD 1976 Settlement* [2011] JRC 243 at [13], on Jersey legislation similar to Trustee Act 1925, s.57. For s.57, see §§ 45–12 et seq.
[60b] *Tam Mei Kam v HSBC International Trustee Ltd* [2008] HKCFI 496; (2008–09) 11 I.T.E.L.R. 246 at [245] (point not mentioned on appeal, [2010] HKCA 197; [2011] HKCFA 34).
[65a] Cf. *Popely v Ayton Ltd*, unreported, October 13, 2008, HC of St. V. and G. (where a corporate trustee purported to exercise a power of exclusion to remove an entire family as beneficiaries so as to stifle a claim brought by them against companies in the same group). For fraud on the power, see §§ 29–255 *et seq.*
[65b] *Curwen v Vanbreck Pty Ltd* [2009] VSCA 284; (2009–10) 26 V.R. 335.
[85a] As in *Re SMP Trustees Ltd* [2012] EWHC 772 (Ch).
[85b] For such powers, see § 11–74.

amendments as are necessary or desirable to cause it to comply with the new proper law.

NOTE 86: INSERT AT THE END: But the test is an objective one and the court does not receive evidence of what the parties actually did consider: *The PNPF Trust Co. Ltd v Taylor* [2010] EWHC 1573 (Ch); [2010] All E.R. (D) 251 (Jun) at [144].

AFTER § 30–60 INSERT THE FOLLOWING NEW PARAGRAPH:

When the purpose of a power of amendment has been identified, trustees **30–60A** cannot be liable for failing to exercise a power of amendment, or to consider doing so, so as to effect some other purpose.[98a] Under a company life assurance scheme, for example, where the trustees had a power to amend the scheme but only with the employer's consent, it was held that the purpose of the power was to facilitate better administration and management of the scheme; hence the trustees were not liable for failing to propose, or to consider proposing, an increase of cover.[98b]

Retrospectivity

AT THE END ADD: Even when a retrospective amendment is authorised by the **30–61** trust instrument, external constraints may prevent such an exercise of the power.[2a]

Alteration of administrative powers

NOTE 3. AT THE END ADD: The Standard Provisions of the Society of Trust **30–62** and Estate Practitioners (2nd edn), para.13, permit trustees to adopt subsequent editions of those provisions themselves, though they do not permit any wider amendment.

8. POWERS OF REVOCATION

Whether fiduciary

AT THE END OF THE FIRST SENTENCE INSERT A NEW NOTE 28a: *Tassaruf* **30–74** *Mevduati Sigorta Fonu v Merrill Lynch Bank and Trust Co. (Cayman) Ltd* [2011] UKPC 17; (2011–12) 14 I.T.E.L.R. 102 at [59]–[62], on appeal from (2010–11) 13 I.T.E.L.R. 1, Cayman CA.

[98a] *Power v Trustees of the Open Text (UK) Ltd Group Life Assurance Scheme* [2009] EWHC 3064 (Ch); [2009] All E.R. (D) 236 (Dec).
[98b] *ibid.*
[2a] *Harland & Wolff Pension Trustees Ltd v Aon Consulting Financial Services Ltd* [2006] EWHC 1778 (Ch) (European Community law, as construed by the European Court of Justice, precluded retrospective amendment of pension trust).

CHAPTER 31

POWERS OF MAINTENANCE

1. SECTION 31 OF THE TRUSTEE ACT 1925

Part 1 of the Family Law Reform Act 1969

31–05 NOTE 36. ADD: The application of the statutory restrictions on accumulations is not affected by Perpetuities and Accumulation Act 2009 since the provisions of that Act do not apply to an appointment made in exercise of a special power created before that Act came into force: s.15(1)(*b*).

Modification or exclusion of section 31

31–06 NOTE 43. AT THE END ADD: *Fine v Fine* [2012] All E.R. (D) 286 (Jul); [2012] EWHC 1811 (Ch) at [10].

NOTE 45. DELETE THE SECOND SENTENCE AND REPLACE BY: The statutory restrictions on accumulations apply to an instrument made before the provisions concerning accumulations in Perpetuities and Accumulations Act 2009 came into force on April 6, 2010 (see Perpetuities and Accumulations Act 2009, s.22; Perpetuities and Accumulations Act 2009 (Commencement) Order 2010 (SI 2010/37)) and also to an instrument made on or after that date in exercise of a special power of appointment created before that date: ss.15 and 16, 21 and Sch.

Terms of the power

31–08 NOTE 51. AT THE END ADD: considered in *Pitt v Holt* [2011] EWCA Civ 197; [2012] Ch. 132 at [33]–[38].

Circumstances to be considered

AFTER § 31–09 ADD A NEW PARAGRAPH AS FOLLOWS:

31–09A Settlements and wills commonly amend section 31(1) in two ways. First, by the replacement of the words in section (1)(i) "as may in all the circumstances be reasonable" by "as the trustees in their discretion think fit". The purpose of this amendment is to replace the constraints of an objective requirement of reasonableness by trustee discretion. This does not mean that the trustees may act unreasonably in applying income for maintenance but rather that trustees may determine in exercise of fiduciary discretion what, if any, income should in their view properly be applied for maintenance taking relevant considerations into account and disregarding irrelevant considerations. Secondly, by the deletion of the proviso to section 31.[54a] There are two objections to the proviso. The first is that the requirement that the trustees should have regard to age of the child and generally to the circumstances of the case is unnecessary since those are relevant considerations to the exercise of discretion which the trustees would have a duty to take into account apart from the proviso. The second is the unduly restrictive nature of the requirement for a proportionate application of income where the trustees have notice that more than one fund is applicable for maintenance. Notice of the availability of another fund for maintenance purposes is a relevant consideration to be taken into account as matter of exercise of discretion, but it may not necessarily be appropriate, even if practicable, for the trustees to be restricted by the requirement of proportionate application. The Law Commission has proposed that the above common amendments to section 31(1) should be put on a statutory basis in relation to all trusts howsoever established, excluding existing trusts, but including trusts in wills made before the proposed reform by testators who die after the proposed reform, and including trusts in advancements or appointments made after the proposed reform under powers conferred by existing trusts.[54b]

Accumulation of income not applied for maintenance—section 31(2)

NOTE 68. AT THE END ADD: The Law Commission has considered but not **31–12** proposed alteration of this rule, see LCCP No.191 (Supplementary) (2011) on *Intestacy and Family Provision Claims on Death: Sections 31 and 32 of the Trustee Act 1925*, paras 3.42 and 3.43.

NOTE 70. FOR THE REFERENCE TO *Theobald on Wills*, SEE NOW (17th edn), §§ 30–008 and 30–009.

Payment of income to adult beneficiaries with contingent interests

Adult beneficiary with vested interest

NOTE 87. DELETE THE SECOND SENTENCE AND REPLACE BY: The statutory **31–17** restrictions on accumulations apply to an instrument made before the provisions concerning accumulations in Perpetuities and Accumulations Act 2009 came into force on April 6, 2010 (see Perpetuities and Accumulations Act 2009, s.22; Perpetuities and Accumulations Act 2009 (Commencement) Order 2010 (SI 2010/37)) and also to an instrument made on or after that date in exercise of a special power of appointment created before that date: ss.15 and 16, 21 and Sch.

[54a] See §§ 29–146 *et seq.*
[54b] Law Commission Report on *Intestacy and Family Provision Claims on Death* (Law Com. No.331, December 14, 2011), paras.4.78 to 4.97 and clauses 8 and 10 of clause 4 of draft Inheritance and Trustees' Powers Bill in Appendix A to the Report.

Contingent interests and intermediate income

Testamentary gifts within section 175 of the Law of Property Act 1925

31–21 NOTE 95. FOR THE REFERENCE TO *Theobald on Wills*, SEE NOW (17th edn), § 30–006.

NOTE 96. AFTER THE REFERENCE TO *Theobald on Wills*, ADD: (not considered in 17th edn: see § 38–005 of that edn).

Other testamentary gifts

31–22 NOTE 2. FOR THE REFERENCE TO *Theobald on Wills*, SEE NOW (17th edn), § 38–003.

NOTE 4. ADD: *Beard v Shadler* [2011] EWHC 114 (Ch); [2011] W.T.L.R. 1147.

Pecuniary legacies

31–26 NOTE 19. DELETE THE REFERENCE TO THE PRACTICE DIRECTION AND REPLACE BY: CPR, Practice Direction, Pt 40A—Accounts & Inquiries, para.15.

NOTE 20. FOR THE REFERENCE TO *Theobald on Wills*, SEE NOW (17th edn), § 38–019.

31–28 NOTE 26. FOR THE REFERENCE TO *Theobald on Wills*, SEE NOW (17th edn), §§ 38–016 to 38–019.

NOTE 28. FOR THE REFERENCE TO *Theobald on Wills*, SEE NOW (17th edn), § 38–019.

CHAPTER 32

POWERS OF ADVANCEMENT

3. THE STATUTORY POWER

Benefit

NOTE 58. *X v A* IS ALSO REPORTED AT [2006] 1 W.L.R. 741. **32–16**

Resettlement

NOTE 65. DELETE THE SECOND SENTENCE AND REPLACE BY: Note that an advance **32–18** into an off-shore trust may be attacked by HMRC on the ground that it does not come within the scope of the power (see §§ 29–216 *et seq.*), or on the ground of fraud on the power (see §§ 29–255 *et seq.*) but not on the ground that it involves a failure to take relevant considerations into account, etc. under the principle in *Re Hastings-Bass* [1975] Ch. 25, CA as restated in *Pitt v Holt* [2011] EWCA Civ 197; [2012] Ch. 132 (see §§ 29–238 *et seq.*). Compare the inability of HMRC to attack an appointment of non-resident trustees. see §§ 14–40 to 14–44.

Non-objects as beneficiaries

NOTE 70. AFTER THE PENULTIMATE SENTENCE INSERT: *Kain v Hutton* was **32–19** reversed on appeal ([2008] NZSC 61; (2008–09) 11 I.T.E.L.R. 130) on grounds which did not involve determination whether the inclusion of non-objects in a resettlement was justifiable, though reservations were expressed (at [42]) whether a resettlement conferring wide powers on the settlor rather than the advanced beneficiary to add and remove trustees and discretionary beneficiaries could be said to be for the benefit of the advanced beneficiary.

NOTE 73. *X v A* IS ALSO REPORTED AT [2006] 1 W.L.R. 741.

Discretionary trusts and dispositive powers

NOTE 78. FOR THE REFERENCE TO Hanbury and Martin, *Modern Equity*, SEE **32–20** NOW (18th edn), § 20–042. FOR THE REFERENCE TO Parker and Mellows, *The Modern Law of Trusts*, SEE NOW (9th edn), §§ 18–032 to 18–036. FOR THE REFERENCE TO Underhill and Hayton, *Law of Trusts and Trustees*, SEE NOW (18th edn), § 80.17. FOR THE REFERENCE TO Thomas and Hudson, *The Law of Trusts*, SEE NOW (2nd edn), §§ 14.42 to 14.45.

Perpetuities

32–21 DELETE THE SECOND SENTENCE OF THE TEXT AND N.85 AND REPLACE BY: Where some, but not all, of the trusts of the resettlement are void for perpetuity in view of the above rule, the advance will nonetheless be valid as regards the trusts of the resettlement which are not void if the effect of the advancement can reasonably be regarded as beneficial to the advanced beneficiary.[85] We do not consider that potential invalidity of some of the trusts (or powers) under wait and see perpetuity provisions[85a] would normally be sufficiently serious as to prevent the advancement from being reasonably regarded as beneficial to the advanced beneficiary.

AFTER § 32–21 INSERT THE FOLLOWING NEW PARAGRAPH AND HEADING:

Resettlement varying part only of the trusts

32–21A The statutory power may be exercised so as to vary the trusts applicable to part only of the beneficial interests in the trust property if that is for the benefit of the advanced beneficiary, for example by applying capital of the trust fund so that it is held on like trusts to the existing trusts save for a variation in respect of contingent interests arising under accruer provisions.[86a]

AFTER § 32–22 INSERT THE FOLLOWING NEW PARAGRAPH AND HEADING:

The statutory power and powers of appointment in favour of a class

32–22A The statutory power is different in character from a power of appointment exercisable by trustees in favour of all or any members of a class of beneficiaries. The statutory power involves no selection of the beneficiary in whose favour the power is exercised. The power is exercisable by the trustees in favour of a beneficiary who has a vested, defeasible or contingent interest in capital and permits that capital in whole or in part to be applied for his benefit before the time when the capital becomes payable to him under the trusts in any way that the trustees properly consider is for his benefit including by way a resettlement for his benefit. A power of appointment exercisable by trustees in favour of one or more members of a class of beneficiaries involves selection of the beneficiary or beneficiaries to be benefited by an exercise of the power who will not necessarily have any interest or eligibility to benefit under the trusts save under the power of appointment, and even if the objects of the power are also interested in capital under the trusts in default of appointment, the power is not exercised because they have those interests but because they are objects of the power.

---

[85]   *Re Hastings-Bass* [1975] Ch. 25, CA distinguishing *Re Abrahams' Will Trusts* [1969] 1 Ch. 463; considered in *Pitt v Holt* [2011] EWCA Civ 197; [2012] Ch. 132 at [39]–[67]. As to the circumstances in which an exercise of the power of advancement (or other power), though falling within the scope of the power, may be set aside on the ground of breach of duty in failing to take into account relevant consideration or taking into account irrelevant considerations, see §§ 29–238 *et seq.*

[85a]   Perpetuities and Accumulations Act 1964, s.3(1); Perpetuities and Accumulations Act 2009, s.7(1) and (2). See §§ 5–38 and 5–38A (including Supplement).

[86a]   *Southgate v Sutton* [2011] EWCA Civ 637; [2011] W.T.L.R. 1235 at [42]–[46].

Accordingly, if trustees purport to exercise the statutory power by way of resettlement, and it appears from the terms of the purported exercise and the surrounding circumstances that the trustees have in mind only the statutory power, the purported exercise of the statutory power, if invalid as an exercise of that power, will not be taken as being a valid exercise of a power of appointment which could have been exercised if the trustees had decided to do so.[88a] Nevertheless, the distinction between statutory power and a power of appointment, though important, should not be exaggerated in circumstances where both powers are capable of being exercised to create the same trusts for the benefit of the same beneficiary. If the trustees purport to create a resettlement in exercise of the statutory power and all other powers enabling them to do so, and the resettlement comes within the scope of a power of appointment conferred on them but not the statutory power, and the trustees take into consideration matters material to the exercise of both powers, we do not consider that the resettlement, expressed to be in exercising of all other enabling powers, should fail by reason of the reference to the statutory power.[88b]

Interest of a beneficiary

AFTER THE FIRST SENTENCE INSERT: It is not enough that the beneficiary is an **32–23** object of a power of appointment over capital which could be exercised to entitle him to capital but has not been exercised when an advancement under the statutory power is purportedly made.[89a]

Consent from beneficiaries with prior interests

AT THE END OF THE FIRST PARAGRAPH ADD: A person entitled to a prior **32–25** interest has no fiduciary obligations in giving or withholding consent. Such a person is entitled to give or withhold consent whether his reasons are good, bad or indifferent, and even if they are or appear to be based on whim or prejudice, like or dislike.[1a]

Extent of power—its exhaustion

AT THE END ADD: The Law Commission has proposed the reform of section **32–27** 32 so that the power to pay or apply capital to or for the benefit of a trust beneficiary extends to the whole rather than one-half of the beneficiary's share in the trust fund, in relation to all trusts howsoever established, excluding existing trusts, but including trusts in wills made before the proposed reform by testators who die after the reform, and including trusts in advancements or appointments made after the proposed reform under powers conferred by existing trusts.[9a]

[88a] *Kain v Hutton* [2008] NZSC 61; (2008–09) 11 I.T.E.L.R. 130 at [27]–[38]. See further § 29–176 (including Supplement).

[88b] For the exercise of powers so expressed, see § 29–173.

[89a] *Kain v Hutton* [2008] NZSC 61; (2008–09) 11 I.T.E.L.R. 130 at [39].

[1a] *PJC v ADC* [2009] EWHC 1491 (Fam); [2009] W.T.L.R. 1419 at [15], *per* Munby J.

[9a] Law Commission Report on *Intestacy and Family Provision Claims on Death* (Law Com. No.331, December 14, 2011), paras.4.61 to 4.73 and clauses 9 and 10 of draft Inheritance and Trustees' Powers Bill in Appendix A to the Report.

4. EXERCISE OF THE POWER

Subject matter of advance

32–32 AFTER THE WORDS "capital money" INSERT A NEW NOTE 18a: The Law Commission has proposed the clarification of s.32 so that it is made clear that trustees may, as well as paying or applying capital money under s.32, also transfer or apply any other property subject to the trust, see Law Commission Report on *Intestacy and Family Provision Claims on Death* (Law Com. No.331, December 14, 2011), paras.4.74 to 4.76 and clause 9 of draft Inheritance and Trustees' Powers Bill in Appendix A to the Report. This proposal is intended to apply to all trusts whenever created or arising, see clause 10 of the draft Bill. Since the proposal is intended to clarify rather than reform the law, it is thought that the reference to property subject to the trust is intended to be limited to property forming capital as distinct from income of the trust.

NOTE 19. AT THE END ADD: Applied by analogy in *Brown v InnovatorOne plc* [2012] EWHC 1321 (Comm) at [996]–[999].

AT THE END OF THE TEXT ADD: While the trustees can advance to a beneficiary property comprised in the trust fund, even though not cash, they cannot advance to a beneficiary (that is make himself entitled to) a beneficial interest in the trust fund created by the trusts of the settlement, such as an interest under accruer provisions in the settlement.[20a] This principle does not, of course, prevent the trustees from applying capital for the benefit of a beneficiary by way of resettlement, if that is for his benefit, giving him an interest freed from provisions that would have applied under the settlement conferring the power had the resettlement not been made.[20b] Nor, in our view, does this principle prevent a reversionary interest in one settlement which has been settled by its owner on the trusts of another settlement from being the subject matter of an advance in the other settlement, since the reversionary interest is the trust fund or part of the trust fund of the other settlement, not an interest in that trust fund.

[20a] *Sutton v England* [2009] EWHC 3270 (Ch); [2010] W.T.L.R. 335 at [44]–[50] (reversed on appeal *sub nom. Southgate v Sutton* [2011] EWCA Civ 637; [2011] W.T.L.R. 1235 but not on this point, see at [43]).
[20b] See § 32–21A (Supplement).

CHAPTER 33

ASSIGNMENT OF EQUITABLE INTERESTS AND PRIORITIES

2. ASSIGNABILITY

An equitable interest can be assigned

Restriction on alienation

NOTE 5. Trusts (Guernsey) Law 1989, s.40(*b*) HAS BEEN REPLACED BY Trusts **33–04** (Guernsey) Law 2007, s.45(*b*) with effect from March 17, 2008.

4. PRIORITY FROM NOTICE—THE RULE IN *DEARLE V HALL*

Notice as between volunteers

NOTE 40. AT THE END OF THE FIRST SENTENCE ADD: , deciding that a person who **33–44** obtains a charging order is not a purchaser, followed in *Hughmans Solicitors v Central Stream Services Ltd* [2012] All E.R. (D) 102 (May); [2012] EWHC 1222 (Ch) at [24]–[26].

Operation of the rule in *Dearle v Hall*

Shares in companies

FIRST SENTENCE: Section 126 of the Companies Act 2006 came into force on **33–58** October 1, 2009: Companies Act 2006 (Commencement No.8, Transitional Provisions and Savings) Order 2008 (SI 2008/2860).

CHAPTER 34

ADMINISTRATIVE DUTIES OF TRUSTEES

1. DUTIES OF CARE

Exclusion and restriction of the statutory duty of care

34–08 NOTE 54. DELETE EXISTING NOTE AND REPLACE BY: See §§ 39–121 to 39–122.

2. GETTING IN THE TRUST PROPERTY

The primary duty

34–14 NOTE 76. FOR THE REFERENCE TO the Standard Provisions of the Society of Trust and Estate Practitioners, SEE NOW (2nd edn), paras.4.9 (deposit of documents), 4.10 (nominees).

Things in action

Duty to press for payment and take proceedings

34–21 NOTE 1. AT THE END OF THE FIRST SENTENCE ADD: *Re Nordea Trust Co. (Isle of Man) Ltd* [2010] W.T.L.R. 1393, Manx HC.

3. SAFE CUSTODY OF THE TRUST PROPERTY

Money and other fungibles

34–34 NOTE 56. AT THE END OF THE FIRST SENTENCE ADD: *Paragon Finance plc v D.B. Thakerar & Co.* [1999] 1 All E.R. 400 at 416, CA.

AFTER THE FIRST SENTENCE INSERT: It has, however, been held, in the context of a commercial trust, that terms agreed between the parties modifying the legal owner's obligation to keep the property concerned separate from his own or other property does not necessarily preclude the existence of a trust relationship, though the greater the extent to which the duty is disapplied, the harder it will be for the court to determine that the parties objectively intended to create a trust relationship.[56a]

[56a] *Re Lehman Brothers International (Europe)* [2009] EWHC 2545 (Ch) at [60]–[63] (affirmed [2010] EWCA 917); *Re Lehman Brothers International (Europe)* [2010] EWHC 2914 (Ch); [2010] All E.R. (D) 232 at [254]–[260].

Custodians

NOTE 61. FOR THE REFERENCE TO the Standard Provisions of the Society of **34–35** Trust and Estate Practitioners, SEE NOW (2nd edn), paras.4.9, 4.10.

4. MANAGEMENT OF THE TRUST PROPERTY

Land

Repairs

AFTER § 34–45 INSERT THE FOLLOWING NEW PARAGRAPH:

If trust land requires repair but there is no cash held by the trust to fund **34–45A** repairs, and other means of funding are not available, such as borrowing or assistance from beneficiaries, then the court will order the sale of the land.[97a]

Shares

NOTE 7. AT THE END ADD: *Jones v Firkin-Flood* [2008] EWHC 2417 (Ch); **34–49** [2008] All E.R. (D) 175 (Oct) at [99]–[100], [242].

NOTE 12. FOR THE REFERENCE TO the Standard Provisions of the Society of **34–50** Trust and Estate Practitioners, SEE NOW (2nd edn), para.16.

NOTE 18. FOR THE REFERENCE TO the Standard Provisions of the Society of Trust and Estate Practitioners, SEE NOW (2nd edn).

NOTE 25. FOR THE REFERENCE TO Cayman Islands Trust Law, SEE NOW (2011 Revision), Pt VIII.

AFTER § 34–50 INSERT THE FOLLOWING NEW PARAGRAPH:

Where the trustees control a company, the prudence of the management is **34–50A** not their only concern. They will ordinarily be bound also to ensure that the directors exercise their management powers over the company in a manner that is consistent with the terms of the trust and any orders of the court concerning the trust.[25a] An anti-*Bartlett* clause in ordinary form is unlikely to protect them if they fail to do so.

5. INSURANCE

Powers to insure

NOTE 30. DELETE AND REPLACE BY: The Standard Provisions of the Society of **34–51** Trust and Estate Practitioners (1st edn), para.3(1) formerly conferred an express power to insure but in the 2nd edition it has been deleted as the statutory power (see § 34–57) is now adequate.

[97a] *Chapman v Bledwin Ltd* [2009] All E.R. (D) 01 (Feb).
[25a] *Banicevich v Gunson* [2006] 2 N.Z.L.R. 11 at [67]–[71], NZ CA (application for leave to appeal refused [2006] NZSC 24; [2006] 2 N.Z.L.R. 25).

6. NOMINEES AND UNCERTIFICATED HOLDINGS

Uncertificated holdings

CREST

34–67 NOTE 84: INSERT AT THE BEGINNING: For a fuller description of the CREST system, see *Palmer's Company Law* (25th edn), para. 6.701 *et seq.* and *Mills v Sportsdirect.com Retail Ltd* [2010] EWHC 1072 (Ch); [2010] All E.R. (D) 111 (May) at [5] *et seq.*

AT THE END OF THE THIRD SENTENCE INSERT A NEW NOTE 84a: If the shares remain uncertificated, transfer of title to them, at any rate when it takes place through the system, is excluded from the operation of Law of Property Act 1925, ss.53(1)(*c*) and 136: see Uncertificated Securities Regulations 2001, reg.38 and *Mills*, above, at [71]. For the application of the rule that a specifically enforceable contract for the sale of shares passes the beneficial interest to a purchaser, see § 10–09 (Supplement).

Nominees generally

Present statutory power

34–73 NOTE 4. FOR THE REFERENCE TO the Standard Provisions of the Society of Trust and Estate Practitioners, SEE NOW (2nd edn), para.4.10.

Extension under trust instrument or variation

34–84 NOTE 35. FOR THE REFERENCE TO the Standard Provisions of the Society of Trust and Estate Practitioners, SEE NOW (2nd edn), para.4.10.

Chapter 35

INVESTMENT BY TRUSTEES

1. Statutory Powers of Investment

The general power of investment conferred by the Trustee Act 2000

AFTER THE FIRST SENTENCE ADD: The statutory power extends to all property **35–02** within the trust, whether at the time in a state of investment or not.[5a]

2. Express Powers of Investment

Such investments as the trustees think fit

AT THE END OF THE TEXT ADD: Where the clause does give the trustees the **35–16** investment powers of a beneficial owner, they have the power to give warranties on the sale of shares in a private company.[56a]

Investment in companies

"Public company"

NOTE 83. Companies Act 2006, s.4 came into force on October 1, 2009: **35–25** Companies Act 2006 (Commencement No.8, Transitional Provisions and Savings) Order 2008 (SI 2008/2860).

4. Auxiliary Powers

Power to vary investments

NOTE 32. ADD: This statement was approved in *Hawksford Trustees Jersey* **35–42** *Ltd v Stella Global UK Ltd* [2011] EWHC 503 (Ch); [2011] All E.R. (D) 154 (Mar) at [124], where it was said that a power to invest extends to a power to sell investments.

[5a] The words, "whether at the time in a state of investment or not" were expressly contained within the provisions of the former Trustee Investments Act 1961, s.1, but their omission in the 2000 Act does not entail any restriction in the statutory power of investment: *Gregson v HAE Trustees Ltd* [2008] EWHC 1006 (Ch); [2009] 1 All E.R. (Comm) 457 at [86].

[56a] *Jones v Firkin-Flood* [2008] EWHC 2412 (Ch); [2009] All E.R. (D) 175 (Oct) at [213]. Where the giving of the indemnities enabled the best price to be obtained, no objection could be taken by the beneficiaries on the ground that the trustee's discretion as to the distribution of the trust fund had been fettered.

5. Exercise of Powers of Investment

The investment power is fiduciary

35–62 NOTE 96. AT THE END OF THE FIRST SENTENCE ADD: *Re David Feldman Charitable Foundation* (1987) 58 O.R. (2d) 626, Ont. Surr. Ct.

Excluding ulterior purposes

35–63 NOTE 2. Companies Act 2006, s.172(1)(*d*), (2) came into force on October 1, 2007: Companies Act 2006 (Commencement No.3, Transitional Provisions and Savings) Order 2008 (SI 2007/2194).

NOTE 3. ADD: For a discussion of the problems occasioned by this rule, and of proposals for its reform, see Thornton [2008] C.L.J. 396.

NOTE 7. AT THE END ADD: Pension trustees cannot, however, use this rule by analogy by contending that they are acting in the interests of the beneficiaries to justify exercising their powers in such a way as to bring about an insolvency event and thus to bring the fund within the Pension Protection Fund: *Independent Trustee Services Ltd v Hope* [2009] EWHC 2810 (Ch); [2009] All E.R. (D) 234 (Nov) at [111]–[113].

Diversification

35–70 DELETE THE FOURTH AND FIFTH SENTENCES AND REPLACE BY: The duty is to review and to consider diversification of the assets of the trust, not a duty to diversify as such. Whilst section 4(3) speaks of diversification as a need, there will be circumstances where the trustees will be justified in retaining an undiversified portfolio, particularly where the initial trust property contains a shareholding in an unlisted company.[30a] The duty in section 4(3) will necessarily be excluded by a direction by the settlor to retain a particular shareholding or other asset.[30b] However, it should be borne firmly in mind that Parliament has referred to diversification as a need. In normal circumstances, a trustee will properly fail to diversify only where there is a compelling argument for such a course of action.

AT THE END OF THE TEXT ADD: A failure to consider at all whether the investments of the trust should be diversified may justify the removal of the trustee.[31a]

[30a] See *Gregson v HAE Trustees Ltd* [2008] EWHC 1006 (Ch); [2009] 1 All E.R. (Comm) 457 at [90]. These comments were, strictly, *obiter dicta*, as the claim was struck out on other grounds.

[30b] *ibid.* at [88].

[31a] *Jones v Firkin-Flood* [2008] EWHC 2412 (Ch); [2009] All E.R. (D) 175 (Oct) at [240], where this was one of the factors said to justify the removal.

Fairness as between beneficiaries with different interests

IN THE FIRST SENTENCE AFTER trustees must INSERT: , subject to the terms of the trust,[52a] **35–74**

NOTE 53. AT THE END ADD: *Jeffery v Gretton* [2011] W.T.L.R. 809 at [68].

DELETE THE FINAL SENTENCE AND REPLACE BY: In a 2004 Consultation Paper,[56] the Law Commission made proposals for the duty to balance the interests of capital and beneficiaries to be put on a statutory basis and also for the trustees to have a power to allocate receipts between capital and income so as to discharge the duty to balance. Both of these proposals were subsequently rejected in a Law Commission Report in 2009.[57]

Review of investments

AFTER THE FIRST SENTENCE ADD: The reference to the investments of the trust is to be read as a reference to the trust property, and was almost certainly not intended to confine the scope of section 4(2).[62a] **35–77**

NOTE 63. AT THE END ADD: The duty is certainly not excluded by virtue of the trustees being given the investment powers of an absolute owner: *Jeffery v Gretton* [2011] W.T.L.R. 809 at [69].

6. INVESTMENT ON MORTGAGE

Trustees should not employ same solicitor as borrower

NOTE 99. AT THE END ADD: *Hilton v Barker Booth & Eastwood (a firm)* [2005] UKHL 8; [2005] 1 W.L.R. 567. **35–119**

7. ACQUISITION OF LAND

Trustee Act 2000

Exclusion of investment in land from the statutory general power of investment

NOTE 17. FOR THE REFERENCE TO Megarry and Wade, *The Law of Real Property*, SEE NOW (7th edn), §§ 23–001 *et seq.* **35–123**

NOTE 23. FOR THE REFERENCE TO Megarry and Wade, *The Law of Real Property*, SEE NOW (7th edn), § 10–030.

[52a] *Canada Trust Co. v Browne* [2010] ONSC 4118; (2010–11) 13 I.T.E.L.R. 648 at [62]–[94] (provisions for income beneficiaries' entitlement to be determined by reference to the total return of trust assets impliedly excluded the duty to act impartially).

[56] Law Commission Consultation Paper No.175, *Capital and Income in Trusts: Classification and Apportionment.*

[57] Law Commission Report No.315, *Capital and Income in Trusts: Classification and Apportionment*, at paras.5.26 and 5.81. See § 25–03 (Supplement).

[62a] See *Gregson v HAE Trustees Ltd* [2008] EWHC 1006 (Ch); [2009] 1 All E.R. (Comm.) 457 at [84].

What land may be acquired under section 81(1) and (2)

35–127 NOTE 91. FOR THE REFERENCE TO Underhill and Hayton, *Law of Trusts and Trustees*, SEE NOW (18th edn), §§ 49.35 to 49.38.

CHAPTER 36

ADMINISTRATIVE POWERS OF TRUSTEES

1. GENERAL

Dispensing with circuity

NOTE 24. AT THE END OF THE FIRST SENTENCE ADD: Applied by analogy in *Brown* **36–07**
v InnovatorOne plc [2012] EWHC 1321 (Comm) at [996]–[999].

2. POWER TO EMPLOY AGENTS

Agency under the Trustee Act 2000

General

NOTE 49. FOR THE REFERENCE TO the Standard Provisions of the Society of **36–14**
Trust and Estate Practitioners, SEE NOW (2nd edn), para.15.

Matters capable of delegation

NOTE 84. IN THE FIRST SENTENCE DELETE a administrative power AND REPLACE **36–19**
BY an administrative power. AT THE END OF THE FIRST SENTENCE INSERT: See
the comments on that decision in *Southgate v Sutton* [2011] EWCA Civ 637;
[2012] 1 W.L.R. 326, where, however, it was common ground (see *ibid.* at
[10]) that the trustees had no inherent power to effect such an appropriation.

Terms of engagement

IN THE THIRD SENTENCE AFTER THE NUMBERED SUB-PARAGRAPHS, INSERT A NEW **36–27**
NOTE 14a: The Standard Provisions of the Society of Trust and Estate
Practitioners (2nd edn), in para. 15, now exclude (or purport to exclude) all
the restrictions in Trustee Act 2000, ss.12 to 15.

Asset management

NOTE 37. ADD AT THE END: The Standard Provisions of the Society of Trust **36–31**
and Estate Practitioners (2nd edn), in para.15, now exclude (or purport to
exclude) all the restrictions in Trustee Act 2000, ss.12 to 15.

AFTER § 36–31 INSERT THE FOLLOWING NEW PARAGRAPH:

It is quite common for the investments of a trust to be held not by the **36–31A**
trustees directly but by a holding company of which all the shares are vested

in the trustees. If the company appoints a discretionary fund manager, he is the agent of the company and not of the trustees and it seems that the special obligations imposed by section 15 of the 2000 Act will not apply to him.

AFTER § 36–33 INSERT THE FOLLOWING NEW PARAGRAPH AND HEADING:

Liability of agents

36–33A An agent duly appointed may, of course, incur a liability to the trustees if he defaults in the performance of his functions. Although an agent may act gratuitously, his liability will typically be for breach of contract and so will depend on the terms of the contract between him and the trustees; there may also be a parallel liability in tort for negligence. A discretionary asset manager, for example, will owe a duty of reasonable care and skill in carrying out his functions unless the duty is modified by the terms of the agreement.[41a] As to other possible liabilities, even when an agent takes possession of trust assets, he will not be treated as a trustee *de son tort* if properly appointed, since he is lawfully in possession of them.[41b] Even if the trustee infringes the limits set by the 2000 Act to the appointment of agents, section 24 probably precludes an agent from being so treated.[41c] But it is possible that an agent may incur a liability as such if he is engaged by a principal who is purporting to be a trustee but has not been properly appointed a trustee and so is himself a trustee *de son tort*.[41d]

3. POWERS OF APPROPRIATION

Sources of powers of appropriation

36–62 NOTE 15. FOR THE REFERENCE TO the Standard Provisions of the Society of Trust and Estate Practitioners, SEE NOW (2nd edn), para.4.15.

Appropriation by trustees under general law

36–66(5) NOTE 32. AT THE END ADD: But such a power may be conferred by the court under Trustee Act 1925, s.57: *Southgate v Sutton* [2011] EWCA Civ 637; [2012] 1 W.L.R. 326. For s.57, see §§ 45–12 *et seq.*

AT THE END ADD: It has been said, however, that such an appropriation is authorised when the power conferred by section 41 is incorporated into the trust instrument and the trust instrument dispenses with the consents required by the section;[32a] and if that is correct the power may well be found useful by trustees.

36–74 INSERT AT THE END: There may on occasion be some practical difficulty in effecting an appropriation and in such a case the trustees will need to adopt such method as the nature of the property permits; where, for example, they

---

[41a] Both at common law and under the Supply of Goods and Services Act 1982, ss.13, 16.
[41b] *Cunningham v Cunningham* 2009 J.L.R. 227.
[41c] See § 36–33.
[41d] *Cunningham v Cunningham*, above; and see § 42–96.
[32a] *Hughes v Bourne* [2012] EWHC 2232 (Ch) at [41].

hold all the membership rights in a company limited by guarantee, an appropriation can be effected by admitting new members.[50a]

7. POWERS OF BORROWING

Borrowing generally

NOTE 3. DELETE ENTIRE NOTE AND REPLACE BY: The Standard Provisions of the **36–94** Society of Trust and Estate Practitioners (2nd edn), para.14, confer a power of borrowing for any purpose at all.

[50a] *Walbrook Trustees (Jersey) Ltd v Fattal* [2010] EWCA Civ 408; [2011] 1 All E.R. (Comm) 647 at [18]–[19], [29].

Chapter 37

TRUSTS AFFECTING LAND

1. Introduction

From 1926 to 1966—settled land and trusts for sale

37–01   Note 3. For the reference to Megarry and Wade, *The Law of Real Property*, see now (7th edn), §§ 10–004, 10–005.

Note 5. For the reference to Megarry and Wade, *The Law of Real Property*, see now (7th edn), § 10–009.

The 1996 Act—trusts of land

37–02   Note 11. For the reference to Megarry and Wade, *The Law of Real Property*, see now (7th edn), § 15–052.

2. Trusts of Land

"Trust of land"

"Settled land"

37–07   Note 38. At the end add: or the 7th edition.

Power to postpone sale under express trusts for sale

"Created by disposition"

37–09   Note 52. For the reference to Thomas and Hudson, *The Law of Trusts*, see now (2nd edn), § 59.35.

3. Powers of Trustees of Land

Consent to the exercise of trustees' functions

37–31   Note 75. For the reference to *Emmet on Title*, see now *Emmet and Farrand on Title*, § 22.020.

Title guarantees

37–50   Note 26. For the reference to *Emmet on Title*, see now *Emmet and Farrand on Title*, §§ 16.001 and 16.002.

4. Rights of Beneficiaries of Trusts of Land

The right to occupy trust land

Note 59. The text referred to in *Emmet on Title* (now *Emmet and Farrand on* **37–57** *Title*) is no longer included within that work.

Excluding and restricting the right to occupy and conditions of occupation

Note 81. After second sentence add: Principles of equitable accounting **37–62** do, however, still apply where the occupation of the co-owner has not been excluded or restricted in accordance with the 1996 Act because he has no right to occupy, as where the co-owner is the trustee in bankruptcy of the co-owner's spouse: *Re Barcham* [2008] EWHC 1505 (Ch); [2009] 1 W.L.R. 1124.

Note 85. Delete and replace by: *Rahnema v Rahbari* [2008] All E.R. (D) 308 (Mar) at [29]; and see § 9–54 (including Supplement).

The powers of the court

Note 3. At the end add: For a case where the obligation to obtain the **37–67** consent of the beneficiaries before sale was removed despite its having originally been included as part of the compromise of a proprietary estoppel claim, see *Page v West* [2010] EWHC 504 (Ch); [2010] W.T.L.R. 1811.

After the text to n.8 insert: An application may be made between separated spouses, but it is better in principle for an issue about the sale of the matrimonial home to be dealt with in ancillary relief proceedings. If the parties will be able to apply for ancillary relief within a reasonable period, the court should not hear an application for an order for sale under s.14.[8a]

Supervision of the court

Secured creditors of beneficiaries

Note 28. Delete and replace by: See *Close Invoice Finance Ltd v Pile* [2008] **37–70** EWHC 1580 (Ch); [2008] B.P.I.R. 1465 at [13] (in application for order for sale by holder of charging order under CPR 73.10, the court must exercise its discretion in a way which respects the right of all those living in the property to have respect for their family life and their home); *Putnam & Sons v Taylor* [2009] EWHC 317 (Ch); [2009] B.P.I.R. 769 at [29] (s.15 compliant with the Convention); *National Westminster Bank plc v Rushmer* [2010] EWHC 554 (Ch); [2010] 2 F.L.R. 362 at [50] (ordinarily sufficient to give due consideration to the factors listed at s.15). See too the cases cited in § 37–73 (including Supplement), there in the context of applications by a trustee in bankruptcy.

[8a] *Miller Smith v Miller Smith* [2009] EWCA Civ 1297; [2010] W.T.L.R. 519 at [18]. Wilson L.J. said that, if there was a measurable chance of the respondent preserving his occupation of the property in the application for ancillary relief, the making of an order for sale under section 14 would almost certainly not be a proper exercise of the court's discretion.

Bankrupt beneficiaries

37–72 NOTE 40. AT THE END ADD: In the absence of exceptional circumstances, the trustee is entitled to an order for possession and the court is obliged to make it unless the bankrupt is in a position to apply for the annulment of the bankruptcy: *Pick v Sumpter* [2010] EWHC 685 (Ch); [2010] B.P.I.R. 638 at [10], [15]. It would appear that the Court retains a discretion, pursuant to Insolvency Act 1986, s.363, to suspend an order for possession: *Re Gonsalves* [2011] B.P.I.R. 419.

Exceptional circumstances

37–73 NOTE 45. AT THE END ADD: The medical condition of the bankrupt's spouse may constitute an exceptional circumstance even where the spouse is himself bankrupt: see *Everitt v Budhram* [2009] EWHC 1219 (Ch); [2010] Ch. 170 (Insolvency Act 1986, s.335A(2)(*b*)(ii)).

AFTER THE TEXT TO N.48 INSERT: The circumstances of the making of the bankruptcy order are irrelevant.[48a] Delay by the trustee in bankruptcy in pursuing an application will constitute exceptional circumstances only where it (a) is inordinate, and (b) materially affects some interest to which the court is directed to have regard.[48b]

DELETE THE FINAL SENTENCE (BUT NOT N.50) AND REPLACE BY: The question whether the Human Rights Act 1998 has altered the interpretation of what constitutes exceptional circumstances is not yet finally resolved. The relevant decisions are all at first instance, but most recently the courts have indicated that the European Convention on Human Rights does not require any modification of the application of section 335A of the Insolvency Act 1986.

NOTE 50. AT THE END ADD: In *Foyle v Turner* [2007] B.P.I.R. 43 at [50], it was said that, "provided that the provisions of s.335A are faithfully followed and applied, there is no need to enter into any separate consideration of Art.8 rights. The priority determined by Parliament, as between the creditors and the bankrupt's family is that save in 'exceptional circumstances', the interests of the creditors prevail.". See *Turner v Avis* [2009] 1 F.L.R. 74 at [16], and *Alexander v Ford* [2012] EWHC 266 (Ch) at [41]–[51].

Rights of occupation after bankruptcy

37–74 AT THE END OF THE TEXT ADD: Where a co-owner continues to occupy the property until or in default of sale, he will usually be liable to pay an occupation rent to the trustee in bankruptcy upon principles of equitable accounting.[57a]

[48a] *Everitt v Budhram*, above, at [30].
[48b] *Foyle v Turner* [2007] B.P.I.R. 43 at [21]; *Turner v Avis* [2009] 1 F.L.R. 74, Ch D at [20].
[57a] *Re Barcham* [2008] EWHC 1505 (Ch); [2009] 1 W.L.R. 1124, applying *Re Pavlou* [1993] 1 W.L.R. 1046. See § 9–54.

Procedure

NOTES 66 AND 67. FOR THE REFERENCE TO *Civil Procedure* (2007), Vol.1, **37–76**
48BPD.1 SUBSTITUTE *Civil Procedure* (2012) Vol.1, 48BPD.1. Supreme Court
Act 1981 is renamed Senior Courts Act 1981 from October 1, 2009, see
Constitutional Reform Act 2005, Sch.11, para.1 and Constitutional Reform
Act 2005 (Commencement No.11) Order 2009 (SI 2009/1604).

5. THE SETTLED LAND ACT 1925

Conveyancing matters

AT THE END OF THE TEXT ADD: It was so as to allow conveyances in such **37–83**
circumstances that the meaning of "settlement" includes any estate or
interest not disposed of by a settlement and remaining in or reverting to the
settlor, or any person deriving title under him.[97a]

6. WHO CAN EXERCISE THE SETTLED LAND ACT POWERS

Person entitled to possession

Right to occupy

NOTE 20. AT THE END ADD: It should be borne in mind that this question may **37–92**
still arise today where the right of occupation was granted before the Trusts
of Land and Appointment of Trustees Act 1996 came into force: see *Amin v
Amin* [2009] EWHC 3356 (Ch); [2009] All E.R. (D) 186 (Dec) at [276]–[279].

Where there is no instrument—unexercised rights

NOTE 29. AT THE END ADD: (not repeated in the 7th edn).   **37–93**

Exercise of powers

AT THE END OF THE TEXT ADD: In Victoria, in a case where the tenants for life **37–97**
were split 14–2 as to whether the settled land should be sold, the court gave
the trustee power to sell the land, subject to certain conditions, under the
equivalent of section 57 of the Trustee Act 1925.[46a]

Overriding qualifications

Beneficially interested

NOTE 60. AT THE END OF THE SECOND SENTENCE ADD: or the 7th edition.   **37–102**

[97a] Settled Land Act 1925, s.1(4); *Ben Hashem v Al Shayif* [2008] EWHC 2380 (Fam); [2009] 1
F.L.R. 115 at [259]. On the meaning of "settlement", see § 37–79.
[46a] *Royal Melbourne Hospital v Equity Trustees Ltd* [2007] VSCA 162; (2007) 18 V.R. 469. The
Victorian legislation contains no equivalent to Settled Land Act 1925, s.93. All parties
agreed that the provision equivalent to Trustee Act 1925, s.57 applied to settled land. It is
doubtful whether this is the position in England. As to Trustee Act 1925, s.57, see §§ 45–12
et seq., and on the question whether s.57 applies to settled land, see § 45–18.

8. General Provisions Affecting the Powers of a Tenant for Life

Exercise of powers cannot be fettered

The effect of section 106

37–146 Note 11. At the end add: For a case concerning the equivalent provision in the applicable legislation in Victoria, see *Royal Melbourne Hospital v Equity Trustees Ltd* [2007] VSCA 162; (2007) 18 V.R. 469 at [292].

At the end of the text add: It would seem that section 75(5) and (6) of the 1925 Act, which require the income from securities representing the investment of capital moneys arising under the Act to be paid or applied as they would have been payable or applicable under the settlement, are to be read subject to the provisions of section 106.[12a]

10. Settled Land Act Powers of Sale and Exchange

The price

37–188 Note 33. For the reference to *Snell's Equity*, see now (32nd edn), § 28–09.

12. Further Settled Land Act Powers

Power to dedicate for streets, gardens, highway purposes, *etc.*

37–232 Note 33. Constitutional Reform Act 2005, s.59 came into force on October 1, 2009: see Constitutional Reform Act 2005 (Commencement No.11) Order 2009 (SI 2009/1604).

15. Application of Capital Money under the Settled Land Act

Power to direct mode of application of capital money

37–292 At the end of the text add: The trustees and the tenant for life are treated as a single person for the purposes of the income tax[99a] and capital gains tax[99b] legislation where the land is vested in the tenant for life and investments representing capital money are vested in the trustees.

[12a] *Royal Melbourne Hospital v Equity Trustees Ltd* [2007] VSCA 162; (2007) 18 V.R. 469 at [296].
[99a] Income Tax Act 2007, s.474(3).
[99b] Taxation of Chargeable Gains Act 1992, s.69(3).

23. CHATTELS

Partition of chattels

NOTE 23. DELETE THE SECOND SENTENCE AND REPLACE WITH: There is no longer a   **37–344**
requirement that such a claim be issued under the Pt 8 procedure, but as it
will be unlikely to involve a substantial dispute of fact, this procedure will
usually be appropriate.

CHAPTER 38

SAFEGUARDING TRUST PROPERTY FROM BREACH OF TRUST

3. STOP NOTICES

Trusts created to facilitate an unlawful and fraudulent ulterior purpose

38–06 NOTE 9. Companies Act 2006, s.126 came into force on October 1, 2009: see Companies Act 2006 (Commencement No 8, Transitional Provisions and Savings) Order 2008 (SI 2008/2860).

4. INJUNCTIONS

Interim injunctions to preserve trust property

38–09 NOTE 29. FOR THE REFERENCE TO *Civil Procedure* (2007), Vol.1, CPR, Pt 25, especially 25.1.9 *et seq.*, SUBSTITUTE *Civil Procedure* (2012), Vol.1, CPR, Pt 25, especially at 25.1.9 *et seq.*

NOTE 36. FOR THE REFERENCE TO *Civil Procedure* (2007), Vol.1, 25.7.24, SUBSTITUTE *Civil Procedure* (2011), Vol.1, 25.1.25 to 25.1.25.13 and Vol.2, 15–2 *et seq.*

Irremediable damage need not be threatened

38–11 NOTE 40. ADD: See *Walbrook Trustees (Jersey) Ltd v Fattal* [2009] EWHC 1446 (Ch); [2010] 1 All E.R. (Comm.) 526 (affd [2010] EWCA Civ 408; [2011] 1 All E.R. (Comm) 647), for a case where an interim injunction restraining a disposal of property rights by trustees was granted and discharged before trial.

5. COMPULSORY PAYMENT INTO COURT

After order for account and for payment of sums to be found due

38–22 DELETE SECOND AND THIRD SENTENCES OF THE TEXT AND REPLACE WITH: It is, however, clear that such a case falls within Civil Procedure Rules, Part 25, rule 25.7(1)(b) as a case where the claimant has obtained judgment against the defendant for a sum of money to be assessed. As soon as an order has been obtained for both an account and for payment of any amount to be found due on taking it, the court can order the defendant to make an interim payment.[79]

NOTE 81. FOR THE REFERENCE TO *Civil Procedure* (2007), Vol.1, 25.7.24, SUBSTITUTE *Civil Procedure* (2012), Vol.2, 15–124.

NOTE 83. FOR THE REFERENCE TO *Civil Procedure* (2007), Vol.1, 25.7.19, SUBSTITUTE *Civil Procedure* (2012), Vol.2, 15–112.

NOTE 85. FOR THE REFERENCE TO *Civil Procedure* (2007), Vol.1, 25.6.1–8 and 25–7.1–29, SUBSTITUTE *Civil Procedure* (2012), Vol.1, 25.6.1–8 and 25.7.1 and Vol.2, 15–99 *et seq.*

6. SUMMARY ORDERS FOR ACCOUNTS

Summary judgment

NOTE 87. Supreme Court Act 1981 is renamed Senior Courts Act 1981 from **38–24** October 1, 2009, see Constitutional Reform Act 2005, Sch.11, para.1 and Constitutional Reform Act 2005 (Commencement No.11) Order 2009 (SI 2009/1604).

Procedure

NOTE 97. DELETE THE FIRST SENTENCE AND REPLACE BY: CPR, Practice Direc- **38–27** tion, Pt 40A—Accounts & Inquiries, para.1.1.

7. APPOINTMENT OF A RECEIVER

Appointment where trust estate unprotected

AFTER THE TEXT TO N.14 ADD: **38–30**

(6) where it would have been difficult to release funds from the trust structure, the trustee was out of pocket and without funds with which to conduct necessary but speculative and contentious litigation, and where there was no practical likelihood of another licensed entity being willing to take on the trusteeship.[14a]

AT THE END OF THE FINAL SENTENCE ADD: or, following the appointment of **38–31** such a representative, in relation to the estate of the deceased person.[16a]

Court reluctant to appoint a receiver

NOTE 17. ADD: For a recent, unsuccessful, application to appoint a receiver **38–32** over trust assets, see *Walbrook Trustees (Jersey) Ltd v Fattal* [2009] EWHC

---

[79] *Pfizer Incorporate v Mills* [2010] All E.R. (D) 96 (May).
[14a] *Re IMK Family Trust* [2008] JRC 136; (2008–09) 11 I.T.E.L.R. 580 at [100], [102] and [106]; affd. [2008] JCA 196; [2008] J.L.R. 430 at [130].
[16a] *Wang Mei Na v Tang Mu Lien* [2011] HKCFI 54.

1446 (Ch); [2010] 1 All E.R. (Comm) 526 at [70]–[100] (no appeal on this point—see [2010] EWCA Civ 408; [2011] 1 All E.R. (Comm) 647 at [18]).

Appointment where trustee guilty of misconduct or insolvent

38–34 NOTE 26. DELETE THE WORDING AFTER THE LAST SEMI-COLON AND REPLACE BY: *Yunghanns v Candoora No.19 Pty Ltd (No.2)* [2000] VSC 300; (2000–01) 3 I.T.E.L.R. 154 at [64]–[95], especially at [84]; *Martyniuk v King* [2000] VSC 319, especially at [14].

38–35 NOTE 35. *Yunghanns v Candoora No.19 Pty Ltd (No.2)* [2000] VSC 300 is also reported at (2000–01) 3 I.T.E.L.R. 154.

CHAPTER 39

REMEDIES AGAINST TRUSTEES PERSONALLY

2. PERSONAL ACCOUNTABILITY AND COMPENSATION FOR BREACH OF TRUST

Introduction

NOTE 2. FOR THE REFERENCE TO Underhill and Hayton, *Law of Trusts and Trustees*, SEE NOW (18th edn), § 87.7.   **39–02**

Scope of account in common form

AT THE END OF THE TEXT ADD: A claim for an account involves at least two   **39–05**
steps. First, at the end of the trial the trial judge gives a judgment that the
defendant do account to the beneficiaries of the trust estate. Later, after
more evidence (usually taken by a Master or district judge, not the trial
judge), there is a calculation. Then there is a judgment for the balance thus
found due.[15a]

Breach of equitable duty of skill and care

NOTE 17. FOR THE REFERENCE TO Underhill and Hayton, *Law of Trusts and*   **39–07**
Trustees, SEE NOW (18th edn), § 87.76.

The basic rule

NOTE 28. ADD: Once the transaction has been completed, in accordance with   **39–09**
the contract governing it, there can be no obligation to restore the fund (*e.g.*
the solicitor's client account) which had been held on bare trust: *Target
Holdings Ltd v Redferns* [1996] A.C. 421 at 436D, HL; *Knighton v Duffle
Haynes Kentish & Co.* [2003] EWCA Civ 223; [2003] All E.R. (D) 198 (Feb);
UCB Home Loans Ltd v Grace, unreported, December 15, 2010, Ch D at
[38]–[40].

NOTE 32. ADD: Not every breach of trust which results in no loss is judicious: **39–10**
Jeffery v Gretton [2011] W.T.L.R. 809 at [84] ("a thoughtless breach of trust
that happens to have turned out well").

[15a] *Brown v Silvera* [2011] ABCA 109 at [152], also representing the practice in England.

What loss is recoverable?

39–13 NOTE 40. ADD: It has been said in New Zealand that the fiduciary has a "limited opportunity" to demonstrate that all or some of the loss would have occurred in any event: see *Stevens v Premium Real Estate Ltd* [2009] NZSC 15; [2009] 2 N.Z.L.R. 384 at [85]. We consider that the position in England is as set out by Elias C.J. in her well-reasoned dissenting judgment: *ibid.* at [32]–[41].

39–14 AT THE END OF THE TEXT ADD: The trustees' performance must, however, not be judged with hindsight.[46a] Furthermore, on principle, compensation for breach of trust cannot be reduced by reason of contributory negligence on the part of the claimant.[46b]

Protectors

39–17 NOTE 54. FOR THE REFERENCE TO Parker and Mellows, *The Modern Law of Trusts*, SEE NOW (9th edn), pp.206–207.

Valuation of the loss

39–19 AT THE END OF THE TEXT ADD: It has been said that the remedy "will be fashioned according to the exigencies of the particular case so as to do what is 'practically just' as between the parties".[66a] This may explain the adoption of different bases of loss in different circumstances, ensuring that the award of equitable compensation operates fairly between the defaulting trustee and the beneficiaries.

The date of the valuation

39–20 NOTE 68. AT THE END OF THE FIRST SENTENCE ADD: *Jeffery v Gretton* [2011] W.T.L.R. 809 at [82]–[83]. FOR THE REFERENCE TO Thomas and Hudson, *The Law of Trusts*, SEE NOW (2nd edn), § 32.29.

Contributory negligence

39–26 NOTE 84. AT THE END OF THE FIRST SENTENCE ADD: *Lloyds TSB Bank plc v Markandan & Uddin* [2010] EWHC 2517 (Ch) at [38]–[43] (see also [2012] EWCA Civ 65; [2012] 2 All E.R. 884, there was no appeal on this point).

[46a] *Nestle v National Westminster Bank* [1993] 1 W.L.R. 1260 at 1276D ("after the event even a fool is wise"); *Power v Trustees of the Open Text (UK) Ltd Group Life Assurance Scheme* [2009] EWHC 3064 (Ch); [2009] All E.R. (D) 236 (Dec) at [30].
[46b] *Lloyds TSB Bank plc v Markandan & Uddin* [2010] EWHC 2517 (Ch) at [38]–[43]. See also § 39–26.
[66a] *Maguire v Makaronis* (1997) 188 C.L.R. 449 at 496, Aus HC, cited with approval in *Sinclair Investments (UK) Ltd v Versailles Trade Finance Ltd* [2011] EWCA Civ 347; [2011] 4 All E.R. 335 at [47].

Examples of liability

Breach of duty in relation to companies in which the trust has an interest— reflective loss

NOTE 7. ADD: *Webster v Sandersons* [2009] EWCA Civ 830; [2009] 2 **39–37** B.C.L.C. 542. See generally on the principles concerning the recovery of reflective loss, Joffe, Drake, Richardson and Lightman, *Minority Shareholders*, (4th edn), §§ 4.78 *et seq.*, and particularly in relation to the case where a wrongdoer causes loss to a company whose shares are held by the trustees of a settlement, at §§ 4.119 *et seq.*

NOTE 14. ADD: See too *Ellis v Property Leeds (UK) Ltd* [2002] EWCA Civ **39–38** 32; [2002] 2 B.C.L.C. 175 at [17], *per* Peter Gibson L.J.

NOTE 16. AT THE END ADD: See too *Freeman v Ansbacher Trustees (Jersey)* **39–39** *Ltd* [2009] JRC 003; (2009–10) 12 I.T.E.L.R. 207 at [97(vi)], where the point was discussed, but not decided. In *Hotung v Ho Yuen Ki* [2010] HKCA 385, it was considered that the applicability of the rule against reflective loss was far from clear in a case where the defendant trustee was merely a shareholder, and not a trustee, of the company.

NOTE 22. ADD: In *Waddington Ltd v Chan Chun Hoo Thomas* [2008] **39–41** HKCFA 86; [2009] 2 B.C.L.C. 82 at [88], Lord Millett N.P.J. expressed the view that *Giles v Rhind* [2002] EWCA Civ 1428; [2003] Ch. 618 was wrongly decided. There is, however, no proper basis for the English courts to decline to follow it, and the decision remains binding at all levels below the Supreme Court, see *Webster v Sandersons* [2009] EWCA Civ 830; [2009] 2 B.C.L.C. 542 at [36]. See Joffe, Drake, Richardson and Lightman, *Minority Shareholders* (4th edn), § 4.178, for the view that *Giles v Rhind* is inconsistent with the decision in *Johnson v Gore Wood & Co.* [2002] 2 A.C. 1, HL.

AT THE END OF THE TEXT ADD: In *Freeman v Ansbacher Trustees (Jersey)* **39–43** *Ltd*,[24a] it was acknowledged that the application of the no reflective loss rule to claims against trustees is uncertain, and the court refused to strike out a claim for breach of trust by the object of a discretionary trust.

Active breaches

NOTE 26. FOR THE REFERENCE TO Atkin's Court Forms, SEE NOW Vol.41, (2009 **39–46** issue), [12].

Accounts on the footing of wilful default

Time for proof

NOTE 41. DELETE THE REFERENCE TO THE FOOTNOTES AND REPLACE BY: nn.39, 40. **39–49**

[24a] [2009] JRC 003; (2009–10) 12 I.T.E.L.R. 207 at [97]. The court described §§ 39–037 to 39–043 of this text as a helpful summary of the current position.

Breaches of trust concerning investment

Investments of unauthorised kinds—options

39–55 NOTE 73. FOR THE REFERENCE TO Underhill and Hayton, *Law of Trusts and Trustees*, SEE NOW (18th edn), § 87.75.

Interest

Interest on compensation generally

39–58 NOTE 82. ADD: See too Ridge (2010) 126 L.Q.R. 279 at 296–300.

Compound interest

39–61 NOTE 4. AT THE END ADD: In *Eden Refuge Trust v Hohepa* [2011] NZHC 730; [2011] 3 N.Z.L.R. 273, compound interest was awarded against defaulting trustees, the court applying a presumption that they had profited from misuse of the trust property.

3. *LOCUS STANDI* FOR A BREACH OF TRUST ACTION

Beneficiaries with an equitable vested or contingent interest under the trust

39–68 AT END OF TEXT ADD A NEW NOTE 32a: See *Freeman v Ansbacher Trustees (Jersey) Ltd* [2009] JRC 003; (2009–10) 12 I.T.E.L.R. 207 at [44], where the text in this paragraph was approved by the court. At [45], it was said that the court has a discretion whether to grant relief in any particular case. The court also expressed the view, at [49], that where a party with standing to bring a claim for breach of trust failed to do so and allowed his claim to become statute-barred, and later procured a beneficiary to bring the claim as his "stool pigeon", relief may be refused as a matter of discretion.

Objects of discretionary trusts and fiduciary powers

39–69 NOTE 36. FOR THE REFERENCE TO *Snell's Equity*, SEE NOW (32nd edn), § 22–005.

Other trustees

39–76 NOTE 64. ADD: The text in this passage was approved by Sir Andrew Morritt C. in *Dalriada Trustees Ltd v Woodward* [2012] EWHC 21626 (Ch); [2012] All E.R. (D) 98 (Jun) at [37].

4. CONTRIBUTION BETWEEN TRUSTEES

Contribution under the 1978 Act

39–78 NOTE 68. *Charter plc v City Index Ltd* was affirmed on appeal on this point, see [2008] EWCA Civ 1382; [2008] Ch. 313.

NOTE 70. DELETE (not repeated in 17th edn) AND REPLACE BY (not repeated in later editions).

Establishing the primary liability

NOTE 74. DELETE AND REPLACE BY: CPR, Pt 6, rr.6.30 *et seq.*   **39–79**

Assessing the contributions

NOTE 85. DELETE THE FIRST SENTENCE AND REPLACE BY: See *Clerk and Lindsell* **39–81** *on Torts*, 19th edn, § 4–12 *et seq.* (not in 20th edn).

6. DEFENCE OF CONCURRENCE, ACQUIESCENCE OR RELEASE AND CONFIRMATION BY A BENEFICIARY

Acquiescence

NOTE 65. AT THE END ADD: See too *Byrnes v Kendle* [2011] HCA 26; (2011– **39–104** 12) 14 I.T.E.L.R. 299 at [24]–[30], [74]–[80] and [126]–[140].

Mere delay

AT THE END OF THE FIRST SENTENCE ADD NEW NOTE 74a: Some sort of detrimental **39–106** reliance will normally be required before it will be practically unjust to give a remedy: *Fisher v Brooker* [2009] UKHL 41; [2009] 1 W.L.R. 1764 at [64], applied in a trusts context in *Brudenell-Bruce v Moore* [2012] EWHC 1024 (Ch); (2011–12) 14 I.T.E.L.R. 967.

7. DEFENCE UNDER EXCULPATORY PROVISIONS

The permitted scope of special indemnity clauses

NOTE 23. AT THE END OF THE FIRST SENTENCE ADD: and see *Fattal v Walbrook* **39–124** *Trustees (Jersey) Ltd* [2010] EWHC 2767 (Ch) at [11] and [67]–[82].

AFTER THE TEXT TO N.25 ADD: Similar considerations apply to other professional trustees.[25a]

NOTE 29. FOR GUERNSEY, Trusts (Guernsey) Law 1989, s.34(7) HAS BEEN REPLACED WITH AMENDMENTS BY Trusts (Guernsey) Law 2007, s.39(7) and (8) with effect from March 17, 2008, and in relation to breaches of trust not covered by statutory provision, see *Spread Trustee Co. Ltd v Hutcheson* [2011] UKPC 13, [2012] 1 All E.R. 251, applying English law as determined in *Armitage v Nurse* [1998] Ch. 241, CA, and not the Scottish cases referred to at the end of n.29. The decision includes an interesting discussion as to the sources of Guernsey trust law, which is beyond the scope of this work.

[25a] *Fattal v Walbrook Trustees (Jersey) Ltd*, above, at [81].

Debenture trust deeds

39–125   NOTE 30. Companies Act 2006, ss.532 and 750 came into force on April 6, 2008: see Companies Act 2006 (Commencement No 5, Transitional Provisions and Savings) Order 2007 (SI 2007/3495).

AFTER § 39–127 INSERT THE FOLLOWING NEW PARAGRAPH AND HEADING:

Directors

39–127A   Section 232 of the Companies Act 2006[34a] invalidates[34b] any provision in a company's articles of association, any contract with the company or otherwise[34c] which purports to exempt to any extent any liability that would otherwise attach to a director of the company in connection with any negligence, default, breach of duty or breach of trust in relation to the company, and also invalidates[34d] any such provision, with certain exceptions,[34e] which to any extent purports to indemnify the director against any liability so attaching to him. No distinction is drawn between dishonest, negligent or innocent breaches of duty or trust. In view of the width of the section it is unnecessary to consider what is the difference in this context between a breach of duty and a breach of trust by a company director.[34f] The section does not, however, prevent a company's articles from making such provision as had previously been lawful for dealing with conflicts of interest.[34g] Nor does the section prohibit the ratification of directors' acts in accordance with prescribed procedures.[34h]

Interpretation of special indemnity clauses

The construction of limiting words

39–134   NOTE 62. ADD: See too *Woodland-Ferrari v UCL Group Retirement Benefits Scheme* [2002] EWHC 1354 (Ch); [2003] Ch. 115 at [68] (wilful default is not the same as fraudulent breach of trust).

Do special indemnity clauses exclude the principle that ignorance of the law is no defence?

39–135   NOTE 69. *Bonham v Fishwick* was affirmed on appeal, see [2008] EWCA Civ 373; [2008] P. & C.R. D14.

[34a]   Replacing Companies Act 1985, s.310 with amendments.
[34b]   Companies Act 2006, s.232(1).
[34c]   See *ibid.*, s.232(3).
[34d]   *ibid.*, s.232(2).
[34e]   *ibid.*, ss.233 to 235.
[34f]   See § 7–16 as to directors as quasi-trustees.
[34g]   Companies Act 2006, s.232(4).
[34h]   *ibid.*, s.239.

8. POWER OF COURT TO RELIEVE A TRUSTEE FROM PERSONAL LIABILITY

Conduct held unreasonable

AFTER THE TEXT TO N.97 ADD: ; and, in the case of a solicitor, paying purchase **39–142** moneys to an apparent solicitor without the consent of a pre-existing charge holder nor obtaining an undertaking that the charge would be redeemed.[97a]

Conduct held reasonable

AFTER THE TEXT TO N.10 ADD: A lay trustee has also recently been excused **39–144** liability for failing to accumulate rents for a beneficiary who would become absolutely entitled at the age of 25, where she honestly believed that she was not required so to account before the beneficiary reached that age.[10a]

The court's discretion

NOTE 18. AT THE END OF THE FIRST SENTENCE ADD: *Cherney v Neuman* [2011] **39–145** EWHC 2156 (Ch) at [321]; [2011] All E.R. (D) 29 (Sep).

9. CIVIL IMPRISONMENT AND CRIMINAL RESTITUTION

The Debtors Act 1869

"Court of Equity"

NOTE 25. Supreme Court Act 1981 is renamed Senior Courts Act 1981 from **39–148** October 1, 2009, see Constitutional Reform Act 2005, Sch.11, para.1 and Constitutional Reform Act 2005 (Commencement No.11) Order 2009 (SI 2009/1604).

Procedure

NOTE 52. FOR THE REFERENCE TO *Civil Procedure* (2007), Vol.1, pp.2045– **39–157** 2069, 2204–2207, SUBSTITUTE *Civil Procedure* (2012), Vol.1, pp.2372–2388, 2494–2501. There is now a Practice Direction which applies to committal applications both in the High Court and in the county court.

[97a] *Nationwide Building Society v Davisons Solicitors (a firm)* [2012] All E.R. (D) 141 (Apr), Ch D. A careful and conscientious and thorough solicitor who conducts a transaction by the book in all respects but fails to discover a fraud is likely to be treated mercifully by the court: *Lloyds TSB Bank plc v Markandan & Uddin* [2012] EWCA Civ 65; [2012] 2 All E.R. 884 at [61].

[10a] *Iles v Iles* [2012] EWHC 919; [2012] All E.R. (D) 147 (Apr). She was not spared liability for the period after the beneficiary turned 25.

CHAPTER 40

REMEDIES AGAINST ACCESSORIES

3. IMPOUNDING TO INDEMNIFY BENEFICIARIES

The general principle

40–06 AFTER THE FIRST SENTENCE INSERT: This principle does not entitle beneficiaries of part of the money in a bank account held on trust to stop the payment to the account holder of other money in the bank account held free from trust in circumstances where the account holder had failed to pay money into that account on trust for the beneficiaries and had instead paid the money into an overdrawn account so that it never became trust property and consequently could not give rise to a right to impound.[22a]

AT THE END OF THE FIRST PARAGRAPH ADD: As to the application of the impounding principle in relation to concurrence by some but not all of the beneficiaries in a breach of the self dealing rule, see § 20–98.

4. DISHONEST ASSISTANCE

General requirements of liability

40–09 AFTER THE TEXT TO N.35 INSERT: Though a dishonest assistant may be personally liable to account for profits made from his dishonest assistance,[35a] it does not follow that such profits made by the defendant become subject to a constructive trust in the proprietary sense, and the remedy of dishonest assistance cannot be used as a route to a proprietary remedy in respect of the profits.[35b]

Basis of liability—*Barnes v Addy* and *Royal Brunei Airlines Sdn. Bhd. v Tan*

40–10 NOTE 37. ADD: For an Australian judicial account of the development of the remedy see *Bell Group Ltd v Westpac Banking Corp.* [2009] WASC 107; (2008–09) 39 W.A.R. 1 at [4627]–[4838].

AFTER § 40–13 INSERT THE FOLLOWING NEW PARAGRAPH AND HEADING:

[22a] *Re BA Peters plc* [2008] EWCA Civ 1604; [2010] 1 B.C.L.C. 142.
[35a] See § 20–53 (including Supplement).
[35b] *Sinclair Investment Holdings SA v Versailles Trade Finance Ltd* [2007] EWHC 915 (Ch); [2007] 2 All E.R. (Comm.) 993 at [109]–[135].

Locus standi

Generally the same rules apply as in connection with breach of trust **40–13A**
claims.[65a] Though a claim will normally be brought by a successor trustee or
a beneficiary, the trustee who has committed a breach of trust has *locus
standi* to bring a dishonest assistance claim against a third party recipient,
even though as between himself and his beneficiary he has committed a
breach of trust and the commission of that breach of trust is a necessary
ingredient in his cause of action against the assistant.[65b] A dishonest assistant may seek a contribution from the trustee.[65c]

Requirement (1)—existence of a trust

Is a fiduciary relationship without any trust property sufficient?

NOTE 70. ADD: In *Dyson Technology Ltd v Curtis* [2010] EWHC 3289 (Ch) at **40–16**
[210] the court accepted, without considering the relevant authorities, a
submission that there had to be in existence a trust fund or property subject
to fiduciary obligation, and held that this requirement was satisfied on the
basis that the property subject to the fiduciary obligation was a bribe
obtained by the fiduciary which had became subject to a constructive trust,
though that would not now suffice, see §§ 20–028A to 20–028C.

AT THE END OF THE TEXT ADD: and at first instance it has been held that a
fiduciary relationship without trust property is sufficient.[71a]

Requirement (3)—assistance by the defendant

NOTE 88. ADD: *Ultraframe (UK) Ltd v Fielding* [2005] EWHC 1638 (Ch); **40–21**
[2007] W.T.L.R. 835 at [1509]–[1510].

NOTE 89. ADD: *Law Society of England and Wales v Habitable Concepts Ltd*
[2010] EWHC 1449 (Ch); [2010] All E.R (D) 156 (Jun) at [23]. As to cases
where the trustee makes a profit from the trust for which he is personally
liable to account but which does not become subject to a constructive trust,
and the assistance is merely in the disposal of the profit (but not in the
breach of duty in making the profit), see § 20–53 (including Supplement).

Requirement (4)—dishonesty of the defendant

The subjective and objective elements of dishonesty

NOTE 95. AFTER THE REFERENCE TO *Att.-Gen. of Zambia v Meere Care &* **40–23**
Desai INSERT: (reversed on facts [2008] EWCA Civ 1007; [2008] All E.R. (D)
406 (Jul)).

[65a] See §§ 39–67 *et seq.*
[65b] See *Montrose Investments Ltd v Orion Nominees Ltd* [2004] EWCA (Civ) 1032; [2004]
W.T.L.R. 1133; *Pulvers v Chan* [2007] EWHC 2406 (Ch); [2008] P.N.L.R. 9 at [380], [385]
and [387]–[395]; and compare § 41–46 on the proprietary remedy and §§ 40–02 to 40–05, 42–
04 to 42–12 and 42–29A (including Supplement) on other remedies by trustees who have
made wrongful or mistaken payments or transfers.
[65c] See § 40–46A (Supplement).
[71a] *JD Wetherspoon plc v Van de Berg & Co. Ltd* [2009] EWHC 639 (Ch) at [503]–[520].

Note 97. After the reference to *Att.-Gen. of Zambia v Meere Care & Desai* insert: (reversed on facts [2008] EWCA Civ 1007; [2008] All E.R. (D) 406 (Jul)).

After the penultimate sentence add: The objective standard of dishonesty is a question of law for determination by the court. It does not depend upon an inquiry into what all as distinct from some normal people regard as dishonest and it is irrelevant that there may be a body of opinion which regards the ordinary standard of honest behaviour as being set too high.[99a]

No need for defendant to be aware of transgressions of ordinary honest standards

40–25 Note 12. After the reference to *Att.-Gen. of Zambia v Meere Care & Desai* add: (reversed on facts [2008] EWCA Civ 1007; [2008] All E.R. (D) 406 (Jul)); *Cunningham v Cunningham* [2009] JRC 124; 2009 J.L.R. 227 at [36]; *Al Khudairi v Abbey Brokers Ltd* [2010] EWHC 1486 (Ch); [2010] P.N.L.R. 32 at [129]–[134]; *Dyson Technology Ltd v Curtis* [2010] EWHC 3289 (Ch) at [194]–[207]. See too *Starglade Properties Ltd v Nash* [2010] EWCA Civ, above, at [30].

Effect of ignorance of the law

40–33 Note 34. At the end add: Compare the effect of ignorance of the law in relation to the proprietary remedy, see § 41–122 and *Sinclair Investments (UK) Ltd v Versailles Trade Finance Ltd* [2010] EWHC 1614 (Ch); [2011] 1 B.C.L.C. 202 at [92]–[98]; [2011] EWCA Civ 347; [2011] 3 W.L.R. 1153 at [102]–[108].

At the end of the text add: It is dishonest for a company director, who knows that the company is insolvent, so as to defeat the claims of a creditor, to cause the company to pay away its assets to other creditors, without obtaining any legal advice as to the propriety of the payments, and his liability does not depend on his knowledge or lack of knowledge of the law concerning voidable preferences.[35a]

Effect of ignorance of the trust

40–34 Note 36. At the end add: *Ultraframe (UK) Ltd v Fielding* [2005] EWHC 1638 (Ch); [2007] W.T.L.R. 835 at [1500]–[1506]; *Starglade Properties Ltd v Nash* [2010] EWHC 148 (Ch); [2010] W.T.L.R. 1267 at [56] (reversed on other grounds [2010] EWCA Civ 1314; [2010] All E.R. (D) 221 (Nov) but no appeal on this point, see at [18]); *Al Khudairi v Abbey Brokers Ltd* [2010] EWHC 1486 (Ch); [2010] P.N.L.R. 32 at [135].

Note 37. Add: See too *Ultraframe (UK) Ltd v Fielding*, above, at [1507].

[99a] *Starglade Properties Ltd v Nash* [2010] EWCA Civ 1314; [2010] All E.R. (D) 221 (Nov).
[35a] *Starglade Properties Ltd v Nash* [2010] EWCA Civ 1314; [2010] All E.R. (D) 221 (Nov).

Pleading dishonesty

NOTE 38. AT THE END ADD: *Cunningham v Cunningham* [2009] JRC 124; 2009 **40–35**
J.L.R. 227 at [37]–[47].

Proving dishonesty

NOTE 42. AT THE END ADD: And see *Ultraframe (UK) Ltd v Fielding* [2005] **40–36**
EWHC 1638 (Ch); [2007] W.T.L.R. 835 at [1508].

Liability of banks for dishonest assistance

NOTE 44. AT THE END ADD: As to when a bank can rely on a suspicion that it **40–37**
would incur liability for dishonest assistance if it acted on a customer's
instructions as a defence to a claim by the customer for breach of contract,
see *Westpac New Zealand Ltd v MAP & Associates Ltd* [2011] NZSC 89.

Registration by companies of share transfers made in breach of trust

IN THE SECOND SENTENCE: delete the reference to the Companies Act 1985 and **40–39**
replace by a reference to the Companies Act 2006.

NOTE 50. DELETE AND REPLACE BY: Companies Act 2006, s.126, replacing
Companies Act 1985, s.360, with effect from October 1, 2009: Companies
Act 2006 (Commencement No.8, Transitional Provisions and Savings)
Order 2008 (SI 2008/2860); Companies (Tables A to F) Regulations 1985 (SI
1985/805), Table A, Art.5.

AFTER § 40–46 INSERT THE FOLLOWING NEW PARAGRAPH AND HEADING:

Contribution

A defendant who is held liable for dishonest assistance, or who enters into a **40–46A**
bona fide settlement or compromise of such a claim, may seek contribution
under the Civil Liability (Contribution) Act 1978[67a] from any other person
liable in respect of the same damage, including the trustee and other persons
held liable for dishonest assistance in the breach of trust concerned. In a case
where a defendant is made vicariously liable for dishonest assistance on the
part of a partner or employee,[67b] the personal innocence of other partners or
the employer is not a factor to be taken into account in apportioning liability between the firm or employer on the one hand and persons who are
not partners and employees on the other hand, though it is relevant to take
into account the undisgorged profits of participants in the breach of trust.[67c]
Where a firm is trustee, the firm may, as between itself in respect of its
liability for breach of trust and an employee in respect of the employee's
liability for dishonest assistance in the breach of trust, expect to obtain a full
indemnity from the employee if the partners are innocent.[67d]

[67a] On which see generally §§ 39–78 to 39–83.
[67b] See §§ 40–43 and 40–44.
[67c] *Dubai Aluminium Co. Ltd v Salaam* [2002] UKHL 48; [2003] 2 A.C. 366; *Pulvers v Chan*
[2007] EWHC 2406 (Ch); [2008] P.N.L.R. 9 at [397]–[405].
[67d] *Pulvers v Chan*, above, at [404].

5. Directors of Corporate Trustee

General position

40–48 Last sentence: delete are and replace by: were formerly.

Note 72. For the reference to Gower and Davies, *Principles of Modern Company Law*, see now (8th edn), Chap.16.

Note 75. After the first sentence insert: Trusts (Guernsey) Law, s.70 was repealed by Trusts (Guernsey) Law 2007, s.83(1) and (3), with effect from March 17, 2008, save in respect of proceedings instituted prior to that date against a trustee in respect of a breach of trust committed by that trustee.

Claims by beneficiaries against directors

40–49 Note 76. At the end add: *McNulty v McNulty* [2011] NZHC 1173; (2011–12) 14 I.T.E.L.R. 361 at [74]–[85].

Note 77. After the semi-colon insert: *McNulty v McNulty*, above, at [86]–[91].

Indirect or "dog leg" action

40–51 Note 83. *Alhamrani (Sheikh) v Alhamrani (Sheikh)* is reported at 2007 J.L.R. 44. At the end add: *Gregson v HAE Trustees Ltd* [2008] EWHC 1006 (Ch); [2009] 1 All E.R. (Comm.) 457 at [22]–[69].

6. Remedies in Tort

Economic torts

40–54 Note 89. For the reference to *Clerk and Lindsell on Torts*, see now (20th edn), §§ 24–90 *et seq.*

Note 91. For the reference to *Clerk and Lindsell on Torts*, see now (20th edn), §§ 24–14 *et seq.*

Note 93. For the reference to *Clerk and Lindsell on Torts*, see now (20th edn), §§ 24–29 to 24–32.

Note 97. For the reference to *Clerk and Lindsell on Torts*, see now (20th edn), §§ 24–70 *et seq.*

Note 98. For the reference to *Clerk and Lindsell on Torts*, see now (20th edn), §§ 24–57 *et seq.*

Conversion, trespass to land and nuisance

40–55 Note 5. For the reference to *Clerk and Lindsell on Torts*, see now (20th edn), §§ 17–06 *et seq.*

NOTE 10. FOR THE REFERENCE TO *Clerk and Lindsell on Torts*, SEE NOW (20th edn), § 19–10.

NOTE 11. FOR THE REFERENCE TO *Clerk and Lindsell on Torts*, SEE NOW (20th edn), § 20–63.

AT THE END OF THE TEXT ADD: Nevertheless, a beneficial owner or co-owner of property who has an absolute beneficial entitlement to or share in the property can sue for reasonably foreseeable loss suffered by him in consequence of negligent damage to the property, provided that the legal owner is joined as a defendant.[12] It has not been decided whether a similar rule applies to a claim in nuisance.[13]

---

[12]   *Shell UK Ltd v Total UK Ltd* [2010] EWCA Civ 180; [2010] 3 W.L.R. 1192 at [111]–[144].
[13]   *Shell UK Ltd v Total UK Ltd*, above, at [151].

CHAPTER 41

PROPRIETARY REMEDY AND TRACING AGAINST TRUSTEES AND THIRD PARTIES

2. GENERAL

Breach of trust and effect of overreaching

41-13 NOTE 24. FOR THE REFERENCE TO Megarry and Wade, *The Law of Real Property*, SEE NOW (7th edn), §§ 6–052 to 6–056

Overreaching and section 2(1) of the Law of Property Act 1925

41-15 NOTE 29. AFTER THE REFERENCE TO Megarry and Wade, *The Law of Real Property*, ADD: (not in 7th edn).

NOTE 32. FOR THE REFERENCE TO Megarry and Wade, *The Law of Real Property*, SEE NOW (7th edn), §§ 12–036 to 12–038.

NOTE 40. FOR THE REFERENCE TO Ruoff and Roper, *Registered Conveyancing*, SEE NOW §§ 13.003 to 13.004.

Imposition of new trust despite destruction of old trust of land through registration

41-16 NOTE 49. AFTER THE REFERENCE TO Megarry and Wade, *The Law of Real Property*, ADD: (not in 7th edn).

Evidence to establish what property or money is subject to the proprietary remedy

General principle in relation to trustee

41-21 AFTER THE FIRST SENTENCE INSERT: This principle does not absolve the claimant from the need to prove that his property can be traced into a particular mixed fund, nor allow the claimant to proceed on the basis that all property held by the trustee belongs to the claimant unless the trustee can prove the contrary.[64a] The principle is of narrow application and concerns identification of property in a particular mixed fund into which it can be proved by the claimant that his money or property went, and the inferences that can

---

[64a] *Serious Fraud Office v Lexi Holdings plc* [2008] EWCA Crim 1443; [2009] Q.B. 376 at [52]–[55].

properly be drawn from the evidence before the court, the burden on the defaulting trustee being no more than a balance of probabilities.[64b]

The proprietary remedy against a trustee

Character of alternative remedies

NOTE 97. ADD: See too *Ultraframe (UK) Ltd v Fielding* [2005] EWHC 1638 **41–31** (Ch); [2007] W.T.L.R. 835 at [1461]–[1469]; *Sinclair Investments (UK) Ltd v Versailles Trade Finance Ltd* [2010] EWHC 1614 (Ch); [2011] 1 B.C.L.C. 202 at [23]–[24] (affirmed [2011] EWCA Civ 347; [2011] 3 W.L.R. 1153).

NOTE 99. ADD: *Serious Fraud Office v Lexi Holdings plc* [2008] EWCA Crim 1443; [2009] Q.B. 376 at [19]–[43].

Locus standi

NOTE 20. ADD: As to the *locus standi* of a trustee who has made a transfer in **41–35** breach of trust to recover the property from a third party, see § 41–46.

Proprietary remedy against purchasers with notice and volunteer recipients

Diplock recipients

NOTE 42. DELETE AND REPLACE BY: See § 41–30. **41–42**

Claim by trustee who has made the transfer in breach of trust

NOTE 58. ADD: Compare § 42–07 on knowing receipt and other personal **41–46** remedies.

Comparison of the proprietary remedy with a constructive trust imposed by the profit rule

DELETE THE LAST TWO SENTENCES AND REPLACE BY: The circumstances in **41–51** which a constructive trust, as distinct from a personal liability to account, is imposed under the profit rule is now narrower than was formerly thought to be the case, and is limited to cases where the asset or money constituting the profit is or has been beneficially the property of the beneficiary, or is property which the trustee acquired by taking advantage of an opportunity or right which was properly that of the beneficiary.[71a]

IN THE SIXTH SENTENCE OF THE TEXT AFTER while under the profit rule INSERT: **41–52** (if applicable—see §§ 20–28 to 20–28C and 41–51 including Supplement).

[64b] *Sinclair Investments (UK) Ltd v Versailles Trade Finance Ltd* [2010] EWHC 1614 (Ch); [2011] 1 B.C.L.C. 202 at [143]–[157]; [2011] EWCA Civ 347; [2011] 3 W.L.R. 1153 at [135]–[141].
[71a] See §§ 20–28 to 20–28C (including Supplement), and *Sinclair Investments (UK) Ltd v Versailles Trade Finance Ltd* [2011] EWCA Civ 347; [2011] 3 W.L.R. 1153.

The proprietary remedy and unjust enrichment

Substituted asset traced into hands of defendant

41–55   NOTE 86. FOR THE REFERENCE TO Underhill and Hayton, *Law of Trusts and Trustees*, SEE NOW (18th edn), §§ 90.6 to 90.9.

NOTE 89. AT THE END ADD: See too *Ultraframe (UK) Ltd v Fielding* [2005] EWHC 1638 (Ch); [2007] W.T.L.R. 835 at [1520].

Defence of change of position

41–57   NOTE 6. AFTER THE REFERENCE TO Underhill and Hayton, *Law of Trusts and Trustees*, ADD: (not repeated in 18th edn, but see §§ 98.40 to 98.44 on defence to personal liability). For the reference to Thomas and Hudson, *The Law of Trusts*, see now (2nd edn), §§ 33–93 *et seq.*

NOTE 12. FOR THE REFERENCE TO *Snell's Equity*, SEE NOW (32nd edn), §§ 12–016 *et seq.*

4. MIXED SUBSTITUTIONS—ACQUISITIONS AND INSURANCE

Introduction

41–69   NOTE 62. DELETE AND REPLACE BY: See § 41–30.

Assets bought with money withdrawn by trustee or other wrongdoer from a mixed bank account—the lien under the *Oatway* rule

41–73   NOTE 75. DELETE AND REPLACE BY: See § 41–30.

Life insurance policy

The remedy

41–82   NOTE 5. DELETE AND REPLACE BY: See §§ 41–30, 41–41, 41–42, 41–44, 41–47.

Indemnity insurance policy

41–88   AT THE END OF THE THIRD SENTENCE ADD: and is sufficiently closely connected with the land or chattels held in trust that it may be described as a graft upon it.[17a]

5. MIXTURES AND PROBLEMS OF IDENTIFICATION

Making new products out of raw material

41–92   NOTE 35. DELETE AND REPLACE BY: See §§ 20–28 to 20–28C, and 41–50 and 41–51 (including Supplement) as to the circumstances in which a trust may

---

[17a]   See §§ 20–28 to 20–28C, 41–51 and 41–52 (including Supplement) for a consideration of the circumstances in which a constructive trust (as distinct from mere personal liability to account) is imposed by the profit rule.

be imposed by the profit rule. The case here is closely similar to cases of graft upon the original trust property.

6. IMPROVEMENTS TO LAND AND CHATTELS

Is there a mixed substitution so that the proprietary remedy is available?

NOTE 45. DELETE AND REPLACE BY: See §§ 41–30, 41–41, 41–42, 41–45.   **41–96**

Improvement of *Diplock* recipient's land or chattels with trust money

NOTE 59. FOR THE REFERENCE TO *Snell's Equity*, SEE NOW (32nd edn), § 44– **41–100**
034.

7. WHEN TRUST ASSETS BECOME UNTRACEABLE

Overdrawn bank account

Purchasing assets with the aid of an overdraft

NOTE 78. DELETE AND REPLACE BY. A constructive trust may not now be **41–108** imposed by the profit rule in the case considered in the text, but a personal remedy would be available, see §§ 20–28 to 20–28C, 41–51 and 41–52 (including Supplement).

Unauthorised employment of trust money in bank trustee's general business

NOTE 93. FOR THE REFERENCE TO Underhill and Hayton, *Law of Trusts and* **41–112** *Trustees*, SEE NOW (18th edn), §§ 90.50 to 90.52.

IN THE FIRST SENTENCE DELETE THE TEXT AFTER N.93 AND REPLACE BY: and attempts to give effect to the dictum have been rejected by the Court of Appeal,[93a] and also, specifically in the context of unauthorised application of trust money by a bank, by the Chancery Division.[93b]

Destruction of leasehold interest on sale of freehold

NOTE 5. DELETE AND REPLACE BY: See §§ 20–28 to 20–28C, 41–51 and 41–52 **41–113** (including Supplement) for a consideration of the circumstances in which a constructive trust (as distinct from mere personal liability to account) is imposed by the profit rule. The case here is closely similar to cases of graft upon the original trust property.

[93a] *Serious Fraud Office v Lexi Holdings plc* [2008] EWCA Crim 1443; [2009] Q.B. 376 at [44]–[58].
[93b] *Re Lehman Brothers International (Europe)* [2009] EWHC 3228 (Ch); [2010] 2 B.C.L.C. 301 at [166]–[198] (reversed in part on appeal on other grounds [2010] EWCA Civ 917; [2010] All E.R. (D) 15 (Aug), and a further appeal to the Supreme Court dismissed [2012] UKSC 6; [2012] 3 All E.R. 1).

8. PURCHASE WITHOUT NOTICE

Requirement (1)—purchase for value

41–115 NOTE 18. FOR THE REFERENCE TO Megarry and Wade, *The Law of Real Property*, SEE NOW (7th edn), § 8–008.

AT THE END OF THE TEXT ADD: Where the transaction by which the property was sold is liable to be set aside for some reason, the recipient can continue to maintain the defence of purchaser for value without notice until the transaction has been set aside.[22a]

Requirement (2)—acquisition of the legal estate

Legal estate taken in the name of nominee

41–117 NOTE 27. FOR THE REFERENCE TO *Snell's Equity*, SEE NOW (32nd edn), § 4–025. FOR THE REFERENCE TO Megarry and Wade, *The Law of Real Property*, SEE NOW (7th edn), § 8–011.

Requirement (4)—purchase without notice

41–120 AT THE BEGINNING OF THE TEXT INSERT: The test of knowledge, as developed in the context of knowing receipt, under which liability depends upon whether the defendant's state of knowledge is such as to make it unconscionable for him to retain the property received, does not apply to the defence of purchase without notice.[37a]

Doubtful equities

41–122 NOTE 46. AT THE END OF THE FIRST SENTENCE ADD: *Sinclair Investments (UK) Ltd v Versailles Trade Finance Ltd* [2010] EWHC 1614 (Ch); [2011] 1 B.C.L.C. 202 at [92]–[98]; [2011] EWCA Civ 347; [2011] 3 W.L.R. 1153 at [102]–[108].

Commercial transactions

41–131 NOTE 76. ADD: *Macmillan Inc. v Bishopsgate Investment Trust plc (No.3)* [1995] 1 W.L.R. 978 at 1000, 1014 (affirmed [1996] 1 W.L.R. 387, CA); *Sinclair Investments (UK) Ltd v Versailles Trade Finance Ltd* [2010] EWHC 1614 (Ch); [2011] 1 B.C.L.C. 202 at [88]–[91]; [2011] EWCA Civ 347; [2011] 3 W.L.R. 1153 at [99]–[101].

[22a] *Independent Trustee Services Ltd v GP Noble Trustees Ltd* [2012] EWCA Civ 195; [2012] 3 All E.R. 210 at [114]. The court acknowledged that the fact of the beneficiaries' claim may cause the transferee not to seek to have the transaction set aside. Once an order for ancillary relief had been set aside in matrimonial proceedings, the wife could no longer claim to be a purchaser for value of property she had putatively acquired under a consent order later set aside.

[37a] *Sinclair Investments (UK) Ltd v Versailles Trade Finance Ltd* [2010] EWHC 1614 (Ch) at [83]–[88]; [2011] 1 B.C.L.C. 202; affirmed [2011] EWCA Civ 347; [2011] 3 W.L.R. 1153.

Requirement (5)—no notice at the time of transfer of the legal estate

Getting in the legal estate after notice without any breach of trust being involved—land

NOTE 85. FOR THE REFERENCE TO *Snell's Equity*, SEE NOW (32nd edn), § 4–026. **41–134**

NOTE 88. FOR THE REFERENCE TO Megarry and Wade, *The Law of Real Property*, SEE NOW (7th edn), § 8–014.

CHAPTER 42

PERSONAL REMEDIES AGAINST RECIPIENTS

1. Scope of Chapter

Remedies against wrongful recipients of trust property

42–01 At the end add: And the courts in England[2a] and Australia[2b] have declined to remould the traditional personal causes of actions into a general restitutionary remedy.

2. Common Law Action for Recovery of Money Paid by Mistake

Recovery by trustee

Claim in equity

42–07 Note 20. Add: And see § 42–29A (Supplement).

5. Knowing Receipt

Receipt based liability of third parties as constructive trustees

42–21 Note 69. Add: For an Australian judicial account of the development of the remedy see *Bell Group Ltd v Westpac Banking Corp.* [2009] WASC 107; (2008–09) 39 W.A.R. 1 at [4627]–[4838].

General requirements of liability for knowing receipt

42–22 Note 71. At the end add: The six requirements were adopted in *Independent Trustee Services Ltd v GP Noble Trustees Ltd* [2010] EWHC 1653 (Ch); [2010] All E.R. (D) 54 (Jul) at [48].

Knowing receipt as a proprietary and personal remedy

42–24 Note 74. Add: In *Ultraframe (UK) Ltd v Fielding* [2005] EWHC 1638 (Ch); [2007] W.T.L.R. 835 at [1486], [1577] knowing receipt was treated as a personal remedy only which applies where the defendant no longer retains

---

[2a]   *Bank of Credit and Commerce International (Overseas) Limited v Akindele* [2001] Ch. 437; *Charter plc v City Index Ltd* [2007] EWCA Civ 1382; [2008] Ch. 313.
[2b]   *Farah Constructions Pty Ltd v Say-Dee Pty Ltd* [2007] HCA 22; (2007–08) 10 I.T.E.L.R. 136.

trust property or its identifiable proceeds subject to the proprietary remedy. The question whether knowing receipt might have any impact on the remedy available where trust property or its identifiable proceeds were still retained by the recipient was not considered.

Basis of liability

Restitution basis

NOTE 78. FOR THE REFERENCE TO Underhill and Hayton, *Law of Trusts and* **42–28** *Trustees*, SEE NOW (18th edn), §§ 98.37 and 98.38.

NOTE 83. FOR THE REFERENCE TO Scott, *The Law of Trusts*, SEE NOW Scott and **42–29** Ascher, *The Law of Trusts* (5th edn), Vol.5, § 29.1.9.

AFTER § 42–29 INSERT THE FOLLOWING NEW PARAGRAPH AND HEADING:

Locus standi

Generally the same rules apply as in connection with breach of trust **42–29A** claims.[91a] Though a claim will normally be brought by a successor trustee or a beneficiary, the trustee who has made a transfer in breach of trust has *locus standi* to bring a knowing receipt claim against a third party recipient, even though as between himself and his beneficiary he has committed a breach of trust and the commission of that breach of trust is a necessary ingredient in his cause of action against the recipient.[91b] A recipient who no longer has the transferred property or its traceable proceeds may, however, seek a contribution from the trustee.[91c]

Requirement (1)—property subject to a trust

Companies and other fiduciary agents—quasi-trustees

NOTE 94. ADD: *Ultraframe (UK) Ltd v Fielding* [2005] EWHC 1638 (Ch); **42–32** [2007] W.T.L.R. 835 at [1487]–[1488].

Property subject to a constructive (or resulting) trust—constructive trustees

NOTE 1. DELETE AND REPLACE BY: See § 20–53 (including Supplement) and **42–33** note that the circumstances in which a profit is subject to a constructive trust is now narrower than was formerly thought to be the case, see §§ 20–28 to 20–28C (including Supplement).

NOTE 7. AT THE END ADD: In principle, there may be knowing receipt of property held on a *Quistclose* trust: *Gabriel v Little* [2012] EWHC 1193 (Ch); [2012] All E.R. (D) 159 (May) at [76].

[91a] See §§ 39–67 *et seq.*
[91b] See *Montrose Investments Ltd v Orion Nominees Ltd* [2004] EWCA (Civ) 1032; [2004] W.T.L.R. 1133; *Pulvers v Chan* [2007] EWHC 2406 (Ch); [2008] P.N.L.R. 9 at [380]; and compare § 41–46 on the proprietary remedy and §§ 40–02 to 40–05, 40–13A (Supplement) and 42–04 to 42–12 on other remedies by trustees who have made wrongful or mistaken payments or transfers.
[91c] See § 42–73A (Supplement).

Requirement (2)—transfer by the trustee

42-35   NOTE 13. For the reference to Gower and Davies, *Principles of Modern Company Law*, see now (8th edn), § 13–35. Companies Act 2006, ss.677–683 came into force on October 1, 2009: Companies Act 2006 (Commencement No.8, Transitional Provisions and Savings) Order 2008 (SI 2008/2860).

NOTE 16. ADD: See Smith (2009) 125 L.Q.R. 338.

Requirement (3)—transfer in breach of trust

Breach of trust by company directors

42-38   NOTE 30. Companies Act 2006, ss.197–214 came into force on October 1, 2007 in relation to transactions or arrangements entered into on or after that date (subject to transitional provisions and amendments of Companies Act 2006, s.205): Companies Act 2006 (Commencement No.3, Transitional Provisions and Savings) Order 2007 (SI 2007/2194); Companies Act 2006 (Commencement No.6, Savings and Commencement Nos. 3 and 5 (Amendment)) Order 2008 (SI 2008/674).

Receipt of property under contract entered into by company

42-39   NOTE 33. ADD: applied *Ultraframe (UK) Ltd v Fielding* [2005] EWHC 1638 (Ch); [2007] W.T.L.R. 835 at [1492]–[1494]. For an inconclusive discussion of the availability of a knowing receipt remedy where property is taken under an unauthorised and hence void contract purportedly entered into by a company, see *Thanakharn Kasikhorn Thai Chamkat (Mahachon) v Akai Holdings Ltd* [2010] HKCFA 64; [2011] HKEC 1692 at [138]–[144].

NOTE 34. FOR THE REFERENCE TO Gower and Davies, *Principles of Modern Company Law*, SEE NOW (8th edn), § 7–2.

NOTE 36. Companies Act 2006, s.39 came into force on October 1, 2009 in relation to acts of a company done on or after that date (subject to transitional provisions): Companies Act 2006 (Commencement No.8, Transitional Provisions and Savings) Order 2008 (SI 2008/2860). Companies Act 2009, s.40 came into force on October 1, 2009: *ibid.*

NOTE 38. Companies Act 2006, s.42 came into force on October 1, 2009: Companies Act 2006 (Commencement No.8, Transitional Provisions and Savings) Order 2008 (SI 2008/2860).

NOTE 39. Companies Act 2006, s.41 came into force on October 1, 2009: Companies Act 2006 (Commencement No.8, Transitional Provisions and Savings) Order 2008 (SI 2008/2860).

"Breach" of remedial constructive trust

42-41   NOTE 42. DELETE THE FIRST SENTENCE AND REPLACE BY: Similar considerations apply to the kind of resulting trust considered in § 42–33, n.7.

Requirement (4)—the receipt by the defendant

Receipt by agent or nominee of defendant

NOTE 49. AT THE BEGINNING INSERT: *Pulvers v Chan* [2007] EWHC 2406 (Ch); **42–43**
[2008] P.N.L.R. 9 at [379].

NOTE 50. ADD: *Ultraframe (UK) Ltd v Fielding* [2005] EWHC 1638 (Ch);
[2007] W.T.L.R. 835 at [1562]–[1563]; *Law Society of England and Wales v
Habitable Concepts Ltd* [2010] 1449 (Ch); [2010] All E.R (D) 156 (Jun) at
[20]–[22]; *Dyson Technology Ltd v Curtis* [2010] EWHC 3289 (Ch) at [132]
and [133].

Receipt by subsidiary company

NOTE 52. FOR THE REFERENCE TO Gower and Davies, *Principles of Modern* **42–44**
Company Law, SEE NOW (8th edn), §§ 8–5 to 8–14.

Requirement (5)—receipt for the defendant's own benefit

NOTE 53. AT THE END OF THE LAST SENTENCE ADD: compare *Thanakharn* **42–45**
Kasikhorn Thai Chamkat (Mahachon) v Akai Holdings Ltd [2010] HKCFA
64; [2011] HKEC 1692 at [143] leaving open whether receipt as pledgee was
enough.

Receipt by trustees of special trust

AFTER THE TEXT TO N.64 ADD: and so too in Australia.[64a]   **42–47**

Requirement (6)—knowledge generally

Company's knowledge

AT THE END OF THE TEXT ADD: Knowledge of a director or other agent of a **42–52**
company will not generally be imputed to a company where that knowledge
arises from a breach, whether or not fraudulent, of the director's or agent's
duties to the company, except where the director or agent exercises exclusive
control over the company and is its human embodiment.[88a]

Pleading knowledge

NOTE 91. ADD: Provided the material facts to be proved as ingredients of the **42–53**
cause of action are all set out, however, it is not necessary to plead the word
"fraud" or some similar term: *Relfo Ltd v Varsani* [2012] EWHC 2168 (Ch);
[2012] All E.R (D) 12 (Aug) at [95].

[64a] *Quince v Varga* [2008] QCA 376; (2008–09) 11 I.T.E.L.R. 939 at [2]–[4]; [54].
[88a] See *Stone & Rolls Ltd v Moore Stephens* [2009] UKHL 39; [2009] 1 A.C. 1391 (not a
knowing receipt case) which contains a comprehensive review of the authorities but differing views as to the circumstances in which knowledge should be attributed to a company
in such a case.

Application of knowledge requirement to knowing receipt

The general rule

42–55 NOTE 98. ADD: applied *Charter plc v City Index Ltd* [2007] EWCA Civ 1382; [2008] Ch. 313 at [7]–[8]; *Thanakharn Kasikhorn Thai Chamkat (Mahachon) v Akai Holdings Ltd* [2010] HKCFA 64; [2011] HKEC 1692 at [127], [128] and [134]–[137]; *Dyson Technology Ltd v Curtis* [2010] EWHC 3289 (Ch) at [79]–[84].

42–56 NOTE 2. For the reference to *Halsbury's Laws of England*, see now (4th edn), Vol.48 (2007 Reissue), § 702.

42–57 NOTE 8. AT THE END OF THE FIRST SENTENCE INSERT: *Papamichael v National Westminster Bank plc* [2003] EWHC 164 (Comm); 1 [2007] 1 Lloyd's Rep 341 at [246]–[248] ("the type of knowledge that is required is actual rather than constructive knowledge").

NOTE 9. ADD: *Imobilari Pty Ltd v Opes Prime Stockbroking Ltd* [2008] FCA 1920; (2009) 252 A.L.R. 41 at [27] ("knowledge of facts that would put an honest and reasonable person on notice (but not merely inquiry) of a real and not remote risk that the transfer was in breach of trust or fiduciary duty or involved the misapplication of trust property").

Transactions entered into by companies involving breach of trust

42–61 NOTE 36. The repeal of Companies Act, 1985, s.711A by Companies Act 2006, Sch.16, came into force on October 1, 2009: Companies Act 2006 (Commencement No.8, Transitional Provisions and Savings) Order 2008 (SI 2008/2860).

NOTE 37. Companies Act 2006, s.40 came into force on October 1, 2009: Companies Act 2006 (Commencement No.8, Transitional Provisions and Savings) Order 2008 (SI 2008/2860).

NOTE 38. Companies Act 2006, s.40(2)(*b*)(iii) came into force on October 1, 2009: Companies Act 2006 (Commencement No.8, Transitional Provisions and Savings) Order 2008 (SI 2008/2860).

NOTE 39. Companies Act 2006, s.40(2)(*b*)(i) came into force on October 1, 2009: Companies Act 2006 (Commencement No.8, Transitional Provisions and Savings) Order 2008 (SI 2008/2860).

Relevant time for determining knowledge

42–64 NOTE 53. ADD: See too *Heperu Pty Ltd v Belle* [2009] NSWCA 252; (2009) 258 A.L.R. 727 at [87]–[174].

Receipt of property claimed to be trust property

42–65 NOTE 54. AT THE END ADD: See too *Sinclair Investments (UK) Ltd v Versailles Trade Finance Ltd* [2010] EWHC 1614 (Ch); [2011] 1 B.C.L.C. 202 at [92]–[98]; [2011] EWCA Civ 347; [2011] W.T.L.R. 1043 at [102]–[108] (proprietary remedy).

NOTE 55. ADD: See *Horler v Rubin* [2012] EWCA Civ 4; [2012] All E.R. (D) 142 (Jan).

Measure of personal accountability of knowing recipient

DELETE THE SECOND SENTENCE AND N.77 AND REPLACE BY: In general a trustee **42–71** who distributes trust property in breach of trust will be personally liable to restore the property, and may be held liable to pay the value of the property at the date of misapplication or, if greater, the value of the property at the date of judgment or when it would sooner have been sold in the proper administration of the trust.[77] It has been held in the Hong Kong Court of Final Appeal, however, that where trust property is distributed in breach of trust and is then sold for less than its value at the date of receipt, though more than its value at the date of judgment, the knowing recipient can be made liable for the amount of the proceeds of sale, but not for the higher value at the date of receipt.[77a] It is thought, however, that in a case where the property received by the knowing recipient is an appreciating rather than depreciating asset, the measure of accountability is not necessarily limited to the amount of the proceeds of sale received by the knowing recipient and that he may be made liable for the value of the property at the date of judgment or the value when the property would sooner have been sold by the trustee in the proper administration of the trust had there been no breach of trust, if greater than the proceeds of sale.[77b] The Privy Council has recently said, on an appeal from the Turks & Caicos Islands, that the recipient is subject to custodial duties which are the same as those voluntarily assumed by express trustees.[77c]

DELETE THE TEXT AFTER N.80 AND N.81.

AT THE END OF THE TEXT ADD: Formerly, the court did not generally award compound interest in the absence of evidence that the defendant had used the money or property received for his own commercial advantage in earning profits in his business.[81] Now, following developments in the law on

---

[77]   See § 39–54.
[77a] *Thanakharn Kasikhorn Thai Chamkat (Mahachon) v Akai Holdings Ltd* [2010] HKCFA 64; [2011] HKEC 1692 at [148]–[155] (Lord Neuberger).
[77b] This is the principle applied in England in the context of dishonest assistance, see *Re Bell's Indenture* [1980] 1 W.L.R. 1217 at 1231–1233, itself applying with modifications the principle of *Re Massingberd's Settlement* (1890) 63 L.T. 296 which applies to express trustees. This principle was not referred to by Lord Neuberger in the *Thanakharn* case, above, though in reaching his decision he was influenced by the consideration that the claimant was better off as a result of the sale since the property in that case would have become worthless had the property been retained rather than sold, as would probably have happened if there had been no breach of trust, see at [153]–[154]. Different considerations apply in the context of an appreciating rather than depreciating asset where a sale by the knowing recipient has the effect of increasing rather than reducing the loss. Though Lord Neuberger was sympathetic to the view that the measure of accountability for knowing receipt should be the same as for common law damages for conversion (see at [155]), he did not have in mind issues of equitable accountability in the context of appreciating property.
[77c] *Arthur v Att.-Gen. of the Turks & Caicos Islands* [2012] UKPC 30; [2012] All E.R. (D) 164 (Aug) at [37].
[81]   *Belmont Finance Corporation Ltd v Williams Furniture Ltd (No.2)* [1980] 1 All E.R. 393 at 419, CA. Compound interest with yearly rests was awarded in *El Ajou v Dollar Land Holdings plc (No.2)* [1995] 2 All E.R. 213. As to compound interest, see § 39–61.

the award of compound interest in restitutionary claims,[81a] compound
interest may be awarded generally.[81b] In a case where there are a number of
knowing recipients in respect of the property transferred in breach of trust,
the liability of each recipient will be limited by reference to what he received,
not what other recipients received, and the remedy will be framed so as to
avoid double recovery.[81c] In a case where the knowing recipient sold
depreciating property which he had previously received, and the measure of
accountability was limited to the amount of the proceeds of sale, compound
interest ran from the date of sale and not the date of receipt, and no interest
at all was payable in respect of the period between the date of receipt and the
date of sale.[81d]

Relief under section 61 of the Trustee Act 1925 and defence of change of position

42–73 NOTE 86. ADD: And see *Bank of Credit and Commerce International
(Overseas) Ltd v Akindele* [2001] Ch. 437 at 456F, CA; *Dyson Technology
Ltd v Curtis* [2010] EWHC 3289 (Ch) at [129].

AFTER § 42–73 INSERT THE FOLLOWING NEW PARAGRAPH AND HEADING:

Contribution

42–73A A defendant who is held liable for knowing receipt, or who enters into a
bona fide settlement or compromise of such a claim, may seek contribution
under the Civil Liability (Contribution) Act 1978[87a] from any other person
liable in respect of the same damage, including not only the trustee who
made the transfer in breach in breach of trust, but also directors and professional persons liable in respect of the transfer.[87b] Though a recipient must
expect to pay back any part of the transferred fund which he has retained, it
does not necessarily follow that, because he received the fund, he cannot
receive any contribution in respect of the part of the fund which he has
transferred away from those liable for the same damage who have received
nothing.[87c]

[81a] *Sempra Metals Ltd v I.R.C.* [2007] UKHL 14; [2008] UKHL 1 A.C. 561.
[81b] *Dyson Technology Ltd v Curtis* [2010] EWHC 3289 (Ch) at [148]–[154].
[81c] *Trustor AB v Smallbone* [2000] All E.R. (D) 624, CA at [63]–[66]; *Ultraframe (UK) Ltd v Fielding* [2005] EWHC 1638 (Ch); [2007] W.T.L.R. 835 at [1577]–[1578]. As to contribution between knowing recipients and others liable in respect of the same damage, see § 42–72A (Supplement).
[81d] *Thanakharn Kasikhorn Thai Chamkat (Mahachon) v Akai Holdings Ltd*, above, at [156]–[160].
[87a] On which see generally §§ 39–78 to 39–83.
[87b] *Charter plc v City Index Ltd* [2007] EWCA Civ 1382; [2008] Ch. 313 at [12]–[33] and [79] (note the somewhat different approach of Arden L.J. at [62]–[72]).
[87c] *Charter plc v City Index Ltd*, above, at [34]–[59], [73]–[77] and [79].

6. TRUSTEE *DE SON TORT*

Generally

NOTE 89. ADD: *Dubai Aluminium Co. Ltd v Salaam* [2002] UKHL 48; [2003] **42–74**
2 A.C. 366 at [135]–[141]; *Cunningham v Cunningham* [2009] JRC 124; 2009
J.L.R. 227 at [21]–[33].

Liability limited to property received

NOTE 99. AFTER THE REFERENCE TO *Pearce v Pearce* INSERT: *Cunningham v* **42–76**
Cunningham [2009] JRC 124; 2009 J.L.R. 227 at [21]–[33].

7. INCONSISTENT DEALING BY LAWFUL RECIPIENTS OF TRUST PROPERTY

Lawful agents of trustees in receipt of trust property

NOTE 16. ADD: *Dubai Aluminium Co. Ltd v Salaam* [2002] UKHL 48; [2003] **42–86**
2 A.C. 366 at [135]–[141]; *Cunningham v Cunningham* [2009] JRC 124; 2009
J.L.R. 227 at [21]–[33].

Inconsistent dealing by lawful agent of trustees acting on instructions

NOTE 29. ADD: For a wider statement of a solicitor's liability not requiring **42–89**
dishonesty, see *Eden Refuge Trust v Hohepa* (2010–11) 13 I.T.E.L.R. 187 at
[191]–[205], NZ HC (authorities on inconsistent dealing not cited or considered) (upheld on appeal, [2012] NZCA 124; (2011–12) 14 I.T.E.L.R. 914).

Other cases of inconsistent dealing by agents who hold trust property

Agent of trustee de son tort

NOTE 46. AFTER THE REFERENCE TO *Mara v Browne* INSERT: *Cunningham v* **42–96**
Cunningham [2009] JRC 124; 2009 J.L.R. 227 at [34].

CHAPTER 43

REMEDIES AGAINST THIRD PARTIES OTHERWISE THAN IN RESPECT OF BREACH OF TRUST

1. THE GENERAL RULE AND DERIVATIVE ACTIONS

Trustees normally proper claimants

43–01 INSERT AFTER THE FIRST SENTENCE: Further, normally beneficiaries have no personal cause of action of action in contract or tort against the agents of the trustees,[1a] though sometimes beneficiaries may bring derivative claims which would otherwise be brought by the trustees,[1b] and sometimes a personal claim in tort is available to beneficiaries.[1c]

NOTE 5. ADD: *Roberts v Gill & Co.* [2007] All E.R. (D) 89 (Apr) at [23]–[24]; affd. [2010] UKSC 22; [2011] 1 A.C. 240 (administrator).

Successor trustees

43–02 NOTE 6. DELETE AND REPLACE BY: See CPR, Pt 19, r.19.2(4)(a).

Bare trust

43–03 NOTE 15. AT THE END ADD: *Roberts v Gill & Co.* [2010] UKSC 22 at [63]–[68] (Lord Collins).

AT THE END OF THE TEXT ADD: A beneficiary of a bare trust has no *locus standi* to bring a petition for the winding up of a company.[17a]

Administration action by beneficiaries

43–04 NOTE 18. AT THE END ADD: *Tsang Yue Joyce v Standard Chartered Bank (Hong Kong) Ltd* [2010] HKCFI 981; [2010] 5 H.K.L.R.D. (statement in text approved at [38]).

[1a] *Royal Sudan Airlines Sdn. Bhd. v Tan* [1995] 2 A.C. 395 at 391, PC; *Roberts v Gill & Co.* [2007] All E.R. (D) 89 (Apr) at [23]–[24]; affd. [2010] UKSC 22; [2011] 1 A.C. 240; *Chvetsos v BNP Paribas Trust Corp. Ltd* [2009] JRC 120; 2009 J.L.R. 217; *Webster v Sandersons* [2009] EWCA Civ 830; [2009] 2 B.C.L.C. 542 at [31]; and cases cited in § 43–06, n.39 (including Supplement).
[1b] See §§ 43–03 to 43–05 (including Supplement).
[1c] See section 2 of this chapter.
[17a] *Hannoun v R Ltd* [2009] C.I.L.R. 124, Cayman GC.

Derivative action by beneficiaries

AFTER THE FIRST SENTENCE INSERT A NEW NOTE 20a: This paragraph was cited **43–05** with approval in *Roberts v Gill & Co.* [2008] EWCA Civ 803; [2009] 1 W.L.R. 531 at [15]; affd [2010] UKSC 22; [2011] 1 A.C. 240.

NOTE 22. AT THE END ADD: *Roberts v Gill & Co.* [2010] UKSC 22; [2011] 1 A.C. 240.

AFTER THE TEXT TO N.23 INSERT: The guiding principle is that there must be exceptional circumstances, which embrace a failure, excusable or inexcusable, by the trustees in the performance of a duty to the beneficiaries to protect the trust estate, or to protect the interest of the beneficiaries in the trust estate.[23a]

NOTE 24. ADD: *Tsang Yue Joyce v Standard Chartered Bank (Hong Kong) Ltd* [2010] HKCFI 981; [2010] 5 H.K.L.R.D. 628 at [44].

DELETE THE TEXT TO N.31 AND REPLACE BY: Where a beneficiary brings a derivative action in his own name, then the trustees must be joined as defendants. The need for joinder of the trustees is not merely a procedural matter, nor merely to ensure that the trustees are bound by the judgment or to avoid multiplicity of actions. The need for joinder has a substantive basis since the beneficiary has no personal right to sue and is suing on behalf of the estate, or more accurately the trustee.

NOTE 31. AT THE END OF THE FIRST SENTENCE ADD: *Roberts v Gill & Co.* [2010] UKSC 22; [2011] 1 A.C. 240 at [42]–[70] (Lord Collins) with whom Lord Rodger agreed at [86] and Lord Walker at [95]–[112], rather differing views as to the nature and absoluteness of the rule being expressed by Lord Hope at [79]–[84] and by Lord Clarke at [121]–[130]. DELETE THE SECOND SENTENCE AND REPLACE BY: The question whether other beneficiaries need to be joined was not considered by the SC in *Roberts v Gill & Co.*, above. The CA in that case, [2008] EWCA Civ 803; [2009] 1 W.L.R. 531 at [48], considered that the beneficiaries must also be joined if this is necessary to avoid a multiplicity of actions. Arguably a derivative action comes within CPR, Pt 19, r.19.6, so as to make a judgment binding on the beneficiaries, on the basis that the trustees represent the beneficiaries and the claimant is standing in the shoes of the trustees, though it is not correct to say that the claimant is the representative of the other beneficiaries. If the claim comes within CPR, Pt 19, r.19.7, a representation order could be made under that sub-rule. Alternatively, it may be argued that, once the trustees have been joined as defendants in their capacity as such, the claim comes within CPR, Pt 19, r.19.7A, and, though the trustee will not take an active part in the proceedings, the beneficiary stands in the shoes of the trustees and the same practice, so far as joinder of beneficiaries is concerned, should be applied as if the trustees were the claimants (as to which see § 43–01 (including Supplement)), especially where the beneficiaries are numerous or include minor,

---

[23a] *Hayim v Citibank N.A.* [1987] A.C. 730 at 748, PC; *Shang v Zhang* [2007] NSWSC 856; (2007–08) 10 I.T.E.L.R. 521 at [12]; *Roberts v Gill & Co.* [2008] EWCA Civ 803; [2009] 1 W.L.R. 531 at [41]; [2010] UKSC 22; [2011] 1 A.C. 240 at [53].

unborn or unascertained persons. Distinct from the question whether the beneficiaries must be joined to avoid a multiplicity of actions is the question whether directions should be given to ascertain the views of the other beneficiaries. This is another question which was left open by the CA in *Roberts v Gill & Co.*, above, at [48]. If there has been no *Beddoe* application in relation to the claim, and there are other beneficiaries with substantial interests who may be prejudiced by the claim, for example if the trust has assets which are vulnerable to a costs order against the trustees if the claim fails, there is a good argument that a procedure should be devised for canvassing the views of the other beneficiaries in a similar way to the *Beddoe* procedure (on which see § 21–130), especially as the CA in *Roberts v Gill & Co.*, above, at [43], did decide that the court must take into consideration the financial impact of bringing the claim on the trust (see the text added below).

AFTER THE TEXT TO N.31 INSERT: If a beneficiary brings a personal claim against a third party, and then seeks permission to amend his claim to a derivative action before the expiry of the limitation period, the amendment may be allowed.[31a] But if permission is sought after the expiry of the limitation period, permission will be refused because the amendment would not be allowed unless the trustees were added as defendants but they cannot be added as defendants since they are not necessary parties to the existing personal claim.[31b] The court must consider the financial impact of bringing the claim on the trust, in particular the vulnerability of the trust order to a costs order against the trustees if the claim fails, and the consequential potential adverse effect of such an order on other beneficiaries.[31c] In *Roberts v Gill & Co.*,[31d] the Court of Appeal considered that an estate which had no assets other than the claim, and its administrator, were not vulnerable to an order for costs where the claim was brought by a legally aided claimant. But, leaving aside legal aid cases, a trust is vulnerable to such an order, and even if there are no assets apart from the claim, the trustee may be personally vulnerable since their liability to pay costs in third party claims is not limited to the trust assets,[31e] and so there may be an objection to a derivative action by a beneficiary of an impecunious trust where there are doubts as to the beneficiary's ability to meet a costs order if the claim fails.

NOTE 35. ADD: but see *Lidden v Composite Buyers Ltd* [1996] FCA 1613; (1996) 139 A.L.R. 549 at [18]–[27].

[31a] *Roberts v Gill & Co.* [2008] EWCA Civ 803; [2009] 1 W.L.R. 531 at [34]–[35]; (point not considered on appeal [2010] UKSC 22; [2011] 1 A.C. 240); and CPR, Pt 17, r.17.4(4).

[31b] *Roberts v Gill & Co.* [2010] UKSC 22; [2011] 1 A.C. 240 at [42]–[70] (Lord Collins) with whom Lord Rodger agreed at [86] and Lord Walker at [95]–[112], rather differing views as to the nature and absoluteness of the rule being expressed by Lord Hope at [79]–[84] and by Lord Clarke at [121]–[130]; CPR, Pt 19, r.19.5; Limitation Act 1980, s.35.

[31c] *Roberts v Gill & Co.* [2008] EWCA Civ 803; [2009] 1 W.L.R. 531 at [43] (point not considered on appeal [2010] UKSC 22; [2011] 1 A.C. 240).

[31d] Above (point not considered on appeal [2010] UKSC 22; [2011] 1 A.C. 240).

[31e] See §§ 21–54 to 21–58.

2. CLAIMS IN TORT BY BENEFICIARIES FOR NEGLIGENCE

Introduction

NOTE 39. AT THE END ADD: And see *Royal Sudan Airlines Sdn. Bhd. v Tan* **43–06** [1995] 2 A.C. 395 at 391, PC; *Roberts v Gill & Co.* [2007] All E.R. (D) 89 (Apr) at [23]–[24]; affd. [2010] UKSC 22; [2011] 1 A.C. 240, [2008] EWCA Civ 803; [2009] 1 W.L.R. 531; *Chvetsos v BNP Paribas Trust Corp. Ltd* [2009] JRC 120; 2009 J.L.R. 21; *Webster v Sandersons* [2009] EWCA Civ 830; [2009] 2 B.C.L.C. 542 at [31].

Assumption of responsibility to beneficiaries

NOTE 58. INSERT AT THE BEGINNING: *Webster v Sandersons* [2009] EWCA Civ **43–09** 830; [2009] 2 B.C.L.C. 542 at [31] and see

Negligent physical damage to trust property

AFTER THE THIRD SENTENCE OF THE TEXT INSERT: Nevertheless, a beneficial **43–11** owner or co-owner of property who has an absolute beneficial entitlement to or share in the property can sue for reasonably foreseeable loss suffered by him in consequence of negligent damage to the property, provided that the legal owner is joined as a defendant.[62a]

[62a] *Shell UK Ltd v Total UK Ltd* [2010] EWCA Civ 180; [2011] Q.B. 86 at [111]–[144].

CHAPTER 44

LIMITATION OF ACTIONS

2. FRAUD AND RETENTION OF TRUST PROPERTY

Where no limitation period applies

"Action"

44–05   NOTE 17. AFTER s.38(1) INSERT: (as amended by Welfare Reform Act 2012, s.108(1), (2)).

Section 21(1)(*a*)

Action "in respect of" fraud

44–10   DELETE THE SECOND SENTENCE AND REPLACE BY: It is now clear that the provision may apply, for example, to the innocent recipient of trust property from a fraudulent trustee. Its scope in that respect is discussed in the section dealing with liabilities under constructive trusts and similar liabilities.[37]

Section 21(1)(*b*)

Trustee in possession

44–12   AFTER THE FIRST SENTENCE INSERT: Hence a trustee who retains rent which ought to be paid to an income beneficiary, or to a beneficiary absolutely entitled, will have no defence of limitation.[39a]

Apart from the Act—laches

44–15   NOTE 53. DELETE THE LAST SENTENCE AND REPLACE BY: See too *Cattley v Pollard* [2006] EWHC 3130 (Ch); [2007] Ch. 353 at [153] (decision disapproved on another point in *Central Bank of Nigeria v Williams* [2012] EWCA Civ 415; [2012] 3 All E.R. 579).

44–16   NOTE 55. DELETE THE REFERENCE TO *Cattley v Pollard* AND REPLACE BY: See too *Cattley v Pollard* [2006] EWHC 3130 (Ch); [2007] Ch. 353 at [154] *et seq.* (decision disapproved on another point in *Central Bank of Nigeria v Williams* [2012] EWCA Civ 415; [2012] 3 All E.R. 579).

AFTER THE FOURTH SENTENCE INSERT: But although detrimental reliance by the other party is not an "immutable requirement" for the doctrine of laches

---

[37]   §§ 44–47 *et seq.*
[39a]   *Iles v Iles* [2012] EWHC 919 (Ch) at [45].

to apply, usually some form of reliance will be a necessary ingredient.[57a]
Laches bars only equitable claims[57b] but it seems that the claims material in
this context will always be equitable.

3. Other Claims

Six-year limitation period for many other claims

When claim is "brought"

Note 63. At the end of the first sentence add: *Page v Hewetts* [2012] **44–18**
EWCA Civ 805.

Claim to recover trust property

Claims to recover trust property wrongly transferred

Delete the fifth sentence and replace by: It is now clear that such a claim **44–20**
does fall within section 21(1)(*a*), so that the defendant, though innocent, will
not be able to raise a defence of limitation; we discuss the point in the
section dealing with liabilities under constructive trusts and similar
liabilities.[71]

In the first sentence after will apply insert: (in the absence of fraud on **44–21**
the part of the trustee).

In the second sentence delete section 23(3) and replace by: section 21(3).

Action "by a beneficiary"

Note 31. Delete the first sentence and replace by: *Cattley v Pollard* **44–31**
[2006] EWHC 3130 (Ch); [2007] Ch. 353 at [98]–[102], quoting and
approving this passage from the previous edition of this work (decision
disapproved on another point in *Central Bank of Nigeria v Williams* [2012]
EWCA Civ 415; [2012] 3 All E.R. 579).

Effect of barring one beneficiary

Note 56. Delete and replace by: Note, however, that laches is a defence **44–38**
only to a claim within Limitation Act 1980, s.21(1) (fraud and retention of
trust property) and not to one within s.21(3) (other breaches of trust), see §§
44–15 to 44–16, 44–44.

Actions against personal representatives

Note 93. For the reference to *Snell's Equity*, see now (32nd edn), § 21– **44–45**
055.

[57a] *Fisher v Brooker* [2009] UKHL 41; [2009] 1 W.L.R. 1764 at [64].
[57b] *ibid.*, at [64], [79].
[71] See §§ 44–54 *et seq.* (knowing receipt), §§ 44–59 *et seq.* (*Diplock* claims) (including Supplement in each case).

4. CONSTRUCTIVE TRUSTS AND SIMILAR LIABILITIES

General

44–49 NOTE 20. AFTER THE REFERENCE TO *Halton International Inc. v Guernroy*, INSERT: *Peconic Industrial Development Ltd v Lau Kwok Fai* [2009] HKCFA 16; (2008–09) 11 I.T.E.L.R 844 at [19]–[23]; *Sinclair Investments (UK) Ltd v Versailles Trade Finance Ltd* [2010] EWHC 1614 (Ch); [2011] 1 B.C.L.C. 202 at [55]–[80] (affirmed [2011] EWCA Civ 347; [2011] 4 All E.R. 335); *Central Bank of Nigeria v Williams* [2012] EWCA Civ 415; [2012] 3 All E.R. 579 (not following *Peconic* as to the application of the distinction).

AFTER § 44–49 INSERT A NEW § 44–49A AS FOLLOWS:

44–49A The application of section 21(1) of the 1980 Act to constructive trustees has proved problematical, since its wording does not express the distinction drawn in *Paragon Finance*. Some general points may be made here:

(1) Both paragraph (*a*) and paragraph (*b*) refer to "the trustee", paragraph (*a*) covering an action "in respect of any fraud or fraudulent breach of trust to which the trustee was a party or privy" and paragraph (*b*) covering an action "to recover from the trustee trust property or the proceeds of trust property ...". The action, by the opening words of section 21(1), is "an action by a beneficiary under a trust"[22a] and the trustee referred to is evidently the trustee of that trust. In both paragraphs, the term "the trustee" must mean either an express trustee or a constructive trustee of the first kind but not a constructive trustee of the second kind, since otherwise the distinction drawn in *Paragon Finance* would fail. Later authorities are consistent with that view, though not altogether explicit.[22b]

(2) Section 21(1) nonetheless has in some respects a wider reach than *Paragon Finance* might suggest. Paragraph (*b*) contemplates an action against "the trustee" in that sense, *i.e.* not a constructive trustee of the second kind. Paragraph (*a*), however, is different: it is sufficient if the action is "in respect of" any fraud or fraudulent breach of trust to which the trustee was a party. After some uncertainty in the authorities, the Court of Appeal has now

[22a] For the words "by a beneficiary", see §§ 44–06, 44–30 to 44–31.
[22b] *Cedric Slack & Partners Ltd v Slack* [2010] EWCA Civ 204; [2010] All E.R. (D) 200 (Feb) (in claim to recover company property wrongly distributed, recipient conceded to be outside s.21(1)(*b*) as being only a constructive trustee of second kind; concession held wrong but *semble* only because recipient was director of company, owing prior fiduciary duties); *Central Bank of Nigeria v Williams*, above (defendant sought to be made liable for dishonest assistance in dishonest breach of trust and s.21(1)(a) held to preclude limitation defence; nonetheless accepted that defendant not a constructive trustee of first kind, see [14]; submission rejected at first instance that defendant was "the trustee" within s.21(1) and not renewed on appeal, see [41]). In *Cattley v Pollard* [2006] EWHC 3130 (Ch); [2007] Ch. 353 it had earlier been held (at [86]) that the reference to "the trustee" in s.21(1)(*a*) did not extend to a constructive trustee of the second kind and though otherwise disapproved in *Central Bank of Nigeria v Williams* (see next note) the disapproval does not seem to have extended to that point.

determined, in *Central Bank of Nigeria v Williams*,[22c] that paragraph (*a*) is not impliedly confined to an action against the defaulting trustee (*i.e.* an express trustee or a constructive trustee of the first kind) but also excludes any limitation period in the cases it mentions even if the defendant is sought to be made liable only as a constructive trustee of the second kind.[22d] Hence the availability of a defence of limitation, where paragraph (*b*) is inapplicable, turns not on the conduct of the defendant but on the conduct of the trustee. It follows, for example, that where it is sought to make the defendant liable for dishonest assistance in a breach of trust, he will have no defence of limitation if the trustee was fraudulent but will do so if the trustee was not fraudulent, despite his own dishonesty; conversely, if it is sought to make the defendant liable as a *Diplock* recipient of property distributed in breach of trust, he will have no defence of limitation, despite his own innocence, if the trustee was fraudulent but will do so if the trustee was not fraudulent.

(3) The distinction between the two kinds of constructive trustee remains important for both branches of section 21(1) but it is not always easy to draw. It is not enough to show that the defendant was a fiduciary before the transaction complained of without also showing that the liability sought to be enforced derived from a breach of that duty. In *Paragon Finance* itself, the defendant solicitors were fiduciaries, holding money paid to them by their client, the plaintiff, on trust for them pending completion of a sub-purchase; but the plaintiff did not and could not assert a breach of that trust, seeking instead to allege that the money which would otherwise have been subject to it was obtained by fraud and seeking to raise a constructive trust in their own favour in its place.[22e] That was a constructive trust of the second kind.[22f] Similarly, a director is a fiduciary but if he is liable for making an unauthorised profit not dependent on any pre-existing responsibility of his for the property of the company he is a constructive trustee of the second kind.[22g]

[22c] *Central Bank of Nigeria v Williams*, above, approving *G.L. Baker v Medway Building and Supplies Ltd* [1958] 1 W.L.R. 1216 at 1221 and *Statek Corpn v Alford* [2008] EWHC 32 (Ch); [2008] W.T.L.R. 1089 at [108]–[126], *obiter*, and disapproving *Cattley v Pollard*, above, and *Peconic Industrial Development Ltd v Lau Kwok Fai* (2009) 11 I.T.E.L.R. 844; [2009] 5 HKC 135, HK CFA (in which the leading judgment was given by Lord Hoffmann N.P.J.) on Hong Kong legislation in terms identical to the English predecessor of Limitation Act 1980, s.21(1).

[22d] Compare the wide meaning given to the phrase "in respect of" where it appears in Limitation Act 180, s.22 (for which see §§ 44–44 to 44–45) in *Re Diplock* [1948] Ch. 465 at 512–513, CA, adopted on appeal *sub nom. Ministry of Health v Simpson* [1951] A.C. 251 at 276, HL.

[22e] See [1999] 1 All E.R. 400 at 408c-d, 409g-h. The plaintiff was applying for leave to amend to make that allegation, which was refused.

[22f] *ibid.*

[22g] See §§ 44–64.

(4) It is generally assumed that every case of constructive trusteeship falling outside section 21(1) will attract the six-year period of limitation imposed by section 21(3). Section 21(3) mirrors section 21(1) in referring to "an action ... to recover trust property or in respect of any breach of trust". The breach of trust is at first sight one committed by a real trustee, that is, an express trustee or a constructive trustee of the first kind, as it is in section 21(1), though as the action need be only "in respect of" the breach the wording will encompass a claim against a constructive trustee of the second kind when, say, it is a liability as an accessory which is sought to be enforced, for the claim will be in respect of the breach committed by a real trustee.[22h] But some liabilities as constructive trustee of the second kind exist where there is no real trust and no real trustee,[22i] *Paragon Finance* being itself such a case, and it is not then easy to say how section 21(3) imposes a period of limitation. Since section 21(1) uses the words "to which the trustee was a party or privy" and section 21(3) does not, the answer may be that the breach of trust referred to in the latter extends to a breach of a constructive trust of the second kind.

Knowing receipt

44–55 DELETE THE SECOND SENTENCE AND NOTES 40 TO 42 AND REPLACE BY: Claims against such a person will not fall within section 21(1)(*b*), even if they are proprietary claims, since the defendant will not be a trustee of the relevant kind; they may fall within section 21(1)(*a*) but only if the trustee was dishonest in making the transfer.[40–42]

Dishonest assistance

44–56 DELETE THE LAST FIVE SENTENCES OF THE TEXT AND REPLACE BY: There have been decisions assuming that the principle of the rule survived not only the Trustee Act 1888 but also the redefinition of the accessory's liability as not dependent on the dishonesty of the express trustee.[47] But such an accessory has not assumed the duties of a trustee and is evidently a constructive trustee of the second kind, though the trust itself pre-dates his involvement. It is now clear from *Central Bank of Nigeria v Williams*[48] that he is to be so treated and hence the application of section 21(1)(*a*) of the 1980 Act depends on the conduct of the trustee: if the trustee was also dishonest (*i.e.* fraudulent within that provision), the accessory is deprived of any defence of limitation but if the trustee was not dishonest then the accessory will be able to raise such a defence. In the latter case, the period of limitation will in

---

[22h] See § 44–49A(2) (Supplement) and *Central Bank of Nigeria v Williams*, above; also *Davies v Sharples* [2006] EWHC 362 (Ch); [2006] W.T.L.R. 839 at [48]–[49].

[22i] See § 44–69.

[40–42] See § 44–49A(2) (Supplement).

[47] *Barlow Clowes International Ltd v Eurotrust International Ltd* (1998–99) 2 O.F.L.R. 42, Manx HC (not followed on another point in *Paragon Finance plc v D.B. Thakerar & Co.* [1999] 1 All E.R. 400 at 411–412, CA); *Schulman v Hewson* [2002] EWHC 855 (Ch) at [44].

[48] [2012] EWCA Civ 415; [2012] 3 All E.R. 579; see § 44–49A(2).

principle be six years from the breach of trust[49] but time does not start running until the claimant discovers the fraud or could with reasonable diligence have discovered it.[50-51]

DELETE ENTIRE PARAGRAPH.   **44–57**

IN THE FIRST SENTENCE DELETE It is to be noted that if a dishonest accessory is **44–58** indeed precluded AND REPLACE BY: It is to be noted that when a dishonest accessory is precluded.

Diplock **claims**

NOTE 65. DELETE THE LAST SENTENCE   **44–60**

DELETE THE LAST THREE SENTENCES OF THE TEXT AND REPLACE BY: If, however, the breach of trust on the part of the trustee was fraudulent, then both the personal claim and the proprietary claim would fall within section 21(1)(*a*) of the 1980 Act.[67-69]

AFTER an extended period INSERT (where time runs at all).   **44–61**

Profiting from a trust

NOTE 74. AT THE END ADD: a point considered "noteworthy" in *Sinclair* **44–62** *Investments (UK) Ltd v Versailles Trade Finance Ltd* [2010] EWHC 1614 (Ch); [2011] 1 B.C.L.C. 202 at [79] (affirmed [2011] EWCA Civ 347; [2011] 4 All E.R. 335).

NOTE 75. DELETE AND REPLACE BY: See §§ 20–28 to 20–28C (including Supplement).

Retention of property

NOTE 82. AT THE END OF THE FIRST SENTENCE DELETE: (see § 20–36). AT THE **44–63** END OF THE SECOND SENTENCE ADD: and (iii) *Metropolitan Bank v Heiron*, along with *Lister & Co v Stubbs*, were followed, and *Att.-Gen. for Hong Kong v Reid* not followed, in *Sinclair Investments (UK) Ltd v Versailles Trade Finance Ltd* [2010] EWHC 1614 (Ch); [2011] 1 B.C.L.C. 202 at [35]–[80] (affirmed [2011] EWCA Civ 347; [2011] 4 All E.R. 335), see §§ 20–28A to 20–28C and 20–36 (Supplement).

AT THE END OF THE PARAGRAPH ADD: The decision in *Central Bank of Nigeria v Williams*,[83a] that a defendant sued as a constructive trustee even of the second kind will be deprived of a defence of limitation if the claim against him is "in respect of" a fraudulent breach of trust to which the trustee (*sc.* an express trustee or a constructive trustee of the first kind) was a party or privy, does not seem to bear on this point, because no such breach has taken

---

[49] Limitation Act 1980, s.21(3).
[50-51] *ibid.*, s.32(1)(*a*), discussed at §§ 44–131, 44–132.
[67-69] See § 44–49A(2) (Supplement).
[83a] [2012] EWCA Civ 415; [2012] 3 All E.R. 579.

place;[83b] and it would seem that the defence is provided by section 21(3) of the 1980 Act.[83c]

AFTER § 44–64 INSERT THE FOLLOWING NEW PARAGRAPH:

44–64A The donee of a power of attorney, including a lasting power or (formerly) an enduring power,[86a] owes a fiduciary duty to the donor and has a power of disposition over the property to which the power extends. We consider that if the donee makes an unauthorised profit (*e.g.* by accepting a commission on the sale of the donor's property) his liability is as a constructive trustee of the first kind.[86b]

Fraud

44–65 DELETE THE LAST TWO SENTENCES AND REPLACE BY: It is true, in the light of *Central Bank of Nigeria v Williams*,[88a] that the latter as well as the former may be deprived of a defence of limitation by section 21(1)(*a*) of the 1980 Act but only where the claim against him is "in respect of" a fraudulent breach of trust to which the trustee (*sc.* an express trustee or a constructive trustee of the first kind) was a party or privy. Absent such a breach, fraud on the part of a constructive trustee of the second kind seems to be irrelevant.[89]

DELETE THE HEADING TO § 44–69 AND THE WHOLE PARAGRAPH AND REPLACE BY:

Fraud, misrepresentation, mistake and undue influence

44–69 Property obtained by fraud or theft is held by the recipient as constructive trustee for the owner and the same applies if he retains money paid by mistake when he knows of the mistake;[99a] property obtained by mis-representation or undue influence may likewise be held on a constructive trust. The defendant in such cases is clearly a constructive trustee of the second kind. We have referred to the difficulty of applying the wording of section 21(3) of the Limitation Act 1980 to such claims[99b] but it seems clear nonetheless that a defendant is able to rely on a defence of limitation even in cases of fraud or retention of the property.[1]

[83b] See § 44–49A(1)–(3) (Supplement).

[83c] See § 44–49A(4) (Supplement). It was assumed in *Page v Hewetts* [2011] EWHC 2449 (Ch) (appeal allowed on a different point [2012] EWCA Civ 805) that a six-year period applied to a claim for a secret profit, though Limitation Act 1980, s.21(3) was not in fact mentioned.

[86a] Granted under Mental Capacity Act 2005 and Enduring Powers of Attorney Act 1985 respectively.

[86b] See § 20–36 (including Supplement) on the possible distinction between cases where the commission derives from the property subject to the fiduciary relationship and cases where it does not.

[88a] [2012] EWCA Civ 415; [2012] 3 All E.R. 579.

[89] Carnwath L.J., a party to the decision in *Koshy*, appears to have disavowed that part of its reasoning: see *Halton International Inc. v Guernroy Ltd* [2006] EWCA Civ 801; [2006] W.T.L.R. 1241 at [22].

[99a] §§ 7–25, 7–26.

[99b] § 44–49A(4) (Supplement).

[1] *Piwinski v Corporate Trustees of the Diocese of Armidale* [1977] 1 N.S.W.L.R. 266; *Paragon Finance plc v D.B. Thakerar & Co.* [1999] 1 All E.R. 400, CA; *UCB Home Loans Corporation Ltd v Carr* [2000] Lloyd's Rep. P.N. 754.

5. FUTURE INTERESTS IN LAND

Registered land generally

IN THE SECOND SENTENCE OF THE TEXT DELETE entitle AND REPLACE BY entitled. **44–109(2)**

Adverse possession and registered land held in trust

No successive barring of equitable interests

IN THE SECOND SENTENCE OF THE TEXT DELETE the trespasser either has an **44–114** entitlement AND REPLACE BY either the trespasser has an entitlement.

6. EXTENSION AND POSTPONEMENT OF LIMITATION PERIODS

Disability

NOTE 35. INSERT AT THE END: As the test of mental incapacity has been **44–123** changed by statute, the relevant test is that in force at the time when the right of action accrued: *Seaton v Seddon* [2012] EWHC 735 (Ch); [2012] All E.R. (D) 93 (May).

INSERT AFTER THE FIRST SENTENCE: If there was no disability when the right of **44–124** action accrued, a supervening disability will provide no extension;[41a] but if one disability (incapacity) supervenes before another (minority) has terminated, the extension provided by the earlier will continue after its termination until the later has also terminated, if it ever does.[41b]

Fraud, concealment and mistake

Fraud

NOTE 75. AFTER THE REFERENCE TO *Beaman v A.R.T.S. Ltd*, INSERT: *Barn-* **44–132** *staple Boat Co. Ltd v Jones* [2007] EWCA Civ 1124; [2008] 1 All E.R. 1124 at [31]–[33].

NOTE 79. DELETE AND REPLACE BY: Assumed in *Cattley v Pollard* [2006] EWHC 3130 (Ch); [2007] Ch. 353 at [103]–[106] (decision disapproved on another point in *Central Bank of Nigeria v Williams* [2012] EWCA Civ 415; [2012] 3 All E.R. 579).

Deliberate concealment

AT THE END OF THE FIRST SENTENCE OF THE TEXT INSERT A NEW NOTE 88a: The **44–135** scope of Limitation Act 1980, s.32(1)(*b*) is discussed in *Williams v Fanshaw Porter & Hazelhurst* [2004] EWCA Civ 157; [2004] 1 W.L.R. 3185.

AT THE END OF THE FOURTH SENTENCE OF THE TEXT INSERT A NEW NOTE 91a: But in a case of active concealment what must have been concealed is a fact relevant to the claimant's right of action, not the right of action itself:

[41a] *Seaton v Seddon*, above.
[41b] *ibid.*

Williams v Fanshaw Porter & Hazelhurst, above. How far the defendant must have been under a duty to disclose the fact is discussed in *ibid*.

Discovery and diligence

44–141   NOTE 10. AT THE END ADD: But a claimant is not expected to take exceptional measures: *Paragon Finance* at *ibid*.; *Biggs v Sotnicks* [2002] EWCA Civ 272; [2002] All E.R. (D) 205 (Jan).

NOTE 11. ADD AT THE END: *Page v Hewetts* [2011] EWHC 2449 (Ch) (appeal allowed on a different point [2012] EWCA Civ 805), where denials from a defendant did not prevent a finding of sufficient knowledge on the part of the claimants. See too *Seaton v Seddon* [2012] EWHC 735 (Ch); [2012] All E.R. (D) 93 (May).

CHAPTER 45

LAWFUL DEPARTURE FROM THE TRUSTS

2. THE INHERENT JURISDICTION

Emergency powers of administration

AFTER THE THIRD SENTENCE ADD: The jurisdiction also extends to the con- **45–05** ferral of powers for the convening of quorate meetings of beneficiaries where the absence of such powers will occasion a deadlock in trust administration.[13a]

Compromises

NOTE 34. FOR THE REFERENCE TO *Civil Procedure* (2007) Vol.1, 19.7.5, SUB- **45–10** STITUTE *Civil Procedure* (2011) Vol.1, 19.7.5.

4. MANAGEMENT AND ADMINISTRATION—SECTION 57 OF THE TRUSTEE ACT 1925

Expediency

NOTE 37. TRANSPOSE THIS NOTE TO THE END OF THE FIRST SENTENCE AND AMEND **45–13** IT TO READ: *Re Craven's Estate (No.2)* [1937] Ch. 431 at 436. The court therefore refused to permit under Trustee Act 1925, s.57 the purchase of a membership of Lloyd's for one of two life tenants.

DELETE THE SECOND SENTENCE OF THE TEXT AND REPLACE BY: This means the same as expedient in the interests of the beneficiaries under the trust.[37a] But, as has been decided in New Zealand[37b] and in England,[37c] this does not mean that that the court needs to be satisfied that the transaction or power in question is expedient or advantageous in the interest of each and every beneficiary considered separately, but rather that taking into consideration the interests of all the beneficiaries the transaction or power in question can

---

[13a] *Grender v Dresden* [2009] EWHC 214 (Ch); [2009] W.T.L.R. 379 at [35].
[37a] *Re Earl of Strafford* [1980] Ch. 28 at 44–45, CA; and to a similar effect see Australian and New Zealand authority *Riddle v Riddle* (1952) 85 C.L.R. 202 at 214, 220–222, Aus. HC; *Re Dawson* [1959] N.Z.L.R. 1360; *Re Sykes* [1974] 1 N.S.W.L.R. 597 at 600; *Perpetual Trustee Co. Ltd v Godsall* [1979] 2 N.S.W.L.R. 785 at 790–791; *Banicevich v Gunson* [2006] 2 N.Z.L.R. 11 at [19], NZ CA (application for leave to appeal refused [2006] NZSC 24; [2006] 2 N.Z.L.R. 25); *Royal Melbourne Hospital v Equity Trustees Ltd* [2007] VSCA 162; (2007) 18 V.R. 469 at [155]–[161].
[37b] *Re Dawson*, above, at 88.
[37c] *Alexander v Alexander* [2011] EWHC 2721 (Ch) at [23].

fairly be said to be expedient in the interests of the trust as a whole. And in Australia it has been held that a transaction or power, otherwise expedient in the management or administration of the trust and interests of the trusts and beneficiaries as a whole, may be authorised or conferred even if its impact may be relatively positive for some beneficiaries and relatively negative for other beneficiaries.[37d] In England too, the conferral of a power has satisfied the test of expediency where it is in the interests of the trust as a whole in that it facilitates better administration against a background of beneficiaries in different jurisdictions, though it is of particular benefit to one group of beneficiaries who are adversely affected by the absence of the power in a way the others are not.[37e] The approach to expediency under section 57 of the Trustee Act 1957 is therefore different from the approach to benefit under the Variation of Trusts Act 1958. Under section 57 a broad approach is adopted so that an assessment can be made of the advantage to the beneficiaries as a whole, while under the 1958 Act each beneficiary or group of beneficiaries is considered separately and appropriate compensating adjustments will need to be made where some beneficiaries, considered separately, do not benefit or, normally, where other beneficiaries benefit disproportionately. But there must be an advantage under section 57 to the beneficiaries as a whole, not merely to the trustees. And so there is no justification under the section 57 jurisdiction for the conferral of a general power on trustees to pay tax liabilities when such liabilities are not enforceable against the trustees.[37f] The court can take into account the wishes of the settlor in considering an exercise of its powers under section 57.[37g]

Management or administration

45–16   DELETE § 45–16(1) AND N.43 AND REPLACE BY:

(1)   in a case where there is no other power, (i) partition or appropriation of trust property between absolute and settled shares under the trust,[43] partition or appropriation between settled shares under the trust,[43a] (ii) distribution of trust property *in specie* in satisfaction of an absolute interest[43b] and (iii) appropriation of a similar nature to appropriation under the statutory power

---

[37d]   *Royal Melbourne Hospital v Equity Trustees Ltd*, above, at [114]–[119] and [162]–[167].
[37e]   *Southgate v Sutton* [2011] EWCA Civ 637; [2011] W.T.L.R. 1235 at [22]–[24] and see at first instance (not reversed on this point) *sub nom. Sutton v England* [2009] EWHC 3270 (Ch); [2010] W.T.L.R. 335 at [23] and [28]; and see too the observations in *Re Downshire Settled Estates* [1953] Ch. 218 at 250, CA (no appeal on this part of the case, see *sub nom. Chapman v Chapman* [1954] A.C. 429 at 465, HL) on *Re Mair* [1935] Ch 562 where the interests of remote unascertained beneficiaries were not taken into account.
[37f]   *Sutton v England*, above, at [52]–[55] (reversed on appeal on other grounds *sub nom. Southgate v Sutton*, above).
[37g]   *Alexander v Alexander*, above, at [33]. Compare § 45–85 on relevance of wishes of the settlor in variation of trust cases.
[43]   *Re Thomas* [1930] 1 Ch. 194.
[43a]   *Re Z Trust* (2010–11) 13 I.T.E.L.R. 843; [2009] C.I.L.R. 593, Cayman GC; *Southgate v Sutton* [2011] EWCA Civ 637; [2011] W.T.L.R. 1235 at [28]–[41], distinguishing *Re Freeston's Charity* [1978] 1 W.L.R. 741 at 752, CA.
[43b]   *Hornsby v Playoust* [2005] VSC 107; (2005) 11 V.R. 522.

conferred on executors by section 41 of the Administration of
Estates Act 1925;[43c]

NOTE 45. DELETE AND REPLACE BY: *Re Salting* [1932] Ch. 57; on which see *Re
Forster's Settlement* [1954] 1 W.L.R. 1450 at 1456–1457 where the court in
special circumstances authorised trustees under s.57 to buy the life interests
under their own trusts so as to stop wastage of the trust fund resulting from
the creation of charges previously authorised by the court. *Re Forster* was
cited with approval in *Royal Melbourne Hospital v Equity Trustees Ltd*
[2007] VSCA 162; (2007) 18 V.R. 469 at [159]–[160], though on the question
of expediency rather than the question of management or administration.
Re Forster should not be taken as authority for any wide proposition that
trustees can buy or sell beneficial interests under their own trusts since, apart
from special circumstances such as arose in that case, such a transaction
would amount to a variation, see § 45–15.

NOTE 47. AT THE END OF THE FIRST SENTENCE ADD: *Re Fell* [1940] N.Z.L.R.
552 (sale prohibited by terms of trust); *Royal Melbourne Hospital v Equity
Trustees Ltd*, above, (power of sale excluded by terms of trust); *cf. Re Smith*
[1975] 1 N.Z.L.R. 495 (application for sale refused because testator intended
land to remain settled and so sale would be a variation of the trusts, *sed
quaere*).

NOTE 49. ADD: *Page v West* [2010] EWHC 504 (Ch); [2010] W.T.L.R. 1811
at [22]–[23].

AFTER § 45–16(8) INSERT THE FOLLOWING NEW SUB-PARAGRAPHS:

    (9) variation of the mechanics for making payments to beneficiaries
without disturbing the underlying interests;[50a]

    (10) extension of powers of appointment of new trustees;[50b]

    (11) conferral of powers on trustees to convene meetings of bene-
ficiaries in the event that quorate meetings cannot be convened in
accordance with the provisions of the trust instrument;[50c]

    (12) authorisation for the trustees to act in accordance with the opinion
of senior chancery counsel, subject to notice being given to adult
beneficiaries, on questions of incidence of future inheritance tax
liabilities.[50d]

[43c] Compare *Russell v I.R.C.* [1988] 1 W.L.R. 834 at 842 where such an appropriation was
classified as administrative.
[50a] *NBPF Pension Trustees Ltd v Warnock-Smith* [2008] EWHC 455 (Ch); [2008] 2 All E.R.
(Comm) 740.
[50b] *HSBC International Trustee Ltd v Registrar of Trusts* [2008] C.I.L.R. N5.
[50c] *Grender v Dresden* [2009] EWHC 214 (Ch); [2009] W.T.L.R. 379 at [33] and [34].
[50d] *Sutton v England* [2009] EWHC 3270 (Ch); [2010] W.T.L.R. 335 at [22] (reversed on appeal
on other grounds *sub nom. Southgate v Sutton* [2011] EWCA Civ 637; [2011] W.T.L.R.
1235).

Land

45–18 NOTE 65. AT THE END ADD: But in a Victorian case it was agreed by all parties that the Victorian equivalent of s.57 applied to Victorian settled land: *Royal Melbourne Hospital v Equity Trustees Ltd* [2007] VSCA 162; (2007) 18 V.R. 469.

Procedure

45–19 NOTE 66. DELETE AND REPLACE BY: CPR, Pt 8, r.8.1(2)(b) and (6); Practice Direction, Pt 8, Section B.

NOTE 67. DELETE AND REPLACE BY: *ibid.*

6. THE VARIATION OF TRUSTS ACT 1958

Jurisdiction to vary trusts

45–31 AT THE END ADD: In the context of the 1958 Act property held on trusts includes property in an unadministered estate, and so the court has jurisdiction to vary dispositions taking effect during the administration period, though not trusts in the strict sense, for instance a contingent legacy given to a minor not carrying the intermediate income.[3a]

Incapacity—adult beneficiaries lacking mental capacity

All other beneficiaries capable of assenting—enduring or lasting power of attorney in existence

45–39 AT THE BEGINNING OF THE LAST SENTENCE INSERT: Notwithstanding a contrary view expressed in a Canadian case,[28a]

Persons who may become entitled to an interest—section 1(1)(*b*)

45–45 AFTER THE PENULTIMATE SENTENCE INSERT: In Jersey (where the provision concerning unascertained beneficiaries is materially different from section 1(1)(*b*) of the 1958 Act) the view has been taken that it is unnecessary for the court to approve an arrangement on behalf of potential beneficiaries under a wide power of addition of beneficiaries conferred on the trustees after the death of the settlor.[47a]

45–46 NOTE 50. FOR THE REFERENCE TO Underhill and Hayton, *Law of Trusts and Trustees*, SEE NOW (18th edn), § 43.44.

[3a]   *Bernstein v Jacobson* [2008] EWHC 3454 (Ch); [2010] W.T.L.R. 559; contrast *Re Davies* (1967) 66 D.L.R. (2d) 412, cited in, but not referred to in the judgment in, *Bernstein*.
[28a]   *Drescher v Drescher's Estate* [2007] NSSC 352; (2007–08) 10 I.T.E.L.R. 352.
[47a]   *Re IMK Family Trust* [2008] JCA 196; 2008 J.L.R. 430 at [99]–[115].

Scope of court's powers

Variation or revocation not resettlement

NOTE 75. ADD: For a wide view in Jersey of the jurisdiction see *Re IMK* **45–54** *Family Trust* [2008] JCA 196; 2008 J.L.R. 430 at [62]–[83].

AFTER THE TEXT TO N.75 INSERT: An arrangement does not constitute a resettlement merely because a new perpetuity period is adopted.[75a]

Purposes of application under the 1958 Act

NOTE 81. AT THE END ADD: *Re DDD Settlements* [2011] JRC 243 at [25]–[32]. **45–56**

Public policy

DELETE THE LAST SENTENCE AND NOTE 91 AND REPLACE BY: For that purpose, **45–57** however, the perpetuity period runs afresh from the date of the court order approving the variation, so that before April 6, 2010 the benefits of the Perpetuities and Accumulations Act 1964 could be made available in relation to settlements constituted before July 16, 1964,[91] or alternatively a new common law period using a life in being at the order date could be adopted.[91a] In relation to a variation approved by the court on or after April 6, 2010, when the Perpetuities and Accumulations Act 2009 came into force,[91b] the 125-year perpetuity period under the 2009 Act[91c] will apply to beneficial interests varied by the arrangement, since the arrangement counts as an instrument for the purposes of section 15(1) of the 2009 Act.[91d] Likewise, in relation to a variation approved by the court on or after April 6, 2010, advantage can be taken of the abolition of the statutory restrictions on accumulations by the 2009 Act. [91e]

Benefit and discretion

AFTER § 45–66 INSERT THE FOLLOWING NEW PARAGRAPH AND HEADING:

Postponement by creation of transitional serial interest or immediate post-death interest in favour of surviving spouse

Normally it will not be for the benefit of beneficiaries with a reversionary **45–66A** interest in capital for their interest to be postponed by the creation of a reversionary life interest which takes priority over their interest. The creation of a life interest for the surviving spouse of a life tenant which qualifies

---

[75a] *Wyndham v Egremont* [2009] EWHC 2076 (Ch); (2009–10) 12 I.T.E.L.R. 461; and on perpetuity periods see § 45–57.
[91] *Re Holt's Settlement* [1969] 1 Ch. 100 at 120.
[91a] *Wyndham v Egremont* [2009] EWHC 2076 (Ch); (2009–10) 12 I.T.E.L.R. 461.
[91b] Perpetuities and Accumulations Act 2009, s.5. See § 5–37F.
[91c] Perpetuities and Accumulations Act 2009, s.22; Perpetuities and Accumulations Act 2009 (Commencement) Order 2010 (SI 2010/37).
[91d] Compare *Re Holt's Settlement*, above, a decision on a similar provision in the 1964 Act.
[91e] Perpetuities and Accumulations Act 2009, s.13, s.21 and Sch. See §§ 5–100A to 5–100D.

as a transitional serial interest within section 49D of the Inheritance Tax Act 1984[16a] will prospectively postpone a charge to inheritance tax until the death of the surviving spouse. That in itself is unlikely to be beneficial to the reversionary capital beneficiaries since they will still suffer inheritance tax before their interest falls into possession. But where the creation of the transitional serial interest facilitates mitigation of inheritance tax and capital gains tax through advances to the reversionary beneficiaries after the life tenant's death, and through cheaper life insurance against the inheritance tax risk under a joint lives policy, the disadvantage of postponement of the reversionary interest may well be outweighed by considerable prospective inheritance tax savings.[16b] There may be similar, and indeed more obvious, benefits for minor beneficiaries under a will trust by the creation within two years of the testator's death of an immediate post-death interest within sections 49A[16c] and 142[16d] of the Inheritance Tax Act 1984 in favour of the surviving spouse for an appropriate period, and the tax saving may be split between the minor beneficiaries and the adults involved in the variation.[16e]

Non-financial considerations

45–80 NOTE 48. ADD: See too *Re H Trust* 2007–08 G.L.R. 118 (disabled young adult); *Wright v Gater* [2011] EWHC 2881 (Ch); [2011] All E.R. (D) 153 (Nov) (vesting of capital in young child under intestacy trusts postponed until age 21 as regards 10 per cent of fund and age 25 as regards remaining fund, but not until age 30 as regards whole of fund with accumulation and maintenance trusts in meantime as initially proposed).

No financial advantage

45–82 NOTE 57. AT THE END ADD: contrast *Re DDD Settlements* [2011] JRC 243 at [20]–[24] (where an application to remove the settlor from an excluded class was held to be beneficial to unborn beneficiaries for tax reasons but not on the ground of an alleged moral obligation).

Practice and procedure

Parties to be joined

45–89 AT THE END OF THE TEXT ADD: Normally an adult beneficiary can decline to give consent or withdraw consent at any time before the court order is made. In a case where there is a doubt whether an adult consent will be forthcoming, particularly where the variation is made in the context of a family or matrimonial dispute, it is prudent to ensure that adults are bound before the application to the court is commenced by contract between the adults and the trustees, or by an irrevocable direction to the trustees.[85a]

[16a]   As added by Finance Act 2006, s.156 and Sch.20, para.5 and amended by Finance Act 2008, s.141(1).
[16b]   *Re RGST Settlement* [2007] EWHC 2666 (Ch); (2007–08) 10 I.T.E.L.R. 754.
[16c]   As added by Finance Act 2006, s.156 and Sch.20, para.5.
[16d]   As amended by Finance Act 1986, s.101(3) and Sch.19, para.24, and Finance Act 2002, s.120(1), (4).
[16e]   *Bernstein v Jacobson* [2008] EWHC 3454 (Ch); [2010] W.T.L.R. 559.
[85a]   *Re IMK Family Trust* [2008] JCA 196; 2008 J.L.R. 430 at [116]–[124].

Persons who need not be joined

NOTE 92. DELETE AND REPLACE BY: As to the relevant CPR rules, see n.85.   **45–90**

The defendants' response and evidence

IN THE SECOND SENTENCE, DELETE THE REFERENCE TO patients AND REPLACE BY   **45–97**
protected parties.

NOTES 25 TO 28. ADD: see too *The Chancery Guide* (6th edn, 2009),
paras.25.12 and 25.13.

Interlocutory procedure

NOTE 32. DELETE AND REPLACE BY: *The Chancery Guide* (6th edn, 2009),   **45–98**
para.6.27.

Substantive hearing

DELETE THE LAST SENTENCE AND NN. 38 AND 39 AND REPLACE BY: Before the   **45–99**
introduction of the Civil Procedure Rules the substantive hearing was
generally in open court.[38] When the Civil Procedure Rules were first introduced, specific provision was made for hearings under the 1958 Act to be
listed for hearing in private, but that provision has been dropped, and now
the hearing will be in open court in accordance with the general rule unless
the judge decides that the hearing is to be in private.[39]

Order

NOTE 43. AFTER THE SECOND SENTENCE INSERT: *The Chancery Guide* (6th edn,   **45–101**
2009), paras.25.11 to 25.14, gives no guidance on these matters, but it is not
thought that the practice has changed.

NOTE 44. FOR THE REFERENCE TO *The Chancery Guide* (2005), SEE NOW *The
Chancery Guide* (6th edn, 2009), paras.25.11 to 25.14.

Costs

NOTE 45. DELETE THE REFERENCE TO Practice Direction 44 AND REPLACE BY: **45–103**
Practice Direction Pts 43 to 48, para.13.2(2).

---

[38]   *Re Chapman's Settlement Trusts (No.2)* [1959] 1 W.L.R. 372; *Re Rouse's Will Trusts, ibid.*;
       Re Byng's Will Trusts [1959] 1 W.L.R. 375.
[39]   For the general rule that a hearing is to be in public, see CPR, Pt 39, r.39.2(1). The
       circumstances in which a hearing may be in private are listed in CPR, Pt 39, r.39.2(3). The
       decision whether the hearing is to be in public or in private is made by the judge conducting
       the hearing, having regard to article 6(1) of the European Convention on Human Rights,
       see Practice Direction, Pt 39A, para.1.4 and 1.4A. Practice Direction, Pt 39A, para.1.5
       specifies a number of hearings which should in the first instance be listed as hearings in
       private, and applications under the 1958 Act were specified in para.1.5(11), but that is not
       so now. Private hearings can be justified only on the basis that they involve confidential
       information (CPR, Pt 39, r.39.2(3)(c)), or are necessary to protect the interests of a child
       (CPR, Pt 39, r.39.2(3)(d)), or perhaps on the basis that they involve non-contentious
       matters arising in the administration of a trust (CPR, Pt 39, r.39.2(3)(f)). A contentious
       issue of fact or law would provide a reason for a hearing (or giving of judgment) in open
       court, as would the absence of any real prejudice to the protection of confidential infor-
       mation or the interests of a child.

DELETE THE REFERENCE TO para.4.11 AND REPLACE BY: para.13.11.

AT THE END ADD: See too *The Chancery Guide* (6th edn, 2009), para.25.14 which provides that where the parties are represented by the same solicitors and counsel from the same chambers the court is unlikely to assess costs summarily unless either the case is a clear one or the value of the trust fund is such that a detailed assessment of costs would be disproportionate.

NOTE 46. DELETE AND REPLACE BY: See CPR, Practice Direction, Pts 43 to 48, para.13.5.

45–104 DELETE THE FOURTH SENTENCE AND REPLACE BY: Normally it cannot come from a beneficiary of full age and capacity because, if the proposed variation is dependent on his consent, it cannot succeed if his consent is withheld; and if it is not so dependent, then his opposition is irrelevant and he should not be a party. However, in a Jersey case an adult beneficiary contested a variation on grounds that he had not given a binding consent and on jurisdictional and other grounds.[48a] We would expect costs of hostile intervention of this kind by an adult beneficiary to follow the event.

NOTE 49. FOR THE REFERENCE TO *Halsbury's Laws of England*, SEE NOW (4th edn), Vol.5(4) (2008 Reissue), § 1429. FOR THE REFERENCE TO *Civil Procedure* (2007) Vol.1, 21.5.1, SUBSTITUTE *Civil Procedure* (2011) Vol.1, 21.5.1.

[48a] *Re IMK Family Trust* [2008] JCA 196; 2008 J.L.R. 430.

CHAPTER 46

TRUSTEES INVOLVED WITH CRIMINAL AND TERRORIST PROPERTY

2. THE LEGISLATION

Principal legislation and regulations

INSERT AT THE END: and by the Serious Crime Act 2007 with effect from early **46–03(1)** 2008.

INSERT AT THE END: and the Terrorist Asset-Freezing etc. Act 2010. **46–03(2)**

NOTE 11. INSERT AT THE END: amended principally by Money Laundering **46–03(3)** (Amendment) Regulations 2007 (SI 2007/3299) and Money Laundering (Amendment No.2) Regulations 2011 (SI 2011/2833) and Money Laundering (Amendment) Regulations 2012 (SI 2012/2298), the last coming into force on October 1, 2012.

NOTE 12. ADD AT THE END: A fourth Directive is in prospect at the time of writing but no draft has been published and it will not be incorporated into English law for some time.

NOTE 15. ADD AT THE END: (3rd edn). **46–03**

4. PROCEEDS OF CRIME

Introduction

NOTE 33. DELETE AND REPLACE BY: Considered at §§ 46–130 *et seq.*, 46–144 *et* **46–09** *seq.*

Criminal conduct

Foreign element

NOTE 48. DELETE AND REPLACE BY: See Proceeds of Crime Act 2002 (Money **46–13** Laundering: Exceptions to Overseas Conduct Defence) Order 2006 (SI 2006/ 1070) providing in art.2 that any conduct punishable by more than 12 months' imprisonment in any part of the United Kingdom if it had occurred there is (with minor exceptions) so prescribed.

Criminal property

The offender's state of mind

46–17 AFTER THE SECOND QUOTATION INSERT: There is no requirement that the suspicion must be reasonable; but a mere feeling of unease is not suspicion.[65a]

Arrangements

46–18 IN THE FIRST SENTENCE, DELETE commit AND REPLACE WITH committing.

AFTER THE LAST SENTENCE, INSERT: But the property must have been criminal property as a result of some conduct occurring before the act which is alleged to constitute the offence under section 328; it is not enough that the property became criminal only as a result of carrying out the arrangement.[69a]

Acquisition, use and possession

46–21 AT THE END OF THE TEXT ADD: Here too the property must have been criminal property as a result of some conduct occurring before the act which is alleged to constitute the offence under section 329; it is not enough that the property became criminal only as a result of acquiring, using or having possession of the property.[77a]

Other defences

46–25 NOTE 86. AT THE END ADD: inserted by Serious Organised Crime and Police Act 2005, s.103(1), (4).

Concealing, disguising, converting and transferring

46–26 AT THE END OF THE TEXT ADD: Here again the property must have been criminal property as a result of some conduct occurring before the act which is alleged to constitute the offence under section 327; it is not enough that the property became criminal only as a result of concealing or disguising the property and so on.[88a]

Defences

46–29 NOTE 94. AT THE END ADD: inserted by Serious Organised Crime and Police Act 2005, s.103(1), (2).

[65a] *Shah v HSBC Private Bank (UK) Ltd* [2009] EWHC 79 (QB); [2009] 1 Lloyd's Rep. 328 at [45]–[48] (affd. [2010] EWCA Civ 31; [2010] All E.R. (D) 45 (Feb)).
[69a] *R. v Geary* [2010] EWCA Crim 1925; [2011] 2 All E.R. 198.
[77a] *R. v Geary* [2010] EWCA Crim 1925; [2011] 2 All E.R. 198.
[88a] *R. v Geary* [2010] EWCA Crim 1925; [2011] 2 All E.R. 198.

5. PROPERTY CONNECTED WITH TERRORISM

"Terrorist property"

Proscribed organisations

NOTE 23. THE REFERENCE TO THE HOME OFFICE'S WEBSITE SHOULD NOW BE TO: **46–39**
http://www.homeoffice.gov.uk/publications/counter-terrorism/proscribed-terror-groups/proscribed-groups?view = Binary

Laundering terrorist property

DELETE THE HEADING TO THIS PARAGRAPH (*The defence*) AND REPLACE BY: **46–47**
Mental element.

AFTER § 46–47 INSERT THE FOLLOWING NEW PARAGRAPH AND HEADING:

Prior consent and disclosure as a defence to sections 15 to 18

There are defences comparable to those under the 2002 Act against criminal **46–47A**
liability for any breach of sections 15 to 18 of the Terrorism Act 2000 if there
is suitable disclosure to an authorised member of the staff of SOCA and that
person's consent is forthcoming.[49a]

6. DUTIES OF DISCLOSURE AND NON-DISCLOSURE

Duties of disclosure under the Proceeds of Crime Act 2002

DELETE THE SECOND SENTENCE AND N.65 AND REPLACE BY: Included in the **46–50(2)**
regulated sector by the 2002 Act are businesses to the extent that they
consist of "the participation in financial or real property transactions concerning ... the creation, operation or management of trusts" by someone
providing legal services by way of business; and the provision to others, by
way of business, of services which extend to "acting, or arranging for
another person to act, as ... a trustee of an express trust or similar legal
arrangement".[65] The business of a professional trustee is therefore included.

NOTE 67. DELETE AND REPLACE BY: Proceeds of Crime Act 2002, s.330(3A), **46–50(3)**
inserted by Serious Organised Crime and Police Act 2005, s.104(1), (3).

NOTE 69. DELETE AND REPLACE BY: Proceeds of Crime Act 2002, s.330(4), **46–50(4)**
inserted by Serious Organised Crime and Police Act 2005, s.104(1), (3) and
amended by Serious Crime Act 2007, s.74(2)(*f*), Sch.8, Pt 6, paras.121, 126.

[49a] Terrorism Act 2000, ss.21ZA–21ZC, inserted by Terrorism Act 2000 and Proceeds of
Crime Act 2002 (Amendment) Regulations 2007 (SI 2007/3398), reg. 2, Sch.1. For the
comparable provisions in Proceeds of Crime Act 2002, see §§ 46–30 to 46–32.

[65] Proceeds of Crime Act 2002, s.330(12) and Sch.9, Pt 1, paras.1(1)(*n*)(v), (1)(*o*), (4)(*d*)(i),
Sch.9 as substituted by Proceeds of Crime Act 2002 (Business in the Regulated Sector and
Supervisory Authorities Order 2007 (SI 2007/3287), arts.2, 3. *Cf.* the definition of "the
regulated sector" in Terrorism Act 2000, see § 46–53, and that of "relevant person" in
Money Laundering Regulations 2007 (SI 2007/2157), see § 46–60.

Defences

46–51(1)   NOTE 75. DELETE AND REPLACE BY: Proceeds of Crime Act 2002, s.330(6)(a), inserted by Serious Organised Crime and Police Act 2005, s.104(1), (3). There does not seem to have been any decision on what is a reasonable excuse in this context.

46–51(2)   NOTE 76. DELETE AND REPLACE BY: See the definition in Proceeds of Crime Act 2002, s.330(14), inserted by Proceeds of Crime Act 2002 and Money Laundering Regulations 2003 (Amendment) Order 2006 (SI 2006/308), art.2.

NOTE 78. AT THE END ADD: and Terrorism Act 2000 and Proceeds of Crime Act 2002 (Amendment) Regulations 2007 (SI 2007/3398), reg.3, Sch.2.

46–51(3)   DELETE 202 Act AND REPLACE BY: 2002 Act.

AFTER § 46–51(3) INSERT THE FOLLOWING NEW SUB-PARAGRAPH:

> (3A) A knows or reasonably believes that the money laundering is occurring outside the United Kingdom, it is not unlawful under the local criminal law and it is not of a kind prescribed by an order of the Secretary of State;[80a] or

46–52   NOTE 82. DELETE Serious Organised Crime and Police Act 2002 AND REPLACE BY Serious Organised Crime and Police Act 2005.

Duties of disclosure under the Terrorism Act 2000

46–53   DELETE THIRD FOURTH AND FIFTH SENTENCES (The definition ... TO ... invest-ment schemes) AND NN.83–87 AND REPLACE BY: The definition of that expression in this Act is the same as that in the 2002 Act, so that it extends to the business of professional trustees, asset managers and legal advisers.[83-86]

46–53(1)   AT THE END OF THE FIRST SENTENCE INSERT A NEW NOTE 87: As amended by Counter-Terrorism Act 2008, s.77(1), (2).

NOTE 88. DELETE AND REPLACE BY: Terrorism Act 2000, s.19(7B), inserted by Anti-terrorism, Crime and Security Act 2001, s.3, Sch.2, Pt 3, para.5(1), (4) and amended by Serious Organised Crime and Police Act 2005, s.59, Sch.4, paras.125, 126.

46–53(2)   NOTE 91. INSERT AT THE END: and amended by Serious Organised Crime and Police Act 2005, s.59, Sch.4, paras.125, 128 and Terrorism Act 2000 and Proceeds of Crime Act 2002 (Amendment) Regulations 2007 (SI 2007/3398), reg.2, Sch.1.

[80a]   Proceeds of Crime Act 2002, s.330(7A), inserted by Serious Organised Crime and Police Act 2005, s 102(1), (5). No such order has been made.

[83-86] Terrorism Act 2000, s.19(7A) and Sch.3A, both originally inserted by Anti-terrorism, Crime and Security Act 2001, s.3 and Sch.2, Pt 3, para.5(4), (6) but the terms of Sch.3A now inserted by Terrorism Act 2000 (Business in the Regulated Sector and Supervisory Authorities) Order 2007 (SI 2007/3288), art.2.

Duties of non-disclosure—tipping-off

DELETE THE SECOND SENTENCE AND REPLACE BY: The offences of that name **46–55**
created both by the 2002 Act and the Terrorism Act 2000 apply only to the
regulated sector;[97a] but both Acts also create offences, not further described
here, of prejudicing investigations which apply outside the regulated
sector.[97b]

Proceeds of Crime Act 2002

DELETE THE ENTIRE PARAGRAPH AND N.98 AND REPLACE BY. **46–56**

The tipping-off offences created by the 2002 Act are concerned with
avoiding prejudice to investigations by the authorities. The investigation
may or may not have been prompted by an authorised disclosure or a
protected disclosure.[98]

DELETE THE ENTIRE PARAGRAPH AND N.99 AND REPLACE BY: **46–57**

Section 333A of the 2002 Act[99] provides, in part:

> "(1) A person commits an offence if—
>
>   (a) the person discloses any matter within subsection (2);
>
>   (b) the disclosure is likely to prejudice any investigation that
> might be conducted following the disclosure referred to in that
> subsection; and
>
>   (c) the information on which the disclosure is based came to the
> person in the course of a business in the regulated sector.
>
> (2) The matters are that the person or another person has made a
> disclosure under this Part—
>
>   (a) to a constable,
>
>   (b) to an officer of Revenue and Customs,
>
>   (c) to a nominated officer, or
>
>   (d) to a member of staff of [SOCA] authorised for the purposes of
> this Part by the Director General of that Agency,
>
> of information that came to that person in the course of a business
> in the regulated sector.
>
> (3) A person commits an offence if—
>
>   (a) the person discloses that an investigation into allegations that

---

[97a] For which see §§ 46–50(2), 46–53.
[97b] Proceeds of Crime Act 2002, s.342, as amended by Serious Crime Act 2007, s.77, Sch.10,
paras.1, 2 and Terrorism Act 2000 and Proceeds of Crime Act 2002 (Amendment) Regulations 2007 (SI 2007/3398), reg.3, Sch.2; Terrorism Act 2000, s.39, as amended by Anti-
terrorism, Crime and Security Act 2001, s.117(1), (3) and Terrorism Act 2000 and Proceeds
of Crime Act 2002 (Amendment) Regulations 2007 (SI 2007/3398), reg.2, Sch.1.
[98] For which see §§ 46–31 to 46–33 and § 46–52 respectively.
[99] Inserted by Terrorism Act 2000 and Proceeds of Crime Act 2002 (Amendment) Regulations 2007 (SI 2007/3398), reg.3, Sch.2.

an offence under this Part has been committed is being contemplated or is being carried out;

(b) the disclosure is likely to prejudice that investigation; and

(c) the information on which the disclosure is based came to the
person in the course of a business in the regulated sector."

Neither offence is committed if the person does not know or suspect that the
disclosure is likely to prejudice an investigation.[99a] There are exceptions for
disclosures made within undertakings, disclosures between certain institutions and between advisers of the same kind (including professional legal
advisers), and disclosures by certain advisers (again including professional
legal advisers) to their clients, though only if made for the purpose of dis-
suading the client from committing an offence.[99b]

Terrorism Act 2000

46–58 DELETE THE ENTIRE PARAGRAPH AND NN.1 TO 6 AND REPLACE BY:

Section 21D of the Terrorism Act 2000[1] is in almost identical terms. It
provides, in part:

"(1) A person commits an offence if—

(a) the person discloses any matter within subsection (2);

(b) the disclosure is likely to prejudice any investigation that
might be conducted following the disclosure referred to in that
subsection; and

(c) the information on which the disclosure is based came to the
person in the course of a business in the regulated sector.

(2) The matters are that the person or another person has made a
disclosure under a provision of this Part—

(a) to a constable,

(b) in accordance with a procedure established by that person's
employer for the making of disclosures under that provision,

(c) to a nominated officer, or

(d) to a member of staff of [SOCA] authorised for the purposes of
that provision by the Director General of that Agency,

of information that came to that person in the course of a business
in the regulated sector.

(3) A person commits an offence if—

(a) the person discloses that an investigation into allegations that
an offence under this Part has been committed is being contemplated or is being carried out;

[99a] Proceeds of Crime Act 2002, s.333D(3), (4), inserted as above.
[99b] Proceeds of Crime Act 2002, ss.333B–333E, inserted as above.
[1] Inserted by Terrorism Act 2000 and Proceeds of Crime Act 2002 (Amendment) Regulations 2007 (SI 2007/3398), reg.2, Sch.1.

(b) the disclosure is likely to prejudice that investigation; and

(c) the information on which the disclosure is based came to the person in the course of a business in the regulated sector."

Again, neither offence is committed if the person does not know or suspect that the disclosure is likely to prejudice an investigation.[2] There are also exceptions comparable to those under the 2002 Act.[3-6]

7. CUSTOMER DUE DILIGENCE AND OTHER SYSTEMS

General

AFTER § 46–59 INSERT THE FOLLOWING NEW PARAGRAPH:

The Counter-Terrorism Act 2008 gives H.M. Treasury powers to impose **46–59A** requirements on business with countries outside the European Economic Area against the risk of money laundering activities or terrorist financing.[8a] The requirements include customer due diligence and ongoing monitoring but also extend to limiting or ceasing business with a specified person altogether. Those powers are confined to credit or financial institutions, however, and are not further discussed here.

Customer due diligence–general scheme

NOTE 23. AT THE END ADD: In June 2011, H.M. Treasury proposed the de- **46–61** criminalisation of "technical" money laundering offences. The proposal was not implemented in Money Laundering (Amendment) Regulations 2012 (SI 2012/2298) (see § 46–03(3) (Supplement)).

Scope of customer due diligence measures

Identifying the customer

NOTE 31. DELETE AND REPLACE BY: Official guidance from the Joint Money **46–64** Laundering Steering Group (*Prevention of money laundering/combating the financing of terrorism: guidance for the UK financial sector, Part I* (Dec. 2007), para.5.3.2) states, "The firm *identifies* the customer by obtaining a range of information about him. The *verification* of the identity consists of the firm verifying some of this information against documents, data or information obtained from a reliable and independent source" (emphasis in original).

Obtaining information about the business relationship

IN THE SECOND SENTENCE, DELETE the BEFORE regulation. **46–66**

---

[2] Terrorism Act 2000, s.21G, inserted by Terrorism Act 2000 and Proceeds of Crime Act 2002 (Amendment) Regulations 2007 (SI 2007/3398), reg.2, Sch.1.
[3-6] Terrorism Act 2000, ss.21E–21H, inserted as above.
[8a] Counter-Terrorism Act 2008, s.62 and Sch.7.

Administration of the trust and third parties

Trusts having a beneficial owner

46–91 IN THE THIRD SENTENCE DELETE will be concerned with the beneficiaries of the estate AND REPLACE BY: will not be concerned with the beneficiaries of the estate.

Controllers as beneficial owners

46–98 NOTE 38. DELETE AND REPLACE BY: Charities Act 2011, s.280. The power of the members is only to withhold approval of a modification resolved on by the trustees but that is sufficient; see § 46–97.

Other systems

Penalties

46–115 AT THE END OF THE FIRST SENTENCE, INSERT A NEW NOTE 86a: IN JUNE 2011, H.M. Treasury has proposed the de-criminalisation of "technical" money laundering offences.

8. GUIDANCE FOR TRUSTEES

Guidance by industry and professional bodies

46–117 IN THE FIRST SENTENCE INSERT (regulated sector) AFTER the 2002 Act.

46–118(1) DELETE THE ENTIRE SUB-PARAGRAPH AND N.90 AND REPLACE BY: The Joint Money Laundering Steering Group of the British Bankers Association has issued guidance, which has been approved by H.M. Treasury.[90]

46–118(2) DELETE THE FIRST SENTENCE AND REPLACE BY: The Law Society has issued successive *Practice Notes* on money laundering, the current version being that of February 22, 2008.

46–118(3) DELETE SECOND SENTENCE AND NN.92 TO 93 AND REPLACE BY: It published *The FSA's new role under the Money Laundering Regulations 2007. Our Approach*[92] but it does not issue guidance on the 2007 Regulations.[93]

When trustees discover that they are holding criminal property

46–126 IN THE LAST SENTENCE DELETE of WHERE IT LAST OCCURS.

AT THE END OF THAT SENTENCE INSERT A NEW NOTE 23a: *Cf.* § 46–17.

AT THE END OF THE PARAGRAPH ADD A NEW SENTENCE: In comparable

---

[90]   See *Prevention of money laundering/combating the financing of terrorism. Guidance for the UK financial sector* (Dec. 2007, with later amendments). The guidance and proposed amendments may be read on the Group's website at *www.jmlsg.org.uk*.

[92]   The publication can be read on the F.S.A.'s website at *www.fsa.gov.uk*.

[93]   The F.S.A.'s earlier *Money Laundering Sourcebook* has been withdrawn.

circumstances, trustees will incur no liability to their beneficiaries if they refuse to make a distribution without the appropriate consent.[23b]

9. CIVIL RECOVERY OF PROCEEDS OF CRIME

Introduction

INSERT A NEW PARAGRAPH AFTER THE HEADING AND BEFORE § 46–130:

The Proceeds of Crime Act 2002 provides two different procedures designed **46–129A** to strip criminals of the benefits of criminal conduct:

(1) One is a confiscation order. It requires a conviction, the confiscation order being made once the defendant is convicted. What is confiscated is not the proceeds of crime as such but a sum equal to the proceeds of "criminal conduct". It does not matter whether or not the property used to satisfy the order derived from criminal conduct. Confiscation orders are discussed in the next section.[33a]

(2) The other is civil recovery of the proceeds of crime. It differs from a confiscation order in that no conviction is necessary. An order may be made there has been no prosecution and even when the defendant has been prosecuted and acquitted; to obtain an order it is enough to discharge the civil burden of proof.[33b] It differs from a confiscation order also in that the claim is a quasi-proprietary one: the property to be recovered must actually be property obtained by criminal conduct or else property representing it. Civil recovery is discussed in the remainder of this section.

NOTE 34. AT THE END ADD: Proceeds of Crime Act 2002 has been amended by **46–130** Serious Organised Crime and Police Act 2005 and Serious Crime Act 2007.

DELETE THE SECOND SENTENCE AND NOTE 35 AND REPLACE BY: It empowers SOCA, successor to the Assets Recovery Agency, to recover in civil High Court proceedings property that has been obtained through unlawful conduct and property representing it.[35]

Recoverable property

AT THE END OF THE TEXT ADD: But an order for recovery can be made only **46–133** against property situated within the United Kingdom.[48a]

[23b] *Cf. Shah v HSBC Private Bank (UK) Ltd* [2009] EWHC 79 (QB); [2009] 1 Lloyd's Rep. 328 (affd [2010] EWCA Civ 31; [2010] All E.R. (D) 45 (Feb)).

[33a] §§ 46–144 *et seq.*

[33b] See § 46–139A (Supplement).

[35] Proceeds of Crime Act 2002, s.243(1), empowering the "enforcement agency" to take such proceedings; and by *ibid.*, s.316, as amended by Serious Crime Act 2007, s.74(2)(*b*), Sch.8, Pt 2, paras.85, 91(1), (2)(*a*), "enforcement agency" includes SOCA.

[48a] *Perry v Serious Organised Crime Agency* [2012] UKSC 35; [2012] All E.R. (D) 252 (Jul).

General exceptions

46–138 IN THE LAST SENTENCE, DELETE (not yet exercised).

NOTE 63. AT THE END ADD: See Proceeds of Crime Act 2002 (Exemptions from Civil Recovery) Order 2003 (SI 2003/336), making exemptions not material for the purpose of this work.

Proceedings for recovery orders

46–139 IN THE FIRST SENTENCE DELETE that is, the Director of the Assets Recovery Agency AND SUBSTITUTE: ordinarily SOCA.

AFTER § 46–139 INSERT A NEW PARAGRAPH:

46–139A To establish a right to a recovery order it is sufficient to discharge the civil burden of proof.[68a]

Application for an interim receiving order or a property freezing order

46–140 DELETE THE HEADING TO THIS PARAGRAPH AND REPLACE BY THE HEADING SET OUT ABOVE.

DELETE THE FIRST TWO SENTENCES AND N.69 AND REPLACE BY: Where the enforcement authority, ordinarily SOCA, may take proceedings for a recovery order in the High Court, the authority may (before or after starting the proceedings) apply to the court for an interim receiving order or a property freezing order.[69] An interim receiving order is an order for the detention, custody or preservation of property and the appointment of an interim receiver. A property freezing order is an order prohibiting any person to whose property it applies from dealing with the property in any way; it was introduced to obviate the need to appoint an interim receiver in every case, though the court may in fact also appoint a receiver (limited to the management of property) when making the order or afterwards.

DELETE THE LAST SENTENCE AND REPLACE BY: The application for an interim receiving order must nominate a suitably qualified person (not a member of the staff of SOCA) for appointment as interim receiver; and if a receiver is to be appointed as part of a property receiving order the application must contain a similar nomination (but in that case the receiver may be a member of the staff of SOCA).

Receivers and interim receivers

46–141 DELETE THE HEADING TO THIS PARAGRAPH AND REPLACE BY THE FOREGOING.

AT THE END OF THE FIRST SENTENCE, INSERT A NEW NOTE 69a: Proceeds of Crime Act 2002, s.247.

[68a] *Gale v SOCA* [2011] UKSC 49; [2011] 1 W.L.R. 2760.
[69] Proceeds of Crime Act 2002, ss.245A, 245E, inserted by Serious Organised Crime and Police Act 2005, s.98(1); *ibid.*, s.246, as amended by Serious Crime Act 2007, s.74(2)(*b*), Sch.8, Pt 2, paras.85, 86. Those sections of the 2002 Act contain provisions summarised in the remainder of this paragraph.

DELETE THE LAST THREE SENTENCES AND NN.72 TO 74 AND REPLACE BY: A property freezing order under which a receiver has been appointed will confer powers on the receiver limited to management of the property. The order may authorise or require the receiver to take any steps which the court thinks appropriate in connection with the management of the property (but they include securing the detention, custody and preservation of the property so as to manage it).[72] Both an interim receiving order and a property freezing order prohibit any dealing with the property on the part of the owner.[73] If the interim receiver or receiver deals with property which he reasonably believes to be covered by the order, he is protected from liability except so far as any loss or damage is caused by his negligence.[74] Both forms of order are registrable as pending land actions.[74a]

Restrictions on dealing

DELETE THE ENTIRE PARAGRAPH AND NN.75 TO 79 AND REPLACE BY: **46–142**

Both a property freezing order and an interim receiving order will prohibit any person to whom the order applies from dealing with the property.[75] Exclusions may, however, be made when an order of either kind is made or on an application to vary it. The excluded property may be described in general terms, a provision which apparently extends to permitting certain expenses to be paid without specifying the precise assets to be used.[76] An exclusion may, in particular, make provision for the purpose of enabling any person to meet his reasonable living expenses, or to carry on any trade, business, profession or occupation, and may be made subject to conditions. The reference to living expenses and the business of "any person" is important for trusts. It enables the court, for example, to allow trustees otherwise forbidden to deal with trust property to pay income to a beneficiary who needs it for living expenses. The power to make exclusions, however, has to be exercised with a view to ensuring, so far as practicable, that the satisfaction of any right of the enforcement agency to recover the property obtained through unlawful conduct is not unduly prejudiced. This, especially the word "unduly", calls for some balancing of the ability of SOCA to recover the property and the ability of the holder of the property, or "any person", to maintain a reasonable standard of living while the proceedings are decided. It is to be assumed that the expenses will be met primarily out of such of the person's assets as are not asserted to be recoverable property.[77] No doubt living expenses will be allowed where that is

---

[72]   Proceeds of Crime Act 2002, s.245F, inserted by Serious Crime Act 2007, s.83(1).
[73]   See § 46–142.
[74]   Proceeds of Crime Act 2002, s.245F(7), inserted by Serious Crime Act 2007, s.83(1), s. 247(3).
[74a] Proceeds of Crime Act 2002, s.248, as amended by Serious Organised Crime and Police Act 2005, s. 109, Sch.6, paras.4, 11.
[75]   Proceeds of Crime Act 2002, s.245A–245C, inserted by Serious Organised Crime and Police Act 2005, s.98(1), s.252. Those sections of the 2002 Act contain provisions summarised in the remainder of this paragraph.
[76]   See *Hansard*, May 13, 2002, col. 114.
[77]   *Director of the Assets Recovery Agency v Creaven* [2005] EWHC 2726 (Admin); [2006] 1 W.L.R. 622.

truly necessary but they will ordinarily be restricted to what is need to maintain the normal standard of living of the person in question.

Legal expenses

46–143 DELETE THE ENTIRE PARAGRAPH, HEADING AND N.80 AND REPLACE BY:

Legal expenses[77a]

Trustees may be made defendants to civil recovery proceedings where SOCA considers that they hold recoverable property in that capacity. They may then have difficulty in funding the defence of the proceedings. In its original form, the 2002 Act contained an absolute prohibition on making any exclusion from an interim receiving order for the purpose of enabling any person to meet legal expenses in respect of proceedings under Part 5 of the 2002 Act itself, *i.e.* proceedings for the civil recovery of property obtained through unlawful conduct.[78] Parliament was apparently under the misapprehension that community funding would instead be available for a defendant.[79] In practice it was not and the prohibition was later modified to permit an exclusion for the purpose of meeting legal expenses.[80] A similar exclusion is permitted from a property freezing order.[80a] The court is now bound to have regard to the desirability of legal representation and to disregard the possibility of community funding[80b] but the exclusion must be limited to reasonable legal expenses, must specify the total amount that may be released and must be subject to conditions laid down in regulations.[80c] It is provided—though only in a Practice Direction, the status of which is doubtful—that the court will not make an exclusion for the purpose of meeting legal costs if the person subject to the interim receiving order can meet the costs out of assets to which the order does not apply.[80d] The legislation says nothing about persons who are sued in the capacity of trustee or in some other fiduciary capacity. It has been held that the omission is not accidental and that the statutory regime is exhaustive; in other words, where an interim receiving order is directed at trust property, the existence of adequate personal assets in the hands of the trustee will disqualify him from seeking an exclusion for the purpose of meeting legal expenses out of the

---

[77a] For provisions as to the assessment of costs payable by the trustee for civil recovery, see The Costs Practice Direction (supplementing CPR Pts 43 to 48), para.49A.1 *et seq.*
[78] Proceeds of Crime Act 2002, s.252(4).
[79] *Cf.* § 46–144 and *Director of the Assets Recovery Agency v Creaven*, above, at [9]; *Serious Organised Crime Agency v Szepietowski* [2009] EWHC 344 (Ch); [2009] 4 All E.R. 393 at [13].
[80] Proceeds of Crime Act 2002, s.252(4), (4A), substituted by Serious Organised Crime and Police Act 2005, s.109, Sch.6, paras.4, 14(1), (3).
[80a] Proceeds of Crime Act 2002, s.245C(5), (6), inserted by Serious Organised Crime and Police Act 2005, s.98(1).
[80b] *ibid.*
[80c] Proceeds of Crime Act 2002, ss.245C(5), (6), 252(4), (4A), 286A; Proceeds of Crime Act 2002 (Legal Expenses in Civil Recovery Proceedings) Regulations 2005 (SI 2005/3382); and see Practice Direction—Civil Recovery Proceedings.
[80d] Practice Direction—Civil Recovery Proceedings, para.7A.4. *Cf.* § 27–05 on the status of the Practice Direction.

trust assets.[80e] The trustee is nonetheless under no obligation to use his own assets for the purpose of defending the trust property[80f] and the proceedings may therefore go undefended. If he does use his own assets, however, and he succeeds in establishing that the trust property is not recoverable property, he will have his ordinary right of indemnity out of the trust fund, by then free of the order;[80g] if he fails, but has acted reasonably, the court still has a discretion to allow his costs to be paid out of the trust fund, either on the indemnity basis or the standard basis, and it is only if he has acted unreasonably that the court will be likely to refuse an order in his favour.[80h] Alternatively, the trustee may be able to arrange for one or more of the beneficiaries to fund the defence.

10. CONFISCATION AND SIMILAR ORDERS

INSERT A NEW PARAGRAPH BEFORE THE HEADING TO § 46–144:

We turn now to the second of the two procedures provided by the Proceeds **46–143A** of Crime Act 2002 designed to strip criminals of the benefits of criminal conduct. A confiscation order may be made under section 6 of the 2002 Act. Such an order is an order for confiscation, not of the specific proceeds of criminal conduct, but of a sum equal to the proceeds of such conduct. It is a monetary order, not a proprietary one, and is made against the person who is either convicted of a criminal offence or found to have benefited from a criminal lifestyle.

Restraint orders under section 41 of the Proceeds of Crime Act 2002

DELETE realizable THROUGHOUT AND REPLACE BY: realisable.   **46–144**

DELETE under section 6 of the Proceeds of Crime Act 2002 AND THE SECOND AND THIRD SENTENCES.

NOTE 82. DELETE AND REPLACE BY: See Proceeds of Crime Act 2002, s.82 (as amended by Serious Organised Crime and Police Act 2005, s.109, Sch.9, paras.4, 5 and prospectively amended by Counter-Terrorism Act 2008, s.39, Sch.3, para.7). Free property includes an interest under a trust, see *R. v Walker* [2011] EWCA Crim 103.

AT THE END OF THE TEXT ADD: But assets belonging beneficially to third parties (other than the recipient of a tainted gift) cannot be used to satisfy the confiscation order, if one is made.[85a] Ordinary principles of trust and

---

[80e]   *Serious Organised Crime Agency v Szepietowski* [2009] EWHC 344 (Ch); [2009] 4 All E.R. 393 at [62]–[65].
[80f]   *ibid.*, at [58], [62]; and see § 34–21.
[80g]   *ibid.*, at [63]. For the right of indemnity, see §§ 21–48 *et seq.*
[80h]   *ibid.*, at [63], relying on Proceeds of Crime Act 2002, s.266(8A), inserted by Serious Organised Crime and Police Act 2005, s.109, Sch.6, paras.4, 15.
[85a]   Proceeds of Crime Act 2002, s.69(3); *Sinclair v Glatt* [2008] EWCA Civ 176; [2009] 1 W.L.R. 1845 at [8], [39], on the predecessor provisions in Criminal Justice Act 1988. *Cf. Gibson v Revenue and Customs Prosecution Office* [2008] EWCA Civ 645; [2009] Q.B. 348.

property law are (save in relation to tainted gifts) applied for the purpose of determining whether assets belong beneficially to third parties.[85b]

AFTER § 46–144 INSERT A NEW PARAGRAPH AS FOLLOWS:

46–144A There is comparable legislation in other jurisdictions for the making of both restraint orders and then confiscation orders. Provision is made under the 2002 Act for the English court, at the request of an overseas authority, to make a restraint order in support of criminal proceedings in the jurisdiction of the authority and to provide for the realisation of the restrained property if in due course a foreign confiscation order is made.[85c] Such orders can be and have been made against trustees. But the English order must be confined to property in England and Wales.[85d]

46–145 DELETE realizable IN THE FIRST SENTENCE AND REPLACE BY: realisable.

DELETE THE LAST SENTENCE AND N.90 AND REPLACE BY: The trust property may therefore be frozen and unavailable to fund a defence by the trustees or the beneficiaries. Parliament was told that community funding would be available instead[90] but in practice it was not. Trustees and beneficiaries will be in the same difficulties as with an interim receiving order or a property freezing order and the solutions already mentioned,[90a] such as they are, will apply here too.

AFTER § 46–145 INSERT THE FOLLOWING NEW PARAGRAPH:

46–145A The Crown Court may appoint a receiver of any realisable property either when the restraint order is made or at any time thereafter.[90b] The remuneration, costs and expenses of the receiver are payable out of the realisable property even if the receiver should not have been appointed at all or the order appointing him is quashed, or the accused is acquitted or his conviction is quashed on appeal.[90c] Property held by the accused is realisable property even if he holds it on trust and has no beneficial interest in it; and hence although it cannot be used to satisfy any confiscation order (unless it belongs to a recipient of a tainted gift)[90d] it is liable to satisfy the remuneration, costs and expenses of the receiver.[90e]

46–146 IN THE SECOND SENTENCE AFTER whole net assets is taken, INSERT A NEW NOTE 90a: Where the assets include an interest under a trust, such as a life interest, it is brought into account at its fair value: *R. v Walker* [2011] EWCA Crim 103; [2012] 1 W.L.R. 173.

[85b] *Larkfield Ltd v Revenue and Customs Prosecution Office* [2010] EWCA Civ 521; [2010] W.T.L.R. 1315.
[85c] Proceeds of Crime Act 2002, ss.444, 447; Proceeds of Crime Act 2002 (External Requests and Orders) Order 2005 (SI 2005/3181).
[85d] *King v Director of Serious Fraud Office* [2009] UKHL 17; [2009] 1 W.L.R. 718.
[90] See *Hansard*, May 13, 2002, col. 112.
[90a] § 46–143 (Supplement).
[90b] Proceeds of Crime Act 2002, s.48.
[90c] *Mellor v Mellor* [1992] 1 W.L.R. 517; *Hughes v Customs and Excise Commissioners* [2002] EWCA Civ 734; [2003] 1 W.L.R. 177; *Capewell v R.C.C.* [2007] UKHL 2; [2007] 1 W.L.R. 386; *Sinclair v Glatt*, above.
[90d] See § 46–144.
[90e] *Sinclair v Glatt*, above.

DELETE THE THIRD SENTENCE AND NN.91 TO 93 AND REPLACE BY: The offender is conclusively deemed to be able to pay the full amount[91] and in default of full payment the order can be enforced as a fine.[92]

NOTE 94. DELETE AND REPLACE BY: See §§ 5–156 to 5–163. **46–147**

---

[91] See *R v Wilkes* [2003] EWCA Crim 848; [2003] Cr.App.R.(S) 98 on the strength of the presumption.
[92] Proceeds of Crime Act 2002, s.35, as amended by Serious Crime Act 2007, ss.74(2)(*a*), 92, Sch.8, Pt 1, paras.1, 19, Sch.14.

INDEX

directors, by, over company business,
3–05
equitable, formal requirements for, 3–18
failed transfer not construed as
declaration of trust, 3–42
land, formal requirements for
benefit of Act, pleading, 3–10
personalty, formal requirements for,
3–19
settlor retaining identical assets, 3–06
trustee, transfer of property to
contingent interests and expectancies,
3–35
equitable assignment generally, 3–27
legal transfer, rights incapable of, 3–33
shares and securities, 3–25, 3–41, 3–42,
3–45
statutory assignment of things in action,
3–27

Foreign element
beneficiary, disability of
minors, 11–99—11–99C
constructive trusts
general, 11–54A—11–54C
express trusts
directors and other fiduciaries, 11–54H
obligations of settlor, trustee or
beneficiary, 11–54D—11–54E
third parties' obligations, 11–54F—
11–54G
governing law
changing, 11–74
default of choice, in, 11–67
effects of, 11–70
Hague Convention
application, 11–56
constructive and resulting trusts, 11–62
governing effects of applicable law, 11–70
governing law in default of choice, 11–67
involuntary trusts, 11–60
mandatory rules, 11–80
matrimonial legislation and variation of
trusts, 11–71
overriding rules, 11–82
recognition,
trusts declared without transfers, 11–63—
11–63A
trusts invalid under English law, 11–89
third parties, 11–76
settlor's choice of law, 11–65
timing, 11–59
validity of trusts, 11–70A
variation of trusts, 11–71
writing, trusts in, 11–61
lifetime settlements of foreign movables,
11–88
lifetime trusts
contractual rights, 11–52
shares in companies, 11–54
validity, 11–49
registration, 11–79
trusts arising in relation to acquisition of
property, 11–54L—11–54M

trusts arising under contracts, 11–54I—
11–54K
Fraud
property obtained by
rescission and rectification, 7–27
Fraud on a power
categories, 29–260—29–264
complainant
powers of appointment, 29–269
general principle, 29–256
powers within principle, 29–272, 29–274

Gardens
settled land, grant of, 37–232

Hague Convention
application, 11–56
constructive and resulting trusts, 11–62
governing effects of applicable law, 11–70
governing law in default of choice, 11–67
mandatory rules, 11–80
matrimonial legislation and variation of
trusts, 11–71
overriding rules, 11–82
public policy, provisions incompatible with
trusts invalid under English law, 11–89
settlor's choice of law, 11–65
trusts declared without transfers, 11–63—
11–63A
validity of trusts, 11–70A
variation of trusts, 11–71
writing, trusts in, 11–61
Hastings-Bass, principle in
see also **Mistake**
acting on wrong advice, 29–248
advancements partially void for perpetuity,
5–90, 31–21
appointment of new trustees, 14–40
compensation, 29–250
discretion and equitable defences,
29–250C—29–250E
examples, 29–244
failure to exercise power, 29–252
fiduciaries other than trustees, 4–60
general, 29–229, 29–230, 29–238, 29–239
history of principle, 29–240—29–243
locus standi, 29–250B
nature and seriousness of mistake or
misapprehension, 29–250, 29–250A
negative application only, 29–252
partial avoidance, 29–250F
power exercisable with third party consent,
29–253
relief available, 29–250F, 29–251
resettlement partially void for perpetuity,
32–21
scope of trustees' duty, 29–246—29–249
third parties, effect on, 29–250E
tax consequence, mistake as to, 4–60,
29–230, 29–239, 29–247
whether exercise void or voidable, 29–245
whether breach of duty requirement,
29–246—29–249
Highway
settled land, grant of, 37–232